Inside the Ford-UAW Transformation

Pivotal Events in Valuing Work and Delivering Results

Joel Cutcher-Gershenfeld, Dan Brooks, and Martin Mulloy

The MIT Press
Cambridge, Massachusetts
London, England

MIT Press books may be purchased at special quantity discounts for business or sales promotional use. For information, please email special_sales@mitpress.mit.edu.

This book was set in Stone Sans and Stone Serif by Toppan Best-set Premedia Limited. Printed and bound in the United States of America.

Library of Congress Cataloging-in-Publication Data is available.
ISBN: 978-0-262-02916-2

10 9 8 7 6 5 4 3 2 1

Contents

Preface

The Ford-UAW transformation builds on a foundation of dignity and respect, and is guided by a True North vision of combining good jobs with high performance.

As an ongoing process of changing the underlying assumptions guiding labor and management, the Ford-UAW transformation is visible through the lens of more than 50 pivotal events over 30 years. These events have transformed practices based on twentieth-century assumptions, which were rooted in narrowly defined roles and functions guided by expert knowledge. It is a transformation into integrated operating systems that benefit from the distributed knowledge of the full workforce, with many more people in a greater variety of expert roles. This transformation model has already demonstrated its value in delivering sustainable results for individuals, families, and communities—in the context of business, labor, government, and society overall. But it is also a transformation that is incomplete—and at continued risk with each new pivotal event.

By presenting this transformation through the lens of pivotal events, our book reflects a persistent realization that came through our many conversations: the success of Ford and the UAW cannot be boiled down to a single strategic choice or causal driver. Certain highly visible, transformative events were in mind when we began the book: the 1982 negotiation that articulated a commitment to mutual growth (chapter 1); the Business Plan Review (BPR) and Special Attention Review (SAR) that enabled enterprise integration (chapter 4); the 2007 negotiation that helped to enable Ford stock to move from junk bond status to investment grade by removing hourly retiree health care costs from the books (chapter 6); the 2008 decision not to take the federal bailout funds for the auto industry (chapters 1 and 6); and the use of charters to bring structure and discipline to quality (chapter 7). Many other pivotal events emerged as we reflected further on factors enabling the transformation, and as we interviewed individuals involved in the events we had identified. In the end, though, we could not ignore that *all* the pivotal events we considered (and potentially others) *combined* to effect the transformation—and so the book includes this full range of pivots.

This is not a linear story of change and it is not a short-term story. While most of the pivotal events were at the enterprise level and planned, about a third of them were unplanned and an equal number were at the plant or division levels. This suggests that enterprise-level planning is essential, but that plant-level planning is also important and that resilience in the face of unplanned events is crucial.

Not all pivotal events included in the book were completely successful; some we have included fell well short of their potential, but even their limitations provided lessons that contributed to the overall transformation. Looking more closely reveals that many of the events that fell short of their potential were still embedded in twentieth-century assumptions—and their undertaking helped point to the assumptions needed for the new century, even if not right away. For example, the 1990s "Ford 2000" initiative (chapter 2) had great potential to accomplish much of what the 2006 BPR and SAR processes achieved in integrating divisions and functions in the corporation. But Ford 2000 was rooted in top-down expert reengineering assumptions and never addressed an underlying management norm in which individual leaders take care of their own issues within their functions. By contrast, the BPR and SAR processes had the embedded norm of open, nonblaming dialogue and action where all leaders shared responsibility for any problems identified. Similarly, the initial exploration of the principles of total productive maintenance (TPM; chapter 5) failed to value fully the role of front-line worker knowledge in such a system or the overarching aim of continuous improvement in the operations—not just maintenance of the equipment. In tracing how people at all levels in the Ford-UAW system learned these and other lessons, we can all gain new insights—which is the primary motivation for the book.

How Our Book Is Organized

We begin chapter 1 with a defining pivotal event for Ford and the UAW, move on to an overview of the ways in which pivotal events shape our story, and then present three pivotal events that introduce us as your guides to the transformation story. In this chapter we also include an orientation to the auto industry context. We organize each of the following seven chapters (2 through 8) in three parts. First, we articulate a guiding principle for each chapter as a "theme," and next present pivotal events that embody the principle and contribute to the transformation. Third, we provide selected supporting materials at each chapter's end, which may be useful in applying the principle in practice. In chapter 9 we look at the pivotal events in the whole book from a chronological perspective, and examine as well how they interconnect and overlap with individual chapter themes.

Each of the pivotal events at the core of the book is presented from the point of view of key individuals at the time. Our aim is to take you, the reader, back to that moment and bring you into the debates and action. Of course, the quotes from people we interviewed are all looking back. In that sense the pivotal events are like scenes in a play with the action in the present tense and the additional voices looking back in the past tense.

While some interpretation of the pivotal events is provided at the end of each event and at the end of each chapter, we have attempted to do this with a light touch—so that there is room to discuss and debate the interpretation and meaning of the events. Great success for us would be to find the material in this book fueling wide dialogue and debate on how to interpret and build on the pivotal events presented here (and similar developments in other organizations).

The classification of the events as "planned" or "unplanned" reflects the point of view from which we present the story. Some "unplanned" events, for instance, were completely unexpected—such as the tragic explosion in the Rouge facility (chapter 2). Others are presented as "unplanned" because that is how the people involved experienced them—as with the potential closing of the Cleveland Engine I Plant (chapter 2)—even if others at the corporate level had made the plan that put the plant at risk. Thus, our classification of a pivotal event as unplanned reflects the point of view from which we present the story.

Just as some events were clearly pivotal to us from the outset, while others were added, some of the guiding principles were also clear from the outset, while others crystalized in the writing. For example, the guiding principle for chapter 3—dignity and respect—was something we had in mind as we began to write. The guiding principle for chapter 8—align and stabilize, then integrate—represents a new insight that goes beyond the standard lean-thinking notion of stabilizing and then improving. We add the notion of alignment because the work of stabilization and integration depends on there first being alignment among the stakeholders—whether labor and management, functions within management, or relations between suppliers and the original equipment manufacturer.

Each guiding principle is intended as a signpost in documenting insights from the Ford-UAW transformation; we hope that each will serve within and outside the auto industry as a high-level indicator to know when you are on the right track.

This book spans many perspectives—from front-line workers to senior union and management leaders. We challenge simple stereotypes. Readers who are critical of the role of management in society will find here some courageous leaders who genuinely strive to do what is right for workers and communities as well as the business. Readers who are critical of the role of unions in society will find equally courageous union leaders who rise above internal politics to be full partners in transformation, with collective bargaining serving as a platform for innovation. Many principles in the book will apply in nonunion settings as well as unionized settings, although some forms of employee voice and collective engagement will be important.

We hope the introductory orientation to the industry context in chapter 1 is sufficient to begin the journey, though the auto industry has terminology and subcultures of great complexity. While the book provides considerable detail on many of the innovations that have characterized the auto industry, our presentation of the material can only provide partial background on all the associated concepts. Thus, when we tell the story of hourly Six Sigma black belts, we don't fully review the belt concept or many of the associated tools and methods. Readers will be more or less familiar with Six Sigma; for those who wish to learn more, we provide some references, as we also do for "lean" concepts in general. Similarly, when we discuss alternative team models relevant to the development of the Ford Production System, we give only a high-level introduction to the differences among offline, sociotechnical systems, and lean-production teams, but we provide an extended reference (in chapter 5) to where the distinctions have been more fully documented. In addition, we include a guide to abbreviations, acronyms, and terminology at the end of the book.

As coauthors, we draw on many decades of experience in the auto industry: Dan's 41 years with the UAW and Ford as a union leader with lead responsibility for implementing high-performance work systems throughout the U.S. operations, as well as advancing all UAW-Ford joint programs; Marty's 34 years with Ford as an executive with global responsibility for labor affairs and who led Ford's negotiations with the UAW during what may have been the greatest business challenges ever faced by the company; and Joel's 33 years of experience with innovation in the auto industry (beginning at the Michigan Quality of Working Life Council) and his 23 years as a consultant to the UAW and Ford, including supporting the implementation of high-performance work systems and a redesign of labor negotiations into more of a problem-solving process.

To tell the story fully, however, we did not rely exclusively on our experiences and memories but conducted more than 40 interviews with individuals who had central roles in the various pivotal events we highlight. It was quickly clear that the people we spoke with saw these conversations as part of a legacy for the next generation—documenting lessons learned to provide a foundation for the future. This was as true of the enterprise leaders as it was of the front-line leaders. We are deeply appreciative for the input from everyone we interviewed.

We use relatively few citations in the book; they are at the end of each chapter. Our aim is to make the book as accessible as possible to diverse audiences—practitioners and policy makers, as well as students and scholars. In many respects, the pivotal events can be thought of as primary source material, which is why we make considerable use of quotes throughout the book. There are even a number of places where we have included quotes from ourselves, in specific instances where the comment was uniquely from one of us who was involved in the event, rather than from the three of us as coauthors.

In parts of the story we present different or even competing accounts, and we try where appropriate to show how the same event could have been seen differently. In some cases, however, we had to exercise our best judgment in presenting the story one way rather than another. Ultimately, we as coauthors are responsible for all of the content of this book. The book does not necessarily represent the views of the Ford Motor Company; the International Union, United Automobile, Aerospace and Agricultural Implement Workers of America (UAW); or the University of Illinois.

Acknowledgments

We thank the many individuals from the UAW and Ford who gave of their time and thoughts in the development of the book. They include Wilhelmina Allen, Mary Anderson, Chris Basmadjian, Dean Blythe, Chuck Browning, Dave Curson, Peter Daniel, Bill Dirksen, Linda Ewing, Ahmad Ezzeddine, Jeff Faistenhammer, Wendy Fields-Jacobs, Bill Ford, Henry Ford III, Bennie Fowler, Brett Fox, Joe Gafa, Mike Geiger, Dick Gephardt, Dick Gross, Jack Halverson, Joe Hinrichs, Anthony Hoskins, Bob King, Roman Krygier, Brad Markell, Garry Mason, Doug Mertz, Bridget Morehouse, Bill Mothersell, Alan Mulally, John Nahornyj, Dennis O'Connor, Harold Pagel, Eric Perkins, Adrian Price, Pete Piccini, Jim Quinlan, Joe Reilly, Jimmy Settles, Anne Stevens, Gregory Stone, James Tetreault, Adrian Vido, Dennis Walkowiak, Rusty Woolum, Armentha Young, and Jerry Young. In this list and throughout the book we use people's names in their preferred form, which are mostly informal (such as Bill, Bob, Jerry, Joe, etc.). This list is relatively evenly divided between Ford and UAW leaders, with a mix of current and past leaders, as well as high level and frontline leaders—all have been important in constructing this book.

Tom Kochan was an initial reader of the manuscript, encouraging us from the outset—and we thank him. Additional readers include Gabe Gershenfeld, John L. King, and Fred Stahl, all of whom provided valuable comments. We thank Rob Scott and Will Kimball of EPI and Kristin Dziczek of CARS for assistance in the analysis of hourly wages and productivity, and Taekjin Shin for the analysis of executive compensation relative to the data in chapter 3. We are deeply grateful to Lorraine Pelc, who facilitated the scheduling of many of the interviews and who handled other project logistics. We also owe a debt of gratitude to Bill Dirksen and Ray Day for their assistance in the production process.

Scott Cooper served as editor for this manuscript, ensuring flow, concision, and grammatical precision. Moreover, he is to be credited for helping bring the pivotal events alive as stories. For all of this, we are deeply grateful. John Covell served as our senior acquisitions editor with MIT Press—confirming our fit, serving as arbiter among the seven very helpful (sometimes divergent) external reviews, and delivering this book to the market—for which we are also deeply grateful. Emily Taber, Marcy Ross, and Susan Clark ably guided us through the production process and Mary Bagg served as copy editor. While the reviewers were anonymous, we appreciate the many ways that the manuscript improved as a result of their thorough feedback.

Roger Komer provided the initial connections that brought all three of us together. He was a local UAW leader who traveled the distance from being a labor radical leading wildcat strikes at the Ford Sterling Plant to being a leading expert in the Ford-UAW system on high-performance work systems. He was responsible for introducing the idea of charters in the Ford-UAW context, partnering in the development of the Joint Alignment and Implementation model (JAI), driving some of the earliest team pilots, and influencing many of the other innovations featured in this book. Although he is no longer with us, he has been very much in our minds in the writing of this book.

As we think of Roger, we also think of the many "Rogerisms" that represent the voice of a change agent in a complex system, including his comments during and following meetings on change, such as: "First, get all the liars in a room"; "One bit of information is not a trend"; "Are you going to package up your broken glassware and take it to the new house?"; and "They must have attended the same different meeting." When it was time for implementation, his comments included what to expect when it became "Hand on the shoulder time"; "The rule of 17—people need to hear it, say it, and do it 17 times before it is real"; and "The initiative may have been implemented, but has it been checked, adjusted, and sustained?" He also had many colorful ways of characterizing different types of missteps, including "crash and burn," "trail of dead bodies," "runaway train," and "shame and blame."

Roger could be particularly colorful upon meeting people. Once, after meeting a new HR manager in his plant, he offered this assessment: "There ain't enough mustard in the whole world to cover that hot dog."

Ultimately, Roger did have key advice for success including, "It's what you say, how you say it, and when you say it" and "Avoid surprises, eliminate disconnects, build capability, and take action." Roger introduced the idea of a "sustaining agent" as a key complement to a "change agent." He was one of hundreds of talented and wise individuals who can be found in the Ford-UAW system—all of whom are also in mind with our focus on Ford-UAW pivots.

Finally, we offer our deepest appreciation to our wives, Susan, Mary, and Janet. It is Susan who first urged us to give this book top priority, and she was joined by Mary and Janet in enabling our progress in countless ways—including their new hobby of reading and providing valuable comments on the manuscript as it developed.

It is with Susan, Mary, and Janet that we join in dedicating this book to our children. For Joel: Gabe and Aaron. For Dan: Chuck, Danielle, Ciera, James, and Tyler (plus grandchildren, Caden, Hayes, Sailor, Logan, Grady, Rowan, Kamren, Harper, Malakai, and Roman). And for Marty: Eileen and Julie—along with all of their "brothers and sisters" in labor and management in the next-generation workforce. It is the next generation who will be navigating the pivotal events to come if we are ever to see a full renewal of what in the United States is called the "American Dream"—a dream of a system that values knowledge and hard work so that one generation can do better than the next. It is a dream that is increasingly a realistic part of the aspirations of people around the world.

1 Pivotal Events: Introduction and Industry Context

For the Ford Motor Company, perhaps the most important pivotal event in the past half century—certainly the most visible—was the decision in 2008 not to take the federal bailout package. The entire U.S. automobile industry was in a catastrophic financial position, and its future hung in the balance, with seasonally adjusted annual sales (SAAR) of cars and trucks having dropped from a projection of more than 17 million vehicles at the beginning of 2006 to under 11 million in 2008. The nation and much of the world was watching. Let's go back to this pivotal moment in 2008: Richard Gephardt has retired from Congress and is serving on Ford's board of directors.

"There was a sense of disbelief," recalls Gephardt. "It was hard to accept that we might lose all three companies."

Once people went past the state of disbelief, which went on too long, then there was blame. There was blame for the business people and blame for the unions. When enough people confronted the fact that it is really going to happen if you don't do something—that jobs will be lost, the supply chain will go down—then we started to see action. You can blame later, but deal with the issues.

Housing and autos are two industries that are essential to the economy. We had lost housing and cars were on their backs. This was no small sector of the economy. People don't think about all that goes into a vehicle. Autos, for example, are the biggest purchasers of silicon chips....

We were on the precipice of a depression. People had to face these hard facts. Facts are stubborn things.

Going back to 2008, Ford's North American Automotive Operations have lost $16 billion and the losses continue to mount, despite drastic cost-cutting measures in the two years prior. The company's primary domestic competitors are about to be driven into bankruptcy and government protection. Ford CEO Alan Mulally testifies in favor of the bailout (see figure 1.1); Ford indicates its concern about the impact on its supply chain were General Motors or Chrysler to go under. But Ford surprises many in Congress and the nation by not taking the money.

Ford remains standing while its competitors were brought to their knees. *How did this happen?*

Figure 1.1
Auto Industry CEOs and UAW President Testifying Before Congress. (From left to right: GM CEO Rick Wagoner; UAW, President Ron Gettelfinger; Ford CEO Alan Mulally; and Chrysler CEO Robert Nardelli.) *Source:* Ford Motor Company.

Ford's decision on whether to take the money is not easy; there is intense internal debate. Led by the chairman Bill Ford; CEO Alan Mulally; the president of the Americas division, Mark Fields; CFO Lewis Booth; the group vice president of Global Manufacturing, Joe Hinrichs, and others, the internal debate is about the very future of the enterprise. On the one hand, if Ford took the money, the Ford family would essentially be giving up family ownership of the firm. On the other hand, there might not be another opportunity. Bankruptcy is a real possibility; already it is clear that this is the worst recession since the Great Depression. Ford's hourly workforce is being cut from more than 90,000 individuals to approximately 40,000. Certainly Ford's domestic competitors—GM and Chrysler—are about to gain an enormous competitive advantage by wiping out considerable debt and liabilities.

But there is much more to the story than just an internal debate followed by a gutsy decision. Business history is littered with bold moves that turned out to be wrong. How is it that Ford was correct in betting the business and not taking the money? How could Ford have been confident of its ability to bring high-quality, energy-efficient products to market without the same bankruptcy protection and the same federal loans provided to its domestic competitors?

Well before the crisis, Ford took an important strategic move, mortgaging the entire enterprise—including the iconic blue oval—for a $23.5 billion line of credit. This move reflected Mulally's experience in the aerospace industry (where the level of credit needed to survive major swings in the economy exceeds what was considered normal in the auto industry), as well as the concerns of Ford's recently retired CFO Don Leclair and newly appointed CFO Lewis Booth, both of whom weighed in on the fragile state of the U.S. credit markets.

Bill Ford, the board chair, reflects back on the decision "Right after borrowing the money, we were at a three-company meeting and the others thought we had lost our mind, borrowing all that money. We said, 'We have a huge restructuring ahead.' They said, 'We've done ours already.'" In retrospect, of course, the measures Ford's competitors thought of as sufficient restructuring was far short of what they needed to keep them out of bankruptcy. As Chairman Ford adds, "At least we recognized the need sooner."

So, by the 2008 congressional testimony, the Ford Motor Company is better positioned to weather the storm with this line of credit and with its recognition that transformational change is needed. But let's unpack the story a bit more. There are a number of pivotal events in the Ford-UAW employment relationship in the years immediately preceding the hearings and the bailout offer. These give Ford a level of confidence not enjoyed by its competitors. For instance, consider events that took place between 2005 and 2006.

Senior Ford and UAW leaders go from plant to plant almost every week to negotiate more than 45 competitive operating agreements that generate what is conservatively estimated to be in excess of $500 million in savings—money that can be invested in new products. None of the other auto companies have been as comprehensive or as successful in moving to more flexible and competitive work practices.

The displacement of approximately 50,000 hourly employees between 2006 and 2008 is done on an entirely voluntary basis, with a combination of voluntary early retirement and voluntary separation packages. No other U.S. employer at the time comes close to this scale of restructuring without some involuntary layoffs of hourly employees. Ford does it on a joint basis with the UAW, with unique education and retraining opportunities for displaced workers. Over the two-year period Ford does not lose a single unit of production, while realizing year-over-year quality improvements the entire time.

In the 2007 national negotiations, Ford and the UAW change the way they bargain. Taking a problem-solving approach to negotiations, they reach agreements that improve on the industry pattern set by GM and Chrysler around a new entry wage and a Voluntary Employee Benefits Association (VEBA). These agreements simultaneously remove retiree health care costs from the books and make the UAW the nation's single-largest private purchaser of health care. These negotiated agreements begin the process of taking Ford's credit rating from junk status back to investment grade. As Gephardt concludes, "Labor relations is an important part of the picture in Ford not taking the money."

Moreover, in 2007, Ford and the UAW can draw on more than a decade's experience developing and implementing integrated operating systems in the factories, which allows production of as many as six different vehicles in a single facility. In the mid-1990s, concurrent production of even two models on the same assembly line had been considered an important accomplishment.

These earlier pivotal events (and many others documented in this book) were all part of Ford's calculus in not taking the money in 2008. Those familiar with the auto industry knew Ford and the UAW had been making considerable progress from near last in quality in 2000, but many in Congress and the general public were surprised to find Ford in a different position than its competitors. And that wasn't the only surprise. Many in Congress and the public were surprised by the role the UAW played as the decision-making process unfolded: Dave Curson, a union staffer on a team supporting UAW president Ron Gettelfinger in Washington, recalls:

These people saw us as a bunch of 300-pound brutes who only got what we got due to the threat of a strike. ... I believe that is how they pictured us going in. ... They were so distant from the hard work that actually takes place in a plant. If they had gone into an auto plant, they would have been amazed by the technology and the workforce knowledge needed. ... As the UAW, we brought knowledge of the supply chain, the distribution system, and the communities where the plants were located, as well as knowledge of the operations. ... They were not prepared for the intelligence of our arguments.

Again, let's return to the Congressional hearings and the Auto Industry Task Force in 2008 and 2009, when the UAW weighs in with expertise on several key issues. The union is particularly effective in detailing the interconnected nature of the supply chain in the industry and the ways in which a collapse of one company can bring down the entire industry. As the UAW's research director Linda Ewing comments, "Many folks on the outside didn't understand the depth of the UAW's knowledge about the auto industry and the breadth of our concern—not just the auto manufacturers but also the supply chain and a deep concern about the communities where our members live and work. There is an intricate web of relationships connecting the suppliers to OEMs [original equipment manufacturers], as well as the tax base that our members represent in their communities."

Formal bargaining also figures in the relationship between the Task Force and the UAW in 2009: the Task Force wants to impose the comparatively low pay scale at nonunion auto plants deep in the U.S. South as the competitive standard for auto wages; the UAW argues that if there was to be any comparison, it should be with the Japanese- and German-owned auto plants in Ohio, Pennsylvania, and Indiana. In the end, a blended rate is imposed as the standard, which keeps auto industry wages higher than the low, southern wages—a key consideration for autoworker families and communities.

The UAW criticizes the Task Force for its focus on managing transitions at the executive levels of the auto companies rather than on addressing the impact of proposed benefit changes on the workforce and the approximately 1 million retirees. Initially, for example, the government seeks to convert the entire active and retired workforce from defined benefit pensions to defined contributions. For the UAW, this is a deal breaker—union leaders testify such a change would trigger a national revolt that would go well beyond the auto industry. As Curson explains:

The government had just one objective, which was getting an agreement. They began to be overwhelmed as they came to see how complicated and interconnected the issues were. It was our job to make sure it wasn't just any agreement, but the best possible agreement.

The UAW agrees to sufficient change to save the industry, but no more. The key turns out to involve first negotiating with Ford and then bringing that agreement back to the government and GM and Chrysler as a pattern agreement (detailed in chapter 6). The union thus surprises many participants and observers by playing a proactive, constructive role, delivering on needed agreements while minimizing the burden on the workforce, retirees, and their communities.

Ford and the UAW have a track record of taking a problem-solving approach to difficult issues and finding mutual gains solutions—even before the company's decisions to establish a $23.5 billion line of credit and not take the bailout money. This track record is pivotal—without it, Ford's leadership would likely not have taken the risk. There are also positive ramifications that could not have been predicted. For example, after Ford makes public that it will not take the bailout money, surveys show a big increase in consumer willingness to consider a Ford as the next car purchase—it goes from approximately one-third of the marketplace to two-thirds. This is a shift of unprecedented magnitude in the industry. When consumers like what they find in the showrooms, it helps Ford transition from a 2006 loss of approximately $16 billion to a profit in 2013 of more than $8.8 billion. States with domestic auto manufacturing operations that are facing dire budget shortfalls now enjoy new, unexpected tax revenues, thanks in part to maintaining retiree benefits and preserving jobs.

In the 2008 hearings, members of Congress are brutal in their treatment of the auto industry,[1] unaware of and inattentive to the genuine progress all the companies and the UAW have been making in the preceding years. Had they known just how different the auto industry is from the banking industry, they may have approached the hearings and bailout differently. Had they known of the unique Ford-UAW partnership, they might not have been so surprised when Ford didn't take the money.

But were the events of 2005 to 2009 an anomaly? How did these pivotal events come about? It turns out a direct lineage can be traced between the decision not to take the money, the immediate stage-setting events for that decision, and nearly 50 preceding pivotal events. Most happened in the decade prior to the recession and the industry crisis, but some date back even decades further. For example, the billions of dollars spent on voluntary separation packages in 2006–2008 had a precedent dating back to the 1982 recession, when Ford and the UAW jointly committed, through partnerships with community colleges and political officials, to retraining and placing in other jobs more than 100,000 individuals who would never again work in an auto plant—and succeeded with more than 90 percent of the workers placed within two years. Similarly, the flexibility to produce multiple models on a single assembly line rested on dozens of pivotal events in the development of team-based work systems, dating back to an initial agreement in 1979 to foster employee involvement on the job.

A further unpacking of pivotal events—some planned and some unplanned—reveals key aspects of the deep culture of Ford, the UAW, and the Ford-UAW relationship, some that became visible beyond Ford only when the nation was in crisis. That Ford is still a family-owned company is important; more important is the sense that most employees genuinely see themselves as part of the Ford family. For instance, in 1999, an explosion at Ford's Rouge power plant killed six people and injured 24. Bill Ford rushed to the scene, over the protests of staff members who said the situation was still dangerous. His response was widely seen within Ford as a family member's response to a tragedy, not just as an official corporate response in a crisis. UAW vice president Ron Gettelfinger joined him at the scene, and the two committed to joint safety initiatives that became integral to the larger operating system. The explosion was pivotal in the immediate, heartfelt mutual response of labor and management and in the long-term constancy of purpose in driving system safety.

Nor has the story stood still following the decision not to take the bailout money. Pivotal events continue to unfold in what are really three parallel and simultaneous transformations: the transformation of the Ford Motor Company into a stronger market leader; the transformation of the UAW into a modern business partner and worker advocate; and the transformation of the Ford-UAW relationship into a generator of good jobs and high performance in the United States, simultaneously. These transformations are not complete. Indeed, they are still at risk at a time of accelerating change in markets, technology, and society. Even the decision not to take the money has yet to be fully judged by history. But the transformations have progressed sufficiently, and the story is so important to the fortunes of the nation, that it is worth tracing the full lineage of pivotal events that enabled the iconic decision not to take the money. That full set of pivotal events is the focus of this book.

Defining and Presenting Pivotal Events

It is traditional to view organizational transformation as the product of immediate proximate events, seeing cause and effect with a relatively tightly focused temporal lens and emphasizing the role of top leaders.[2] Within the reengineering literature, for example, transformation is typically presented within multiyear, rather than multidecade, time horizons.[3] While there may be some large-scale transformations that involve a single pivot or a few preceding events, it is clear in the Ford-UAW case that transformation has been the product of an extended set of pivotal events that have built on one another over many years, enabled *both* by top leadership and by distributed knowledge throughout the workforce.

We define *pivotal event* as follows: A pivotal event is a time-bound situation with highly consequential potential.

Note that an event is pivotal if it has the *potential* to be highly consequential—even if that potential is not realized. Not all events can be recognized as pivotal in advance; only those that are planned interventions have this characteristic. Unplanned events can also be pivotal, though they will only be recognized as such in the moment or in retrospect.

Transformation is not specified in this definition since we see transformation as the product of multiple pivotal events.

The focus on pivotal events builds on an earlier study of a transformation in the relationship between Xerox and the Amalgamated Clothing and Textile Workers Union, which represents many of Xerox's manufacturing employees.[4] In that 1988 study, commissioned by the U.S. Department of Labor, there were seven pivotal events that added up to a transformed union-management relationship in manufacturing operations. In *Healing Together*, which describes the decade-long Kaiser Permanente partnership with a coalition of unions, the concept of pivotal events is again employed to document a transformation in service operations.[5] Similarly, the manufacturing transformation documented in *Worker Leadership* by Fred Stahl involves a succession of what we are terming *pivotal events*, first at the plant level and then at the corporate level.[6] In comparison to these and other workplace transformation studies, we are more systematic in structuring our entire book around pivotal events. In part, we are drawn to the word *pivot* because of its growing use with respect to entrepreneurial enterprises, seen as making multiple pivots or changes in direction before matching their innovation with the right customers.[7] A large, established organization also pivots, but not everything at once as with a startup organization. That is a key point of the book: it takes many pivots to transform a major multinational corporation or an international union.[8]

The use of the term *pivotal event* is common, of course, in historical analysis,[9] which includes pivotal events that extend over long periods (such as a world war), or immediate events (such as the 9/11 attacks, which in the United States were experienced in an instant even if they had long-term ramifications).

In medical science, the term *pivotal event* is commonly used to refer to a component cause contributing to a fundamental shift in health status—such as an event that contributes to a heart attack or amputation or the cure of a disease.[10] The use of the concept of pivotal events in medicine parallels the use in history and our use at organizational and institutional levels of analysis in the sense that the pivot is seen as embedded in a larger sequence of events. A related concept, "critical emotional incidents," is introduced in a recent study of trust building in multi-stakeholder partnerships.[11] Just as we find transformation to be the product of multiple pivotal events, trust in this analysis is the product of multiple critical emotional incidents.

In *The Transformation of American Industrial Relations*, a transformation from more traditional, adversarial relations is seen as possible only with integrated changes at three levels: the workplace level, the collective bargaining level, and the strategic level.[12] Such a transformation is presented as essential to move to an employment relations system that combines good jobs and high performance. There is debate among scholars and practitioners over the degree to which economic recessions represent a necessary or critical context for unfreezing relations or accelerating such a transformation.[13]

The Ford-UAW pivotal events documented here are at all three levels—workplace, collective bargaining, and strategic—and there are essential links among the levels. These pivotal events do validate the transformation thesis and suggest that a transformation can be decomposed into a series of pivotal events. While economic recessions certainly have "unfreezing" or enabling roles in many of the pivotal events, strategic choices and leadership at these moments are revealed as essential (in other words, unfreezing alone is not enough), and pivotal events involving strategic choices and leadership occur during other phases in the economic cycle as well.

Not only is a transformation revealed as the product of a series of pivotal events, but also the fulcrum of each pivot, if you will, is around assumptions about work and relationships. Of particular importance are what we refer to as "operating assumptions," such as assumptions around prevention (rather than inspection of quality or safety), or assumptions about standardization and stability as a necessary foundation for innovation and continuous improvement. Closely connected are assumptions about the inherent knowledge and capability of the distributed workforce, assumptions about the role of a union with respect to continuous improvement in workplace operations, and assumptions about the role of a company with respect to families, communities, and society.

In *The Human Side of Enterprise*, in 1960, Douglas McGregor taught us to "tune our ears" to listen for underlying assumptions about people in organizations.[14] In 1985, in *Organizational Culture and Leadership,* Ed Schein documented how such assumptions represent the deep, often unstated foundation on which organizational culture rests.[15] The pivotal events we selected for our book are pivotal in that these assumptions about work and relationships, which include valuing the distributed knowledge of the workforce and the cooperative potential in the union-management relationship, could be advanced (in comparison to more traditional, adversarial assumptions), making possible a transformation combining good jobs and high performance.

Some of the pivotal events we present were intended to be transformational, but fell short of their potential. The Ford 2000 initiative in the 1990s (detailed in chapter 2), fell short of its potential, for example, because the full scale and scope of the change was greater than was understood at the time. Ultimately, however it was foundational in Ford becoming an integrated, global corporation. Others, in retrospect, proved transformational in unexpected ways. For instance, the 2003 Ford-UAW national negotiations were a relatively low-profile round of bargaining. But contained within the negotiations was the use of an interest-based approach on one issue—quality (presented in chapter 6)—which proved pivotal in a transformation that enabled Ford to go from near last in quality to industry leadership (a story presented in chapter 8), and which set the stage for a problem-solving approach to collective bargaining on all issues in 2007.

We feature two types of pivotal events. *Planned* pivotal events involve intentional change. For example, Alan Mulally's 2006 Business Plan Review (BPR) and the Special Attention Reviews (SAR) in chapter 4 were planned interventions designed to focus the company's Global Business Units and Functional Teams on "One Ford" as a global enterprise. Others involve *unplanned* change, typically shocks to the system—like the 1999 explosion in the Rouge power plant, the response to which became pivotal. Of course, a planned change for some may be experienced as unplanned by others. For example, top leaders experienced the "Way Forward" plan as a planned pivotal event, but the workforce initially experienced the associated plant closings with shock and surprise. For them, this was unplanned change. Additionally, what is pivotal for some may not be pivotal for others. Closing the Green Island Plant (discussed later in this chapter) was pivotal for the workforce there but not for the larger system, because another Ford-UAW plant picked up much of the work. We make the distinction between planned and unplanned pivotal events based on the concepts of planned and unplanned change outlined in the change management literature, illustrating the importance in transformation, both of planned interventions and of adaptive responses to unplanned developments.

Seeing transformation in a larger context is a key point of this book. The individuals we spoke with concerning the pivotal events we selected are knowledgeable, and their experience is illustrative. Our aim is to provide an inside perspective that reveals the dynamics associated with each pivot—not just the externally visible features. But these events and perspectives are not exhaustive.

The pivotal events we present in this book do not constitute a deterministic path. The fact that approximately one-quarter of the pivotal events were unplanned signals the crucial roles of leadership, strategic choice, and improvisation.[16] Indeed, pivotal events represent crucibles for leadership[17] in which a mix of inherited institutional, economic, and technological structures combine with individual agency.[18]

Most pivotal events we document in this book are planned events at a system/enterprise level, which is as to be expected. A transformation on the scale and scope of the UAW and Ford requires many such instances of planned change at this level. On their own, events at the plant/division level would not add up to a transformation without changes at the system/enterprise level. The events selected at the plant/division level were all selected as harbingers of larger system level changes, many of which were codified through collective bargaining or other institutional and policy decisions.

We assembled the pivotal events into nine chapters:

1. Pivotal Events: Introduction and Industry Context
2. The Case for Change
3. Dignity of Work
4. Business Fundamentals
5. Knowledge-Driven Work
6. Negotiated Change
7. Joint Alignment
8. Integrated Operating Systems
9. True North: Good Jobs and High Performance

Each chapter presents pivotal events in chronological order to convey *sequence* around a given theme. Not all pivots build on earlier events fully or directly, but they always flow over time. In many cases, events relating to one theme, such as "negotiated change," interweave with other themes, such as "business fundaments" or "joint alignment." In some cases, the chapter themes have a direct, one-step connection. For example, figure 1.2 indicates that "the case for change" (the theme for chapter 2), is a foundational connection for the changes that are the focus of chapters 3–8.

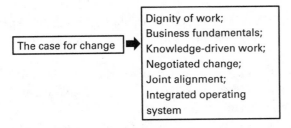

Figure 1.2
Chapter Themes (tied to The Case for Change).

In other cases, there might be two steps. For example, figure 1.3 indicates that pivotal events around the "dignity of work" (the theme for chapter 2) are a direct foundation for pivotal events around "knowledge-driven work" (the theme for chapter 5), which, in turn, are a direct foundation for the "integrated operating systems" (the theme for chapter 8).

Ultimately, the connections can involve three steps, with interweaving at some of the steps. For example, figure 1.4 indicates that pivotal events around "business fundamentals" and "knowledge-driven work" (the themes of chapters 4 and 5, respectively), interweave with each other. Together, these pivotal events are reinforced and extended through "negoti-ated change" and "joint alignment" (the themes of chapters 6 and 7), which combine to

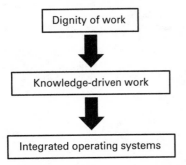

Figure 1.3
Connecting Chapter Themes (beginning with Dignity of Work).

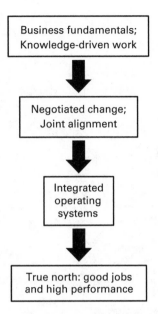

Figure 1.4
Connecting Chapter Themes (beginning with Business Fundamentals and Knowledge-Driven Work).

enable "integrated operating systems" (the theme of chapter 8), making possible the combination of "good jobs and high performance" (which is characterized as "True North" in chapter 9). We identify these and other connections throughout the book; readers will certainly see additional links that are all woven into the larger fabric of transformation.

Auto Industry Context

Over a half century ago, Peter Drucker documented in *Concept of a Corporation* how another iconic auto company, General Motors, was an exemplar for the modern twentieth-century corporation, with all of its internal complexity.[19] At the time, it was indeed plausible to state, as did the popular paraphrase of a GM president's testimony before the U.S. Congress, "As GM goes, so goes the nation." The correspondence between the auto industry and the twentieth-century mass-production, mass-market industrial model (and the foundational role of the Ford Motor Company) is so strong that scholars in Europe and certain fields in the United States still refer to the mass production model as "Fordism."

While autos were a defining industry in the twentieth century,[20] no such hubris is possible in the global knowledge economy of the new century. Auto production in the United States is no longer limited to domestic manufacturers, and the market share of these domestic companies has been eroding for more than two decades, as is illustrated in figure 1.5.

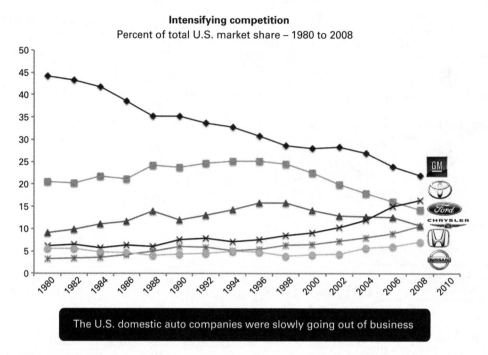

Figure 1.5
Briefing Slide on Auto Industry Competition, 1980–2008. *Source*: Ford Motor Company.

The recession that began in 2008 threatened the very viability of this industry in the United States—for domestic and foreign manufacturers. This book tells a transformation story in which the embrace of knowledge-driven principles and a labor-management partnership in one of these companies has proven essential for survival—a starting point much more dynamic and uncertain than the context for Drucker's *Concept of a Corporation*. The implications of this book are particularly relevant for organizations facing transformational challenges.

While the implications go beyond the auto industry, it is important to understand the industry context. Transformation can best be understood in context. The auto industry has a substantial footprint in the United States. Not only are there original equipment manufacturers (OEMs) such as Ford, GM, Chrysler, Toyota, Hyundai, VW, Mercedes Benz, Mitsubishi, and Honda, but there is also a vast supply chain. A typical car has more than 10,000 component parts, with better than half produced at what are called Tier 1, Tier 2, and Tier 3 suppliers. Tier 1 suppliers contract directly with the OEMs and are supported in turn by Tier 2 suppliers, who may have Tier 3 suppliers. Nationwide, an estimated 8 million workers and their families depend on the auto industry (a multiple of the 1.7 million people directly employed in the industry). Each year, the industry generates $500 billion in paychecks, while generating $70 billion in tax revenues across the country. Approximately 1 in every 17 U.S. jobs depends on the auto industry.[21]

The auto industry involves highly stereotyped jobs in our society: captive assembly line worker, domineering supervisor, commanding plant manager, contentious union leader, creative car designer, and many others. However, the work in all these jobs—and every other job in the industry, for that matter—has changed in profound ways. The more visible pivots by Ford and the UAW rest on deeper shifts in the nature of the work itself.

Consider the unrelenting heartbeat of the assembly line, where any lost production can exceed $10,000 a minute in lost profit. Yet, the frontline assembly worker is no longer a replaceable cog in the machine, hired just for his strong back. Today, that man or woman may be an elected team leader who is tracking safety, quality, delivery, cost, capability, environmental performance, and other measures; his or her knowledge of daily operations is central to continuous improvement in the enterprise. The plant manager and local union leader are more likely to be partners, sharing responsibility for hundreds of millions of dollars in sales in a facility that faces global competition for each product it produces and is one of the community's leading employers. The two may have disagreements, as in any partnership, but their destinies are bound in ways that have fundamentally changed the work they do, now emphasizing their roles as leaders and teachers. So, too, have the car designers changed; they are now part of what some estimate to be the nation's single-largest research and development enterprise at a time when the automotive experience involves an inexorable move toward greater integration of people and technology.

Box 1.1 serves as primer for readers who may be less familiar with the basic terms, structures, and operations in the auto industry today.

The U.S. auto manufacturers (Chrysler, Ford and General Motors) are highly unionized. The focus of this book is on the transformation involving both Ford and the UAW. The principles developed in this book, however, are not exclusive to the auto industry or even to unionized workplaces. In any setting, work and relationships can be transformed to deliver results through a series of pivotal events—some planned and some unplanned. Nevertheless, we have kept our lens tightly focused on the auto industry and particularly on the labor-management relationship between Ford and the UAW. It is important first to understand events and developments in the institutional and industry context, which is our aim here.

Pivotal Events in This Chapter

This chapter highlights three pivotal events for Ford and the UAW (two at the plant level and one at the enterprise level). Two were unplanned and one was planned. One pivot was unsuccessful, ending up in a plant closing; one was successful, ending up in a plant-level transformation; and one was (and is) foundational for many aspects of the enterprise-level transformation. We highlight these three because they are among the first pivotal events we each experienced directly—all in the early 1980s. They are early harbingers of key themes

Box 1.1
Auto Industry Terms, Structure, and Operations

Many aspects of the auto industry, as well as Ford and the UAW as organizations, involve unique terminology and concepts that are integral to an understanding of the pivotal events. This includes aspects of high-performance work systems, lean and Six Sigma principles, collective bargaining dynamics, change management processes, human resource practices, internal union structure and operations, and other matters. For example, North American manufacturing operations in the Ford Motor Company are organized around three major divisions—Vehicle Operations (VO), which includes assembly plants building the final products (cars and trucks); Stamping Division, which includes metal stamping plants producing doors, hoods, trunks, roof panels, and other major components; and Powertrain Operations, producing engines, transmissions, axles, drive train, gears, and other related components. At various times over the past decades there have been other relevant divisions, including plastic and trim products, and the Automotive Components Holdings (ACH), as well as other major parts of the enterprise, including product development, Ford Motor Credit, parts depots, and others. These structural aspects of Ford are integral to some of the pivotal events because some of the earliest pilot examples of team-based work systems were in powertrain plants, while the assembly operations were the most challenging to change.

Within the UAW, a vice president is assigned to the Ford Department, with international representatives servicing multiple plants. Within a plant, there will generally be both a local union president and the chair of the local bargaining committee, as well as other local officers. Instead of stewards (a term used in many unions), there will be bargaining committeepersons (previously committeemen) who serve on the local bargaining committee and provide direct assistance to union members in the plant with grievances and other matters. Although the local officers and bargaining committee representatives are all elected, there are also many appointed UAW positions in an auto plant, focusing on issues of safety, quality, and other matters. Formal joint programs always list the UAW first. In this book, when we are not discussing the formal joint programs we list Ford first to indicate that we are not discussing a formal joint program.

Note: A listing of abbreviations, acronyms and terminology is included prior to the notes at the end of book.

throughout the book and they are formative events for each of us. Because of our close personal connections with these three pivotal events, they serve to introduce us and give the reader a sense of where we're coming from as narrators for the rest of the book.

The Monroe Stamping Plant illustrates the challenges facing a facility and its leadership when the business is at risk; we document the pivot of the local union leadership from a stance of opposition to constructive engagement with the business challenge. The Green Island story involves a comparable plant-level business challenge, but in this case local union and management leaders were unable to escape their adversarial relationship. Ultimately, the plant could not adapt to changing business realities. Finally, the employee-involvement and mutual-growth programs represent an enterprise-level pivot that was foundational in transforming the Ford-UAW relationship.

In addition to introducing us as coauthors, all three of these introductory pivotal events illustrate the "case for change" (chapter 2). The Monroe Stamping Plant also illustrates aspects of "knowledge-driven work" and "negotiated change" (chapters 5 and 6). The 1979–1982 pivotal event on employee involvement and mutual growth serves as a foundation for the "mutual growth" guiding principle in chapter 4 on "business fundamentals," as well as the dynamics of "negotiated change" and "joint alignment" (chapters 6 and 7).

As in subsequent chapters, we first summarize the pivotal events to be presented. Also, as was the case at the beginning of this chapter, the pivotal events are presented as though readers were there at the time, even if some of the interwoven quotes are looking back in the past tense.

Chapter 1 Pivotal Events	Overview	Type, Level
Monroe Stamping Plant, 1981	A formative event for Dan Brooks occurs in his home plant, the Monroe Stamping Plant, where he and other UAW leaders and members face the fundamental challenge of relaxing contractual work rules to preserve jobs. This is a precursor of pivotal choices facing the entire UAW in later years.	Unplanned, Plant Level
Green Island Plant, 1981	Marty Mulloy's initial assignment to Ford's Green Island Plant involves the potential for a pivot similar to Monroe Stamping, but the productivity, flexibility, and cultural issues are not joined in this location, and ultimately the plant is closed. There is a case for change, but not the required leadership.	Unplanned, Plant Level
Employee Involvement and Mutual Growth, 1973–1982	The 1979 UAW-Ford agreement to support Employee Involvement (EI) and the 1982 agreement around "mutual growth" set the stage for joint activities that value the work of UAW members in enabling business success. For Joel Cutcher-Gershenfeld, witnessing the behind-the-scenes dynamics is a formative experience.	Planned, Enterprise Level

Monroe Stamping Plant, 1981

It is 1981 and Dan Brooks is in his first term as president of UAW Local 723, which represents workers at the Ford Monroe Stamping Plant. Ford and the UAW have begun implementing 1979 UAW-Ford contract language advancing the idea of "Employee Involvement." Japanese management practices are getting increased attention for producing high-quality products through the use of quality circles and other practices. In many plants such as Monroe, the new contract language is seen as part of a move to be more like the Japanese—a notion not generally embraced.

In a newsletter article to his membership, Dan writes, "Monroe is not the land of the rising sun." He promises his members will never see "fish heads and rice" on the cafeteria menu—rejecting Employee Involvement as a company-run program that will undermine the local union's agenda, diminishing its power and strength.

Shortly afterward, a member of UAW vice president Don Ephlin's staff visits Dan in his office and challenges the article's premise. Speaking for Ephlin, he points out that Employee Involvement could work as a powerful tool for the local union to improve the quality of work life for its members. It's a way, he says, to address issues on a weekly basis in "good and welfare" meetings that would otherwise have to go through the local grievance procedure or wait until local negotiations, which take place every three years. And he insists this is not a Japanese quality improvement process, but is a response to the "blue collar blues" and worker alienation that have been in the news—workers seen as having been hired only for their "hands," not their "heads."

"Making a shift like this was incredibly difficult," Dan recalls today. "You get elected on one platform and now it's a roll of the dice whether people will still support you after the change."

In response, Dan and others in the local union leadership begin to meet with management for weekly "good and welfare" meetings where issues are raised such as cleaning up break areas, installing fans on the floor, improving safety practices, and other matters relating to the quality of work life of the union members. Soon, improvements begin to take place around the factory. Suggestions from members flow through the union leaders onto the meeting agendas. At the same time, the company begins to share with the union leaders more information on the pressures facing the business. With this forum in place, the parties are prepared to have a pivotal strategic conversation.

It is the same year the "oil crisis" rocks the United States, out of which comes what are termed "Corporate Automotive Fuel Economy" (CAFE) standards required for all auto companies. This puts a spotlight on vehicle weight. Most Monroe Stamping Plant workers produce steel car bumpers, steel wheels, and front-end collision absorption systems.

CAFE requirements have a huge impact on Monroe. Within a year, work disappears and the local union membership plummets from more than 3,000 to fewer than 1,400. Rumors begin to circulate: Monroe is on a list of facilities to be closed.

Suddenly, the good and welfare meetings have a very different focus. The union leadership asks plant management if there is new work to make up for the lost jobs. The plant manager says he's willing to pursue any available work, but in return needs a commitment from the union to change work practices—relax job classifications for production workers and what are termed "lines of demarcation" for skilled trades. Essentially, he asks the union to be more flexible in how things operate on the floor to enable bidding on new work.

At the core of the challenge facing the union is the need to fashion an agreement that still values the work of its members even as changes are contemplated. The local union leaders schedule meetings with the membership to explain this proposal and the potential changes. They gain approval to continue the discussions with the company and return with details—which they do. First, though, local union leaders report to UAW International on the potential terms of an agreement—and there are concerns. Is the local union setting a precedent that will create problems for others?

The International sends representatives to Monroe Stamping to learn more. They return to Solidarity House, the UAW's headquarters in Detroit, persuaded that the agreement makes sense.

Local leaders take the agreement to the membership for ratification. It is approved, overwhelmingly.

At a meeting of the UAW-Ford Council, which represents workers in Ford-UAW facilities across the United States, leaders from other locals roundly criticize the Monroe leaders. Meanwhile, though, Ford—with agreement in hand—is living up to its commitment to bring in new work, producing new stampings, new springs, catalytic converters, and other work. As jobs begin to grow, though, the full recession of 1982 hits the entire region. Suddenly, the same local leaders who had criticized Monroe are on the phone asking for specifics of the local agreement that paired flexibility with job growth.

Ultimately, by the late 1980s, Monroe grows back in size to make up for nearly all the lost jobs, thanks to everyone coming to appreciate the need for change: local union leaders, local managers, local members, the international union and, ultimately, even leaders from other UAW locals.

✳ ✳ ✳

In retrospect, the strategic choice by local union leaders to recommend fundamental change involved a clear-eyed assessment of the situation, with access to relevant data suggesting greater risk in maintaining the status quo. Once local leaders understood this, they had to make the same case for change to their membership. Managers in a nonunion firm will prefer to have such a conversation without a union involved. Consider, though, the power of moving forward with changes in work operations after a clear expression of support from the workers achieved through their elected leaders.

As a pivotal event, the Monroe Stamping Plant involved an unplanned shock to the system—as the market shifted and work was discontinued in the plant—as well as planned change through local negotiations to set the stage for bringing in new work. The union was able to retain and expand good jobs by more fully contributing to high performance.

Green Island Plant, 1981

In 1923, Henry Ford founded Ford Motor Company's Green Island Plant on the banks of the Hudson River across from Troy, New York, where he had once shared a camping site with Harvey Firestone, John Burroughs, and Thomas Edison—they called it Camp Fordson. The potential water-generating power from the Mohawk and Hudson Rivers was the determining factor to build the plant at this location.

The plant, organized by the UAW-CIO in 1941, initially manufactured automotive springs, radiators, pistons, and batteries, but was turned over to Pratt and Whitney to build aircraft engine parts and tank turrets during the war—after which the plant was returned to Ford and its original focus on automotive components. From the outset, worker-management relations in the plant were adversarial, as supporting material item 1.1 illustrates—the dialogue in a 1944 meeting between the local union leadership, local management, and an outside corporate representative, most likely while Green Island was still engaged in wartime production. By the early 1980s, work in the plant concentrated on building radiators and heater cores.

Going back to this time, Marty Mulloy transfers to Green Island Plant in 1981. The adversarial culture is well established; there are third-generation employees working in the factory. The hourly workforce is exclusively male (there is one salaried female supervisor) —which at times creates a toxic culture where compromise and joint problem solving are seen as weaknesses of character. After 40 years of collective bargaining, management and labor have settled into traditional roles. Many managers in the plant are former military officers who value command and control of all plant operations, whereas hourly employees are former enlisted men and immigrants from Irish, Italian, and Russian families. They distrust management and have a class view of social interactions within the plant. A skilled tradesman may earn more than an accountant, but each belongs to separate social class—the former identifies with the working class, expecting to be exploited by management; the latter identifies as a member of management, assuming that the working class is not committed to the business.

Ford has several "problem plants," but Green Island stands out as among the company's worst. Marty Mulloy, before coming to Green Island, had been a labor relations representative at Ford's Sheldon Road Plant (SRP) in the Detroit suburb of Plymouth, which built air conditioning components as part of a product line-up similar to that of Green Island. SRP also had a similar number of hourly and salaried employees. But at SRP Marty had an average of 10–20 active grievances at any point; Green Island's active grievance load averages 1,500 per labor relations representative! At SRP, grievances were settled amicably—common sense was the litmus test for sorting through the "right" way to address issues. SRP had another advantage: its workforce was a diverse mix of rural/urban, black/white, and male/female employees. No prevailing culture dominated the plant; with few exceptions, employees felt they were very fortunate to work at the Sheldon Road plant.

During Marty's first week on the job at Green Island, he is baptized into the plant's toxic culture. After working the day shift, he is called back into the plant at 9:00 p.m. *Trouble is brewing*, warns the superintendent. Walking through the plant to the superintendent's office after he arrives, Marty tells the superintendent he sees nothing unusual on the floor.

"There will be in a few minutes," the superintendent responds. Apparently, this afternoon-shift superintendent gets bored and likes to "stir things up a bit." Fully aware of the physical capabilities, skill level, and personal preferences of the workers, he reassigns selected employees to jobs they either cannot physically perform or prefer not to do.

There are just two hours remaining in the shift. The assembly process on the plant floor is humming along perfectly fine. But the superintendent makes the change.

"All hell broke loose," Marty later describes.

Two hours of shouting and threats ensue, and then the superintendent magnanimously reassigns the workers to their former positions.

Marty recalls asking the superintendent the point.

"I wanted to send a message to the employees and the union," says the superintendent, "of how much control I have over them, and furthermore I cannot stand the morning shift superintendent and he's the guy that will have to clean this up in the morning."

This abuse of the superintendent's authority reinforces hourly employees' perception that they need a union to protect them from capricious acts of management.

Local union leaders also demonstrate dysfunctional behavior. A new technology in the building of radiators—the core product of the plant—is introduced, reducing the number of production steps by more than half. The old manual operation of radiator assembly involves the largest number of workers in the plant in any single job classification. The national and local contracts provide a process to measure the time standards of this new operation: a Ford industrial engineer and a UAW Time Study representative stand beside the radiator assembler to determine the proper rate of build that can be done fairly and safely. But the union instructs all radiator assemblers to slow down their build rate with the new technology to match the existing manual labor rate, thereby keeping the number of radiators built per hour to the same level as with the manual process—and avoiding potential layoffs.

The plant manager, a recent transfer into the plant, does not overreact but instead calmly shows the build rate at the supplier by a similarly skilled radiator assembler. He walks the union leaders through the investment made in the new equipment, and also explains the company's ability to move the equipment to a new location and have the radiators built at another facility. The fate of the plant rests on the union's willingness to work cooperatively and acknowledge the changes in technology that make the plant more efficient.

Months go by, during which the union refuses to put forth an honest effort to build the radiators with the new technology, so the equipment is moved to the Sheldon Road Plant and employees are offered an opportunity to transfer to Michigan. A handful of salaried and hourly employees transfer, and by 1989 the entire Green Island Plant has been shut down—with the jobs permanently lost to the community.

For Marty Mulloy, the experience has an indelible impact. "Green Island," he says, "illustrates how not to treat people, as well as the deep challenges in changing an organization's culture."

***

This pivotal event illustrates the story of many plants: a case for change, but one in which there was insufficient leadership from either union or management to make that change. At Green Island, the pivot's potential was never realized. "Good jobs," as we call them, were lost to the community.

Employee Involvement and Mutual Growth, 1973–1982

In the 1970s, with the civil rights and women's rights movements in full swing, attention turned as well to other issues affecting the workplace, such as "blue collar blues" and worker alienation. The 1972 strike over a "speed up" at the General Motors plant in Lordstown, Ohio, put a spotlight on worker discontent, one of the catalysts for our next pivotal event.

Within the UAW, Vice President Irving Bluestone approaches General Motors about addressing some of the underlying issues. Building on experiments in GM's plant in Tarrytown, New York, and other locations, the UAW proposes new contract language in 1973 on the Quality of Working Life (QWL). Six years later, in 1979, the UAW and Ford reach a similar agreement, but use the term Employee Involvement (EI).

"People have more to offer than the strength of their bodies," says Ernie Savoie, Ford's Director of Labor Relations Planning and Employment Office. "When given the opportunity, the time and the training, they can and will contribute mightily in terms of positive ideas the solve work-related problems, improve the work environment, and enhance work relationships."[22]

The UAW's QWL program with GM and EI program with Ford involve voluntary weekly meetings of groups of workers from a given area of the plant to make suggestions on workplace improvements. The process is explicitly set up as separate from collective bargaining—a distinction that later proves limiting and is ultimately rejected by labor and management. While some of the early suggestions focus on improving the physical environment, such as suggesting the need for more water fountains and fans in the summer, a growing number of worker suggestions do result in improvements around safety, quality, and productivity.

The initial efforts are challenged in 1980 when the United States enters a severe recession—a second catalyst for this pivotal event. The future of the domestic auto industry is in question. U.S. auto sales are in an unprecedented slump that began three years earlier, as *Automotive News* recalls.

Auto sales were off to a rousing start in 1979. Sales of domestic vehicles in the first 10 days of the year were up 23 percent. Then all hell broke loose. On Jan. 16, 1979, the Shah of Iran was overthrown, and the Ayatollah Khomeini came to power. He cut Iran's oil production, which reduced shipments of crude oil to the United States. Gasoline prices soared, and the American economy plunged into a recession.[23]

Sales of the more fuel-efficient Japanese cars took off, and combined car sales of the top-three Japanese brands—Toyota, Datsun (now Nissan), and Honda—rise from 1.1 million in 1978 to 1.4 million in 1982, a 29 percent increase. Indeed, in 1982, Japan surpasses the United States, even if only briefly, as the world's largest producer of cars and trucks.

Management presses for concessions from autoworkers, driving deep divisions between the UAW in the United States and Canada, where the recession is less severe. Ultimately, these tensions lead to the break up of the union and the formation of the Canadian Auto-workers Union (CAW).

At Ford, the situation is eerily similar to the later 2007 recession. Ford's car sales drop 47 percent, from 2.5 million in 1978 to 1.4 million in 1982. The company had already lost $1.5 billion in 1980 and $1.0 billion in 1981 (equivalent to $4.6 billion and $2.7 billion, respectively, in 2014 dollars), with hourly employment dropping by 46 percent during the same period; nearly half the workforce is laid off. Several plants are shut down and others are slated to close. Ford leads the auto industry—just as it did 40 years later—in providing retraining and placement assistance to approximately 100,000 workers who will never again work in an auto plant. More than 90 percent are placed in new jobs by the end of 1983.

The case for change is clear (the focus of chapter 2). In an unprecedented move, the 1982 auto negotiations begin six months earlier than scheduled. The automakers are looking for concessions from the UAW—particularly the end of the Annual Improvement Factor that provides for a 3 percent annual wage increase (separate from a cost-of-living increase) based on a 3 percent growth in productivity. At the same time, the UAW wants increased job security for the remaining active workforce.

Writing the lead article for the inaugural issue of *Work Life Review*, a journal launched by the Michigan Quality of Work Life Council in 1982, Ernie Savoie—vice chairman of Ford's 1982 negotiations committee (Pete Pestillo was the chair)—summarizes key features of the 1982 negotiations and describes the bargaining dynamics.

The need for action was compelling. In January 1982, the UAW started early talks simultaneously with General Motors and Ford, but concentrated immediately on GM. The UAW and GM shortly thereafter announced an agreement in principle on a "Framework for a New Agreement." A couple of days later, this Framework appeared on the Ford table. But our review of it convinced us that because of the differences in our size and structure, the GM approach would have resulted in a serious competitive price disadvantage in the marketplace for Ford. As a result, Ford counter-proposed with its own approach—something that had not occurred in the auto industry in 25 years.

When the negotiations at GM terminated without a new contract, our counterproposal was still on the table, very much alive. Since it addressed all the key concerns the Union and employees had been talking about, it became the new focal point for auto industry bargaining.[24]

The break in pattern bargaining, with Ford replacing GM as the lead company, is unprecedented in the industry. It is also a strategic move by Ford to gain competitive advantage over GM.

By January 1982, Ford completes most of the layoffs it needs to match workforce size with reduced demand—something GM has not yet fully done. By reaching an agreement that includes certain income security guarantees for the remaining workforce, Ford responds to a primary UAW concern and gains a cost advantage over GM that lasts for nearly a half-dozen years. But it is possible only because Ford's counterproposal represents a compelling alternative to the initial "Framework for a New Agreement" the UAW began discussing with GM.

Joel Cutcher-Gershenfeld, then on staff at the Michigan Quality of Work Life Council, recalls, "Ernie Savoie served on our research advisory committee. We had a regularly scheduled meeting after the UAW had targeted the bargaining with GM. Ernie was at the meeting and right after shared his view that Ford had to get the UAW focused in a different direction. He indicated he and others at Ford were prepared to table a proposal for something dramatically broader than anything going on in the industry."

In the *Work Life Review* article, Savoie describes the agreement that the UAW reached with Ford.

A final agreement emerged out of two-and-one-half weeks of intensive problem-solving negotiations. The bargaining produced a network of interlocking programs that fit together in a complementary way. The network, the Mutual Growth Program, was symbolized by a "Gear Chart" that represented the matrix of cooperation, which would yield success for employees, the Ford Motor Company, and the UAW.

Figure 1.6, the Gear Chart to which Savoie refers, shows the Mutual Growth Program's full scope.

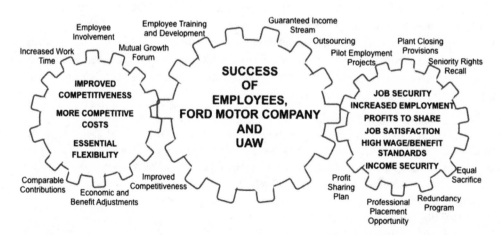

Figure 1.6

UAW-Ford Mutual Growth Program Gear Chart. *Source:* Ernest J. Savoie, "The New UAW-Ford Agreement: It's Work Life Aspects," *The Work Life Review,* 1982.

"Ernie was in a rush to get the gear chart drawn once the negotiations had concluded," Joel Cutcher-Gershenfeld recalls. "While all the right words were on the diagram, there was some criticism in the plants that produced gears and axles for Ford, since the gears were drawn in such a way that if real, they would not mesh properly." In fact, it would take the full transformation to realize the full potential of having the gears fully meshed.

Don Ephlin, the UAW's lead bargainer with Ford in the 1982 negotiations, writes a foreword to Ernie Savoie's article and comments:

It is impossible to understand the UAW-Ford agreement and the Mutual Growth Program that it establishes without an understanding of our joint Employee Involvement (EI) program. Although the UAW went to the bargaining table to do everything possible to make the jobs of the UAW-Ford members more secure, this was not negotiation in the normal sense of the word. We were engaged in precisely the kinds of joint problem solving that has characterized our most successful EI efforts.

The 30-month agreement, reached six months in advance of the contract expiration without the threat of a strike, does set aside the Annual Improvement Factor. In lieu of a percentage increase in the base wage, the union wins lump sum wage increases—the very issue over which Canadian UAW members split to form the CAW. The U.S. workforce also secures a profit-sharing program along with a Guaranteed Income Stream (GIS) that gives the remaining workforce assurances of income security in a future downturn in exchange for a willingness to accept transfers to different jobs in their plants or at other locations. The existing EI program is reinforced with new training investments.

Two new institutional arrangements are also established. First are the Mutual Growth Forums at national and plant levels. Ernie Savoie describes the new arrangement in his *Work Life Review* article.

Designed to function at both the national and local levels, the Forums are an adjunct to the existing collective bargaining process. They will provide a new framework intended to promote sound management-union relations through better communications, systematic fact-finding, and advance discussion of certain business developments that are of material interest to the union, the employees, and the company.

The Forums, which will meet at least quarterly, are in the vein of certain Japanese and European joint consultative meetings that take place regularly throughout the year between management and unions. They represent an extension of the informal meetings on business operating matters that have always occurred at Ford at the national level and in many local settings as well. This will provide an opportunity for preventative problem solving and can serve as an early warning system.

As part of the letter of agreement on the Mutual Growth Forums, Ford invites the UAW vice president and director of the Ford Department to address the company's board of directors twice a year.

Characterizing the Mutual Growth Forums as an "adjunct" to collective bargaining is significant. Both the EI program at Ford and the parallel QWL program at GM were explicitly set up in 1979 as separate from collective bargaining. This is an important connection between worker participation and the negotiation of wages, hours, and working conditions. Most important, it connects the union formally to the fortunes of the business.

Savoie also describes the Employee Development and Training Program (EDTP), the second new institutional arrangement established in this negotiation.

To our knowledge, there is nothing like it anywhere in American industry. It is a new, jointly administered program designed to: (a) provide training, retraining, and developmental opportunities for active employees; (b) arrange for training, retraining, and developmental assistance for employees displaced, or laid off because of new technologies, new production techniques, shifts in customer product preferences, facility closings, or discontinuances of operations; (c) sustain and support local and national Employee Involvement efforts; and (d) provide opportunities for the exchange of ideas and innovations with respect to employee development and training needs.

Funding for the joint programs is set initially at five cents per hour worked for all U.S. hourly employees and hence is termed the "nickel fund." As EDTP's scope expands in subsequent years, the hourly increment is increased. The arrangement builds on the parties' joint experience providing retraining and placement for the massive number of employees laid off in 1980 and 1981, with the focus expanding to include the active workforce. In other auto companies and in other industries, similar joint training funds and programs are established based on the UAW-Ford model. It is notable that among industrial relations and personnel professionals in management, these funds in later years are valued for the way they protected investments in training, which are otherwise usually the first parts of budgets to be cut in a downturn.

Ernie Savoie sums up the agreement as follows.

The 1982 Ford-UAW agreement represents a major demonstration of the new work-life spirit; of the transference from *we versus they* to *us*; from adversarial to converging; from rigidity to flexibility; and from partisan to common interest.

✳ ✳ ✳

Both the UAW and Ford demonstrated essential leadership in the face of an economic crisis that has many echoes of the 2007 recession. There were instrumental motivations for both parties as well—Ford to gain competitive advantage over GM and the UAW to make the best possible deal for the active workforce. It was a genuine challenge and took more than three decades to see the full potential represented by all the parts of the 1982 agreement. The scale and scope of what both parties constructed represented a compelling vision and framework that continues to guide innovation today.

Recap: The Pivotal 2008 Bailout Decision

In this chapter we place the focus on a highly visible and highly consequential decision—Ford not taking the bailout money. That was not an isolated event. It was possible only because it rested on the shoulders of dozens of preceding pivotal events in a story still unfolding. Presenting these pivotal events represents a journey inside the Ford-UAW transformation, which is the aim of this book.

Beginning the journey, we present three pivotal events in this chapter—primarily to introduce ourselves as coauthors, but also as early harbingers of the pivots to come. Two plant-level pivots are presented—one in which transformative change was achieved and one in which it was not, with the plant closing as a result. The third pivotal event is at the enterprise level and marks the foundation for the principle of "mutual gains" in the Ford-UAW system—a theme of enduring importance.

The balance of this book represents our best effort to capture that story and set the stage for what is yet to come. We tell the story through pivotal events, each of which provides a unique window into the culture of Ford and the UAW as well as the dynamics of change. What was and remains at stake in the pivotal events in this book goes far beyond Ford and the UAW. It is the very ability of the United States to retain and grow manufacturing jobs. It is a key enabler of the American Dream—the ability to have good jobs and high performance go hand in hand in a way the preserves and grows the middle class in society.

What is at stake is the ability of one generation to have confidence that the next generation will be able to do better. Increasingly, that dream is not limited to America but is a hope for the future shared by people throughout the world.

SUPPORTING MATERIALS

1.1 Green Island Archive

> *Corrected Copy**
> Labor-Management Meeting
> Ford Motor Company—Green Island, New York
> January 14, 1944
>
> | Representing Labor | Representing Management |
> |---|---|
> | Frank Murphy, President Local 930 UAW-CIO | J F Ringwald, ITO Labor Rep'tve |
> | Frank Cox, Vice President Local 930 UAW-CIO | J F Doocey, Plant Protection Head |
> | Louis Sanders, Recording Sect'y Local 930 UAW-CIO | J L Sandford, Employee Man |
> | Committeeman, Messier Boudreau | Foreman Carlow and Dailey |

Doocey: Mr. Ringwald has come down here to try to help us find out what our difficulties are and see if he can't help us to be a happy family down here one way or another. Only one way to find out what's what is to find out what grievances are on the fire etc. He'll do what he can to try and help us. From now on it's up to you fellows to talk to him and tell him our difficulties, or differences.

Murphy: As far as we are concerned we have no differences.

Ringwald: Just what are your grievances now? We're here to discuss them.

Murphy: We'll discuss them in the regular way at the proper time.

Ringwald: Just what is the regular way and the proper time?

Murphy: In the first place, we don't want anything to do with you. You're just a visitor as far as we are concerned. We know your record. We know what you are and you're not bluffing anybody.

Ringwald: So you think I'm bluffing?

Murphy: I don't think, I know your bluffing.

Ringwald: Well, I'll show you whether I'm bluffing or not. Joe, does this man do any work when he's not settling grievances?

Doocey: No

Ringwald: Well, assign him a job and see that he works on it. If he don't, fire him. I came down here prepared to discuss your grievances with you in a business-like way, if you want to make it a personal matter why that's OK with me. We'll play with you any way you want. If you want it personal then it'll be personal. There are several parts of the agreement you have violated. There is too much lost time on the job, committeemen are not doing enough work, are off the job more than just settling grievance matters, the minutes cost is too high on the Pratt & Whitney job. Now if you want to discuss these things, all right, we're here to discuss them. If you don't, that's all right too.

Murphy: Just what do you want us to do?

Ringwald: Bring out your grievances. I understand there are plenty of them down here.

Murphy: We don't want to deal with you, and we don't have to deal with you. We'll bring up our grievances at the regular meeting on Tuesday afternoon at 2 o'clock. We didn't know you were coming; we had no time to prepare ourselves and get our grievances ready.

Meeting descends to personalities. Ringwald states he does not Murphy's attitude. Murphy states he doesn't like Ringwalds. In the discussion Ringwald call Murphy a liar, says he's yellow, asks Murphy if he'll come out in front with him. Murphy states he'd be a fool to go out and make a spectacle of himself so that Ringwald could go back to Dearborn a hero etc. etc. Ringwald then asks Murphy if he'll stand up to him inside. Murphy says what for. Takes off his glasses and lays them on the table …

Ringwald: Murphy, I'd like to see you get a better idea of what bargaining means.

Murphy: I don't want any suggestions from you. I know who you are and what you are. Why you ought to be ashamed to look in the glass

*Excerpted from the original Minutes as recorded by the Union Secretary. No changes of any kind have been made.

POSTSCRIPT: At the time of this meeting Local 930 was barely three years old. Predictably, leadership for both labor and management would face some tough go-arounds as they begin to learn the fine art and disciplined skill of listening in one another, of communicating effectively, of dialogue, of negotiation. The progress of more than forty years is clearly evidenced by such outstanding accomplishments in our plant as Special Early, EI, EAP, RAC, health and education fairs, career advising, and instructional programs and service.

Source: Ford Motor Company

Comments:

This set of transcribed minutes from a 1944 interaction in the Green Island Plant has been presented in the same format as used in the local union newsletter years later. It illustrates just how contentious and even abusive traditional union-management relations were in the early years at Green Island—on both sides.

2 The Case for Change

Guiding Principle: Courageous Leadership

Why change? Consider the alternative. Why leave things unchanged?

We know change is difficult. It's not that alternatives aren't promising. It's that change involves letting go[1] and heightens uncertainty. In any pivotal event when change is on the table, someone early on is bound to ask why. Leaders envisioning change must have a convincing answer. Advancing change takes courage. So, too, do contemplating change, accepting change, embracing change.

This chapter focuses on pivotal events in which making the case for change is particularly central to the pivot. Generally this is at the early stages of a pivot. Each pivot illustrates the courage required or the consequences when the case for change is not sufficiently clear.

Workplace leaders—labor or management—making the case for change to others must begin by looking inward and persuading themselves of the real need for change.[2] In 2002, UAW and Ford leaders had to have this inner conversation when the company had what many saw as a "burning platform" on global quality and its product lineup was earning mixed reviews. Around 2008, considerable progress had been made on quality, but it was clear the industry was about to face its worst collapse since the Great Depression of the 1930s. Another case for change would be needed, and another inner conversation required.

Key changes by labor and management in expanding partnership—at times of great labor-management conflict in society—enabled Ford to achieve world-class, industry-leading quality, with best-in-class products on energy efficiency and design. UAW and Ford leaders who saw the need for change in 2002 and again in 2008 are celebrated today for their vision, dedication, and the results achieved—which set the stage for Ford not taking the bailout money. But it wasn't so clear at the time, and it certainly wasn't easy.

Making the case for change first requires establishing a sense of urgency. Leaders begin within their own hearts and minds and then extend the sense of urgency across the enterprise. A sense of urgency doesn't imply complete agreement among all leaders on the ultimate goal or aim (we get to joint alignment in chapter 7), but it does imply agreement that the current state—the direction in which things are headed—is inadequate. This is where courage comes in—it takes some courage to be among the first to state that the status quo is inadequate, and it takes much more courage to point in the direction of a new aim, vision, or approach.

You would have been angry had you been a UAW leader back in 2002. The challenges of the post–9/11 recession were compounded by the preceding decade during which Ford invested vast sums in international acquisitions rather than its core U.S. business. The company you work for, and that your mother or father likely worked for, is spread too thin and had made itself more vulnerable than most other automotive manufacturers to the downturn. Beyond the big strategic issues, you'd be angry about day-to-day things like supervisors pitting workers against each other on performance, managers pitting one shift against another, and the company pitting plant against plant. It would be so easy to play to your membership audience, feed their anger, and fix the blame squarely on management.

If you were a supervisor or manager or executive, you could be blaming the union leaders and the rank-and-file workers. You'd be aware that workers mistreat co-workers. You'd point to excessive absenteeism on Mondays and Fridays, and workers tolerating unsafe behavior on the job. Blaming aging capital equipment wouldn't require you to look very far either. You'd fault suppliers for dropping the ball when they'd been asked to take on more responsibility for engineering design. The finger pointing would extend to complaints about dealer customer service and the reluctance of some dealers to reinvest in their facilities.

There would also be blame to go around at the societal level as well. UAW leaders and Ford managers alike would find it easy to resent southern states competing for investment and automotive jobs by offering lucrative tax breaks to foreign manufacturers—while domestic automotive manufacturers that had been in U.S. communities for decades received much more limited government economic incentives. Compounding this inequity in public investment, the domestic union and management leaders alike would begrudge these foreign companies for the fact that they didn't carry enormous "legacy costs"—pension and retiree health care costs. Such legacy costs actually benefit American society through retiree purchasing power, but these same costs weaken the balance sheet and available investment funds of the domestic companies. If these leaders were particularly patriotic—and most would be—they would also wonder about, and probably resent, public incentives given to foreign companies from the very countries the United States fought during World War II. Why, they might ask, aren't we investing as much in skills for the U.S. workforce or in ensuring the competitiveness of the U.S. manufacturers?

Back in 2002, blame was the easy path. Much more difficult would be for a union leader to work cooperatively with management to fix the problems, much harder for management would be to share decision making with the union as a full partner. Labor and management would both find it challenging to value front-line work in ways that make continuous improvement possible. Sure, everyone can grasp a joint effort on safety. But tackling quality means giving up power and autonomy while taking on full, shared responsibility for current performance gaps. Acknowledging interdependency and acting together responsibly begins as a personal courageous decision, one leader at a time.

If in 2002 you showed courage and made the tough decision to work jointly to accelerate the implementation of quality and safety operating systems, by 2008 you would be rightfully proud of having produced an historic turnaround. Ford rose from near-last place in global quality to overall best in class. Dozens of assembly plants, each building a car a minute, valued work, engaged frontline teams, had aligned internal functions, and were delivering positive results. But the handwriting was already on the wall, and you would soon face as profound a challenge as in 2002: there was about to be a major collapse in the marketplace and a number of those very successful plants would be at risk of closing.

Workers, union leaders, and managers who had made the difficult leadership decisions were about to be rewarded with massive change—involving approximately 50,000 hourly workers. Once again, it would be easy to find others to blame.

If you had succeeded in setting aside blame in 2002, could you have done it again in 2007? You'd need to internalize the sense of urgency in your head and in your heart, and then you'd have the challenge of communicating that sense of urgency to others. People who are confronted with data on competitive pressures and the need to change typically respond first with denial. They may even blame the messenger. Persist with them, and they may shift to questioning the data. For leaders trying to create a sense of urgency, that questioning can feel like more rejection of the message. In fact, though, it's a good thing—an important shift—because people are at least engaging the question. Courageous leaders know to welcome challenges to the data with open arms; it's a necessary step in people accepting the data (or insisting on additional data) that allows for a more broadly shared sense of urgency. In other words, making the case for change requires the courage to accept and even embrace hard questions.

Leaders in large corporations such as the Ford Motor Company and major unions such as the UAW have considerable formal authority when it comes to committing resources and making strategic decisions. That authority, though, is only enough to insist on compliance when it comes to making the case for change. It is of little use in winning commitment. Winning the commitment needed in 2002 and 2008 requires leadership not by authority but by influence.

The first item in the supporting materials for this chapter (2.1, the transition curve for a cycle of change), illustrates the journey people generally follow before being willing to consider change. They give up notions of their own competency on a given issue or matter. Shock, denial, awareness, and acceptance are all steps that come before engagement with the change process. This is a journey traveled on the basis of influence more than authority.

Of course, the challenges of 2002 and 2008 were preceded by numerous economic and social shocks in the auto industry, all with an associated sense of urgency around change. The effects of the 1980s oil embargo, coupled with the availability of fuel-efficient, high-quality Japanese vehicles, dramatically reduced market share and profit margins for U.S.

automakers, representing the first shock to traditional relations. While contractual language promoting Employee Involvement (EI) was first drafted in 1979 by the UAW and Ford, reflecting an earlier aspiration to improve the quality of work life, it was the economic shocks of the 1980s that created a sense of urgency around connecting EI with a need to improve the economic performance of the business.

The pivotal events in this chapter all illustrate the importance of the case for change—both the compelling force when it is clear and the limiting constraints when it is not. In making the case for change, leadership is essential. Often, the exercise of leadership involves ambiguity and risk—leaving behind comfortable assumptions and operating in new ways. For these reasons, we highlight the courageous leadership needed in the early stages of a pivot when the case for change is on the table.

Pivotal Events in This Chapter

We focus on six pivotal events in this chapter, beginning with a pivotal event that had transformative potential in the business but that fell short in a number of regards. Each of these pivots could be in other chapters as well: the Ford 2000 pivot could be in chapter 4 on "business fundamentals"; the Cleveland Engine Plant 1 pivot could be in chapter 5 on "knowledge-driven work"; the pivot on competitive operating agreements could be in chapter 6 on "negotiated change"; and so forth with the others. We chose them for this chapter to illustrate the many dimensions associated with making the case for change, and also because they signal substantive types of change that are relevant for many parts of the book. We present these events, and the pivotal events in other chapters, as though you were there at the time.

Chapter 2 Pivotal Events	Overview	Type, Level
Ford 2000, 1993–1995	Launched as a reengineering initiative to transform global design, manufacturing, and production, Ford 2000 reveals how challenging that goal will be. In the process, the pressure for efficiencies undercuts the Ford-UAW partnership in important ways—and a potentially transformational pivot falls short.	Planned, Enterprise Level
Cleveland Engine Plant 1, 1996–2002	In this plant, there is both the case for change and the needed leadership. The lessons from the changes echo as recently as the 2011 national Ford-UAW negotiation with respect to team-based work systems (chapter 6).	Unplanned, Plant Level

Chapter 2

Pivotal Events	Overview	Type, Level
The Rouge Explosion, 1999	Also at the plant level, this pivot has much broader implications. The case for change in the 1999 Rouge explosion is unambiguous. It is foundational in what ultimately becomes the safety operating system. Equally important, however, the instant and courageous response of then chairman and CEO Bill Ford reinforces the sense of family in what is America's most prominent family-owned firm in ways that also prove pivotal when the entire business is at risk of bankruptcy.	Unplanned, Plant Level
Competitive Operating Agreements, 2006–2007	This negotiation directly involves most of the U.S. facilities with the formal development of case-for-change presentations in each plant, as well as the exercise of courageous local leadership by management, the union, and the workforce.	Planned, Enterprise Level
Ford Puts All Cards on the Table with the UAW, 2007	When Ford puts all the cards on the table with the UAW in 2007, an explicit case for change is made and courageous leadership is shown at the highest levels of both organizations. This is an unprecedented level of information sharing by the company and an equally constructive response on the part of the UAW.	Planned, Enterprise Level
Frontline Leadership, 2013	A frontline hourly leader exemplifies the personal changes and courage involved in transitioning from a traditional assembly line job to leading issues of quality, diversity, supplier relations, and continuous improvement based on Six Sigma methods.	Unplanned, Plant Level

Ford 2000, 1993–1995

"Ford 2000," launched in January 1993, aims to improve Ford's operating practices world-wide. Its leader Robert Transou—Group Vice President for Manufacturing—is building on earlier steps taken in Powertrain Operations (PTO), sourcing common components in engines on a global basis. Transou's initial preparations catch the attention of CEO Alex Trotman, who had previously headed up European operations. In Europe, the business is divided along country and product lines, creating many inefficiencies. Trotman instantly sees the importance for Ford beyond Powertrain or manufacturing, and it becomes his signature initiative.

"We called this reengineering how we did our work," explains Roman Krygier, who led the manufacturing aspects of Ford 2000. This reengineering model of change underlies Ford 2000, which primarily takes a top-down approach.[3] A reengineered Ford Product Development System (FPDS) is created as part of Ford 2000 to improve quality, cost, and time to market by sharing platforms and components on a global basis.[4] Ford 2000 also sets the stage for what would become the Ford Production System (FPS).

While Ford 2000 is a precursor to transformational changes to come for Ford and the UAW, its immediate impact is mixed. The complexity of the change proves overwhelming, including an enterprise-wide shift to a matrix organizational structure; fundamental changes in the relationships among product development, manufacturing, purchasing and other functions; and restructuring of union-management joint activities.

The Ford 2000 case for change centers on the potential efficiencies associated with global product platforms. "Globalization was providing a different emphasis on how to be successful," Krygier says. "The company had to be focused on managing its business on a global basis. Otherwise the business would be vulnerable."

The challenges are considerable. "If you are designing cars," Krygier adds, "you want to leverage design in manufacturing around the world—all aspects have to come together. If a vehicle is successful in one market it is easier to transfer to other markets by adapting, rather than starting from scratch.... This was a huge change. We had so many different areas of the company—North America, Europe, Asia, Australia, South America. Some things were similar, but many things done differently."

Initially, a core group of people is removed from their jobs and brought together on one floor in Ford's world headquarters. "There were 25 people initially," says Krygier, "each responsible for touching all aspects of what they did in their functions, as well as the related functions of other people in the group. My responsibility was to deliver all the definitions of the common processes for manufacturing, as well as the roles and responsibilities of the people doing the processes."

For Krygier, this involves defining and improving processes in common ways across the world, as well as strengthening relations across functions. "The goal," he says, "was to reduce the time from design to manufacturing—every process involved relationships among people and how they did their individual work."

The case for change in Ford 2000 also involves addressing Ford's country and function "fiefdoms"—done through a formalized matrix structure throughout the company.

Says Krygier, "Ford 2000 was definitely a pivotal event in going after our processes in two ways—the process within each function (such as manufacturing) and the relationship among the functions (manufacturing to product development, for example). In both cases the goal was to streamline how things get done."

Constantly improving processes, notes Krygier, "really means improving relationships. It was about getting our act together in how we did work."

One major change is in reporting relationships. Many who once reported to a single person now have dual reporting relationships. Krygier, for instance, goes from reporting only to Bob Transou (head of Manufacturing), to reporting both to Transou and Jacques (Jac) Nasser (head of Product Development) as a part of the Ford 2000 initiative. Some people end up with as many as three or four reporting relationships.

When the Ford 2000 case for change is made more broadly, it is on a top-down basis—with no broad education or engagement. This gap is compounded by an incomplete understanding of the full magnitude of the challenge. As Krygier recalls:

People need to report within the function and across functions. This had to work at every level in the organization. This was hard to do—it was one of the most difficult things. You're changing from a highly autocratic culture....People got confused about roles and responsibilities. It wasn't easy. Some people couldn't buy into this new system—these were fundamental relationship changes.

In retrospect, notes Krygier, "It was a bigger thing than we realized....The human interfaces were not given enough attention....It's not that we didn't give them attention. It's just that we didn't understand the dynamics of all the effects Ford 2000 would have on people."

The degree to which Ford 2000 did not fully achieve its objectives can be seen in one of its most visible pilot initiatives. The Ford Escort is redesigned and launched under Ford 2000, but beyond the Ford oval on the car's front it does not share fully a single other component in all markets. Conflicting regulatory requirements and persistent organizational fiefdoms mean the Ford Escorts sold in Europe, the United States, and other markets still differ from one another in many substantial ways.

Perhaps most problematic, though, is the top-down approach to change. By centralizing all product-sourcing in Dearborn, the company undercuts the authority of country and regional leaders around the world. The decision-making bottleneck that results, without input from people close to the source, proves unmanageable.

"In the course of the whole effort," Krygier notes, "we were so focused on the common processes that we didn't think about what had to be altered regionally. When you talk about purchasing, for example, you need to give regions more flexibility. If it all had to come back centrally you lose the quickness of getting things done....The system wasn't robust enough to take into account all the factors."

The Ford Product Development System (FPDS) that is created as part of Ford 2000 ultimately becomes the foundation for transformational change in new product development. Ford moves to a limited number of flexible platforms, replacing platforms that support only one or two products with platforms that each support as many as a half dozen. The realization of that vision takes more than twice as long as the initial year 2000 target, however; many factors contribute to the delay, including some having to do with work and relationships.

First, the way automotive design engineers are rewarded and promoted creates problems. Instead of being rewarded to stay with a product from design through launch and production operations, they are promoted from one new product design to the next, often moving across specialty areas. What may be a great strategy for developing enterprise leaders does little to build the end-to-end understanding that design engineers need if product development is to be fully transformed. Second, the limited input production workers have into the early stages of the design process makes it difficult to advance the principle of "design for manufacture." More often, workers and managers in production operations complain about design engineers throwing unrealistic designs "over the wall" for production to sort out. In both cases, the lack of a shared appreciation for the need to change is reflected in results.

Ford 2000 is not a change that would be made in partnership with the UAW. It is a global management reengineering initiative. Ford's human resource and labor affairs professionals play a limited role, and thus get no opportunity to address potential complications with cross-functional relationships, career paths, and union-management relationships that ideally would be fully integrated into the design and development of Ford 2000. The case for change is never presented to the frontline workforce in a way that addresses their interests.

The reengineering logic of Ford 2000, with its emphasis on finding efficiencies through the redesign of operations, actually has negative implications for the Ford-UAW relationship during the mid-to-late 1990s, by which time a typical week in the Ford-UAW facilities with strong joint programs involves numerous joint meetings on employee involvement, health and safety, quality, preventative maintenance, and other topics. Five or more such meetings each week are a considerable time commitment for plant managers, HR managers, and local UAW bargaining committee chairs. Some local union and management leaders see them as a waste of time; many meetings don't live up to their potential, and these leaders want fewer of them. So, under the Ford 2000 banner, these meetings are compressed into a single weekly joint meeting—in the name of efficiency. The new format, though, means packed agendas dominated by update reports with little time for genuine dialogue or problem solving.

At the UAW's highest levels, there is not resistance to the erosion of the joint processes at Ford. Steve Yokich, who leads the UAW from 1994 to 2002, rejects many of the joint activities pioneered at Ford under the banner of Employee Involvement (EI) and at General Motors under the banner of improving the Quality of Work Life (QWL). While some union leaders and managers at the local level are committed to the joint pursuit of mutual gains, and use "good and welfare" meetings and other meetings for these objectives, Ford 2000 makes it easier for other less-committed local leaders to side-step mutual gains. It takes the tragic explosion at the Rouge plant (discussed below) to reintroduce separate safety meetings focused on problem solving. The quality function follows by reestablishing its own separate meetings, and ultimately there is a full "time and data management" structure for quality, safety and other parts of a balanced scorecard (presented in chapter 7).

Still, overall, the reengineering approach of Ford 2000 is a step back for joint programs. By the late 1990s it is arguable that the Ford-UAW locations are more variable in the joint activities than at the beginning of the decade. There are pockets of exceptional innovation at the plant and enterprise levels (as we show later), but there are also pockets of highly traditional relationships.

On the management side, with the year 2000 approaching and results falling short of their potential, senior Ford leadership shifts focus to acquiring brands to enhance the Ford portfolio, including purchasing Land Rover and Volvo in 1999, and a larger stake in Mazda.

✳✳✳

Ford 2000 was foundational for the Ford Product Development System and for what would become the Ford Production System. It was the first attempt to organize operations on a global basis, which would ultimately be achieved under the banner of "One Ford" in the mid-2000s.

More than a decade and a half after Ford 2000's launch, the systematic changes in the work and the relationships needed to transform product development show results. Increased flexibility in the production facilities, achieved by Ford in partnership with the UAW, is integral to the success, as is a shared appreciation of the need to change throughout the engineering and design operations. The relationship ultimately changes between manufacturing and new product design, as well as the underlying appreciation of the need for change.

The case for change was strong. But as Krygier notes, "It was much more complicated than was understood at the time." In particular, the case for change never reached all of the relationships, including the union-management relationship, the supplier relationships, the cross-functional relationships, the dealer relationships, and others that needed to be aligned for change at this scale.

Ford 2000 was pivotal, but it was also a lesson for what could and could not pivot under the banner of a single initiative at this time.

Cleveland Engine Plant 1, 1996–2002

In 1996, Cleveland Engine Plant 1 faces a fundamental crisis. Ford has slated the two engines it produces to be discontinued, placing the plant at risk of closing. By the mid-1990s, Cleveland Engine Plant 2 and the Romeo Engine Plant (see chapter 5) are already experimenting with work groups and elected team leaders. But the work group approach has not been deployed in Cleveland Engine Plant 1, the older part of the complex.

How the plant faces the crisis is pivotal to the Ford-UAW transformation. The crisis motivates union and management leaders to embrace lean production practices as embodied in the Ford Production System; it becomes the first wall-to-wall implementation of FPS. Further, the union—more so than management—is the driving force for change, altering the stereotypical narrative about unions. Even with the galvanizing threat of a potential plant closing, however, there is still resistance to change and success is far from assured.

A number of years earlier, another engine plant in Windsor, Ontario, faces a similar threat. Windsor works to be the highest-scoring plant on the Q1 quality audit, which proves key to that facility winning new products and avoiding a closure. This serves as a model for the UAW at Cleveland Engine Plant 1, although management initially rebuffs the union. John Nahornyj, UAW's Employee Resource Coordinator, is a driving force in the implementation.

"We thought in Plant 1 that if [Windsor] could do it, we could," Nahornyj recalls. "Q1 was a memory and the new thing was the FPS and work groups. We decided we would do everything and anything to improve upon what was happening."

In 1995, Ford and the UAW convene a briefing at Detroit's Renaissance Center on the idea of Modern Operating Agreements (MOAs). Ford's aim is to achieve some flexibility in work rules. As discussed further in chapter 6, the move is controversial—the union sees it as "pitting plant against plant." While there are some uncompetitive practices in the plants, as Nahornyj acknowledges today, there is also resistance to being forced into "the Japanese model." The Cleveland site local leadership attends the Detroit briefing as well as an additional weeklong training on MOAs offered by the company and the union, and conducts benchmarking visits to other locations operating in this way. They conclude that since they are already sharing information and working together in some of the same ways as at the MOA locations, they can go the MOA route in local negotiations.

"I spoke with the building chairman of Plant 1 about the need for change," Nahornyj recalls, "and we both agreed that we can't stand here and just watch. We needed to take control of the future of the plant. We decided to follow the Windsor Plant 2 approach. Tim [the UAW chairperson] was able to take that idea to Ford leadership. There were those high in the organization who laughed in his face and said the plant would close and never reopen. I don't believe anyone thought we could do it."

Going back to before 1996, plant employees are working with steady demand for the products. Most are skeptical of any risk to the plant's future. They treat closure rumors as nothing more than doom and gloom designed to frighten people. But the UAW leadership knows that the threat is real and looks for ways to extend the life of the plant. Participating in the corporate rollout of FPS and scoring the highest ranking in the FPS audits appears to offer the best opportunity for success.

Nahornyj continues his account:

Corporate FPS saw us as a closing plant, so no funding for FPS rollout was dedicated to Plant 1. There was a rapid deployment plan in the Lima Engine Plant and for other locations. I recall talking to people in HR indicating our interest and we were flat out told "no."

[The year] 1996 was a contract year. It was also the year production of the 4.9 liter engine was scheduled to end. We were invited up to Detroit where we were told, "You can negotiate a traditional agreement and you will not get any work. You will rot on the vine." We were told there was no new work at this time. We were also told, "If you negotiate a Modern Operating Agreement and new work becomes available, you will be in the running."

We looked at Romeo and Windsor, MOA plants with new work. We negotiated both an MOA and a traditional agreement. At the eleventh hour, we decided to go with the MOA. Then there was the issue of how to make the transition.

Once the contract is agreed to, a plan for implementation is developed within the framework of the FPS. This means migrating the plant's culture from traditional work practices to a modern, team-based facility. The transition to work groups is to occur incrementally, with the Engine Assembly Department developing functioning teams within the first year of the contract and the remainder of the plant to follow in the final two years of the agreement. Additionally, lean-manufacturing principles will replace the mass production methods of the past. Corporate FPS agrees to assist by providing coaching and periodic audits to measure progress.

The cornerstone of this initiative is to engage and educate the 1,000 employees working in the plant. "We scheduled all hourly and salaried employees to attend meetings in groups of 50 people to explain the current state of the plant and to define our strategy for saving the plant," Nahornyj recalls. "The meetings were led by UAW-Ford plant leadership. The loss of the 6-cylinder was painful and now the employees were told the 5.0 was also slated to shut down in 1999. The impact on morale was devastating at the outset. But there was a plan in place and most of the people agreed that something had to be done and were willing to fight for the future of their plant."

The MOA grandfathers those with the job classification "panel operator" into the role of team leader, since they are already filling in, reporting issues, and performing some other team leader–like tasks along many sections of the assembly line. As openings become available through retirements or individuals moving to other jobs, team leader positions are established and UAW members can bid on the jobs (that is, request consideration for the new role). This builds up a cadre of individuals who meet the team leader criteria on a more permanent basis. In other plants, team leaders are elected by team members, but at Cleveland Engine Plant 1 they are selected based on established criteria, though the specific roles and responsibilities are still being hammered out during implementation. The learning process, Nahornyj recalls, makes it imperative to specify the training for these individuals.

We had a basic idea, but there was no standardized training available for team leaders. There was a great deal of learning as we implemented. We didn't have much time. The 6-cylinder had been shut down. All we had left was the 5.0-liter. We also knew that training needed to be developed and delivered if we were to be successful. At this point it was clear we were tackling a large beast.

Then, by 1997, the training has to be delivered plant-wide because the entire workforce is now part of the strategy to save the plant. At the same time, the company indicates it plans to reduce production on the 5.0-liter and lay off 92 people. This, according to Nahornyj, leads the local union and management leaders to propose a bold solution.

Rather than cutting production and laying people off, the idea was to work four days a week at the original hourly production rate and dedicate one day a week for training. There was a total of 120 hours of training needed, so this was a perfect solution. We took this to the production manager, who took it to corporate. Within a week, we had approval, and now there was interest from Dearborn. We managed to train the entire plant—workers, engineers, supervisors—all mixed together. We had a thousand people in the plant—so everyone had a different training day to use the learning center. Everyone then had time to implement the principles in their work area for three weeks following training in one of the disciplines of FPS (quality, safety, materials, cost, etc.). Then they would move on to the next discipline. They would learn a concept and then apply it in their work area.

We knew people had to be able to talk with one another to set objectives. So we were building teams during the training, while reinforcing the learning. There was all the forming, storming, norming, and performing. We were teaching people about these behaviors. They realized their reactions were normal. Before you know it, they were achieving things.

Under the Q1 quality initiative and in some of the early experiments with work groups in many plants, there is first an "initial application area" that serves as a pilot for the change process. As is generally the experience with pilot experimental areas, diffusion beyond the pilot can be more challenging than the initial pilot (which often benefits from extra resources and more focused attention). In the case of Cleveland Engine Plant 1, the parties begin with a broader implementation, rather than a single pilot area.

"There was resistance like you wouldn't believe," Nahornyj notes.

Q1 was based on initial application areas, and this is where the politics came in. Some wanted it to be section A of the assembly line and we were recommending something else. Some wanted the whole assembly line as the FPS initial application area, but that was too big. At this point the leadership came to understand that it was the real deal and not just a dog-and-pony area. Recognizing some of the difficulty we were having at Engine Assembly, the leadership of Cylinder Head Machining volunteered—after discussing this with the hourly and salaried workers in the department—their final air test section was selected to be the initial application area. The shift to this new area accelerated and focused our initiative immensely by eliminating the political constraints in the previous area and by virtue of the fact that the people chose to be involved.

Nahornyj recalls a UAW committeeman suggesting that continuous improvement on safety be plant-wide from the outset, since everyone can agree on safety. At first, only a few people in each work area attend the voluntary safety meetings. As safety issues are prioritized and addressed, however, participation increases. Nahornyj states, "We had maps of each area and used color dots for accidents—contusions, falls, lacerations. The meetings would be around the boards. The visuals helped teams to focus their attention. There was full support from the company on this."

There is also *active* resistance to the change from some in labor and management. "Some managers," Nahornyj explains, "were sabotaging the effort: withholding funding; overriding ideas that would be beneficial; and not coming to steering committee meetings, which we had agreed would be the deciding body to drive the process. Managers would not show up or come in late to be disruptive. It impacted the morale and the enthusiasm. At the same time, there were UAW committeemen on the floor going behind people's backs and saying they didn't support this."

Even *support* can be problematic if it involves traditional adversarial or command-and-control approaches. "I can't tell you how many one-on-one meetings I had with salaried and union guys who went back to old ways and pounded the table to insist on new behaviors," says Nahornyj. But he also recalls some individuals opposed to the change who chose not to act as barriers.

We adopted a policy of inclusion throughout this endeavor. Organizations have formal leaders and informal leaders, opinion leaders. There was a man on the block line who was the number-one grievance writer in the plant. He was critical of the changes as "Japanese claptrap." We would go back and forth discussing this. One day he came up to me and said, "I don't see anything wrong in what you guys are doing, but for me it is too late to change." Then he said, "I will not get in your way."

This was an influential opinion leader, and his being willing not to impede was a major success. As for the appointed team leaders, Nahornyj reports this role was not handled clearly.

As the teams on the plant floor were evolving, we continued to struggle with the weekly team leader meeting. It was only later that we realized the team leaders were a team in themselves. Initially, their meetings were among the most dysfunctional. So we talked through this with them, and then we started to have more functional meetings. It was a transition from a group of egos to a real working meeting—sharing ideas and helping each other. That is when we began to more precisely define roles and responsibilities.

Cleveland Engine Plant 1 becomes the first plant to specify the roles and responsibilities of a team leader under the FPS, and later decides to apply for one of the 2001 national joint UAW-Ford recognition awards. These awards are for innovation that can be replicated by other plants in the system, based on the plant's organizational design document and the established team leader roles and responsibilities. Results are important in this process. Nahornyj recalls, "Once the data began to reflect cost savings, the cynicism went into hiding. We took over $110 in cost out of a mature product. At 100,000 engines that is $1 million." Production on the 5.0-liter engine has been briefly extended; still, its end is looming—which means closing the plant. The hope is the award will win the plant a reprieve from closure; while that is not the award's purpose, the Windsor Engine Plant had earlier earned a new lease on life with the top Q1 award. Approaching the award as a way to help make the case for survival is a form of institutional creativity on the part of the local union and management leaders.

The plant wins the 2001 award, but nevertheless closes in 2002. Still, that is an extension of its life well beyond initial expectations.

The shutdown turns out to be brief. During a plant visit at the time, the Manufacturing vice president Roman Krygier has in hand a booklet with team leader testimonials. He states, "What if I were to take the front cover off of this booklet so that you didn't know what plant it was from? What would you say?" People there at the visit don't know if this is a rhetorical question or not. Krygier answers his question: "You would say, only close that plant long enough to put new work in there." Indeed, this is what happens—Cleveland Engine Plant 1 has made the business case for new work and it has another lease on life.

As Nahornyj recalls:

We had been flying by the seat of our pants. We didn't have time to breathe. Then we got the prize of new work. We learned not to take anything for granted. It was some of my most exhilarating work at Ford. We had developed a sense of urgency and we maintained it. We trained team leaders during the [new product] launch period. There were focus groups with production and skilled trades, which helped to clarify roles and responsibilities. We developed an Organizational Design Document with the help out outside consultants where we documented our growth strategy and the roles and responsibilities of all the employees in the plant.

We were surprised by high-seniority people, who were most willing to jump in. By contrast, some of the younger ones were most against change because of messages from their parents at home, who had previously been in the system. You will never get 100-percent support, but as long as you have 100-percent of the people not impeding the growth you can be successful.

✳ ✳ ✳

As a pivotal event, Cleveland Engine Plant 1 stands out as the first wall-to-wall implementation of FPS principles in an existing facility. Winning agreement for the transition from a traditional plant to a high-performance operation was not easy—even with the clear case for change, based on the threat of a plant closing. There was still active resistance to change and new learning required for everyone in the facility. It is notable that at several key junctures it was the union more than management making the case for change. In the end, the plant earned a second lease on life and continues as an effective team-based work system.

The Rouge Explosion, 1999

At 1:00 p.m. on Monday, February 1, 1999, "clouds of black smoke and bursts of red flames billow for several hours above the Ford Rouge Plant" following a massive explosion in a power plant boiler.[5] Six employees die. Another 24 are injured.

Bill Ford, the chairman and CEO at the time, wants to head over to the site immediately, but the staff urges him to hold back, pointing out that the situation is full of uncertainty and potentially still dangerous. He rejects the guidance and, within two hours of the explosion, is at Rouge.

"It was heartbreaking," Ford says. "It's about the worst feeling you could ever have."

UAW vice president Ron Gettelfinger joins Bill Ford and UAW Local 600 president Jerry Sullivan at the scene. Together, they comfort the bereaved families and co-workers.

Employees throughout the complex donate blood, food, and money to the families of the dead and injured.

Years later, the incident has assumed near-legendary status among Ford employees, but Bill Ford indicates he doesn't want to "make a big deal" out of this. "When that event happened, my first thought was what can I do—how can I help."

Further, "Ron [Gettelfinger] came down and we agreed right there on a renewed focus on health and safety."

Shortly afterwards, Gettelfinger addresses a joint Health and Safety meeting held in Romulus, Michigan, involving plant managers, human resources managers, local union presidents, and plant chairpersons from all locations. He "accepts the responsibility for safety" and, focusing on the UAW leaders in the room, adds, "If we do not fix safety, the UAW delegates to the next UAW Convention are obligated to vote against me." This was not hyperbole—the elected union leaders in the room knew Gettelfinger meant exactly what he had said.

Subsequently, every U.S. Ford location holds a "safety stand-down" that begins with meetings of the Ford operating committees and all elected and appointed UAW representatives, with UAW staff members and their Ford counterparts in attendance. It is made clear that any employee caught working in an unsafe manner will be penalized, as will their immediate supervisor. Gettelfinger indicates that every appointed UAW official will be reassigned from his or her current duties to safety if needed. Workplace safety becomes Job 1 in every UAW-Ford location.

*** *** ***

The event is pivotal in two respects. First, even though the joint UAW-Ford health and safety programs had been in operation for decades as one of the first joint programs between the company and the union (the apprentice program was the other), the response following the incident elevated the attention given to safety and marked the beginning of a shift into a safety operating system (detailed in chapter 8). Ultimately, the emergence of the safety operating system involved replacing the reactive "inspection" operating assumption with the comprehensive embrace of "prevention" as a more proactive approach.

At the time of Rouge explosion, Gettelfinger praised Ford for putting people above profits in the tragic situation. "Ford Motor Co. has never raised the issue of production throughout this crisis....We've started discussion about getting the operations back. They have dealt with the human side of the story, and I want to applaud Ford Motor Company."[6]

Looking back, Gregory Stone, a physician who had been in Ford's top health and safety position for less than three months at the time of the explosion, comments, "The response to the Rouge explosion set the tone, and that has not wavered at all. There was no finger pointing. It was just about tackling what needed to be tackled."

The second aspect that makes this a pivotal event is the way it reinforced the Ford Motor Company's unique role as the largest and most prominent family-owned firm in the United States. Hourly and salaried employees say they "work at Ford's" (not "for Ford") when asked about their place of employment. The Ford family shares this view. "I have never seen our employees as white or blue collar, union or nonunion," says Bill Ford. "We are all Ford. Yes, the UAW represents people for bargaining, but we are all an extended family."

Going directly to the scene of the explosion within hours of the incident evidenced leadership on the part of Bill Ford. His advisers made strenuous attempts to keep him from doing so. He went despite that first responders and, indeed, everyone there continued to face personal risk because it was not clear whether the site was safe. This response was also emblematic of what any family member would do at a time of family crisis. Ford personally comforted the families who had come to learn the fate of their loved ones.

Holding himself personally accountable for safety evidenced leadership on the part of Ron Gettelfinger. He was prepared to be voted out of office if no progress was made on this issue.

When the entire enterprise was at risk eight years later, during the Great Recession, this sense of family and personal responsibility were integral to the responses across the enterprise, with many citing the response to the Rouge incident as pivotal. It takes certain courage to put the situation above self, which was evident from both labor and management in this case.

UAW-Ford Competitive Operating Agreements, 2003–2007

By January 2006, more than a year and a half before national auto negotiations open, the UAW knows Ford faces deep financial difficulties. Anticipating strong pressure for concessions, the UAW makes a strategic move. Three years earlier, the 2003 agreement formalized the sort of constructive engagement that had happened on an ad hoc basis in 1981 in Monroe and again in 1996 in Cleveland, during which local unions negotiated with the company to modify local work practices. Still, such changes are controversial. While it would be easier to be reactive on a plant-by-plant basis, the union is mindful of its strategic priority, which is to preserve existing work in the Ford-UAW plants and, where possible, bring in new work. Chuck Browning is the member of the UAW's international staff who is given responsibility by Vice President Bob King to be proactive in this situation. When participating in a 2008 panel reflecting on the negotiations, he explained:

So, rather than have to try and muscle Ford Motor Company into bringing work into an uncompetitive environment, we took an approach that we're going to create an environment and create a cost structure where it's a positive for Ford Motor Company to put work in our plant. Also, if we're doing work with competitive labor costs, we thought we'd be a lot better off in national negotiations. If we could reduce some of the costs with competitive work practices, it can reduce having to reach into the members' pockets and pull money out of their wages or money out of their benefits.[8]

Joe Hinrichs, who was then Ford's vice president of Manufacturing, notes management's engagement of the union as a partner. "We worked hard to treat the [UAW's] national Ford department as part of the solution, not part of the problem. It would have been easy to blame the union just as it would have been easy to blame the company for lots of things in the past."

The union arranges for its own financial expert, Eric Perkins, to examine the company's financial situation. Perkins meets with the top executives of the company and is given access to the most confidential aspects of the business plan. He concludes that the situation is even worse than the company is saying.

The UAW and Ford negotiators embark on a marathon set of negotiations involving local union and management leadership in 41 separate plants—approximately one plant a week throughout 2006. This represents nearly all of Ford's U.S. assembly, stamping, and power-train production facilities. While there is a history of negotiating what are sometimes termed "competitive operating agreements" (COAs) or "modern operating agreements" (MOAs) at auto plants, most are one-at-a-time negotiations. This set of 41 sequential local COA negotiations in the space of less than one year is unprecedented in the history of U.S. collective bargaining.

Perkins prepares briefings for the union membership on behalf of the UAW. His message is blunt. "I told the membership that the company was in terrible shape. They should prepare for the worst. There were flexible body shops only running one product. Money had been wasted on share buybacks and special dividends, rather than investment in new products. Purchased component costs (two-thirds of vehicle costs) were roughly $2,000 higher for Ford than for Toyota and maybe a thousand higher than they were at GM on equivalent vehicles, primarily because of lousy volume predictions at the time of product approval. There was too much complexity in the design. Their time to market was two to three years longer than the Japanese and one year longer than GM. Ford had generated many innovative products such as the Explorer and the Expedition, but the success covered up underlying problems. Further, most of the Big 3 market share loss since 2001 had been at Ford, and this included the very profitable products such as Explorers, Expeditions, and even pickups—product segments Ford had once dominated. I said this company is on the verge of bankruptcy and they needed to make a radical transformation. Purchasing and design accounted for more of the problem than labor. I said that though we were only 20 percent of the problem, every penny counted. Many UAW members owned stock and identified with Ford. People thought of themselves as working for a great company—so it was a difficult message to deliver."

The bargaining delivers on the promise of generating substantial cost-savings; the efficiency changes are valued at more than $500 million. The local union and management leadership in each plant, as well as the frontline workforce, also develop much more comprehensive appreciation of the competitive situation of Ford's products in the marketplace. The process begins with the union's independent economic analysis of the company and a series of union meetings with divisional manufacturing management leadership. In these meetings, the union first asks for detailed information on what is needed in each location to get their part of the business in order financially. Then the union and management jointly explore what new work might have the potential to be brought in. With this information in hand, the international union then meets with local union leaders—having a clear vision of what management needed to improve economic performance and what new work might be possible for the location.

Each local union needs authorization from its members to open up the local agreement for negotiations. The entire workforce must be persuaded of the need for change, which involves a membership briefing on the competitive situation of the company and their plant. Many of the sessions hear a presentation from Eric Perkins, the independent expert selected by the union who has been given virtually unrestricted access to the corporation's financial information, as well as a presentation by a senior manufacturing executive—often Joe Hinrichs. It's particularly important that each briefing be consistent with the others. As Hinrichs recalls:

We wanted to have an honest-to-goodness real business conversation with the workforce. They were scared just like we were. We owed it to them to say where we were; it wasn't a scare tactic. I have always had the most success when . . . we had direct conversations as a business partner—town halls or otherwise. We were not threatening and not jumping to solutions. Some people booed, but most of the time the feedback was positive—people appreciated the honesty and transparency.

"The data were very credible," says Chuck Browning. "The union checked it out. The company checked it out. All the stakeholders were saying the same thing. That's pretty powerful when that happens. It's not always identical, I should say, but it is still consistent. Also, we had clear targets. That made things easier to do."

It is not, however, just a one-way or top-down process, as Browning elaborates:

As smart as we all think we are, it's always our strong opinion that it's the people in the plants at the end of the day who make everything happen. They know my opinion up here might be pretty good, but I guarantee it's not as good as somebody that's actually building the car or a supervisor who's going to oversee the operations. We took all the knowledge that we had from a higher level, went into each facility and talked to the local union, talked to each operating committee, and got their input on what needed to happen to make that particular location cost effective. So, we incorporated everybody at every level, into what needed to be done.

The union also approaches the negotiations with an eye toward other possible contract language changes (beyond what was related to potential new investment or work in the location) that might be important to the local union. "Since we were changing the old way of doing business," recalls Browning, "you know, guess what? Some things did not work that well for us. Even though the company was driving what they needed to change for business reasons, we took the time to say, *If we are going to change, why don't we improve some of the things that haven't worked for us either contractually.* And we did that."

The actual negotiations involve "locking" the bargaining teams in a room for anywhere from 17 to 35 hours while they address an agenda that includes work rules, operating practices, and potential future investment in the plant. In each case, an agreement is reached that is then brought back to the local membership for ratification. Most agreements are ratified by around 80 percent of the members in each location; some win more than 90 percent.

Again, more than half a billion dollars in savings are achieved though operational improvements, without any changes in pay or benefits. In return, the union wins specific commitments to invest in operations. Also, local unions are able to address specific operating issues important in that location.

Overall, the bargaining process establishes important norms, including full transparency by the company on the economic situation and investment picture for each plant. The traditionally adversarial issue of work practices becomes an opportunity for constructive dialogue. "It was problem-solving rather than passing things back and forth," says Browning. "The company had an initial list, but it had to move beyond that to a business case as the goal. The key was seeing the list as just suggestions. That put the local union at ease—it was not specific demands. But the jolt of the list did unfreeze things, with the understanding that different ways were all on the table to get to the goal. The local union had to be able to bring its issues to the table as well, [which built] in some win-wins. An example: overtime agreements that addressed sources of grievances or failed implementation of past contract language."

✳✳✳

The COA experience was pivotal in at least three ways. First, in advance of the 2007 national negotiations, during which there were going to be severe concessionary pressures, labor and management generated a running start—with over $500 million in savings. Second, the combination of transparency and problem solving reinforced a break from traditional, adversarial negotiations. Third, labor and management in each facility developed a shared appreciation of the work that people do on a daily basis and the business realities facing the operation. Reflecting back during a 2008 presentation on the negotiations, Browning comments, "There's just an extreme amount of pride on both sides in what was accomplished. Both the local management teams and the local unions were faced with the reality that this was a case where it is 'really resting on you. You're the leadership that's here at this point in time to make a difference.' And they did. They really saved a lot of these locations." Ford's executive director for Labor Affairs, Bill Dirksen, adds, "The COA negotiations were a watershed series of events for Ford and the UAW. The changes were important for each plant and the sum was even greater in the way it set the stage for what followed."

Ford Puts All Cards on the Table with the UAW, 2007

In advance of the 2007 national auto negotiations, Ford determines that the company's very survival depends on two key substantive outcomes: reducing costs with the current workforce, and reducing retiree costs. A $16 billion loss in 2006 convinces Ford that the scale of change it needs goes far beyond the normal give and take of collective bargaining. Experts suggest Ford would have no choice but to declare bankruptcy—anathema to the Ford family and its workforce. Making the case for change in this context is not just about pointing to a burning platform or using threats and intimidation. It requires a compelling case for change *and* a credible, sustainable way forward.

For three years prior to the 2007 negotiations, top UAW and Ford leaders—including UAW president Ron Gettelfinger and Ford's president of the Americas Mark Fields—meet in a monthly "Action America" forums (detailed in chapter 6) that establish a level of dialogue and information sharing with the union that exceeds that of all other auto companies. The discussion that begins on May 11, 2007, builds on the Action America pivot.

On May 11, the top UAW leaders—Ron Gettelfinger, president, and Bob King, vice president responsible for the UAW's National Ford Department—meet with the top Ford executives in a small conference room at the Dearborn Inn. They expect what the negotiations literature calls "attitudinal structuring" or "managing expectations"—a typical company briefing prior to the start of national negotiations. What happens instead is not entirely typical.

Gettelfinger and King sit down with Ford CEO Alan Mulally, the vice president for North American Operations, Joe Hinrichs; CFO Don Leclair; the vice president for Labor Affairs, Marty Mulloy; and the group vice president for Human Resources, Joe Layman. Mulally begins with what the UAW already knows: the average labor cost for an hourly employee at Ford is more than $70 an hour, including all wages, all benefits, social security and other legally mandated costs, and "roll-up." At the Japanese transplants operating in the United States, the average is approximately $40 an hour. Why such a difference? A major portion of this differential is retiree pension and health care costs. The "Penny Sheet" used to compare labor costs has been seen by union leaders previously. They disagree with aspects of the comparison, but this is not new information.

Given declining sales and predictions of further decline, the Ford executives explain there are at least two assembly plants—Louisville and Michigan Assembly—at risk of closing. New investment, they say, is likely to go to Mexico. Moreover, Ford Motor's credit rating has plummeted to Caa1—eight notches below investment grade, and considered speculative grade. Ford Credit's commercial paper is at junk bond status, making it more expensive to acquire cash needed to reinvest in new products, wholesale vehicles to dealerships, and provide financing for Ford Credit's retail customers.

Again, none of this is new information to the UAW, but clearly the situation is dire. What happens next, though, *is* new.

Mulally is using the top half of a flip chart page to highlight Ford's uncompetitive manufacturing cost position compared to U.S. operations of Toyota and Honda. On the bottom half of the page, he begins to share his vision for Ford as a global enterprise. This includes selling off nearly all the brands acquired in the 1990s under Jacques Nasser. Some of what he presents is already public knowledge, but some is still highly confidential. He lists one brand after another and then draws lines through most of them. He indicates that the financial and human capital invested in these overseas brands will be redirected to Ford and Lincoln—something long urged by the UAW.

Mulally takes a considerable risk sharing this information. He is staking his job and reputation on the UAW engaging in constructive dialogue while keeping the information confidential.

At the end of the session, the UAW expresses appreciation for the information but makes no commitments other than to return in a few days for a second meeting—also held at the Dearborn Inn. There, Hinrichs goes through the entire cycle plan of new products, along with a plant-by-plant review for where the new product programs will be sourced in the future. Gettelfinger and King have never seen such a level of detail, unprecedented in advance of negotiations. They are being made privy to strategic business decisions about new products and manufacturing plans.

The UAW leaders grow uncomfortable. This is no simple attempt to soften them up for the contract negotiations. The company is putting all its cards on the table.

Ron Gettelfinger expresses a concern that further meetings at the Dearborn Inn could draw media attention. So, for the next meeting, the group convenes at an unoccupied building in Commerce Park, near the Detroit Lions practice facility in the town of Allen Park, Michigan. Everyone arrives in a different car at a different time. They switch up the entrances they use. It is clearly understood: this meeting will involve very serious pre-negotiations discussions.

At this third session, CFO Don Leclair reviews the financial situation. If Ford is to avoid financial collapse and return its credit rating to investment grade, he explains, the company needs to restructure its balance sheet. Approximately 25 percent of Ford's labor cost is categorized as "Other Post-Employment Benefits" (OPEB)—primarily of post-retirement health care. A key idea is floated: why not create UAW Voluntary Employee Benefit Association (VEBA) to assume the cost of retiree benefits? Actuaries could help determine the amount of funding the company would need to put up (it turns out to be about $15 billion).

This is a relatively new idea. Goodyear had set up a similar plan with the United Steel Workers, but there are few other examples. It is an arrangement that will make a UAW VEBA one of the nation's single-largest purchasers of health care services and place all ongoing responsibility for retiree healthcare with the VEBA Trust. (This is detailed further in chapter 6.)

The VEBA idea is challenging: it's relatively new and the financial calculations are complicated. The second idea put on the table, though, is even more challenging and politically volatile.

Ford and the UAW have agreed to offering different, creative incentives for voluntary reductions aimed at ultimately cutting the workforce of over 90,000 employees nearly in half (detailed in chapter 3). It's being done with unprecedented separation packages and opportunities for retraining. However, the company wants the union to agree to something more complicated: a lower entry wage—that is, a two-tier wage system. Ford indicates that this could keep work scheduled to go to Mexico in the United States, and bring work slotted for nonunion suppliers to UAW-Ford plants. The result: an increase in the number of UAW manufacturing jobs in the United States.

These are not abstract threats and promises. In their second secret meeting, Joe Hinrichs had already shown the specific plant-by-plant implications of not making this change.

"Starting the dialogue around where we needed to go was important," Hinrichs recalls, "but it was equally important for the UAW to see that we were listening to what were the concerns of their members—such as the packages for displaced workers and working together on safety and quality. They had to see that it was possible to develop a plan that honored the commitment we had to each other—a cycle plan that was the best plan possible—with some insourcing."

The union leaders register deep concerns around potential plant closings. They'll have to have specific commitments of products and investment, they say, if the union is going to discuss an entry wage for new workers. And they make clear that while they appreciate the importance of ensuring Ford's viability, the VEBA idea will need considerable study and analysis.

The union has credibility in this discussion, thanks to the gains already achieved in the COA negotiations. The union emphasizes its commitment, even in a concessionary situation, not to cut the wages of the current workforce.

As UAW president, Bob King reflects on this process, "No one has more at stake in the success of the company than white collar and blue collar front line workforce. He calls the UAW-Ford relationship "one of creative problem solving—and that is what took place in 2007."

The goal of the meetings is not to negotiate the actual agreement (which is presented in chapter 6). The actual negotiations involve restructuring the entire bargaining process to better address the interests of the parties, departing in some ways from the tradition of pattern bargaining in the auto industry, while still maintaining key economic patterns. Instead, the goal is to ensure that the union fully understands what is at stake for the company in the negotiations and ensure that the company fully understands the union's concerns in this context.

"This is the way we do business," says Mark Fields. "It is not just a transaction with the union. The UAW leadership is part of the team for delivering the business."

✳ ✳ ✳

Two years later, when the three Detroit automakers and the UAW testified before Congress, legislators tried to portray the industry as having been inattentive to competitive pressures. That may have been a fair accusation in the 1990s, but it was certainly not the case for the UAW and Ford by 2007. Consider the contrast between the inattention to the bundled mortgages in the financial sector and the scale of the change, as well as the internal transparency, that characterized the 2006–2007 COA negotiations and Ford's decision the put all the cards on the table in 2007.

The initial flip chart page Mulally used at that May 11 meeting at the Dearborn Inn was later framed in his office—a testimonial to trust, transparency, and pivotal change.

"The reason we are still making cars in the U.S. is that we are competitive—competitive with respect to quality, fuel efficiency, safety, and design," says Mulally. "Together with the UAW, we have earned the right to be in this business in the United States."

Ford has since fully funded the VEBA, which was indeed instrumental in returning Ford's credit rating to investment-grade status. Controller Peter Daniel notes, "From a financial perspective, [the VEBA] was one of the most significant things we have ever done in the company in improving the balance sheet."

Ultimately, too, Ford and the UAW reached an agreement on the entry wage, which has made it possible for Ford to create a projected 18,000 new jobs in the United States. Many of these would not exist were it not for the company putting all of its the cards on the table and the union responding in a constructive way.

Frontline Leadership, 2013

Perhaps the most pervasive pivot, but the least visible, involves the many thousands of individual workers whose work lives have shifted toward being valued for the knowledge and expertise they bring to the job. As we present more fully in chapter 5, this is a shift to a knowledge-driven work system. At the individual level, the case for change is made one person at a time. Amid the change at the individual level, there are some who lead the way—who make the case for change in what they do, not just what they say. We present this as a pivotal event, although it is actually a series of many pivotal events in the life of an individual, Armentha Young, all of which add up to a fundamental change in her work and relationships. Young's experience exemplifies many such pivotal changes at the individual level.

Since 2004, Armentha Young has been a Quality Operating Systems Coordinator (QOSC) in the Dearborn Truck Plant. As an hourly employee with plant-wide responsibility for adherence to the Quality Operating System, she must constantly make the case for change. She has demonstrated her ability to see major process improvement through from conception to results—and earned her Black Belt in Six Sigma systems. Her journey to her present role and how she fulfills that role today illustrates the case for change at the individual level.

"When I became a QOSC," Young says, "an important part of my responsibilities to the hourly workforce was to inform and familiarize them with the terms used in the plant—for example, first time through (FTT), rejects per 1,000 (R/1000), cost per unit (CPU), things gone wrong (TGWs)—and to reference data regarding the Quality metrics. I want the workforce to feel empowered by enabling informed discussion. I also coach people in problem-solving decisions and I let them know why a change is in discussion. In a lot of cases the operator is the "subject matter expert" regarding his or her job and the defects associated with it. I help people understand that they are critical in this process."

Being an hourly co-worker of those people, not a salaried manager, is important. "I am in the role of being a person who is close to you—a union sister—who can explain why the company does what it does. I let you know that you can even make suggestions of what you would do if you were the boss, but mostly I make sure we value the work people do."

For Young, it "all comes down to these internal and external data points in how we run business." Her work involves ensuring that frontline teams have feedback on quality performance. "Not everyone gets it, but many do."

Hers is a coaching role to both hourly and salaried workers. It can be challenging, given traditional hourly and salaried roles, to confront frontline supervisors.

"Even though I am hourly," she says, "part of my job is to point out where something has gone awry. I tell supervisors that I am not here as a tattletale to your boss. I am here so that we are all better able to be proactive in responding to problems."

Thus, in making the case for change—supporting the Quality Operating System —a key part of Young's role is as a bridge between the hourly and salaried workforce.

She begins her journey to this role in 1994, when she is first hired as an assembly line worker. Within a few years, she works her way up to be an inspector for quality in her plant's final assembly area. That's when she begins to question how the larger systems work.

"As I became accustomed to understanding what defects were and what the plant's expectations were and what was needed for customer satisfaction," she recalls, "I wanted to learn more. Then I wanted to know how the company used the information to run the business."

At the time (during the 1990s), her plant has what is termed "mass relief"—everyone takes breaks and conducted meetings at the same time, stopping the assembly line. This makes it possible for her to attend the daily Ford Customer Product Audit (FCPA—now termed GFCPA since it is Global) for the final assembly area, where she asks questions about the quality issues being discussed. The local union and management leadership alike note her interest, and she is asked to serve in the supplementary role of Vehicle Concerns Resolution Specialist (in addition to her regular job). This peer-to-peer program involves hourly workers assisting other hourly workers who purchase Ford products from Ford dealers. It is an appointed position (part-time in most plants) established under Appendix Q of the national agreement between the UAW and Ford to better connect all workers with the products they produce, as well as provide the company with feedback on the sales experience in the showrooms. This, Young notes, helps her "understand another segment of the business."

To be able to facilitate change with respect to quality, though, she first has to undergo her own change process—learning about all aspects of the business. This happens when she is among dozens of hourly workers invited to represent the UAW and Ford at the Detroit Auto Show in a display called "Working Together for Quality"—something she recalls as "a little intimidating."

At the time, she is working in the Dearborn Assembly Plant (before it converted to the Dearborn Truck Plant as part of the 2001 Rogue revitalization discussed in chapter 4), the home of the Mustang, and her role at the auto show is to find out what customers want to see in the vehicle. When she returns to the plant, Young is asked to give a presentation on what she learned.

I presented to the plant leadership. The chief Mustang engineer came from Vehicle Operations. I said that I talked to a number of older customers who were still loyal to the vehicle, but wanted additional features such as illuminated buttons. The experience was a plus for me in that I could connect the assembly process with the role of data, the role of dealers, and now the customer connection.

As she expands her understanding of the full system, Armentha Young also gains an appreciation for the need to pull together in a team-based work system. This is reinforced when she is selected to help drive a major plant-wide diversity initiative in 2000 as one of six people who will provide diversity training to hourly and salaried employees (more information on the diversity training is provided in chapter 3).

"I could see how there wasn't the harmony that was needed—hourly to salaried and among the hourly," she recalls. With the training, however, people were better able to "see the differences in skill sets, culture, and values."

All these differences, she says, are "part of quality. You see how people who are valued come to work more and are more engaged in work."

Out of the diversity training, it becomes ever clearer to management that the change needed in the plant includes a change in how the frontline workforce is perceived. "Not everyone wants to be in management," says Armentha, "but everyone has something to bring to the organization; we all have various levels of skills and talents. But you would never know it unless you engage in conversation. You might find out that they have knowledge or experience about something you value."

The diversity training, she notes, "became a valuable part of quality. People were engaged. People began to see that differences were not something to fear, but something to appreciate. Getting people to respect each other had a big effect on company success."

The capstone for Young is completing a college degree and then earning her Six Sigma Black Belt certification, which occurred on October 19, 2010. As she comments:

Black Belt training has empowered me. People in management do respect you more. Some didn't believe a person without a statistics background could pass. When I did pass, some begrudgingly shook my hand. You could see it in their faces: they were amazed. I thought, "You've got to be kidding me." They were, like, "Oh my god, she passed and did it on the first time."

The comment is a little insulting—there are plenty of people who could do this. People have skills that managers don't know anything about. One should never be comfortable making an assumption about another person's skill set or talents simply by their classification, association with a group or a particular organization and/or appearance.

✳ ✳ ✳

Of course there are many in Armentha Young's plant, and in the broader system as well, who celebrate the accomplishments of people like her. But she reminds us that the journey is far from complete. There are still deeply embedded assumptions around hourly and salaried roles, and the case for change begins with an appreciation for what any individual can accomplish when they have the drive and desire to learn that Young embodies. The story also illustrates the powerful combination of an individual who asks questions about how the business works and a system that rewards such interest with increased opportunities. It is for all these reasons that we have highlighted Armentha Young's story as illustrative of the pivotal events involving courageous leadership at the individual level—a process that can involve many individual pivots over a lifetime and which add up to being a key pivot for the entire system.

Recap: Guiding Principle for Chapter 2—Courageous Leadership

Pivotal events in the UAW-Ford transformation feature the courage of countless individuals. There is the courage of the union leader who advocates for politically unpopular changes. There is the courage of the management leader to put all the cards on the table, providing complete transparency in a dire business situation. Both have been highlighted in this chapter, and in both instances the case for change was clear. Also in both cases, courage can be seen not just in making the case for change, but also in the response of others who have to travel the distance to engage constructively with the potential changes.

Pivotal events are crucibles for individual leadership,[9] but these events are not only defined by individual agency (that is, individual initiative). Ford 2000 featured deep systemic and institutional barriers to overcome: the structure of career paths for engineers; the flexibility of manufacturing operations; the fiefdoms in different parts of global operations. Leadership in Ford 2000 meant the willingness to acknowledge the full scale and scope of the challenge, learn from the limitations of the approach, and sustain a change that took a decade or more to realize its full potential—long after the initiative had ended.

Negotiating the Competitive Operating Agreements involved a more immediate form of courage. Union and management leaders both had to face a tough town-hall meeting audience every week or two and engage the entire workforce of a plant in a data-driven dialogue on its future. The individuals in the plants—labor and management—then had to step forward and take increased responsibility for their future, adopting new operating assumptions in the process. It was an extended, long-term form of courage with which Armentha Young and others like her reached beyond stereotypes of the hourly workforce to earn Six Sigma Black Belts and lead major change initiatives.

Courageous leadership in making the case for change permeates the pivotal events throughout this book. And the individuals in leadership positions we feature here are only a fraction of those making the case for change in fundamental assumptions in order to transform work and relationships to deliver results.

SUPPORTING MATERIALS

2.1 Ford Executive Education Transition Curve

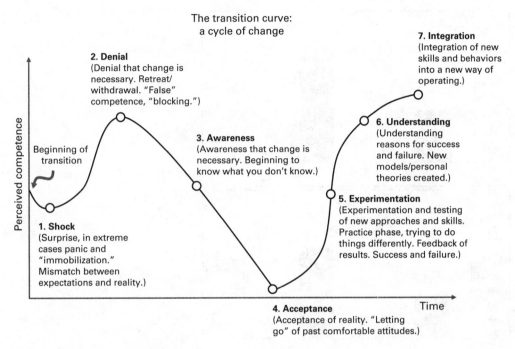

The transition curve:
a cycle of change

7. Integration
(Integration of new
skills and behaviors
into a new way of
operating.)

2. Denial
(Denial that change is
necessary. Retreat/
withdrawal. "False"
competence, "blocking.")

6. Understanding
(Understanding
reasons for success
and failure. New
models/personal
theories created.)

3. Awareness
(Awareness that change is
necessary. Beginning to
know what you don't know.)

Beginning of
transition

5. Experimentation
(Experimentation and testing
of new approaches and skills.
Practice phase, trying to do
things differently. Feedback of
results. Success and failure.)

1. Shock
(Surprise, in extreme
cases panic and
"immobilization."
Mismatch between
expectations and reality.)

Perceived competence

Time

4. Acceptance
(Acceptance of reality. "Letting
go" of past comfortable attitudes.)

Source: Ford Motor Company

2.2 U.S. Assembly Plants 2002 vs. 2009/2010 Comparison

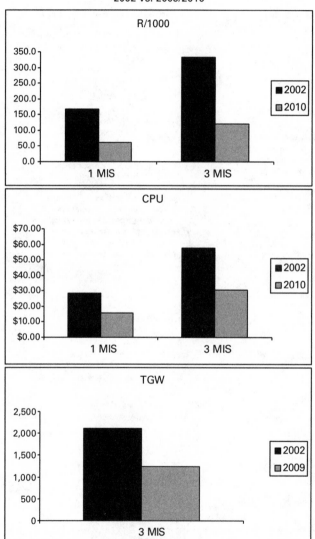

Vehicle operations – US assembly plants
2002 vs. 2009/2010

Key: Rejects/1000 (R/1000), Cost per Unit (CPU), and Things Gone Wrong (TGW).
Source: Ford Motor Company and UAW.

3 Dignity of Work

Guiding Principle: Dignity and Respect

Since biblical times, work has been appreciated for its essential dignity and value—"The slothful person desires but has nothing; but the soul of the diligent will be sated" (Proverbs 13:4). Work has been deplored, for just as long, as hard, degrading, and even the product of original sin—"By the sweat of your brow you will eat your food until you return to the ground, since from it you were taken; for dust you are and to dust you will return" (Genesis 3:19).

Over the centuries, work in any occupation became increasingly intertwined with Protestant conceptions of faith, salvation, and material well-being.[1] The father of modern sociology, Max Weber, documented this with the rise of the Industrial Revolution, and it is this Calvinist conception that Henry Ford echoes in his 1922 autobiography.

The natural thing to do is to work—to recognize that prosperity and happiness can be obtained only through honest effort. Human ills flow largely from attempting to escape this natural course....I take it for granted that we must work...since we must work it is better to work intelligently and forehandedly; that the better we do our work the better off we shall be.[2]

The UAW, in the preamble to its founding constitution, emphasized a conception of work that went beyond its purpose in improving one's economic status to include dignity and self-worth.

Essential to the UAW's purpose is to afford the opportunity for workers to master their work environment; to achieve not only improvement in their economic status but, of equal importance, to gain from their labors a greater measure of dignity, of self-fulfillment and self-worth.[3]

The UAW and Ford leaders we interviewed for this book are, for the most part, either deeply religious, value-driven, or both. While not unique to Ford and not characteristic of everyone at Ford, the culture does tend to draw people who view hard work as part of one's moral character and who see respect and dignity in the workplace as paramount. This perspective seems to transcend whether one is on the hourly or salaried sides of the company.

As UAW vice president Jimmy Settles develops more fully in chapter 9, work plays a foundational role for families in our society, enabling what is known as the American Dream. He comments:

Work brings dignity, hope and excitement. You know that if you stay the course you can accomplish your goals. You begin with a family structure. When the parents have a job, the kids come to understand the importance of earning a living and taking care of a family. Good jobs give you the opportunity to make a better standard of living for your kids. It gives you options to live in a different area than where you grew up, so your kids can go to better schools.

Henry Ford's "five-dollar-day" pay policy, announced in 1914, was twice the daily wage at the time. Famous for enabling the workers to buy the product they were building, the policy didn't just draw a connection between mass markets and mass production, but it also signaled dignity and respect for workers as consumers and reflected Ford's values in promoting family life. In the Detroit area, Henry Ford is also well known for his pay equity policy for black workers, which dates as least as far back as 1918. The wages paid at the Ford Motor Company made the company the preeminent and largest U.S. employer of blacks in the pre–World War II period. In 1939, the average wage of a Ford black employee was not only nearly twice the average of all black employees in the United States, but exceeded the average of *all* workers in the United States.[4] Like the five-dollar day, the pay-equity policy also served the business, enabling Ford to attract a higher-caliber workforce than its competitors. Many pivotal events in this chapter had this dual character—a combination of key values and helping advance the business. Of course, there were other dimensions where Henry Ford's views were not as progressive, such as in his anti-Semitic views and his initial response to unionization, though pivots on these and other aspects of dignity and respect have long since shifted the culture at Ford in positive ways.

We have assembled these pivotal events, in part, because they do reflect foundational aspects of the UAW and Ford cultures, but we also show a direct line connecting these pivotal choices with the operation of the team-based work systems so central to the successes the parties have achieved. It is literally the case that a transformation in work and relationships rests on a foundation of the core values of dignity and respect.

The pivotal events in this chapter reveal that articulating the value of work is only a first step in making dignity and respect in the workplace part and parcel of the way an organization functions. Even if most individuals hold these values, it does not necessarily follow that the system will always deliver on the values. Indeed, as we document in this chapter, the changes required to ensure dignity and respect in the workplace have been massive in scale, nothing short of transformational in impact, and still incomplete. These very human aspects of work are often seen as incidental or separate from business transformation; here we focus on dignity and respect not just as worthy ends in themselves, but also as essential building blocks for subsequent pivotal events, such as the implementation of team-based work systems.

Of the eight pivotal events in this chapter, the first two center on gender. The rest involve race and other aspects of dignity at work.

Chapter 3

Pivotal Events	Overview	Type, Level
Selection of First Female Plant Manager, 1996	This event offers a window into how the case for change is made in a male-dominated world.	Unplanned, Plant Level
Chicago Sexual Harassment Lawsuits, 1999	Lawsuits unveil local leaders in both Ford and the UAW who tolerate unacceptable and illegal behavior in the workplace. The event is pivotal in the scale, scope, and depth of both organizations' responses, with positive implications for an effective team-based work system.	Unplanned, Plant Level
Pivot on Affinity Groups, 1999	Ford does an about-face in its policies on affinity groups—a pivotal event that also illustrates courageous leadership.	Unplanned, Enterprise Level
Same-Sex Partner Benefits, 2000	Ford provides same-sex partner benefits earlier than many other companies. This pivot takes on new meaning as state laws change on same-sex marriage.	Planned, Enterprise
UAW-Ford United in Diversity (now Equality and Diversity) Program, 2000	A planned pivotal event becomes the vehicle through which every Ford U.S. manufacturing employee undergoes diversity training. More than a decade later, the principles covered in that training are still part of everyday conversations at Ford.	Planned, Enterprise Level
9/11 Zero Tolerance Response, 2001	Ford reinforces its zero tolerance policy around anti-Muslim or anti-Arab expressions immediately following the 9/11 terrorist attacks.	Unplanned, Enterprise Level
Atlanta Zero Tolerance Intervention, 2002	A targeted pivot on racial issues illustrates an intervention from the union on a specific diversity situation.	Unplanned, Plant Level
Voluntary Separation Packages, 2006–2008	Tens of thousands of individuals lose their jobs during the Great Recession. Ford offers voluntary separation packages (in consultation with the UAW) that not only show concern for the dignity and respect of individuals about to lose their jobs, but also for families and communities that would otherwise have been even worse off.	Planned, Enterprise Level

Selection of First Female Plant Manager, 1996

Women working on assembly lines during World War II achieved iconic status in American society—think Rosy the Riveter—but the postwar decades saw the return to a nearly all-male environment in factories. That began to change in frontline operations in the 1970s and 1980s, but change came more slowly in the engineering and managerial ranks.

The role of the plant manager is highly visible and the subject of considerable debate every time it is filled. All the pressures of production—producing a new car every minute—combined with the pressures on cost, quality, safety, schedule, morale, and environment are concentrated on this one role. The plant manager is accountable to the corporation, workforce, and community. By the mid-1990s, Ford has a number of female area managers, quality managers, and assistant plant managers, but no female plant managers.

The appointment at the Dearborn Engine Plant of the company's first female plant manager is not part of a formal plan or an intentional move to increase diversity. "We had three candidates for the position—one woman and two other male candidates," recalls Jim Quinlan, who was then a divisional human resource director. "The operating team for the group was meeting and they were arguing for one of the males who was a good person—no question about it. I said, 'What about the female?' and they said that she didn't have the right background."

This pivotal event is driven entirely by merit. "We had a slide ready with her background and the backgrounds of the others," says Quinlan. "Hers was clearly stronger. The person who had been the biggest obstacle said, 'I can't argue with that.'"

That is the turning point that led to Linda Miller becoming Ford's first female plant manager.

"Some knew who the best candidate was but weren't saying anything," Quinlan notes. "Once the facts were evident, however, it became okay to speak up. These guys were results-oriented and you had to put it in black and white—that is how they did business."

The relationship between a plant manager and the chair of the local union bargaining committee is an intense one. When a new plant manager is appointed, there is always an initial jockeying between these two key leaders. In this case, the initial welcome is a bit different.

"Her first day on the job," Quinlan recounts, "the chairman came in with a bouquet of flowers."

✳ ✳ ✳

This event is pivotal as a milestone in the journey away from discrimination or even just habit based on gender, race, or other factors. One promotion such as this, however, does not change the system. While a number of women were promoted to plant managers in subsequent years, and then to higher-level officer positions in the corporation, there were serious instances of sexual harassment in some Ford plants during the same period (as the next pivotal event describes).

Chicago Sexual Harassment Lawsuits, 1999

Women working in Ford's Chicago Stamping Plant and the Chicago Assembly Plant register complaints internally about sexual harassment, but neither the plant management nor the local unions treat the complaints as credible. So the women file complaints with the Equal Employment Opportunity Commission (EEOC). The ABC television newsmagazine *20/20* airs an exposé on December 19, 1999. Finally, the women file lawsuits, which proves to be a pivotal event in the way they galvanize both Ford and the UAW into actions that ultimately changed the culture in both organizations.

Dick Gross, Ford's assistant general counsel at the time, is assigned to investigate.

Things were happening prior to the *20/20* exposé, but that put further pressure on us to find resolution. When we investigated the situation, we found a number of the charges were factual. We presented our findings to senior management—Jim Padilla and Bob Transou.

"Devastated" is the best way to describe their reaction. We found that plant management had been aware of what was going on and did nothing. The executives were fully supportive of our taking action. Then we met with Ron Gettelfinger and went through what we had found and what we planned to do. He indicated unequivocal support from the UAW.

We might disagree with the UAW on other issues, but on this issue we all committed to the same goal.

Ford commits to comprehensive training in the two Chicago facilities as part of the settlement of the lawsuits and the EEOC cases. Jim Padilla, the group vice president for Global Manufacturing, goes further and commits to training Ford's entire U.S. workforce. Dick Gross recalls Padilla telling him, "Don't just fix the problem; prevent something like this from recurring." This is a key operating assumption in quality and safety—prevention—being applied to the social system.

Leaders are educated as trainers, using a curriculum developed by the law firm Sayfarth Shaw that employs colors to indicate conversations or situations that are acceptable (green), borderline (yellow), or inappropriate (red). Meanwhile, Human Resource professionals in the plants are trained in how to investigate a harassment claim properly, using HR and General Counsel's office material developed internally. On top of all this, Ford establishes a zero tolerance policy that is added to the national contract with the UAW later that year.

Using collective bargaining as a forum to reinforce the company's commitment to preventing continued sexual harassment in the plants goes beyond how most employers and unions approach this institutional arrangement. For Ford and the UAW, it involves more than simply adding language on zero tolerance to a contract. In the 1999 negotiations, Ford allocates additional incremental heads (additional offline staffing) to this issue and allocates the time for development and delivery of eight hours of training for every employee. This is unprecedented for any issue.

The training begins the next year. Dick Gross recalls the big challenge: culture change.

I started off in the Cleveland Casting Plant in 1973, and there were no women working in the factory. A few years later, women began to work in the factories, but it was still an environment where there might be inappropriate pictures on toolboxes and inappropriate behavior in the plant.

Even with the training and the zero tolerance policy we found that there had to be a way for issues to surface through the layers of management. It was first in the Kentucky Truck Plant that we developed a 14-question employee relations survey to get a view into the climate. We also developed a harassment hotline. With the combination of the survey, the hotline, and any EEOC complaints, we had an early warning system to see if a facility was headed in the wrong direction.

When a facility does head in a negative direction, a coordinated intervention takes place that involves the office of the General Council, either Labor Affairs (if hourly workers are involved) or Human Resources (for the salaried workforce), and the UAW. This is in addition to the training.

"Initially, the 'Red-Yellow-Green' was almost like a joke," recalls Dan Brooks, the first UAW representative assigned to co-lead diversity efforts. "Someone would say something and others would say 'you are now in the red zone' or 'you are in the yellow zone.' Over time, however, it became a learning process."

Marty Mulloy adds, "Still today, people will be in a meeting and someone will say, 'It is getting yellow.' The interesting thing with this is that you don't have to accuse the person of being sexist or racist. You just say it is yellow or red and that is enough."

✳✳✳

The Chicago lawsuits were an unplanned pivotal event, contributing to the transformation of the UAW and Ford in multiple ways. First, by responding in a comprehensive way, the climate across U.S. operations did improve—other harassment situations were identified and addressed, while the risk of such situations in the future was reduced. Issues around sexual harassment, racial mistreatment, or other types of discrimination, as well as basic respect and dignity, are a continuing challenge, of course, but the response to the lawsuits marked a fundamental shift from an environment in which polices and practices were variable and incomplete to one with consistent, comprehensive policies and practices.

Second, tools and techniques utilized to address this issue had application in other domains. For example, the same company that developed the hotline for harassment issues helped to develop the hotlines established in later years for quality and safety (as part of the operating systems discussed in chapter 8). Further, the experience of this pivotal event taught lessons about what not to do. Having all U.S. employees receive eight hours of training had a clear impact. However, the parties also learned that delivering training on such a scale was expensive and variable in its impact. As detailed in chapter 8, a model for targeted training emerged that involved more systematic use of assessments to determine what people already know and then to focus training on filling gaps. The diversity training experience was commonly cited as a motivation for developing the targeted training model.

Third, the lawsuits ended up being pivotal because the diversity training they spurred became foundational in the move toward a team-based work system. Indeed, many of the diversity trainers (e.g., Armentha Young, introduced in chapter 2), went on to become team leaders or quality representatives. It is notable that several of the women involved in the Chicago lawsuits also went on to become team leaders. Chapter 5 details the pivotal role of diversity when work becomes more knowledge driven.

Affinity Groups, 1999

The 1990s sees so-called affinity groups gaining currency in U.S. corporations—people coming together into loosely connected groups based on shared profession, race, gender, nationality, sexual identity, interests, or other characteristics. By 2005, for example, 90 of the *Fortune* 500 firms have lesbian, gay, bisexual, and transgender (LGBT) affinity groups.[5] In some ways, they are a form of collective action that is more palatable to U.S. corporations than unions, and in other ways they represent new forms of community based on various forms of personal identity.

At first, these groups pose a policy challenge for many companies. Will these collective entities coalesce in an oppositional way? Will they be complementary to the corporation? Even within Ford, with its 30-year history of partnership with the UAW, some in the human resources function are concerned these groups will turn into collective bargaining agents on behalf of salaried employees.

Termed "resource groups" within Ford, the first such groups are established in manufacturing and engineering. The oldest is the Ford-employees African-Ancestry Network (FAAN), founded in 1994 and described on the Ford corporate website.

FAAN champions workplace diversity at Ford by making a positive impact on the African-American community, and by actively promoting and supporting the Ford brand throughout the community. For its constituents, FAAN promotes leadership development through seminars, mentoring, counseling, and Dialogues on Diversity with senior management. Our members support summer internship programs, recruiting at minority-focused career events, and collaborate with the Company to produce a spectacular annual Black History Month celebration.[6]

In 1997, the Ford Asian Indian Association (FAIA) is established with a similar mission to that of FAAN: professional development and outreach representing Ford in Asian and Indian communities. The Ford Chinese Association (FCA), which can trace its roots back to 1983, is formally recognized as a resource group later.

While managers at various levels support the groups, there is still resistance to them in parts of the HR community. "Manufacturing and engineering saw the need, but HR was not leading," says Jim Quinlan, HR director for Global Manufacturing. "It was a wake up call for our community."

In 1999, at a corporate meeting of HR leaders, the issue of resource groups becomes the focus of discussion. Quinlan ends up playing a key role.

"People were going back and forth about the resource groups," recalls Marty Mulloy. "Then Jim spoke up and said, 'Whether you like it or not, these groups are forming. We can either fight it as a company or work with them and embrace diversity.' That changed the whole tenor of the meeting. If Jim hadn't stepped forward at the time, it could have been a mess. If the company had not acknowledged their existence, these groups could have become protest groups."

Many resource groups have since formed at Ford. "The groups that do the best don't expect anything in return—like career promotions," says Quinlan. "Instead, they are focused on 'what can I learn?'"

Quinlan points to the Ford Chinese Association as an example. The group promotes educating Americans on Chinese culture and American culture within the Chinese community, and also promotes Ford products. Quinlan notes that Ford Gay, Lesbian, or Bisexual Employees (GLOBE) has "helped the HR managers and the unions get out in front on workplace bullying." He says of resource groups:

It is amazing how you can talk to production workers or the technical community and [see that] all share the desire to do what is best for Ford Motor Company. These groups bring diverse people together. …over the years all the groups have been tweaked and some have changed dramatically, but the basic issue of respect in the workplace is the bottom line that hasn't changed.

✳✳✳

We highlight this pivot as representing a key shift within a support function—HR—from ambivalence or resistance to support. There was no planned strategy to form the groups in the first place, but as they came together it was a pivotal decision whether to acquiesce to the groups or embrace and support them. Had Ford not embraced the groups, it would have diminished dignity and respect. Doing so reinforces these values.

Including those mentioned above, additional Ford resource groups today include:

• Ford Employees Dealing with disAbilities (FEDA)
• Ford Hispanic Network Group (FHNG)
• Ford Interfaith Network (FIN)
• Ford Parenting Network (FPN)
• Ford Veterans Network (VET_NG)
• Middle Eastern Community @ Ford Motor Company (MEC@Ford)
• Professional Women's Network (PWN)

Note that the Hispanic group has faced challenges from encompassing so many different nationalities and cultures. This illustrates an enduring challenge when organizing collective interests based on diversity categories. In that sense, future pivots can be anticipated as different forms of identity become more or less salient in the workplace. In important ways, the affinity groups are a form of collective action based on identity as compared to unions, which may have initially organized building on different immigrant groups but came to be centered more on economic or class distinctions.

Same-Sex Partner Benefits, 2000

In 1996, the CEO at the time, Alex Trotman, issues a policy statement that sexual orientation is protected under Ford's existing antidiscrimination policies. The next year, retired CFO Allen Gilmore discusses in a *Fortune* magazine interview his experience of being gay—something he had kept private for much of his career at Ford.[7] These events acknowledge the presence of LGBT employees at Ford and ensure protection against discrimination, but they do not represent a full pivot on dignity and respect for this community.

The emergence of the Ford Gay, Lesbian, or Bisexual, Employees (GLOBE) group in 1999 (see previous pivotal event) further increases visibility. In many companies, the formation of an LGBT affinity group is followed by a policy change on same-sex partner benefits.[8] In Ford's case, the policy change indeed follows quickly, though the full pivot takes a decade to reach resolution.

In 2000, Ford announces that same-sex partners of Ford employees are entitled to health benefits through the company. This reverses the previous limitations for Ford employees in the degree to which they could extend health care coverage, pension, and other employee benefits to their same-sex partners (which was possible with some benefits and not with others).

The decision to extend same-sex partner benefits, led by CEO Jacques Nasser and HR vice president David Murphy, is not just about fair treatment for a group of employees. It is also a business decision. Ford is mindful of the economic power of the gay community.

The change is well received by many in the Ford workforce (although Marty Mulloy recalls losing an employee who said he could no longer work for a company with such policies, because of his religious beliefs). Gregory Stone, the physician whose career included his role as the senior executive sponsor of Ford GLOBE, comments, "I wasn't involved in the lead-up to the 2000 policy change, but I do understand that it would not have happened without the UAW support. The auto companies were among the first to offer same-sex partner benefits."

In some quarters, though, the decision is controversial. Although there is not a visible response for five years, the American Family Association (AFA) does announce a boycott of Ford products in 2005. Ford does not change the policy, but is seen as reducing the visibility of its advertising and sponsorship in the LGBT community. Ford states that the change is for economic reasons; AFA claims it is the result of a negotiated agreement to end the boycott. Either way, the reduction in advertising generates criticism from GLOBE and from groups outside the company.

For the next five years, the benefits stay in place, but there are competing views on Ford's advertising policy. Then, in 2011, there is a clear resolution. As the Motor City Gay Pride celebration moves from Ferndale, Michigan, to Hart Plaza in Detroit, Ford joins other auto companies as a visible presence. In 2013, Ford also has a presence at the Louisville Pride event, and an hourly leader in GLOBE from Ford's Chicago plant attends the Louisville Pride event to learn more about how Ford might be featured in Chicago area events. By this time, a growing number of states have legalized gay marriage.

Stone comments, "I am surprised that the larger societal changes have happened in my lifetime. As a kid I didn't understand why you couldn't marry who you want."

With the legalization of same-sex marriage, there is an additional twist to the story. Now same-sex partners in these states can only get access to employee benefits if they are married—otherwise it would be unfair to opposite-sex partners who are living together in that state but are not married. This was codified in a recent announcement to all Ford salaried employees, which read, in part, as follows:

Purpose of This Communication: To communicate to Salaried Employees an update to all Company benefit plans.

What You Need to Know: The definition of Spouse has been revised for all Company benefit plans, including all Health, Welfare, and Retirement plans.

This update conforms with recent changes to Federal rules and guidance regarding recognition of legal same-sex marriages for Federal law purposes. As of June 26, 2013, all Company benefit plans define a Spouse as an individual legally married under the laws of the state or foreign jurisdiction where the marriage took place. Legally married same-sex spouses will be eligible for all the same Ford benefits that presently are offered to legally married opposite-sex spouses. This includes eligibility for a surviving spouse benefit under the General Retirement Plan (GRP), as a beneficiary under the Savings and Stock Investment Plan (SSIP) and Ford Retirement Plan (FRP), and spousal health benefits.

✳ ✳ ✳

The decision to provide full benefits to same-sex partners was pivotal. It anticipated and reflected increasing societal acceptance of equal treatment for LGBT employees. It was also pivotal as a business decision in which there were two market segments that could not both be satisfied and for which Ford had to make a choice. The policy decision was a planned pivotal event, although the subsequent set of competing collective interests was not planned and took more than a decade to reach a clear resolution.

UAW-Ford United in Diversity (now Equality and Diversity) Program, 2000

The sexual harassment lawsuits at the Chicago facilities prove costly in a number of ways. The payout to plaintiffs, the public embarrassment, and the directive by the EEOC to train the workforce on the subject of sexual harassment causes Ford and the UAW to address the issue of diversity in the workplace more broadly. Meanwhile, the company is already well on its way to creating team-based work systems to assist in the transition from mass to lean production. Each employee in the facilities has received eight hours of Continuous Improvement Work Group (CIWG) training. While the training gives employees the skills necessary to work together in groups, it becomes apparent that there is a gap in people's skill to appreciate differences within a team and act accordingly.

This mix of issues puts diversity on the agenda in the 1999 UAW-Ford negotiations. While wages and benefits get the most attention, collective bargaining is also a platform identifying and launching innovative initiatives. So, in that spirit, the 1999 UAW-Ford Agreement includes a letter of understanding establishing The National Joint Diversity Committee, with several responsibilities: develop a training process and initiative to boost employee awareness of diversity; oversee the training; and develop any additional initiatives needed to address diversity issues.

As the then UAW vice president Ron Gettelfinger explains in a video prepared by the UAW-Ford National Diversity Program, which was presented to every hourly and salaried employee in North America:

Diversity is our strength and our future.... We're proud of the fact that we are on the cutting edge of developing and maintaining a workplace where each person is treated with respect and dignity.... The training supports our position that everyone and I mean everyone, regardless of sex, race, age, national origin, sexual orientation, military status, or union involvement, has a right to work in an environment free from harassment and discrimination and where their ideas can be shared equally.... Embracing Safety, Quality and Diversity must become our way of doing business and our way of life.[9]

Dennis Cirbes, then executive director of Ford Labor Affairs, leads the negotiation for the company. In the same video he states, "If we are to remain competitive we all must actively value diversity and embrace improvement. Diversity is not just the right thing to do...it's the only thing to do."[10]

Dan Brooks, the first UAW representative assigned to co-lead diversity efforts, recalls his initial surprise at being given the job. "When I received the call from Vice President Gettelfinger I have to admit I was confused. Why would I be asked to lead this type of initiative when historically it was always a female or minority who did. As I thought it through it became clear.... Who better to lead than a white male? It would send a signal to others like me."

Brooks, his company counterpart Tom Andersen, and staff first convene focus groups to determine their needs. They hire a consultant to work with the committee to develop the training. Anderson comments in the video, "This is a big step, we need everyone's help and assistance. Our focus group participants told us we needed to concentrate on training and education, respect, communication, and zero tolerance."

Brooks elaborates in the video. "The ideal result of the training is the recognition of prejudices and biases we may have learned along the way. Ultimately it is changes in our behavior that lead to better working relationship. If we can learn to get rid of discrimination and harassment we can build better relationships. Our goal is to create an environment where all employees regardless of their differences feel more comfortable and accepted so we can work more effectively to improve safety, quality and diversity."

The committee develops the United in Diversity program, which goes well beyond the typical cultural awareness approach. Its central idea is that if people become more aware of how others are different from them, they will be more sensitive about who others really are when they relate to them. The aim is not just fewer instances of bias, discrimination, and harassment, but ultimately to provide skills to build better working relationships. The training has eight one-hour modules:

1. What is diversity
2. The business case for diversity
3. Prejudice, bias, and stereotypes
4. Organizational environments
5. Behavior and conduct that fosters an inclusive environment
6. Communication for personal and interpersonal growth
7. The true meaning of inclusion
8. Behavior awareness and personal action

Each plant location identifies hourly employees (including Armentha Young, featured in chapter 2) to undergo "train the trainer" sessions delivered by the national committee. The Red- Yellow-Green concept used after the Chicago lawsuits is employed (see the sample module in the supporting materials for this chapter). This turns out to be far easier for employees than calling a statement or behavior "sexist" or "racist," sending a signal to change without having to use a highly charged label or explain further. To this day, people at Ford use the colors to monitor their interactions.

The stipulation that eight hours of mandatory training be delivered to every employee in every U.S. UAW-represented facility by the end of the contract is met; this also complies with the EEOC directive. The training is completed successfully by the start of 2003 negotiations, and continues to be used in the single-point lesson format that follows the Targeted Training Model (presented in chapter 8).

✳✳✳

The diversity training was a planned, enterprise-level intervention that was pivotal in addressing a core component of dignity and respect—being free from discrimination and harassment. It was also pivotal in an unexpected way. Diversity training turned out to be foundational for the successful functioning of a team-based work system. While the training was not developed and supported with this in mind, it had unplanned and unanticipated benefits.

9/11 Zero Tolerance Response, 2001

Ford and the UAW, like all U.S. corporations and unions, are shocked by the 9/11 terrorist attacks. This unanticipated pivotal event would have long-term implications, but leaders at the time are facing the initial challenge: make sense of what is going on and identify needed responses.

Although the corporation has many different types of emergency response procedures in place, nothing exactly matches this situation. Anne Stevens, the vice president of North American Operations, has a very specific concern. Marty Mulloy is in her office at the time.

"Anne was very concerned that Americans would overreact and target people of Middle Eastern descent as responsible," Mulloy recalls. "Since we have America's highest Arab American population in Dearborn, we were particularly worried about backlash right here in the Rouge."

"We set up a call-in number," says Stevens, "and started holding conference calls every other hour so that people could call in with information. It was initially targeted for directors of manufacturing and plant managers, but there were quickly several hundred people on the line, even Bill Ford. Initially people needed a place to be consoled, but there were lots of emotions. A few directors almost ended up in fistfights due to all the pent up emotion. We didn't want that emotion to go into hatred and blame—that is what motivated our response."

Less than 24 hours after the attack, Ford announces a zero tolerance policy for any statements or actions targeted against people of Middle Eastern ethnicities or the Islamic religion. The company is one of the first to anticipate and address the hatred and blame that emerges in many parts of American society. The policy announcement sends a clear signal very quickly that reinforces Ford's commitments to diversity and inclusion already well underway between the company and the union.

✳ ✳ ✳

In the days and weeks following 9/11, there were countless other immediate challenges for the company, such as getting parts trucks from Canada across borders with heightened security, as well as longer-term challenges as the economy deteriorated. We highlight the immediate zero tolerance policy announcement here because it illustrates how leadership during a cataclysmic crisis can provide direction and mitigate additional harm while also reinforcing core values.

Atlanta Zero Tolerance Intervention, 2002

By 2002, the Red-Yellow-Green training and the related training on diversity are taking hold throughout Ford. As expected, calls to the hotline surge—and some complaints present complications for local union and management leaders.

"A complaint came in from a number of workers about an individual who worked on the line in the Atlanta Assembly Plant," recalls Dan Brooks, then the UAW leader of the joint diversity programs. "This individual used the way he dressed as an expression of his views, and wore shirts and bandanas with the confederate flag. He had tattoos that sent the same message. Other workers found his offensive."

Rather than file a complaint with the Employee Equal Opportunity Commission about a hostile environment, the workers first register the complaint internally. This immediately comes to the attention of the plant HR manager and, since the complaint line is jointly administered, it also comes to the attention of the local union leaders and the international union.

It's clear management has to intervene. The union's role, though, is less clear. Local elected union leaders are divided. Workers hold strong views, and the union's duty is fair representation of all members. This includes the offended and the person who dresses offensively.

Local union leaders contact Dan Brooks from the international union, who flies to Atlanta right away to meet with the workers who are involved in the complaint.

"When you are outside the plant you can express your views however you do," Brooks says in response to the worker's insistence of his constitutional right to free speech, "but you don't have the same freedoms in the plant. Here you have to comply with the rules. I am not here to enforce the rules for the company, but I am here to say to you as a union brother that you can be disciplined and even discharged for not following the rules. This includes the rules for the kind of work environment that we have."

The individual decides to change the way he dresses and make sure his tattoos are covered.

✳ ✳ ✳

Union and management leaders made hundreds of interventions and had many very difficult conversations in their efforts to ensure dignity and respect in the workplace. Each of these is pivotal; they reinforce and extend Ford's policy. The pivotal nature of these events, though, goes even further. In the case illustrates, the union defines a role that advances a policy to which it is jointly committed as it attends to the risks facing a union brother who is contravening the policy. In some ways it would be easier for the union to stay out of the issue and let management administer discipline; by stepping forward the union is demonstrating leadership with respect to its own core values around dignity and respect.

Voluntary Separation Packages, 2006–2008

Needing to cut its U.S. workforce in half by approximately 50,000 workers between 2006 and 2008, Ford provides voluntary separation packages to all hourly employees. The various packages combine cash, health care continuation, and, if desired, education tuition support; they far exceed anything offered by other major U.S. employers going through downsizing at the same time.

Painful though the separations are, they are done with respect and appreciation for the individual employees, their families, and the communities in which they live. This is a pivotal event not only in that the reductions are essential to Ford's avoiding a catastrophic bankruptcy, but also in how they are handled—they actually strengthen the company's relationship with its workforce and the UAW.

When Mark Fields becomes President of the Americas (the CEO for Ford in North and South America) in September 2005, the need to reduce the size of the workforce comes into sharp focus. His task is to restore Ford North America to profitability and generate cash for new product investment in the Americas and around the world. It is clear that if Ford doesn't survive in the U.S. automotive market it will likely perish globally.

By the end of 2005, Ford's automotive operations lose $3.9 billion. The company faces a projected $17 billion loss the next year. These losses result primarily from a shrinking market share. In 2000, the company had built 4.7 million units and commanded 23.7 percent of the market, but by 2006 Ford builds only 3 million vehicles and sees its market share drop to 16 percent—despite roughly the same number of manufacturing facilities and workforce size.

Fields has limited options. He must address the company's cash burn immediately. Product Development, led by Derrick Kuzak, is embarking on a massive global restructuring effort that will eventually improve Ford's product lineup. Jim Farley, the group vice president of Marketing and Sales Operations (and recently hired from Toyota), is revamping Ford's marketing strategies and developing a plan to reduce the number of dealers. In parallel, Tony Brown, the vice president of Purchasing, is scrambling to deal with suppliers, who are overcapitalized in their operations because of the loss of Ford's volume. Ultimately, reducing Ford's supplier footprint will take years and more than a billion dollars, which is a longer-term element of cost savings. In the meantime, the only short-term way to stem the losses involves reducing the number of employees and the number of manufacturing facilities.

As Fields contemplates the workforce reductions, the challenge is daunting. In 2005, Ford has approximately 90,000 hourly and 45,000 salary employees, with 15 assembly plants in the United States. The vast majority of the U.S. salaried employees are nonunion and can be reduced through the company's reduction-in-force policies. Reducing UAW hourly employees, however, is another matter. Beginning in 1982 and reinforced in 1984 and 1987, the UAW agreements with the auto companies include what is termed a Guaranteed Income Stream (GIS) and a Job Opportunity Bank (JOB), both established in exchange for the UAW's support of the Employee Involvement (EI) program and mechanisms in which employees contribute productivity improvement suggestions as part of the *kaizen* process (detailed in chapter 5).

At the time of these 1980s agreements, leading nonunion firms such as IBM are known for avoiding layoffs as a way of fostering high levels of employee commitment. By 2005, however, IBM has long abandoned its no-layoff practice. Meanwhile, the steep declines in market share for all U.S. auto companies results in employees receiving 95 percent of their contracted wages and benefits even though they are not needed in the factories. Some are loaned out to nonprofit organizations contributing to community service, or some take classes through local community colleges, but most employees are just sitting in cafeterias without any work to do.

The bottom line: if the parties don't agree to some alternative plan, the company will continue to carry a surplus of what was estimated at the time to be more than 30,000 hourly employees with a combined average wage and benefit cost estimated at $3 billion per year. (In fact, more than 50,000 hourly employees would ultimate separate from the company between 2006 and 2008).

Ford's challenges are compounded by General Motors' demographics, which gives GM a distinct advantage when it comes to dealing with the problem of too many production workers. GM workers as a whole are closer to retirement: more than 60 percent of GM hourly employees have 25 or more years of service; Ford's number stands at 30 percent. Ford needs to come up with an innovative strategy to reduce the number of active employees. Relying on traditional incentive retirement programs is not going to achieve the number of separations required to reduce headcount to match customer vehicle demand.

"Mark Fields told me he had no other option," recalls Marty Mulloy. "Regardless of what the contract stated, we had to reduce our manufacturing footprint and downsize immediately or we would go bankrupt. Fields asked that we break through the constraints and come up with a plan."

A week later, Joe Hinrichs, Ford's group vice president for Manufacturing and Labor Affairs, assembles his team to develop a restructuring plan for Manufacturing Operations, which is immediately shared with senior UAW leadership. As indicated in chapter 2, the UAW is busy doing its own due diligence of the Ford's finances. The union determines Ford isn't bluffing—there must be immediate action to protect active workers and retirees from a Ford bankruptcy.

These events all precede the 2008 economic collapse that triggered the federal government's intervention to save the domestic automotive industry. Bankruptcy in 2007—the loss of more than 50,000 high-paying union manufacturing jobs, loss of retiree postretirement benefits, the potential reduction in retiree pension benefits, and limited capacity for severance payments—is tantamount to liquidation.

Ford closes or sells 27 plants to restructure its U.S. manufacturing footprint to match capacity to customer demand. The human suffering of employees and adverse impact on the communities affected cannot be overstated; however, the UAW and Ford agree to work together to minimize the harm.

Ford Labor Affairs and the UAW National Ford Department work collaboratively on a voluntary employee separation plan to reduce headcount, based on three principles: (1) all reductions will be voluntary; (2) a variety of separation packages will be offered to address employees' unique circumstances; and (3) employees leaving the company will be staggered over a year to avoid any adverse impact on product quality. Ford understands that the challenge in constructing any voluntary separation program is *balance*: offer enough of an inducement to attract the needed volunteers while maintaining the level of resources needed to invest in the future of the enterprise.

Meanwhile, the domestic auto market continues to deteriorate, and as the separation program is being developed and implemented the target size of the workforce reduction continues to grow.

Over a two-year period, Ford offers 14 distinct separations programs for retirement- and non-retirement-eligible employees; Figure 3.1 shows a briefing slide with some examples.

Among the most innovative, the Educational Opportunity Program offers non-retirement-eligible employees four years of $15,000 per year in tuition assistance, half their average base pay, full health care benefits, and $50,000 life insurance. Employees taking advantage of this program attend a wide variety of educational institutions, from vocational schools to Harvard and Oxford universities.

This, says HR director Jeff Faistenhammer, "was a transformational agreement by the UAW with the company."

EMPLOYEE SEPARATION PROGRAMS - Description

- **Special Early Retirement (SER)**
  - Retire at age 50 if 10+ years of seniority
- **Special Retirement Incentive (SRI)**
  - $35,000 lump sum contingent upon immediate retirement
- **Pre-Retirement Leave (PRLP)**
  - 85% of straight-time pay for maximum of 24 months while on leave prior to retirement
- **Special Termination of Employment Program (STEP)**
  - $100,000 lump sum and 6 months of basic health insurance
- **Enhanced Special Termination of Employment Program (ESTEP)**
  - $140,000 lump sum and 6 months of basic health insurance
  - Requirements: 10+ years seniority and waive post-retirement health insurance
- **Educational Opportunity Program (EDOPP)**
  - 50% of straight-time pay and $15,000 tuition reimbursement for 4 years max
- **Focused Educational Opportunity Program (FEDOPP)**
  - 70% of straight-time pay and $15,000 tuition reimbursement for 2 years max
- **Family Scholarship Program (FSP)**
  - $100,000 scholarship for eligible dependents and 6 months of basic health insurance

Figure 3.1

Sample Voluntary Separation Packages. While there was no precise formula for setting option levels, Ford knew that all options had to be generous enough compared to an offer of continued work at full salary. The educational opportunity programs, in particular, were distinctive and sent a clear signal to the workforce and their families about the intrinsic value of work. *Source:* Ford Motor Company.

We started talking about a couple different packages based on the current contract—doing things in the traditional way. Marty [Mulloy] kept saying we need to come up with many more packages and we need to come up with more money and more options if we are going to get the numbers we needed. He talked about people who wanted to have other career options—that it was more than money that was needed. Mulloy would not be knocked off center because of his background having experienced his father being involuntarily laid off in the steel industry when he was growing up.

If we hadn't put this together as we did, we would have ended up having to lay people off. In the end, the company was able to book billions of dollars in savings and it was the right thing to do for the people.

By partnering with the UAW, the company benefits by having additional inputs into what the workforce will value. Both parties are able to send a clear signal on the way work is valued. Mike Geiger, the UAW appointee responsible for job security, notes that earlier contractual voluntary separation programs offered payouts of around $8,000 to $10,000, and workers who accepted those payouts regretted the earning potential they gave up. The large take-up of the voluntary packages, he says, happens once the payouts associated with the packages exceed $50,000.

Geiger praises his management counterparts for how they handled the process. "I always had good people to work with on the company side—we worked together," he says. "It was not table pounding—we worked through the problems and presented the information together. We always got complements in this being clear and understandable. I credit the company wholeheartedly for their work with us." He also notes that neither GM nor Chrysler had the same focus on generating as many options or on offering packages as generous—although the arrangements at all of the auto companies are far more generous than nearly all other major U.S. companies at the time. Indeed, the auto industry separation packages stand out in the U.S. context for the ways in which they reduce the burden on individuals, families, and communities.

By the end of 2006, 40,000 Ford hourly employees—half each retirement- and non-retirement-eligible—accept separations packages. An additional 10,000 employees depart the next year. Ongoing cost savings, estimated to exceed $4 billion per year, are accomplished without a single hourly employee being forced out.

And what about "survivor guilt" among the remaining Ford workers? This is always a key concern with workforce reductions. Since departures are voluntary and the packages are generous, this case has no negative blowback. Indeed, quality performance during this time shows continuous improvement (detailed in chapter 8).

"We went through a huge transformation," says Mark Fields. "We had to say goodbye to almost 50 percent of the hourly workforce and almost 40 percent of the salaried workforce. The key thing about the transformation is that we did not miss a unit of production during this time and quality went up."

Fields praises the union's role as a partner in the process—a role he says is not unusual but just standard operating procedure. "I always love the questions when I meet people outside the industry. It is always about us having to deal with the UAW. I am dumbfounded. We are all part of the Ford family. We all have Ford Motor Company on our paychecks. It is the way we were brought up. There is a reason we haven't had a strike or work stoppage since 1976."

Board chairman Bill Ford echoes this sentiment and praises the leadership of then UAW president Ron Gettelfinger. "Ron could have laid in the tracks and it would have been a different outcome. He didn't roll over. Anyone who knows Ron knows he is principled and tough. But he cared about the future for his members and the future of Ford. His leadership was pivotal."

✳ ✳ ✳

Notably, GM's demographic advantage never materialized. Ford's separation program strategy resulted in more voluntary separations and greater cost savings than GM achieved. This pivotal event was a key contributing factor to Ford avoiding bankruptcy—both in terms of the cost savings and in terms of the operational capability (quality and production) during the recession.

Approaching the UAW as a partner in the face of the crisis, rather than as an adversary, strengthened the relationship between Ford and the union. Over the next five years, the UAW and Ford would meet four times at the national bargaining table to resolve complex business issues. The relationship built in creating and executing the separation program established a level of mutual trust and respect between the parties that became a touchstone as other challenges were faced. This was one way in which the voluntary separation program was pivotal. It was also pivotal in enabling Ford to maintain production and improve quality even with the disruption wrought by separations on such a scale.

As we note in chapter 1, Ford would not have likely had the confidence to turn down the federal bailout money had it not had the foundation of this joint approach to change.

Recap: Guiding Principle for Chapter 3—Dignity and Respect

Dignity and respect in the workplace, as we note in this chapter's opening, are foundational in society and integral to the identity of Ford and the UAW. The pivotal events in this chapter suggest, however, that simply stating these values is not enough. Pivotal moments arise in which they are on the table, and the choices made at these moments will either reinforce or undercut these core values.

While it was inevitable that Ford would eventually have a female plant manager—women were rising in the ranks of plant leadership—zeroing in on the specific moment shows that it was not predetermined. Forces of habit and conservatism lined up against a woman candidate's stronger record, and it took leadership for that stronger record to prevail. Similarly, the pivotal events around affinity groups, zero tolerance after 9/11, and zero tolerance in Atlanta all illustrate moments in which the commitment to dignity and respect had the potential to either be reinforced or undercut. These are just some examples of countless instances where values are either undercut or reinforced. Further, the diversity training and the joint UAW-Ford Equality and Diversity Program that followed the sexual harassment lawsuits are foundational to the pivotal events on dignity and respect during the past decade.

Dignity and respect was central to the way the company approached the very difficult challenge of reducing the hourly and salaried workforces to match market demand. It was handled in a way that provided a measure of stability for individuals, families, and communities—balancing dignity and respect with economic necessity.

SUPPORTING MATERIALS

3.1 Sample United in Diversity Materials

On the Road...

To Mutual Respect

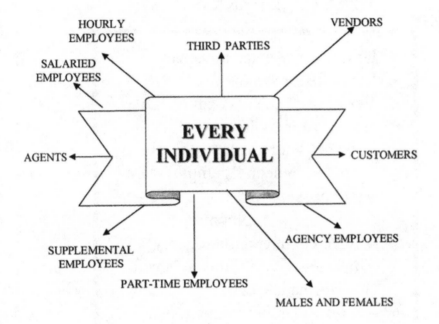

OUR POLICY APPLIES TO:

HOURLY EMPLOYEES

VENDORS

THIRD PARTIES

SALARIED EMPLOYEES

EVERY INDIVIDUAL

AGENTS

CUSTOMERS

SUPPLEMENTAL EMPLOYEES

AGENCY EMPLOYEES

PART-TIME EMPLOYEES

MALES AND FEMALES

Ford

2

U.S. EQUAL EMPLOYMENT OPPORTUNITY COMMISSION
DEFINITION
OF SEXUAL HARASSMENT

- Unwelcome sexual advances
- Requests for sexual favors
- Verbal or physical conduct of a sexual nature, when:
  - Submission explicitly/implicitly affects someone's employment
  - Submission/rejection affects someone's employment
  - Such conduct unreasonably interferes with someone's work performance, or
  - Creates an intimidating, hostile, or offensive working environment

29 CFR 1604.11

3

Ford Anti-Harassment
Policy Scavenger Hunt
PART I

1. Ford Motor Company's Anti-Harassment Policy states that Ford has a zero tolerance for what?

2. Who does Ford's Anti-Harassment Policy protect?

3. List five (5) examples of conduct that is prohibited.

4. List five (5) examples of actions that constitute forbidden retaliation if motivated by an employee's good faith complaint or cooperation in an investigation.

5. What are the consequences for violating Ford's Anti-Harassment Policy?

6. What are the consequences for retaliation?

Ford

Ford Anti-Harassment Policy Scavenger Hunt
PART II

1. What are the four (4) responsibilities every employee has to make the Anti-Harassment Policy work?

2. Who <u>at Ford</u> should employees report violations of the policy to?

3. What should you do if you observe someone else being subject to harassment or retaliation?

4. What will Ford do once an alleged violation of the Policy is made?

5. Complaints will be handled as confidentially as

   _____.

6. What is the toll-free hotline number to report violations of Ford's Anti-Harassment Policy?

Ten Danger Zones

DANGER 1. Comments on personal appearance

DANGER 2. Jokes: such as sexual, racial, religious, or national origin

DANGER 3. Work-related off-premises conduct

DANGER 4. Nicknames

DANGER 5. Stereotypes

DANGER 6. Touching

DANGER 7. Dating/initiating personal relationships

DANGER 8. Retaliating

DANGER 9. Cartoons, posters, pictures, apparel, T-shirts

DANGER 10. E-mail, Internet

Ford

6

Ford Motor Company's Commitment to Equal Employment Opportunity

No employee will be considered for promotion

into any salaried position:

- For a period of two (2) years after being disciplined for engaging in Covered Discrimination, or

- For a period of three (3) years after being suspended for such conduct.

♦ ♦ ♦ ♦ ♦ ♦ ♦

No supervisor or manager will be considered for promotion:

- For a period of two (2) years after being disciplined for failure to meet the obligations described on the previous page, or

- For a period of three (3) years after being suspended for such conduct.

Ford is committed to equal employment opportunity.

7

Source: UAW-Ford National Joint Programs

Guiding Principle: Mutual Growth

For three decades following World War II, the U.S. auto industry experienced dramatic growth, reflected in what could be called the "operating assumptions" that guided the role of labor relations in the economy. The key operating assumption was that of stable, continued growth in the marketplace. This enabled certain institutional arrangements to develop in the auto industry that directly influenced other key industries, such as steel, and set the tone for the nation.

Over the subsequent three decades, from 1980 forward, these assumptions and the associated institutional arrangements have been breaking down. Constructing new institutional arrangements that enable success and mutual growth has become a challenge Ford and the UAW have faced together.

Perhaps the most important institutional arrangement during the first three postwar decades was the Annual Improvement Factor (AIF)—a 3 percent annual wage increase justified from a business point of view by fairly steady 3 percent annual growth in productivity. This was a product of the 1950 "treaty of Detroit" in which U.S. automakers traded steady wage growth for labor peace.[1] While not matched by all employers in all industries, it was an arrangement that was sufficiently well distributed across leading employers in the economy so as to have the societal effect of growing the middle class. The concomitant increase in purchasing power this afforded had a self-reinforcing effect of stimulating increasing demand for products and services.

In 1982, the United States experienced the effects of a global recession that had begun in the late 1970s. It was not the first economic downturn since World War II, but it had some characteristics that called into question the assumption of continued growth. In the auto industry, the shock of the oil embargo, combined with rising Japanese imports, suggested the auto marketplace was changing in substantial ways. In the United States, the recession marked the end of the Annual Improvement Factor and led the parties in collective bargaining to articulate their goal of mutual growth and to begin the search for new ways of achieving it.

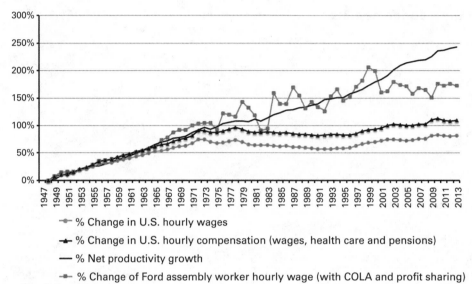

Figure 4.1

Cumulative Percent Change in United States Productivity, United States Hourly Earnings, and Ford Assembly Line Worker Hourly Earnings: 1947–2013[7].

Source: Economic Policy Institute analysis of unpublished Total Economy Productivity data from Bureau of Labor Statistics Labor Productivity and Costs program, Bureau of Labor Statistics Current Employment Statistics, Bureau of Labor Statistics Employment Cost Trends, and Bureau of Economic Analysis National Income and Product Accounts; updated from: Figure 4U in *The State of Working America*, 12th Edition, an Economic Policy Institute book published by Cornell University Press in 2012. Hourly compensation is calculated using a compensation-to-wage ratio the National Income and Product Accounts data. Production/nonsupervisory workers in the private sector and net productivity on the chart are for the total U.S. economy. "Net productivity" is the growth of output of goods and services less depreciation per hour worked. UAW-Ford data are from 2011 National Negotiations UAW-Ford Media Fact Book.

Figure 4.1 tracks U.S. productivity and hourly wages and shows how hourly wages for a UAW-Ford assembly worker fared after World War II. It is important to note that the figure tracks the *cumulative percentage change over time indexed to 1947*, not the actual value of wages or productivity. Also, all values have been adjusted for inflation, since our aim is not to show actual wage levels but, again, the degree of change over time.

Over two and a half decades, real hourly wages for U.S. workers grew every year, matching productivity growth. Beginning in the mid-1970s the cumulative percentage change in wages went flat. For another half decade, benefits continued to grow over and above wages. Some of this was due to substitution of benefits for wages, and some to actual growth in benefits. Eventually, though, benefits also went flat. Incidentally, though it is not on the chart, household wages continued to grow for another decade as women entered the workforce in large numbers, but they flattened by the 1980s. After the 1980s, productivity continued to demonstrate year-over-year increases even as U.S. wages did not keep up. When this connection to productivity growth broke down, it led many consumers to take on greater debt, which became a key precipitant of the Great Recession in the United States beginning in 2007. Although it is not represented on the chart, executive compensation grew dramatically beginning in the 1990s as the proportion of compensation tied to stock options expanded— contributing to wage inequality in society.

The greater variability in the cumulative percentage change in the hourly wages of a typical UAW-Ford assembly line worker (with cost of living increases and profit sharing included) reflects the fact that wage increases were negotiated and adjusted every other year or, in some cases, every third year. In addition, the cost of living increases and the profit sharing fluctuated from year to year. Still, even with this variability, autoworker compensation continued to track national productivity growth much better than that of most U.S. workers.[2]

The cumulative percentage change for autoworkers in recent years has, like that for other workers, been relatively flat—reflecting moderated wage demands in recent negotiations in exchange for increased investment in jobs and new technology, as well as a focus on ensuring retiree health care (detailed in chapter 5). This explains, in part, the growing pressure from autoworkers for increased compensation. A challenging question centers on whether a link can be reestablished with productivity in the coming years.

In the 1982 recession, the UAW and Ford declared their commitment to continued "mutual growth," a commitment that needed to be articulated because it could not be assumed as an outcome in the future. Figure 4.1 indicates mutual growth was much more of a reality for the UAW-Ford assembly line worker than for most other U.S workers. Stable growth was no longer a valid operating assumption in the economy generally, and the resulting end of the annual improvement factor and related patterns across the economy broke the self-reinforcing connection between wage growth (i.e., growth in purchasing power) and growth in the economy.

For Ford and the UAW, restating mutual growth as a goal meant increased attention to business fundamentals would be necessary. To contribute to mutual growth, union representatives had to ride up a learning curve on how the business functions. Management had to attend to the fundamentals to ensure business success.

This commitment was reaffirmed in the 1999 national UAW-Ford negotiations with a letter of agreement stating, in part:

The UAW-Ford relationship is dramatically different today than it was when the Union and the Company signed their first Collective Bargaining Agreement. Both parties recognize that the need for change continues—that prosperity, secure employment, and the mutual interests of all depend upon our ability to meet the competitive challenge of today's market through growth, development, and adaptation. Perhaps most of all, the parties realize they must explore new methods of resolving their honest differences in orderly, rational ways.

Both parties also recognize that positive change is possible only when progressive, cooperative attitudes exist at all levels of our two organizations. Where we find such attitudes are lacking, the Company and the Union must work vigorously to instill them.

During these negotiations, the parties continued their commitment to the Mutual Growth Forum principles and concepts. The Mutual Growth Forum constitutes a joint process for labor-management consultation, communication, and mutual problem solving. It complements other joint endeavors, as well as the collective bargaining process itself.

This Forum does not replace collective bargaining, nor does it interfere in any way with the parties' Grievance Procedure. Rather, it provides a framework designed to promote better management-union relations through better communications, systematic fact finding, and advance discussion of certain business developments that are of material interest and significance to the Union, UAW-represented Ford employees, and the Company.

The parties regard the Mutual Growth Forum as a major progressive step. It promotes understanding, improves relationships, and prevents disputes by providing for ongoing, constructive, and cooperative problem solving. Both the Company and the Union have pledged to bring good faith diligence to the process and to be responsive to issues and concerns raised by the other party.[3]

This chapter traces various dimensions of the Ford-UAW commitment to mutual growth—a principle that, during the 1990s and 2000s, was eroded in many other parts of the U.S. economy. The full set of mechanisms to deliver on this promise for the UAW and Ford didn't come together until the early- to mid-2000s, with codification of performance metrics and the introduction of the Business Plan Review and Special Attention Review processes. These and other pivotal events in this chapter are presented as follows, again presented as though you were there at the time, with some quotes looking back:

Chapter 4 Pivotal Events	Overview	Type, Level
Plastic and Trim Products Cross-Functional Alignment, 1995	This is a pivot that doesn't happen—the effort to align the internal functions around a shared view of the value stream falls short, due in large part to barriers in the form of deep cultural "chimneys."	Planned, Division Level
Policy Deployment—SQDCME, 1999–2002	The "balanced scorecard"—a key building block of business fundamentals—is essential for internal alignment, as is extending the metrics all the way to frontline teams.	Planned, Enterprise Level
Rouge Revitalization, 2001	Ford revitalizes the iconic River Rouge operations into the world's most energy-efficient auto assembly building—with a flexible assembly production process.	Planned, Plant Level
UAW FPS Total Cost Stand Down, 2002–2003	As the UAW becomes more of a partner in the business, it begins to challenge the labor cost and overhead system of accounting—illustrating the union's deeper engagement in operations.	Unplanned, Enterprise Level

Chapter 4

Pivotal Events	Overview	Type, Level
Lean Manufacturing Managers and the Lean Implementation Network, 2001–2003	Increased capability in the social system (in addition to the technical aspects of lean manufacturing) comes with developing in the next generation of leaders a deep appreciation of lean production principles, combined with a network for shared learning.	Planned, Enterprise Level
BPR and SAR Processes, 2006	Alan Mulally's arrival as CEO is pivotal in many ways, with the Business Plan Review and Special Attention Review processes at the core. Ford pivots away from separate chimneys or fiefdoms and toward a culture of integrated, open problem solving on business fundamentals.	Planned, Enterprise Level
Quality Operating Committee, 2006	Inviting Dan Brooks to be a regular member of Ford's Quality Operating Committee signals the integration of the union in the business operations—based on demonstrated, relevant expertise.	Planned, Enterprise Level
One Ford, 2007	Mulally defines employee behavioral expectations and reduces the number of brands, integrating everything under the mantra of "One Ford"—and Ford successfully navigates the worst economic downturn since the Great Depression.	Planned, Enterprise Level

Plastic and Trim Products Cross-Functional Alignment, 1995

Although the Ford Production System is not fully developed by 1995, many of the underlying lean principles are beginning to influence the way the company does business. Motivated by an early appreciation of the idea of "customer pull," the Plastic and Trim Products Division (as it was then called) organizes an offsite meeting to align internal support functions in support of the customer. It includes division leaders from several support functions:

• Finance
• Human Resources (HR)
• Manufacturing Operations
• Materials Planning & Logistics (MP&L)
• Product Development
• Purchasing

The division's line management leaders convene the meeting, and plant managers from the various plants in the division also attend.

The offsite session begins with a review of some of the lean production principles and the main support function roles: regulatory/compliance role; service delivery/support; and change agent/transformation. The session then shifts to developing a so-called interdependency matrix that will show what each support function depends on from the others and what others can depend on from them. The idea is to forge "reciprocal social contracts" (that is, agreements among those in support-function and operating roles) to ensure the delivery of value to the end customer.

Joel Cutcher-Gershenfeld facilitates the session. It is during the interdependency exercise, he notes, when a complication arises.

I made what I thought was a self-evident statement: since manufacturing delivers the end product to the customer, the work on interdependencies should all be aligned to support manufacturing and, through manufacturing, the customer. One by one, each support function agreed—Finance, HR, Manufacturing Operations, MP&L, and Purchasing. However, Product Development disagreed. The leadership from this function stated that the division produces two products—manufactured components *and* engineered designs. Because of that the NPD engineers stated that all the support functions should be aligned to support them just as much as they were aligned to support manufacturing.

The entire meeting breaks down. Is there one value stream or two? No agreement can be reached. Bill Mothersell, the lead internal change agent from HR for the session, recalls the dynamic. "There were still many people who didn't understand lean production. They could talk about it, but couldn't fully piece it together."

Lean ideas are still relatively new, but the debate goes beyond a simple lack of understanding. Mothersell continues, "At the same time, the top engineering and production guys were jockeying for position. Meanwhile, we're doing this exercise around what each party owes to the other. That was where it started to unravel. We were making real progress up to that point and then it unraveled."

This collapse is emblematic of a problem that plagues Ford for much of the 1990s. The company is highly profitable for many of these years, but the various divisions and support functions each focus on their own priorities, with far too little attention to how they are all integrated in one business. Even though the principle of "mutual growth" had been incorporated into the collective bargaining agreement more than a decade earlier, the principle of mutual growth is not even fully operational within management—let alone between labor and management—during these years.

*** *** ***

We highlight the Plastic and Trim Products offsite session because it had the potential to be a pivotal event, but fell short. Had all the support functions aligned around a "customer pull" through manufacturing it would have advanced progress toward integrated operating systems by at least a decade. The impact of such as change in one division would have been modest, but the example, if followed by the full corporation, would have been transformational. In this case, however, the event illustrates some of the embedded dynamics throughout Ford that were barriers to transformation.

Policy Deployment—SQDCME, 1999–2002

In the aftermath of the 1973 oil embargo and the accompanying onslaught of Japanese vehicles to the United States, all three domestic car companies send teams of experts to study the product development and manufacturing processes of Japan Inc. (Toyota, Honda, Mazda, Datsun). It is from the Japanese that U.S. manufacturing teams learn about using statistical process controls by frontline machine operators (not just industrial engineers) to ensure process capability (standardized, dependable processes), which is essential for the delivery of quality parts.

Ford rolls out its own Statistical Process Controls (SPC) program companywide in 1983, followed immediately by Ford's Q1 program, a comprehensive quality assurance program that includes plant quality audits and certification requirements to demonstrate adherence to quality processes (presented in chapter 8). These initiatives dramatically improve quality at Ford to levels approaching that of the Japanese competition, and also introduce Japanese terms and concepts such as *kaizen* (a central focus of chapter 5) into the everyday Ford vernacular (even as Ford and UAW leaders diligently find substitute English language terms given continued anti-Japanese sentiments in the hourly and salaried workforce).

One Japanese term surfaces early on, but is not fully appreciated: *Hoshin Kanri*—translated as "policy deployment." The term refers to a "catch-ball" process (i.e., a division director "catches the ball" from a vice president and then a plant manager "catches the ball" from the division director); the "ball" is goals on a balance scorecard[4] in the form of performance metrics. This cascades down the levels, across the enterprise. The process involves agreements on the metrics that apply at each level: from the full enterprise to frontline teams, followed by a series of exchanges—the "catch-ball" reference—in which higher-level leaders communicate the goals for each metric, and the next level down either accepts them as stated or signals potential factors that may require the goals be adjusted. Once that "catch" occurs, it moves to the next level. The enterprise objectives for the next year are usually set around October, with division objectives set about November, and plant objectives set around December. In the past, the frontline teams would never learn how these objectives translated to the goals in their work area. As a result, the full *Hoshin Kanri* process has not been followed.

By the late 1990s, Jim Padilla, the group vice president of the Global Manufacturing Operations, becomes the driving force behind Ford's quality improvement efforts and the Ford Production System (FPS), which include building the foundation for a more systematic approach to policy deployment. His experience in product development and quality control provides a holistic systems perspective of FPS. Padilla selects Roman Krygier to be Vice President of Powertrain Operations, who brings his experience as the director Advanced Manufacturing Engineering and Director of Stamping Operations. It is in Powertrain that the first applications of the policy deployment process are implemented.

Krygier is a hands-on, blue-collar executive known for "working the floor," which is rooted in his appreciation for the hard work and dedication of Ford's hourly employees. He understands the latent talent in both the production and skilled trades workforce. Benchmarking trips to Toyota's Georgetown Kentucky plant and automotive supplier Nippondenso provide Krygier with some key insights into the policy deployment process.

Benchmarking on policy deployment, though, is not limited to Japanese operations. "It was the trips to Volvo after it was acquired by Ford that were most helpful to us in the UAW in learning about bringing performance-measureable data to front line teams," recalls Dan Brooks. Volvo's team-based model (discussed in chapter 5) is based on the use of semi-autonomous teams, such as a group of people with full responsibility for building an entire car engine. It is an approach that contrasts with the lean production teams at Toyota and Nippondenso; in many respects, the need for team-level performance data is highest with the semi-autonomous team model at Volvo.

The first step in the policy deployment process at Ford involves establishing the metrics, which are in the form of a balanced scorecard that applies at all levels. This takes place in early 2000, when Ford's Global Manufacturing Operations team adopts a set of production metrics that initially highlight Safety, Quality, Delivery, Cost, and Morale (SQDCM). Within about a year, "E" is added for "Environment." A new "M" is added for "Maintenance" (shown in figure 4.2). In 2010, the "M" for "Morale" is replaced with "P" for "People," which includes skill as well as motivation.

Today, these are the key production metrics for evaluating Manufacturing Operations at Ford:

• Safety—Zero Fatality and Serious Injuries
• Quality—Zero MIS and Cost per Unit (CPU)
• Delivery—Lean Material Flow and On-Time Delivery (OTD)
• Cost—World-Class Efficiency
• People—Skilled and Motivated People
• Maintenance—100% Utilization
• Environment—Green Enterprise

The Powertrain Division pilots these metrics as part of the "catch-ball" policy deployment process, as visualized in figure 4.3.

Were you to walk onto the shop floor of the Romeo Engine Plant in the early 2000s, you would see a "continuous improvement" display board that looks something like the one in figure 4.4, with columns corresponding to the SQDCME metrics (the initials at the time). The pages on the board are updated daily or weekly, depending on the metric being tracked.

The administrative offices of the Romeo Engine Plant have a corresponding board with the same SQDCME columns, but with the results for the full plant (figure 4.5).

"The key was to communicate to the workers on the factory floor the performance of their operation in a consistent, measurable, and easy to understand way," notes Krygier.

FORD MANUFACTURING – BEST IN THE WORLD

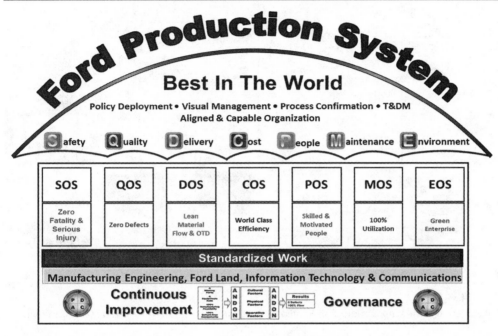

Figure 4.2

SQDCPME Briefing Materials. This corresponds to a balanced scorecard of performance metrics relevant at the enterprise, division, plant, area, and work group levels. Each category also corresponds to a supporting operating system (the primary focus for chapter 8). *Source:* Ford Motor Company.

"Continuous Improvement (CI) boards were set up in work locations—the natural breaks in the flow of production operations determined the size and scope of the work groups."

Visual management principles are used to make sure the information is easy to understand. Initially, salary supervision and staff perform the SQDCME (now SQDCPME) data collection. As the process develops, hourly employees take on greater degrees of responsibility. Eventually, hourly work group leaders are selected and assigned greater levels of engagement in managing the work group's production process and adherence to objectives.

When the process first begins, there is a high degree of variance in the "catch-ball" process across locations. Some teams do not learn of the team-level version of the plant's annual objectives until June or July. By 2002, however, the Lean Implementation Network (discussed later in this chapter) takes the leadership for this process and most locations have frontline teams learning of the balanced scorecard objectives by late January or February. How overall business objectives are translated into a format consistent across levels, with regular feedback

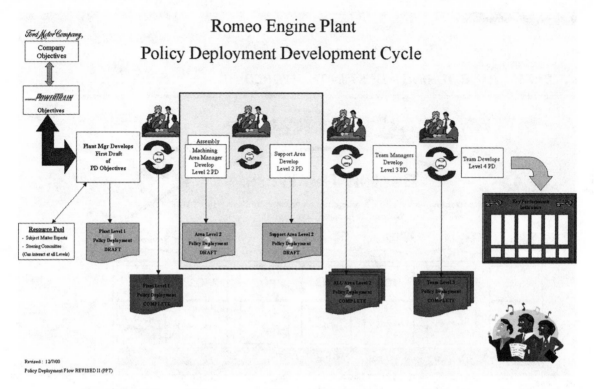

Figure 4.3
Policy Deployment Visualization from Romeo Engine Plant. *Source:* UAW-Ford National Joint Programs.

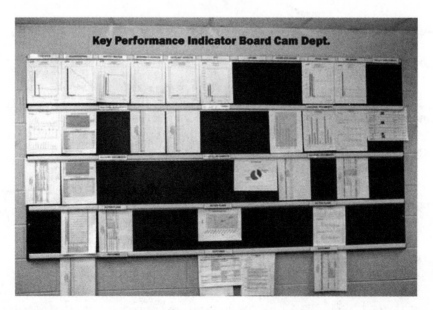

Figure 4.4
Work Area Continuous Improvement Board. *Source:* UAW-Ford National Joint Programs.

Figure 4.5
Plant Visual Display Board. *Source:* UAW-Ford National Joint Programs.

on performance to goal, is a key building block for the transformation of work and relationships to deliver results. For the frontline workforce, policy deployment enables engagement and ownership of their part of the business.

"The CI boards are like reading the box score from a baseball game," says one hourly employee. "At one glance, you know immediately how well the team has performed."

✳✳✳

The next step beyond policy deployment was what Ford and the UAW termed "time and data management" (detailed in chapter 7). Not only were there standardized metrics at all levels of the operation, but also there were standardized forums, on a set schedule, in which people were engaged with the data. Policy deployment on SQDCPME is thus pivotal as a building block for the very heartbeat of the enterprise.

Rouge Revitalization, 2001

The River Rouge complex represents the very beginnings of Henry Ford's vision of a vertically integrated operation that builds on mass production principles. Construction begins in 1917. By the time of completion in 1928, it is the world's largest integrated factory. Beginning with raw iron ore and other raw materials, the site includes a steel mill, glass factory, foundry, component operations, engine production, and almost everything else needed to produce finished automobiles. At its peak, in the 1940s, approximately 120,000 people are employed in the complex.

The Rouge complex has a lot of history for the UAW as well. The pedestrian bridge between one of the parking areas and the complex is the site of the 1937 "Battle of the Overpass," when Ford's internal "Service Department" violently removes UAW organizers (including the future, iconic president of the union, Walter Reuther) posing for a *Detroit News* photographer while distributing leaflets. Photographs of Ford security men coming up behind unionists and beating them with clubs shift public opinion in favor of the union.

By the mid-1990s, Ford faces a key strategic decision about this aging facility, desperately in need of revitalization. There are advocates for investing in a new facility; they propose a wide range of locations across the company and around the country. A new "greenfield" location, or adding on to a newer location, may well involve a lower capital investment. But revitalizing this iconic site has symbolic meaning.

Bill Ford Jr., board chair, leads the decision making not just to refurbish this complex, but also to make it once again an exemplar—this time as the world's greenest auto production complex. It is this decision that we highlight as pivotal. It honors the past and elevates environmental issues as a strategic priority for the business. It also solidifies the awareness in the workforce that the Ford family is influencing business policy with a long-term orientation.

The architect William McConough is hired in 1999 to redesign Ford Rouge Site. Completed in 2002, it features a 1.1-million-square-foot truck assembly plant (producing the F-150) with a 10-acre "living" roof covered with sedum, a low-water ground cover alternative to grass. The sedum retains and cleans rainwater for reuse (generating 20 billion gallons of water per year for industrial use), while also helping reduce building energy costs. The plant is even a designated wildlife habitat. The new Rouge has the capacity for building six different models concurrently (on a given platform)—a level of production flexibility never previously known to Ford.

Early on, there is push back from some executives over the extra cost associated with launching a plant with such flexibility. Today, though, this modular platform approach to manufacturing is the global standard.

"Cultures are not static – but truths continue," says Bill Ford, speaking about the combination of doing things in new, innovative ways in the Rouge complex (particularly the environmental footprint of the facility), while also honoring the past. "The enduring truths have to be re-expressed for the next generation. We have to keep it relevant."

✳ ✳ ✳

The Rouge revitalization was pivotal as the embodiment of Bill Ford's commitment to the environmental issues that he recognized would come to be increasingly important to customers and society. It was also pivotal as an investment in flexible platform-based manufacturing—a goal first embraced in the early 1990s under Ford 2000, but that took more than half a decade to be reflected fully in the redesign and operation of Ford's signature assembly plant.

UAW FPS Total Cost Stand Down, 2001–2002

The Ford Production System (FPS) is not a joint UAW-Ford program, in contrast to issues of safety, quality, employee involvement, and other topics. For Ford management, management rights is at the core of what drives production operations, and as such should not be subject to joint decision making. For the UAW's elected leadership, decisions about production, including efficiency improvements that can reduce headcount in a work area, are politically controversial. However, the UAW and Ford agree on the importance of business success—and union leaders' growing expertise in lean manufacturing principles is valued.

This pivotal event documents the intersection of increasing union expertise in the work system and more traditional union caution with respect to the Ford Production System. A debate arises in 2001 over the underlying assumptions in the accounting system—not something traditionally discussed in union-management relations. The union comes to see the accounting system more clearly based on its work with management around the production system. The UAW has concerns, and there are some in management who are sympathetic. Management, though, is unwilling to make changes—even at the cost of losing union support for FPS.

Implementation of the Ford Production System is not meeting desired expectations by 2001. In part, senior management leadership is not fully oriented around this lean initiative. In parallel, CEO Jacques Nasser launches the Business Leadership Initiative (BLI), modeled on GE's process reengineering principles and featuring Six Sigma tools and methods. This is coupled with a highly controversial performance-ranking process, also copied from GE, with a forced ranking system managers must apply to all of their direct reports. Nasser steps down in October 2001, but BLI and Six Sigma continue to exist in parallel with FPS, along with Ford 2000 (launched in the mid-1990s and presented in chapter 2). Each program has its proponents within Ford, and there is debate as to which is the lead for transformation. Of all these concurrent management initiatives, the union is most deeply engaged in FPS—particularly since FPS is more clearly dependent on continuous improvement through frontline work groups.

One of FPS's selling points is management's willingness to examine system barriers jointly, including using a "total cost" approach to manage a plant's yearly "task." This is in contrast with the established "labor and overhead" approach. Under the latter, a typical plant's operating budget is based on workforce costs (hourly compensation and benefits) plus the overhead for operating the plant (salaried workforce compensation and benefits, energy consumption, and investments in new technology and equipment). The cost of purchased parts, raw materials, and the associated engineering and design of the components are in the budgets of the Purchasing function, new product development, and other parts of the company.

The difference between the two accounting methods is considerable. Using just labor and overhead, hourly and salaried labor accounts for about 70 percent of a typical automotive assembly plant's budget. Using the total cost approach, that number drops to about 30 percent.

The UAW and Ford management alike find the labor and overhead approach stressful. Each plant is given a flat percentage—its "task" for the year—that has to be achieved regardless of facility issues, product, or design mix. A plant launching new products is better able to make headcount reductions by the end of the year, for example, because there are some additional resources associated with the launch that can be let go. But a plant with a three-year-old product absorbs three years of headcount reductions and does not see as many opportunities for efficiency gains. Similarly, a plant with older equipment needs to allocate more people to maintenance than a newer plant—a difference not reflected in the yearly "task."

The underlying principle behind the labor and overhead approach is a valid one—the expectation that all facilities make year-over-year productivity improvements. It is a principle at the very core of the Annual Improvement Factor discussed at the outset of this chapter. When administered mechanically though, the labor and overhead approach drives a wedge in local Ford-UAW relationships. The parties end up contending over which areas of the plant can absorb headcount reductions rather than partnering on efficiency improvements.

In early 2001, a joint union-management study group is set up to examine total cost, aimed at expanding the focus of the accounting system in manufacturing operations so a plant might meet its annual task with cost savings in purchasing or improvements in component parts, or through other savings not tracked under the labor and overhead system. This is how many of the Japanese competitors operate—a plant is credited with all efficiency improvements associated with its operation, not just labor and overhead savings.

Joe Gafa, the UAW coordinator of Continuous Improvement, leads the joint effort on the UAW side. Senior Ford leaders involved include the vice president for North American Operations at the time, Anne Stevens; Marty Mulloy, the director of Human Resources, Global Manufacturing; the comptroller Peter Daniel; and others—all of whom participate even though they are skeptical about how much of a change is possible. Daniels is most vocal on the negative side. He recalls:

Total cost—I was against it. No one could define what total cost was. Is warranty part of it? There could be cost issues that were an engineering design issue? Would the plant want to be responsible for that? It could go on you either way. When you looked in detail most of the cost issues were generally the engineering, not the plants. I had a problem with the concept from a plant perspective.

Consider one of today's quality issues. Ford's quality has taken a hit due to Microsoft's "My Touch" system. Should that be on the plants? My view is, "Why don't you control what you can control?" I was pushing that if you are going to do total cost, do it within the four walls. I must admit that I fought it for two years.

Daniels raises challenging questions. If the UAW wants to take credit for efficiency gains achieved beyond the plant's four walls, will the union also take responsibility for losses from these same sources? And what about the Purchasing function, which also has annual efficiency improvement goals? Won't Purchasing want to take credit for savings associated with suppliers?

Still, the study group makes progress. It identifies some aspects of plant operations beyond labor and overhead that could be considered as part of meeting the annual task. For example, frontline teams might be credited for some gains with suppliers, energy use, and other matters.

The Wayne Assembly Plant conducts a pilot experiment. With the support of Anne Stevens, Bennie Fowler (the plant manager at the time), agrees to use a percentage of efficiencies made in productivity, materials, and power consumption as part of the calculation of his annual task.

"For total cost," Fowler recalls, "I tried to lay out every dollar it took to build a car and have each department understand each element in their department. We had a single agenda for safety as we did for quality. We did value stream mapping to see where the waste was. We then had learning labs with input from customer on quality. The hourly FTPM appointee led on maintenance. On labor cost we would teach about the differences among cost of 'value add,' 'non-value add but necessary,' and 'waste.'"

In 2002, Fowler is promoted to become the director of Manufacturing Operations. His successor at Wayne does not continue the pilot experiment. By then, the joint study group has been looking at the issue for over six months. Internal UAW debates on this issue go back more than two years. It is at this point that the issue becomes entangled with the UAW's FPS activities.

The UAW National Ford Department has never publicly supported the FPS Lean Initiative, but Ron Gettelfinger—the UAW's Ford department director and vice president at the time—had assigned four full-time staff members—Joe Gafa, Jerry Young, Chuck Browning, and Bob Trockley—and eight hourly coaches to assist in the process. The full-timers worked with local leadership, attempting to keep the momentum going and raising implementation concerns with FPS management.

At an early 2002 joint conference in Las Vegas, Gettelfinger issues an ultimatum regarding FPS to Ford leadership: if no resolution on total cost is achieved by that Friday, the UAW's support for the lean initiative will cease. Immediately, a high-level meeting is convened with the union and the company to identify what would constitute resolution of the issue. Matt DeMars, a director of Manufacturing Operations, makes a presentation to UAW leadership on the elements of the total-cost approach. Ford Finance, though, is opposed; Daniels says Finance considers it impossible to come up with an enterprise-wide format.

Jim Padilla adds that he is only responsible for what goes on within the four walls of a plant. As a result, that is all that can be included in the total-cost formula.

Some in the UAW favor going forward on this basis, but Gettelfinger is not satisfied with Ford's response. He tells the four full-time UAW representatives to stand down from their work in support of FPS. The eight hourly coaches return to their home plants.

The UAW protest over total cost links this issue to union support for FPS at the enterprise level. However, at the plant level, the UAW communicates a different message. As the moratorium on UAW involvement with FPS at the enterprise level continues, the UAW International union staff encourages local union leaders and local support staff to continue to work on the FPS lean implementation.

Even at the enterprise level, the four UAW representatives turn their efforts to applying FPS principles in two glass plants that are being put up for sale by Ford (documented in chapter 5). This signals continued UAW engagement with FPS, even if they are simultaneously protesting the response on total cost.

Joe Gafa is promoted to assistant director of the National Joint Programs and Dan Brooks transfers from the Equality and Diversity program to become the coordinator of Continuous Improvement, a role in which he promotes Appendix I of the national UAW-Ford collective bargaining agreement that includes continuous improvement but does not mention FPS specifically. Gettelfinger signals a continuing commitment to Ford's success as an enterprise, even as he protests the specific issue of total cost.

The UAW's active support for the Ford Production System resumes after Gettelfinger assumes the union presidency and Gerald Bantom replaces him as the new vice president responsible for relations with Ford in June 2002. By that fall, the four full-time UAW appointees are reengaged with the enterprise-wide FPS initiative. Indeed, in the 2003 national negotiations, Anne Stevens (who was at the time the vice president for Vehicle Operations at Ford), cites the "Total Cost" efforts in a letter of agreement regarding VO Cost Objective Efforts to Gerald Bantom:

Company and Union recognition of work group involvement and the impact on cost objectives was demonstrated by the significant work of the VO Total Cost Pilot Committee, and local plant committees that embraced the opportunities of continuous improvement. The parties would like to acknowledge and recognize the work of these committees. Through the efforts of these groups a full range of cost elements that are essential to meeting the competitive challenges in the auto industry have been identified.

The efficient and effective utilization of our people is critical to the continuous improvement process. In this regard, VO will continue to utilize work group contributions to support the elimination of waste and the establishment of a continuous improvement mind-set. This process may at times include the identification of productivity enhancements that result in available labor, which will be addressed in accordance with the provisions of the Collective Bargaining Agreement.[5]

Today, the total-cost approach by the corporation continues under the auspices of this letter, which allows for some more flexibility in defining total cost than was the case during the 2001–2002 pivotal event, but still primarily operates within the "four walls" of a plant.

❋ ❋ ❋

The total-cost issue is pivotal in the way it illustrates the increased sophistication of the union and the willingness of the company to explore the underlying assumptions of its accounting system jointly with the union. At the same time, it also reveals the limits of traditional union power tactics. While there was not management unanimity on the issue, it is likely that the union's stand down created more unity among Ford's leadership and drove a more negative response. In the end, influence trumped raw power in bringing about the changes. Collaboration (more so than threats) delivered the results that were possible for the union on this issue.

Lean Manufacturing Managers and the Lean Implementation Network, 2001–2003

In 2001, two Ford executives—Anne Stevens, then vice president of North American manufacturing, and Marty Mulloy, then director of Human Resources, Global Manufacturing—determine that an accelerated implementation of lean manufacturing principles is needed across North American operations. The impetus is, in part, what Stevens describes as a "total breakdown in quality" with the launch of the Ford Focus the year before, just as she assumed her vice president position.

The Focus, launched first in Europe, is fraught with problems as a "carry over" launch, which should have been less complicated than a new launch. In fact, more than half the suppliers are new. The product is "under resourced and under funded."

"Within the first couple of months, there were 17 product recalls," Stevens says, "in what was supposed to be an easy launch.... All the stakeholders were angry. The UAW knew there were problems on the floor that were not being attended to. The dealers were up in arms—first they couldn't get products and then we had the recalls. The company was unhappy that the launch was costing more than expected."

Moreover, the Focus launch was not an isolated event. Ford was trailing its competitors on quality in many product categories. Ford 2000 has been abandoned as the leading change initiative, but the underlying issues of internal fiefdoms within management are at the root of the issues with the Focus launch. Additionally, the 2001 rollover lawsuits involving the Ford Explorer and Firestone tires dominate the news. Within Ford, there are competing factions advocating for Six Sigma or the Business Leadership Initiative (BLI) as the leading change initiative, rather than lean manufacturing.

The acceleration, Stevens and Mulloy tell the UAW, requires change within the management organization and joint efforts for frontline operations. "You have to have a burning platform to accelerate change," says Stevens. The myriad problems with the Ford Focus launch are symptomatic of a burning platform. The UAW will have a role in this initiative, but it is primarily a case of internal management alignment.

Ford continues its practice of imposing on the manufacturing operations a regular "task" to reduce operating costs by a certain percentage. The challenge, then, is to fix the quality problems *and* cut costs. Stevens pushes back: she can address the quality issue, but not guarantee the task for 2002. In fact, though, she ends up delivering most of the task and initiates a transformation in quality operations (many aspects of this quality transformation are detailed in chapter 8).

The management organization, however, needs to be realigned. "[Group Vice President] Thursfield gave me the backing to change the culture," Stevens recalls. "We were able to retire some of the directors of Manufacturing Operations (DOMs) and some plant managers who were part of the old culture." Further, diversity training was linked to lean training (a pivotal event highlighted in chapter 2).

As a key step in the internal alignment, Stevens creates a new position: all North American manufacturing plants will have a lean manufacturing manager (LMM) as its number-two management leader. Some senior executives push back, but Stevens argues that the plant managers are focused on current operations and vary considerably in their ability and orientation toward driving a lean transformation.

"We established the LMM role and I personally interviewed every one," recalls Stevens. "We had to make sure they [would bring] the right values, principles, and culture. Also, I needed to let them know that they had a place to go if they were getting resistance."

In most assembly and stamping plants, the assistant plant manager position has been eliminated in prior waves of headcount reductions, so creating an incremental additional management leadership position is highly valued in the plants. "It was a big deal to add structure," notes Stevens. Most of the engine plants, though, still have assistant plant managers—and many have their titles simply changed to the new LMM position. So, in these plants, the reaction is more mixed.

To evaluate the LMMs, Stevens introduces a balanced scorecard with four quadrants—safety, quality, cost, and behaviors—and ties each to 25 percent of short-term pay. Plus, says Stevens, "We flipped the long-term bonus to focus just on behavior and culture change. An individual who delivered results with brutal behavior would be in the bottom quartile."

As Marty Mulloy recalls:

The measurement of behavior and culture was based on a 360-degree assessment, which included informal feedback from UAW partners. The views of the UAW had never previously been a factor in management leadership assessments and, importantly, this decision was driven by line management, not HR. Senior management recognized that a lean transformation was not possible if a leader did not have a constructive relationship with their UAW counterparts.

Deep cultural norms work against openly sharing difficulties and complications. It is typical for plant managers to fix problems in a way that keeps them invisible to the directors of Manufacturing (DOMs) to whom they report. Meanwhile, the DOMs focus on fixing things so they won't be visible to senior executives such as Anne Stevens. By handpicking the new LMMs in Vehicle Operations, Stevens has a direct channel into operations.

Once the LMM positions are established and filled in nearly all of the 48 North American plants, there is the question how they will be supported in the new role. Stevens and Mulloy step forward as champions for a new Lean Implementation Network (LIN). Change agents from the Ford Production System, including Mary Anderson, Lee Sanborn, and others, join with external consultants Joel Cutcher-Gershenfeld and Roger Komer to facilitate the process.

Each LMM is instructed to partner with his or her plant's HR manager, which begins the process of forming close relations between HR and the next generation of Manufacturing Operations leaders. It also forces the HR managers to accelerate their learning on lean manufacturing principles. Together, the LMM and HR manager are asked to identify an additional individual to be their designated internal change agent—a concept modeled after Roger Komer's experience in a similar role at the Sterling Axle Plant. In the many plants that already have individuals active as change agents, the selection is clear. In other cases, individuals are elevated to this role.

Taken together, the Lean Implementation Network involves more than 150 individuals who are charged with the accelerated implementation of lean principles across North American Operations.

At LIN's first two quarterly offsite meetings in Dearborn, the agenda combines plant case studies and train-the-trainer sessions on key lean principles. Beginning with the third LIN meeting, the venue shifts to a series of host plants—assembly, stamping, and engine—and the agenda involves additional train-the-trainer modules in the mornings and an afternoon "go-and-see" format in which small groups of LIN members fan out across the facility and spend an hour or more in a given area. They observe frontline operations, speak with operators about their use of SQDCME data, and talk about lean principles in use. They then debrief with a panel of senior leaders—usually both union and management—from the plant. Sometimes, they also debrief with panels of team leaders, which allows LIN members to check their assumptions about what they've observed.

Innovations seen in one plant becomes part of the LIN's work. For example, they incorporate one plant's "Neighborhood Watch"—in which teams track aspects of what is termed the "visual factory"—into learning materials so it can be adopted by others. Support innovations from HR, Finance, Maintenance, Material Planning and Logistics, Product Development, Purchasing, and others are all captured.

Hosting a LIN session is a major event for a plant. LIN members are all highly knowledgeable observers, and they miss very little on the floor. A plant making positive progress has a chance to achieve system-wide recognition and respect very quickly.

Mary Anderson, one of the lead internal facilitators, recalls, "The LIN was a way to start really understanding and leveraging best practices and to create a community of practice that allowed us to learn from each other. There was the value of the look-and-see approach in each plant. You can talk about 'Neighborhood Watch' and support systems for production teams, [but when] you see it, it makes all the difference."

Each plant's LMM, HR Manager, and designated change agent returns from each quarter's LIN meeting with new ideas and a renewed commitment to driving the lean transformation. Often, they schedule subsequent visits to host plants for other members of their plant's Operating Committee. After the session at the Kentucky Truck Plant, for example, Anderson recalls, "there were 25 people on the company plane, and one of the biggest resisters on another OCM [Operating Committee Meeting] said at the session, 'We need to do this now.'"

For the staff in the Ford Production System, the LIN represents a shift from pushing lean principles to responding to a pull for training and support from plants across the system. After three years, the accelerated transformation is well underway. With the departure of Anne Stevens in 2006 to become CEO of Carpenter Technology, the LIN sessions formally halt. Many informal cross-benchmarking trips follow, building on network connections established among members of the LIN.

Today, LIN's legacy survives in the system: many of Ford's plant managers are former lean manufacturing managers and some have risen even higher in the ranks. One of the former LMMs, Anthony Hoskins, went on to become plant manager in the Chicago Assembly Plant and is now a director of Manufacturing. In reflecting on the LMM role, he notes its correspondence with the UAW's appointees who also had responsibility for culture change:

When we aligned all the elements together within management (including FPS, the LMM role, time and data management, and other elements), and as the UAW become even more aligned with the company, it made a total transformation possible. Prior to our putting on the Lean Manufacturing Managers and getting aligned with the UAW, we hadn't really taken on the cultural transformation. It was a better platform to begin the transformation on the cultural side. The UAW already had people who had the cultural piece as their role and now we had this in management. Cultural transformation takes a different set of muscles.

✳ ✳ ✳

Courageous leadership is evident throughout the LMM and LIN story. It begins with Vice President Stevens committing to a culture change on quality. This was only possible, she notes, with the burning platform on quality—a key ingredient in making the case for accelerating change. Leadership then extended to the joining together of new lean manufacturing managers, HR managers, and change agents, all with responsibility for accelerated implementation of lean principles. Finally, it involved countless frontline team leaders, supervisors, and team members who hosted LMM visits and discussed honestly what was and was not working during the "go-and-see" sessions.

Individuals on both sides of these conversations had to set aside rank in favor of genuine dialogue, which may be an even more important enduring legacy of the Lean Implementation Network.

BPR and SAR Processes, 2006

Appointing a new CEO is nearly always intended to be pivotal in some way. In 2006, it is understood that hiring a new CEO for the Ford Motor Company is more than just a pivot. The future of the enterprise is at stake. Bill Ford had been serving as both CEO and chairman of the board, but he felt the company needed additional leadership to meet its many challenges. The previous year, U.S. auto sales had begun to decline, a sign of the Great Recession to come.

I went to the board in 2005, wearing all the hats, and indicated we needed help. We were still making money at the time, but we could see that the U.S. consumer was tapped out. It was clear that there was a need for a huge restructuring ahead. When you have a huge fixed asset base, which is the case with an auto company, it is hard to pivot quickly.

All I have ever cared about is the success and reputation of the Ford Motor Company, I told the board. Nothing else matters. If I can help, I will. If I need to step aside, I will.

That fall, Bill Ford retains his position as board chair, and the board supports his offer of the CEO position to Alan Mulally—then CEO of Boeing Commercial Airplanes and a Boeing corporate executive vice president. When Mulally arrives, the groundwork for a major restructuring has already been laid in the form of the 2005 Way Forward plan led by Mark Fields, who at the time was Ford's president of the Americas.

I was new, and I had committed to Bill to put together a plan in the next 60 days. We involved everyone—there was a clear burning platform. We knew we needed to reduce capacity, which would involve closing plants. At the same time, we were committed to maintaining a productive relationship with the UAW. We were prepared to go above and beyond what was required by the law or the contract. Still, it was going to be difficult to say goodbye to so many people.

Mulally inherits a management team of significant talent. Ford has long recruited from the best universities in the world, and the company's talent development model is benchmarked as an industry best practice. The talent level and work ethic of these executives is among the best in the industry. With one exception, Mulally retains the entire senior level management team.

As talented as these individual executives are, however, the company's overall performance is abysmal. In 2006, Ford loses approximately $12.7 billion—then the biggest loss in its 103-year history. Losses for 2007 are projected to exceed $17 billion. Mulally immediately recognizes what the Ford team needs to be better aligned. He implements a new corporate governance framework to ensure the company functions like a symphony orchestra, not as individual musicians playing their own tunes.

In the fourth quarter of 2006, Mulally establishes the Ford Global Business Plan Review (BPR). This simple but eloquent corporate governance process is foundational in Ford's revitalization. It is pivotal both as a structural change (clarifying the matrix structure of the

Figure 4.6
"One Team" for the Business Process Review (2013). *Source:* Ford Motor Company.

corporation) and as a change process (establishing a culture of transparent, non-blaming, problem-solving dialogue and action at the highest levels of the corporation).

Mulally's 37 years at Boeing had taught him the value of process stability. When you are making airplanes, the margin of error is so slim and the consequences of failure so devastating that it is essential to establish robust processes that ensure continuing process capability. The BPR he introduces provides alignment, accountability, and assistance, as well as camaraderie—key elements lacking under Ford's existing governance structure.

"You have to follow the process," says Mulally. "It is all about the process. You can't game it. You have to be accountable. We chose to be in the auto business and we have to make cars and trucks that people will value. How do we do this? It begins with following the process."

The key to profitability in the global automotive industry is scale, and the key in managing the complex global operation that makes cars is alignment across business units and functional skill teams. So, the BPR process drives internal alignment. At the time, the Ford Motor Company has global revenues exceeding $150 billion, with facilities around the world operating at a level of great technical complexity and production intensity. A car has more than 10,000 separate components and the time from start to finish is about a day, with an output rate of about one car per minute. One vehicle platform supports product development for up to seven distinct models, requiring an integrated effort by the Product Development and Manufacturing leaders at all levels.

Mulally schedules mandatory BPR meetings every Thursday morning at seven o'clock, and they last about four hours. They include leaders from Ford's four Global Business Units (The Americas, Ford of Europe, Asia Pacific & Africa, and Ford Credit), and functional skill teams such as Product Development, Manufacturing, Marketing and Sales, Purchasing, Finance, Government Affairs, and other support functions (see figure 4.6).

The BPR process involves both accountability and assistance. It is a weekly report-out on how the business is performing to plan and, when things are not going according to plan, it is a non-blaming, problem-solving format. At the meetings, each business unit and function gives a brief status report using a common reporting system to ensure simplicity and consistency. The reporting format is color-coded: blue bars represent the five-year business plan, which is updated each year; stars indicate the most recent forecast to the business plan; and colored dots show actual results (green for on-plan, yellow for off-plan but correctable, and red for failure to meet plan objectives).

Mulally encourages his team to bring issues to the surface, openly discuss constraints, and work together to address business challenges. Rarely is failure to achieve the plan the sole responsibility of a single business unit or function. Overwhelmingly, the business challenge is a systems issue that crosses several business units and/or functions—such as a typhoon in Asia that shuts down multiple suppliers and which forces rationing of existing parts to powertrain and assembly plants.

Open discussions like those encouraged by Mulally run counter to the operative culture and norms at Ford's executive level. At the early BPR sessions, virtually all the charts are green, with some yellow spots. The dominant norm is that executives handle their own problems within their function—traditionally all are expected to take care of their part of the business and issues are only discussed as a last resort, when they can no longer be contained. This is a deeply embedded assumption in the culture that will need to change.

About two months into the process, the Ford Edge launch is only a few weeks out. Bennie Fowler's quality team finds a problem with a grinding noise during tests that remains unsolved. The norm is to say nothing and concentrate on resolving the issue within Vehicle Operations, with every effort made to not delay the launch (which then makes the problems visible). But Mark Fields does what would be a risk in the existing culture: he shows up with a red box on his chart for the Ford Edge launch[6]—the first time red appears at a BPR meeting.

Mulally's response sets the tone for success with the BPR. He is hard on the problem, but not on Fields. The group is invited in a nonblaming way to address the issue. The Edge launch is delayed until more people are contributing together to find a solution and the quality concern is resolved.

Most senior executives are by nature competitive, with a high desire for achievement and recognition. Such competitiveness may serve a company externally, but if not managed correctly it can become a destructive force internally, dividing a corporation along functional and business unit boundaries. The subtle impact of the BPR is that the senior executives attend together as a team and openly surface tough issues, which minimizes backroom squabbling and "turf wars." Ultimately, the BPR process builds mutual respect and camaraderie among the senior team—quite an accomplishment, and essential to the survival of the enterprise.

Some issues are too complicated and/or time consuming to be covered in the BPR meetings, so they are addressed in Special Attention Review (SAR) meetings that immediately follow. These meetings include only senior managers involved directly in the issues at hand. Again, the governance structure and the underlying tone of these meetings facilitate open discussion and cross-functional cooperation.

Combining BPR and SAR fosters horizontal alignment across all functions and domains and ensures detailed attention to complex issues. It is not unusual for an issue to surface in the BPR, move to the SAR for further attention, and then reappear back on the agenda for integration and action.

❋ ❋ ❋

Taken together, the BPR and SAR were pivotal not just as process innovations, but also as interventions that took on directly a culture of fragmented functions and operations paying insufficient attention to the interdependencies. The BPR and SAR achieved what Ford 2000 had identified as needed change and what The Way Forward plan had begun to address. While the integrated forum on Thursday mornings is important, the underlying shift in operating assumptions is more important—from each person striving to contain their problems, to all sharing responsibility for the success of the enterprise in an open, non-blaming way.

Quality Operating Committee, 2006

The UAW's involvement in quality dates back many decades. In the early 1980s the UAW is featured prominently in one of Ford's most successful advertising campaigns: "Quality is Job 1." The ads build on the Q1 quality certification initiative (discussed on chapter 8) and feature people throughout the Ford system giving a "thumb's up" on quality being "Job 1." Every ad features a worker with the Ford and UAW logos prominently on his or her coveralls, which is key to the ads' success.

In 2003, Ford and the UAW achieve a pivotal breakthrough on quality in the national negotiations (detailed in chapter 6). This leads to the appointment of Quality Operating System Coordinators in each plant, as well as the testing and certification of hourly UAW Quality Representatives. By 2006, the discussions begin on certifying hourly Six Sigma black belts, such as Armentha Young from chapter 2. Local elected union leaders are part of each plant's time and data management system, which includes regular quality meetings. In these and other ways, the UAW becomes a strong and active partner with management on quality. But can the UAW's expertise be recognized at the highest levels of the corporation?

Dan Brooks of the UAW frequently plays a lead role on quality issues, whether in negotiations or in operations. In 2003, he is the co-chair of the National Quality Committee in UAW-Ford National Joint Programs. Adrian Vido is Ford's manufacturing director responsible for quality, and describes their relationship as a partnership.

I had spent a lot of time with [Canadian Auto Workers] folks previously, so I was used to working with a union partner. I found this guy wanted to listen. Even as a senior director, I couldn't always get the structure to listen. In quality, it was important to understand what workers might think. Dan could be forceful but would also listen. I found I had a partner. We began to build a relationship. When we got into quality we realized that the horsepower of the two of us could really make a difference. We knew we needed to standardize our approach and document what we learned.

Building on his partnership with Adrian Vido, Brooks focuses the UAW's quality efforts around achieving Ford's quality business objectives—a shift from the more superficial focus on quality training and other inputs. With support from the UAW leadership, the commitment is to taking joint responsibility for quality outcomes. Brooks partners with Dean Blythe, Ford's labor affairs representative to the National Joint Programs, as well as with Vido as the line manager for quality. When Blythe and Vidro move on to other positions, Brooks works with new counterparts on quality and joint programs, Gary Johnson and Gary Vebahn. Still, the overall leadership on quality at Ford is at a higher level.

Bennie Fowler is a former manufacturing manager just named in 2006 as the group vice president for Quality, he reports directly to Alan Mulally, the new CEO. He brings the BPR-SAR process to how he runs the quality function, with a weekly Quality Operating Committee Meeting (OCM) that follows the BPR process. This is expected of him. What is not expected is that he invites Dan Brooks to be a formal member of the Quality OCM. And he expands the scope of the Quality OCM beyond the United States. Fowler comments: "As I look at the world today, I see I was mostly regional in my thinking previously—focused on North America. Now I have the chance to look at the whole notion of quality across the globe. There are so many cultures across Ford, around the world."

Fowler's invitation to Brooks comes after a UAW-Ford National Joint Conference at which Fowler challenges participants to do all they can improve product quality. Previously, the UAW had attended Quality meetings at the corporate level, but these invitations had been more symbolic than substantive, with no clear responsibilities for the UAW that came with attendance. Inviting Brooks to be a regular, active member of the Quality OCM, with clear responsibility for helping drive quality worldwide, is a pivotal event.

Brooks arrives on the Quality OCM just as Fowler is introducing the BPR-SAR process. It is not a simple change. The approach to quality varies in different regions of the world and in different Ford businesses and divisions. Volvo differs from Ford. Powertrain, Stamping, Vehicle Operations, and other groups all vary. On top of this, data presented in the BPR doesn't match what is coming in from dealers or customers.

Fowler takes the leaders of corporate divisions to Special Attention Reviews for what he calls a "wire brushing"—of the many mindsets. The weekly meetings become highly productive and, with accurate data, Fowler is able to assist these managers to get items marked in red for "failure" into green "on-plan" status.

Toward the end of 2006, as other members of the Quality OCM are scheduling their annual performance reviews with Fowler, Brooks asks for one as well—even though is it not required. "It made sense to serve on the Quality OCM" after the UAW's 2003 decision to work toward achieving Ford's Quality Business Plan," recalls Brooks, "and it made sense to have Bennie review my performance. I wanted to make certain I was doing what was necessary to make Ford number 1 in Quality. As a UAW representative, I know that being number 1 in Quality is true job security."

Fowler shares Brooks' perspective. "Dan had the approach of a partner," he recalls, "not being a disruptive force. We could both learn and move forward: we had to walk the talk. We had a joint UAW-Ford relationship—a joint quality committee and Dan was the UAW's leader on Quality and I was the head of Quality for Ford—so this was already agreed to. The challenge was…getting comfortable with both [of us] looking at the data, and the more we did that, the more it was okay. I feel if you say you are going to be a partner then you have to do that, which is why it made sense to do the annual performance review. Now that Dan has retired, Dave Berry and Reggi Mills are in the role. There is nothing to hide; everyone sees the same data. It is great that the UAW agreed to come and help us in the journey."

Dan continues to serve on the Quality OCM, attending weekly meetings, through his retirement in 2010—after which Dave Berry and Reggi Mills take on his role, and by which time Ford achieves best-in-class quality performance worldwide.

✳ ✳ ✳

A UAW member serving on a management quality operating committee is certainly a much smaller pivotal event than the BPR and SAR or the Rouge revitalization. It is an event that would not even be visible to all but a relatively small number of union and management leaders. But it is still pivotal. For the union, the agreement to serve on the committee signaled a shared commitment to business success and a degree of integration into business operations that, while comparable to that found in many European nations, is rare in the United States. For Ford, including the union at this level signaled trust and transparency in regular operations, not just in a crisis.

One Ford, 2007

Planned pivotal events include *structural* changes, such as creating the Lean Manufacturing Manager role or adding a UAW representative to the Quality Leadership Team, and *process* changes, such introducing the BPR-SAR process. Some planned pivotal events involve articulating and building a shared vision for success. Under Alan Mulally's leadership, such a vision is codified in 2007.

The core of the vision is a simple statement: One Ford: One Team, One Plan, One Goal. Its power is in the fact that it takes on directly the company's *fiefdoms*, *chimneys*, *turfs*—all terms used in Ford to describe what is a big problem. A core vision statement, though, must be more than mere words. It must be both inspirational and reflected in action. Otherwise, it quickly feeds cynicism.

The new vision statement is distributed globally on laminated 3×5 cards, and later on wallet-size cards, with the following text placed under the Ford logo:

ONE FORD

ONE TEAM ● ONE PLAN ● ONE GOAL

ONE TEAM

People working together as a lean global enterprise for automotive leadership as measured by: Customer, Employee, Dealer, Investor, Supplier, Union/Council, and Community Satisfaction

ONE PLAN

- Aggressively restructure to operate profitably at the current demand and changing model mix
- Accelerated development of new products our customers want and value
- Finance our plan and improve our balance sheet
- Work together effectively as one team

ONE GOAL

An exciting viable Ford delivering profitable growth for all

Several features of this vision statement are noteworthy. First, it focuses Ford well beyond its shareholders; investors are one of seven key stakeholders making up "One Team." Customers, essential to business success, are listed first, followed by employees, as you might expect. But note that unions are also listed—a departure from the norm in most U.S. corporations. Dealers, the face of the company with customers, are listed along with investors. Suppliers, with whom Ford has a historical reputation for adversarial relations, are also listed. Finally, the list notes Ford's presence in communities, which reinforces more than a century of community service.

A message like this requires mechanisms engaging each stakeholder group as a team member. Mulally revitalizes forums and other outreach with dealers and engages employees and the union in the business in new, fundamental ways. He establishes a greater focus on partnership with suppliers. And he prioritizes metrics for assessing stakeholder satisfaction.

The "One Plan" language is remarkably blunt and direct on the need to restructure operations, as well as specific on the role of financing—two points that do not typically make their way into vision statements. The aim is straightforward—stop the cash burn by reducing fixed

Box 4.1
Ford Expected Behaviors

Foster Functional and Technical Excellence

- Know and have a passion for our business and our customers
- Demonstrate and build functional and technical excellence
- Ensure process discipline
- Have a continuous improvement philosophy and practice

Own Working Together

- Believe in skilled and motivated people working together
- Include everyone; respect, listen to, help and appreciate others
- Build strong relationships; be a team player; develop ourselves and others
- Communicate clearly, concisely, and candidly

Role Model Ford Values

- Show initiative, courage, integrity, and good corporate citizenship
- Improve quality, safety, and sustainability
- Have a can do, find a way attitude and emotional resilience
- Enjoy the journey and each other; have fun—never at others' expense

Deliver Results

- Deal positively with our business realities; develop compelling and comprehensive business plans, while keeping an enterprise view
- Set high expectations and inspire others
- Make sound decisions using facts and data
- Hold ourselves and others accountable for delivering results and satisfying our customers

---

Source: Ford Motor Company

cost and increase revenue by filling the product development pipeline with cars and trucks consumers want to buy. Eventually, Ford closes or sells 34 plants in North America and reduces its hourly and salary headcount by 50 percent (discussed in chapter 3) while completely overhauling its product lineup with fuel-efficient vehicles based on global vehicle platforms that command industry's best margins.

Nothing summarizes Mulally's business philosophy better than "profitable growth for all"—the "One Goal." The rewards for all the hard work are distributed to the entire Ford team of stakeholders. Building on the 1982 articulation of "mutual growth" as the framework for the employment relationship, the reward for each employee (and the union) is an industry-leading profit-sharing check in 2013 of $8,500.

Paired with the "One Ford" message were a set of expected behaviors that were on the other half of the 3×5 cards and on the back of the wallet cards (box 4.1).

Figure 4.7
Wallet Card for "One Ford." *Source:* UAW-Ford National Joint Programs

Many corporations have statements of behaviors and values. What makes the "One Ford" vision different is that it depends on supporting behaviors that are tied to underlying values, and Mulally holds all leaders accountable for adherence to the behaviors and values.

Figure 4.7 shows the front and back of the wallet card.

✳ ✳ ✳

"One Ford" is pivotal as a vision primarily because it went beyond being just a statement. It was connected to a plan and a set of expected behaviors—many of which had been coming together for more than a decade—that corresponded to actions and priorities at the highest levels of the corporation.

It is easy to offer up slogans; doing what Ford did is more difficult. "One Ford" built on the 1982 articulation of mutual growth, the Ford 2000 goal of global integration, and prepared the entire Ford stakeholder team for the necessary shared sacrifices during the national recession.

Recap: Guiding Principle for Chapter 4—Mutual Growth

The principle of mutual growth recognizes interdependence and signals a commitment to progress. It drives information sharing and requires accountability. Even though it was articulated formally in 1982 in collective bargaining, there were times at which Ford or the UAW (or both) did not fully operate consistently with this principle. Over more than three decades, though, a succession of pivotal events has given full meaning to the phrase.

Today, the concept of mutual growth is reflected in a projected 18,000 new jobs created since the national recession that began for autos in 2006 and for the nation as a whole in 2008. It is reflected in $8 billion-plus corporate profits in 2013 that translated into $8,800 profit-sharing checks for UAW members.

One wonders how the United States might be different if all corporations were to operate on the basis of mutual growth as a guiding principle.

SUPPORTING MATERIALS

4.1 Support Function Alignment

Source: Ford Motor Company

Comments:

This diagram was used to illustrate the role of support functions for the operations at every level in a plant. For some functions, such as quality, maintenance, materials planning and logistics, and cost, there might be a designated work group member responsible for each element. The illustration also shows the internal customers of the support functions (note that team leaders as internal customers did not apply in all cases).

Support functions have three primary roles: *oversight* regarding adherence to standards, policies, and laws; *service* that involves providing data, support, and other services; and a *transformation or change* role that involves leadership and facilitation. As this chart suggests, all these roles are being enacted concurrently and need to be aligned.

4.2 Sample Business Fundamentals Briefing Materials

Trend of credit ratings for Ford

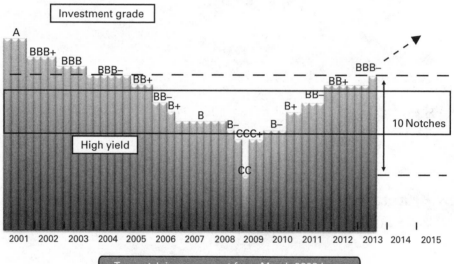

Source: Ford Motor Company

Comments:

This is an example of a chart used to educate managers, union leaders, and workers on Ford's credit rating. It tracks the descent into "junk bond" status and the ascent back to "investment grade."

5 Knowledge-Driven Work

Guiding Principle: Continuous Improvement

Increasingly, it is the knowledge-driven nature of work that defines the postindustrial global economy.[1] As a result, a broad range of jobs are becoming ever more knowledge driven. Within the auto industry, skilled trades positions, such as tool and die makers, electricians, machine repair technicians, and others, along with engineering and design professionals, have always been valued for the knowledge and skills that are integral to their work. In the body shop, where the tiniest imperfections can affect the fit and finish of a car or truck, the need for specialized knowledge and skills has always been understood. It is on the assembly line itself where the real challenge in fully harnessing the knowledge and skills of the workforce arises.

Assembly jobs in the auto industry can be monotonous and physically demanding. Industry cost pressures make what is called "mass relief"—shutting down the assembly line for breaks and meetings—uncompetitive; mass relief on an assembly line making a high-customer-demand vehicle with healthy profit margins can cost about $10,000 a minute in lost profit. Avoiding mass relief and instead pulling people off the line for team meetings to study performance data and make continuous improvement suggestions requires backfilling those positions on the line, which in turn means higher staffing levels. Scheduling meetings before a shift begins or after it ends means overtime. Additional options can include meetings of team leaders and the designation of lead workers on a team for special topics such as quality, safety, cost, and schedule in what is termed the "star point" model (with each role illustrated as one of five points on a star).

The bottom line: in an auto assembly plant, any way of organizing team meetings involves added direct costs. In many other jobs, meeting times can be scheduled as part of the regular flow of work; in engine machining operations or stamping operations, workers have time between cycles of the machinery to study quality data or attend to other tasks. Not so on the assembly line.

This chapter documents a series of pivotal events that mark the journey toward achieving a very challenging objective: enabling the distributed knowledge and expertise of Ford's full

Figure 5.1
Kanji Characters for *Kaizen. Source:* workpress.com.

frontline workforce to drive continuous improvement—often designated by the Japanese word *kaizen*. This concept—popularized in *The Machine That Changed the World*[2] as a central pillar in the Toyota Production System—is represented in Japanese by the kanji characters in figure 5.1.

Kaizen comprises the characters *kai* (meaning "change") and *zen* (meaning "good"—but note that the character is not the same as the one used for Zen Buddhism). Together, they are meant to suggest change for the better. In the context of organizational change, *kaizen* often is modified by "continuous"—continuous change for the better.

The term "*kaizen* event" has entered the common parlance in many industries. It refers to a gathering of individuals with relevant knowledge and expertise who come together for as little as a half day and as long as a few weeks to map the flow of work and identify improvement opportunities. Even though implementation may then take weeks or months, this is still a "time-bound" change, which may seem like a contradiction with "continuous." In fact, a *kaizen* event is a discrete event akin to process reengineering. The Ford-UAW experience with continuous improvement is a combination of "top down" process reengineering, "bottom up" frontline, team-based process improvement efforts, and additional improvements made possible through innovations in engineering and design.

The terminology of transformation in the U.S. industry is today a mix of English and Japanese terms. We review the terminology, in part, because these words are helpful in understanding the role of knowledge-driven work in the Ford-UAW transformation. More important, these terms help in understanding the models of change that are in play, including the tensions among them. However, the Japanese terms were not always well received in the U.S. context, though *kaizen* is now commonly used.

The idea of a knowledge-driven work system poses a challenge both to management and organized labor in the United States. The National Labor Relations Act (NLRA) of 1935 defines the role and responsibilities of management to include supervision and engineering, while hourly employees primarily execute manual labor tasks presided over by white-collar supervision. The drafters of the NLRA never foresaw a day when hourly employees would take on responsibilities of planning production schedules, directing operations, and accepting accountability for a team's performance—all responsibilities the NLRA attributes to management.

Beyond the NLRA, clearly defined lines of demarcation that were established over decades separate the responsibilities of management and organized labor. The idea of job classifications was, nearly a century ago, a managerial initiative with Frederick Taylor as the leading proponent for breaking down the work of skilled craft workers into component parts for more-efficient assembly work. Although the idea was initially resisted by craft unions, it was later embraced by industrial unions as a protection against arbitrary treatment by supervisors. The separation of hourly and salaried roles also reinforced traditional class distinctions. It was not uncommon, as a result, for management to act dictatorially and labor to respond by doing no more than what was minimally expected. Further lines of demarcation existed between production workers and the skilled trades. These distinctions are still reflected in today's wage and hour laws, as well as in the supervisory distinction in the National Labor Relations Act. Thus, the movement toward knowledge-driven work systems documented in this chapter represents a challenge to deeply embedded assumptions in the law and the institutions of employment relations.

This chapter highlights nine pivotal events:

Chapter 5

Pivotal Events	Overview	Type, Level
Ford Total Productive Maintenance Roots, 1982	The first exposure to the knowledge-driven aspects of predictive and preventative maintenance are eye opening for some, but ignored or discounted by others. It takes more than 15 years for this pivot to realize its potential.	Unplanned, Enterprise Level
Mazda Flat Rock, 1987	Ford's partial ownership of Mazda leads to the launch of the Flat Rock, Michigan, assembly plant, which provides Ford managers, UAW leaders, and U.S. workers with direct experience with the Japanese-style, team-based continuous improvement work system. Hiring for the line from professions adds to the knowledge-driven system, but the physically demanding and often monotonous work creates complications.	Planned, Plant Level
Romeo Engine Plant, 1988	Romeo Engine's learning environment demonstrates the possibilities as Ford's first fully team-based U.S. plant. But technical and cultural differences between the Powertrain Operations and Vehicle Operations (assembly) divisions limit the impact.	Unplanned, Plant Level

Chapter 5 Pivotal Events	Overview	Type, Level
Continuous Improvement and FPS Rollout, 1996–1999	A series of events, culminating with the initial rollout of the Ford Production System (FPS), is foundational for later advances in quality, but the absence of a burning platform supporting the case for change makes things more difficult.	Planned, Enterprise Level
Team Start and Stop Designations, 1999	A key decision allows team size to vary based on the nature of the work.	Planned, Enterprise Level
UAW Glass Plants, 2002	The UAW's experience providing technical assistance to two glass plants helps improve operations in advance of a planned sale (enabling continuity for the UAW as the representative for the workforce) and reinforces expertise within the union.	Planned, Plant Level
Hourly Six Sigma Black Belts, 2003–2007	Some in management oppose enabling hourly workers to earn a Six Sigma black belt, but ultimately this reinforces the value of frontline knowledge driving continuous improvement in the operations.	Unplanned, Enterprise Level
Powertrain Plant of the Future, 2007–2008	Many innovations at Ford have roots in the Powertrain Division, partly reflecting the highly skilled nature of the work itself and partly reflecting the culture reinforced by successive leaders. A vision for the plant of the future emerges.	Planned, Enterprise Level
Team-Based Agreements, 2011	Team-based aspects of the 2011 negotiations codify the role of knowledge-driven work in daily operations, including integrated attention to production and skilled trades work.	Planned, Enterprise Level

Ford Total Productive Maintenance Roots, 1982

Howard Adams faces a dilemma. A leader in Ford's Total Productive Maintenance program (FTPM), he sees the potential to pivot toward a more knowledge-driven approach in preventative and predictive maintenance. He sees the value of the full workforce being involved in anticipating when equipment will need to be repaired or replaced as part of a larger system of continuous improvement. This contrasts with a limited number of specialists, acting after a failure, focused only on maintenance as their specialty area. Others, though, don't initially see what Adams sees as the future of FTPM.

It is 1982. Adams works in the Ford Corporate Plant Engineering Office at Ford's World Headquarters as part of a group assigned to three-week onsite maintenance-productivity evaluations. He is frustrated because each of these visits to a plant results in a report that is either ignored or directed down to the lowest possible level of the plant leadership for implementation. He requests involvement in developing a new tool for recognizing outstanding efforts in preventive and predictive maintenance. The approach was named the Ford Preventive Maintenance Excellence (PME) program. As Adams describes it:

PME was a step forward. It was a management tool, with 15 criteria. It was a step forward within the Ford box that we all knew as the Ford way to perform maintenance. The 15 PME criteria were all assigned values that totaled to 100 points and plant recognition of PME was attained with a minimum score of 85. Within a short amount of time, all plants had been recognized with an award ceremony for PME. Plant productivity did not improve and in fact, PME turned into just another soapbox pageant. Everyone got the lingo and knew how to get minimum 85 percent on the scorecard, but they did not address the core issue of how maintenance of equipment impacts plant productivity performance.

One day, Adams gets a brochure for a class delivered by Ed Hartmann on the Japanese concept of Total Productive Maintenance (TPM), funded by the Japanese Management Association. "I had never heard of total productive maintenance before this session," recalls Adams, "but it opened my eyes to one of the greatest opportunities for improvement in manufacturing. The seminar focused on the big picture—we were taught to focus on everyone and every operation in the plant when it comes to eliminating waste—*muda* in Japanese."

We were taught to measure OEE, Overall Equipment Effectiveness, which was a product of various factors. Most important, [Hartmann] said, was small group activity. This meant involving people from the floor to give input on losses and then train them to use tools for loss analysis and loss prevention. Then he went on to indicate the importance of training people to identify constraints in the system and set priorities for improvement efforts.

This was so different than anything I had ever seen before. Up until this time, our focus was entirely on critiquing plant maintenance productivity writing standards for machine maintenance.

It is seven years before the writings of Seiichi Nakajima, the chairman of Japan Institute of Plant Maintenance and the leading expert on TPM, are translated into English[3] and 10 years before publication of a complementary book by Ed Hartmann, the organizer of the class, aimed at maintenance operations with a U.S. workforce.[4]

Bill Scollard, then Ford's vice president of manufacturing, met with Nakajima and toured a number of different operations in Japan, including Toyota. Adams recounts his conversation with a mid-level manager after Scollard's trip.

A plant engineering office manager called me into his office and asked if he remembered correctly that I had taken a class on TPM. Now that a senior executive [Scollard] was interested, suddenly this manager and others were interested. He asked if I thought it had potential for Ford and I said "absolutely."

Then the manager comments that "it smacks of conflict with the UAW." I said there was no way they would see this as a conflict—it provided more opportunities for hourly workers to be involved.

Then he said there was a chairman down at the Louisville Assembly Plant—a fellow named Ron Gettelfinger—who might be open to this.

Of course, Ron Gettelfinger eventually becomes vice president of the UAW working with Ford and later UAW International president.

Later on, Scollard meets with Harold "Red" Poling, then CEO of Ford, to advocate for the broad TPM approach. Poling suggested that TPM was important enough that a policy should be written, which ultimately becames Policy Letter 18—a directive from the chairman to all operations to implement TPM. Before the letter was written, it was decided that Ford Motor Company needed ownership and as a result, TPM became FTPM. Ron Gettelfinger is indeed involved in the development of concept and, as Adams comments, "Mr. Gettelfinger's involvement was instrumental in the approval and early development of FTPM."

For the first training event, Ford brings Nakajima from Japan for a two-day seminar. Adams remembers it as a fiasco:

Division managers and other leaders were brought in. Training was over at the Corporate Learning Center in Dearborn. Nakajima-sensi didn't speak English, so the two days of lecture and support slides were all in Japanese with a translator. About an hour into the program, I looked around the room and half the attendees were either sound asleep or straining to understand what was being delivered. It was the wrong kind of comedy. At the end of the second day, the attendees all raised their hands and said that they would commit to instituting FTPM, but hardly an attendee in the room knew what they were expected to do except, follow Policy Letter 18. There was a near unanimous undertone of resentment that corporate leadership had brought in the Japanese to teach Americans how to improve their business.

An opportunity is lost with Seiichi Nakajima, the man revered today as the father of TPM, and for whom an annual prize is named. Meanwhile, the potential for a full embrace of TPM at Ford seems to dissipate. What follows in the late 1990s are programs in Basic Equipment Wellness (BEW), which use some TPM principles, but no training in how to identify operational constraints or any small group activity in which the full workforce is focusing on and tracking measurable improvements. These come much later. Even the training for Basic Equipment Wellness, however, leaves much to be desired, Adams recalls.

We thought if you delivered training, you automatically delivered learning. Wrong, wrong, wrong. It was just butts in chairs. When people went back on the floor or in the office, did they bring anything with them?

We began to go out and coach with small group activity boards. The idea was to locate the board where the greatest opportunity was—the constraints in the operation. However, people put up boards everywhere to show they were with the program. There was even one in the rest room of one facility. They wondered: Why are we not seeing improvement in the plant performance?

People were telling us what they thought we wanted to hear.

In response, Ford flies in a team from the Japanese Institute of Preventative Maintenance to see some of the plants. By now, in the late 1990s, the term FTPM—for Ford Total Productive Maintenance—is being used. The members of the Japanese team discuss the terminology, which leads to deeper learning about the knowledge-driven nature of TPM. As Adams recounts, the members of the Japanese members of the team touring the plants asked about the Ford terminology.

They said, "What is this thing FTPM? What is wrong with TPM?" We said it was about ownership; that "F" was for Ford ownership and identity.

"How do you interpret TPM?" they asked.

We said, "Everyone involved in raising maintenance to the highest level."

The Japanese are very interesting. They never say you are wrong, but they keep asking questions until you see it.

Ultimately, we learned that TPM is about everyone (T) involved in maintaining (M) the highest possible level of productivity (P). It is about "maintenance" (M) shifting from a noun and to the verb "maintaining," and with productivity (P) as the ultimate goal. It was really about how to grow and sustain with *kaizen* (continuous improvements), a term we had purposefully ignored because it was Japanese rather than English. This too, was an eye opener.

It doesn't make sense to have all these tools if you don't have people's hearts. That is why Small Group Activity (SGA) was the center of this paradigm shift. We thought SGAs were just about creating all these work groups and giving them a box full of analysis tools. What we didn't understand was that it was about creating a different culture in the workforce. It was ultimately learning that culture and commitment to continuous change had to come first, before the analysis tools are introduced.

✳ ✳ ✳

Ultimately, Nakajima's teachings would be incorporated into the Ford-UAW FTPM approach, as well as into the broader Ford Production System model. In that sense, these early experiences were foundational. But it took a full two decades after the initial exposure to these ideas before Ford moved to a full knowledge-driven approach to maintenance work—and so this pivotal event fell short of its full potential at the time.

Initially, there were many limiting assumptions. The focus was on maintaining equipment, rather than on continuous improvement in the operation. Small group activity was seen as an add-on feature, rather than the central knowledge engine driving continuous improvement. Training was seen as passive learning rather than as active application. Shifting these assumptions would ultimately involve letting go of a segmented view of management functions (where maintenance as a function is separate from production) and equally segmented views of the roles of labor and management.

Mazda Flat Rock, 1987

The Mazda automobile assembly plant opens in 1987 in Flat Rock, Michigan, built on a site previously home to a Ford casting plant that had supplied V8 engine blocks. Walking into this newly renovated facility, the contrast with other domestic assembly plants is immediate. The cafeteria has a glass-enclosed courtyard with a Japanese rock garden. There are as many Japanese food choices as American. All along the assembly line, team meeting areas are delineated by visible boards with charts and graphs that track quality, safety, cost, and other performance indicators in each area. The "doors off" assembly operation—the correct doors are matched to the correct cars late in the assembly operation—is unusual for Ford, but indicates the commitment to quality. Pull cords on the assembly line allow operators to request help whenever they sense a potential threat to quality. One pull brings over a team leader or supervisor. Two pulls stops the line.

More than 10,000 people apply for just over 1,000 jobs at the new plant. Mazda decides to hire people with no manufacturing experience, but who can bring their higher levels of education and problem-solving skills from their work as teachers, social workers, and in other professions. New hires like these make up some 80 percent of the workforce—drawn by the available jobs and the higher wages.

The team-based work system and the principles of *kaizen*, continuous improvement, are embraced at the plant.

Chuck Browning is one of those first hires. He eventually becomes chair of the plant's UAW bargaining committee and later a leader on the UAW International staff servicing UAW members in this plant and other Ford facilities in the U.S., which was his role when reflecting on this early experience.

I graduated high school in 1982, in the middle of the last auto crisis in Michigan. I joined the Air Force, married my high school sweetheart and, after my four years in the service, wanted to go into Ford. My grandfather had been in the coalmines and then worked for Ford on the railroad, as my dad did. I heard about this plant two miles from where I grew up and put in an application.

It was a year after the military that they called me. It was an elaborate interview process, with a group brought in who watched how we worked as a team. I was asked about the business and asked if I had problems pitching in, which I didn't. There was simulated work and we were evaluated on that. After we were hired, we were not put right on a job, but in an orientation for three weeks during which we were taught the philosophy of the company. There was no effort to keep the union out—right on the first day we had two hours with management and then a meeting with the union and the chance to sign authorization cards. From the outset they indicated that they were going to attend to worker needs.

We learned some basic industrial engineering and teamwork principles. It was clear that this was different from everything I had heard from my family. People were proud of it. There were greater expectations of employees and people were conscious of quality and operations prior to their operation. People would speak out if a part were not installed properly.

Unfortunately, as the plant begins the initial ramp-up to launch new products, two factors come together to produce what comes to be called the "long hot summer." First, many of the workers are not ready for the physically demanding and monotonous work. Second, the norm in Japanese assembly plants is to accumulate ergonomics and safety issues during launch, but not address them until afterward. In the United States, the norm is to address such issues immediately as they arise so there are no ongoing health and safety violations. The Japanese managers put off addressing what the U.S. workers experience as work intensification, which leads to mounting tensions—and eventually to a wildcat strike.

In part, the long hot summer is the product of cross-cultural misunderstanding, but it also reflects the challenge of achieving the full potential with knowledge-driven work in a manufacturing setting. Just having a workforce oriented to problem solving is not enough—the workforce also must be oriented to handle the difficult work.

Some workers leave the plant. Japanese managers adjust how they supervise a U.S. workforce with different expectations about how ergonomics and safety issues should be addressed. Within two years, the plant features active teams using problem-solving tools to drive continuous improvement—tools that spill over into the community. One worker reports following the same multistep problem-solving process in a church committee. Others tell of similar positive spillovers into their community activities and even in the way they are raising their children. The problem-solving tools are also in evidence in local union meetings, where members want to use root-cause analysis to explore how the union spends the dues it collects.

The union leadership has to learn how to represent workers skilled in root-cause problem solving. As Browning notes, the union's focus shifts to match the different work context.

All the workers liked having that input. Within two years, however, it became hard for the commitments to be made. The volumes were low and there was pressure to cut costs. The union was then in place and it embraced lean manufacturing. The union began to bargain for language that would insist on following the lean practices, even though this was contrary to the focus of negotiations in the big three at the time. We bargained in order to secure time for people to meet, ensuring ability to participate in work design, and ensuring commitment to continuous improvements.

I started as a worker and then a committeeman, then a bargaining committeeman and then a chairman. We were able to be a full partner in the system. We would cooperate on the business and represent the members at the same time.

Mazda was a one-plant bargaining unit. There were no transfer options or GEN pool [job bank for dislocated workers]. There was not even much attrition, since it was a young workforce. The only job security was to bring in new work. Job security for me as a unionist from Day 1 is working with the company on the business items, but not at the expense of the worker.

The plant needs a more flexible approach to job classification, as Browning elaborates:

We just had one classification for production, plus team leaders. There were still issues of people wanting to work in desirable areas based on seniority—but we had to address that issue in a different way. There was a seniority structure within the classification, but without lines of demarcation. There was flexibility to utilize workers—as long as someone was "able and capable." Once that condition was met, then seniority could operate. That put the appropriate pressure on the union to ensure that people had equal opportunity to receive training—pressure points that were good for the operation of the plant.

I developed a good sense for what would make the company more efficient and, at the same time, improve the quality of work life for the employee. When we became a Ford location, it was really interesting for me—I had experience with this already and could say to chairman in other locations that this will have a happy ending.

Ultimately, Browning concludes that this approach with the workforce and the union provides competitive value for the company.

To me, this is the competitive advantage—there is no one who understands better what does and doesn't work in building the vehicle than the employee. Continuous training is linked to continuous improvement. It helps when management understands things from the employees' perspective. If the worker thinks from management's perspective, that also makes a difference—it helps in making choices around where to focus improvement. Ford is passing Toyota with the advantage of the communication network that the union brings—including the insistence that things be done the right way in a continuous improvement work system.

✳ ✳ ✳

By 1992, Ford had purchased a 50 percent share in the plant, renaming it Auto Alliance International. Ford purchased the remaining 50 percent in 2012, and the plant became the Flat Rock Assembly Plant. Since then, as part of the 2011 Ford-UAW Agreement, the Ford Fusion is insourced into the plant and more than 1,400 new jobs have been added to the facility, which continues to be a high-performing lean production facility.

As a pivotal event, Flat Rock teaches the great potential for cross-cultural learning, as well as the complications that can happen with cross-cultural disconnects. Moreover, we see how the logic of a knowledge-driven work system can reach beyond the plant into people's personal lives, as well as the positive implications for a union operating in this context and the value that a union can add to the operation.

Romeo Engine Plant, 1988

Originally a factory of 2,500 people producing small tractors and agricultural implements, and acquired by Ford in 1973, the plant in Romeo, Michigan, operates at 35-percent capacity by November 1986, facing declining sales. With only 825 employees.[5] Pete Piccini, the local union chairman, hears the rumors that a closure may be imminent.

The plant manager called my office and wanted me to come to his conference room. We knew something was coming down. The VP was there from the tractor division. We were told the line would shut down in 20 minutes and they would announce the plant was closing. This was before the plant closing law [the U.S. Worker Adjustment and Retraining Notice Act].

People were being sent to other locations around the United States. We had 66-year-old men crying that they had lost their job and were not ready to start all over. There were four or five heart attacks and four deaths. It was tragic stuff.

We had a huge meeting with employees and spouses to find out what people would like to be trained in while the plant was being shut down. It was called the "Last Supper." It was the first time a manager spoke at a union function. One area of training was employee involvement.

The focus on employee involvement, at first rather ambiguous, ends up being a precursor to the launch of Ford's first plant-wide team-based work system. As Piccini notes:

[Earlier,] the plant manager had pulled me aside one day and said, "You have to make hard decisions as a leader. I can't tell you anything. Sometimes a few people have to be sacrificed at the expense of a lot."

I said, "What are you saying?"

He couldn't say.

I had heard an announcement from International staff that there might be a new engine plant.... Mind you, I am coming from tractors and this is very different—engines are a much faster operation. Then Steve Yokich from the International Union gets a hold of me. We spoke with a manager, George Pfeil from Powertrain Operations. He said they were thinking about bringing an engine to this plant, but changes would need to be made. We would need to downsize skilled trades and condense them into 11 basic trades. We would need to operate teams, an empowered workforce, and job rotation.

I said, "What are you guys talking about?" No one was doing anything like this at the time. I asked, "How will you do it?"

The answer from George was, "We don't know." He also said, "We need your help."

"We count on you to run the plant," I said. "Our job is to critique."

It was clear that this was going to be different.

The pressure for a simpler work system is not limited to skilled trades. There are approximately 600 hourly workers who would continue in the plant.

"We had 76 or 77 different production classifications," says Piccini, "and we were told they would like to condense them to three or four—machine operators, team leaders, maintenance, and skilled trades. We had no idea what machining was. I am running for election and don't have enough seniority to stay in the plant if I lose. No one had survived an election with a plant shut down."

The initial launch agreement is codified in a mission statement (figure 5.2) that expresses a shared vision of success for the company and the union. The list of items under "joint efforts in operational efficiency" signals the highly joint approach to the design and launch of the facility.

Additional letters of understanding on job classifications and other matters follow. Many of the letters of agreement on how to operationalize the team-based work system—such as agreements on job classifications—are reached quickly. Agreements on the structure of compensation for work in the plant, however, are much more difficult.

Initially, Ford offers to pay team leaders an extra $2 per hour. The response from Joe Reilly, then representing the International, is unexpected. "I said, bullshit, that would make them supervisors."

Agreement on how to pay the team members and team leaders continues to be elusive. There is no agreement on pay, but management wants people to work in new ways.

"We brought it down to those four classifications," recalls Piccini. "Then we went three years without a local agreement because I wouldn't agree on any of the wage negotiations. They wanted everyone to learn eight or nine jobs, rotate jobs, and keep the same wage. I was getting heat from the floor because we didn't have a local agreement, so lots of things couldn't be grieved. People were on my case. It was the worst time in my life. I lost friendships over this. People thought I had more power than I had."

ROMEO ENGINE PLANT MISSION STATEMENT

The purpose of the Romeo Engine Plant is to produce the highest quality
production engines in the world, that meet all of our customer's requirements
at a cost lower than the competition, and to develop teams of employees who are
the best engine builders in the world.

JOINT EFFORTS IN OPERATIONAL EFFICIENCY

In order to achieve and retain the Best-In-Class Quality, Production, and Cost
objectives necessary to ensure we are not only competitive but a world leader
in building engines, joint efforts will be directed toward establishing:

* Quality goals that will achieve Best-In-Class objectives.

* Productivity goals that will assure a competitive engine per employee ratio.

* Machine efficiency and cost objectives that are competitive on a world-wide
  basis.

* Just-In-Time efforts to keep inventories low and material moving in the most
  efficient manner.

* Visits by team members to other Ford and competitive locations to keep
  abreast of changing technology.

The undersigned reaffirms their commitment to the principles identified above
and mutually agree that all local negotiation matters are hereby resolved.
This agreement shall remain in effect through the expiration of the 1990 Master
Bargaining Agreement.

FORD MOTOR COMPANY   INTERNATIONAL UNION, UAW
Romeo Engine Plant   Local 400

Date: _____   Date: _____

1

Figure 5.2
Mission Statement for the Romeo Engine Plant. *Source:* UAW-Ford National Joint Programs.

Ultimately, Piccini grows so frustrated with the lack of an agreement that he walks into the employee-relations manager's office and says, "Just give me 10 cents extra for everyone."

Corporate headquarters and the UAW International are both contacted. They are negotiating a team-based work agreement in the Wayne, Michigan, integrated stamping and assembly (ISA) plant. This is too low for the Wayne facility and Ford management is looking for common levels of pay in these two team-based facilities. Romeo is told that 10 cents won't work and the offer is rejected.

That, Piccini recalls telling the employee relations manager, will be "the most expensive dime he had ever given up in his life."

In the end, the plant settles on a 50-cent premium for team leaders, as well as pay levels for the new classifications that generate three years of back pay for all 600 hourly workers, with some individuals receiving checks as high as $20,000.

"The corporate wage and hourly people were worried about equity issues with other plants," recalls Lee Sanborn, the launch training coordinator from Ford. "The union was concerned to not have too big a distinction and have people be suck-ups with management. At the same time, the union also wanted to pay people what they were worth for a hard job. The labor relations people didn't understand what we were proposing—they just saw [the team leaders] as relief men."

There are other conflicts in the launch process. When people are told that they don't have enough seniority to remain in the plant in an assembly line job (and so must transfer to another UAW-Ford location), they *are* given the option of staying in the plant in the new team leader role. Later, however, Ford decides to select leaders based on a competency test, rather than seniority. While Piccini had supported the principle of a competency test, he is upset when told that 54 high-seniority people who had been promised team-leader positions will actually have to go back into the "GEN pool" for reassignment to another plant.

"They say you have no enemies in a burning house," Piccini recalls. "The plant closing was a traumatic event.... We were in it together. Still, there were some promises they couldn't keep. They should not have talked to me before I was done eating. [When they told me about 54 people going into the GEN pool] I threw my plate against the wall."

Eventually, an agreement is reached: the 54 can remain in the plant and serve in roles other than as team leaders.

"All that happened at Romeo was a series of pivotal events," notes Sanborn. "Before the launch, the preceding two or three launches at engine plants had been fiascos—late on schedule and couldn't get the quality. We were told that if we couldn't get this right—that is, at Toyota quality levels—they would order the engines elsewhere (outside of Ford Powertrain Division)."

What makes things so difficult? The workforce and union carry over from the tractor plant, but the work is very different. Both the company and the union must learn about entirely new ways of operating. Sanborn notes:

We had the current employees and union, but the tractors were produced one every 20 minutes and all were special order. We had to convert the operation to make one engine every 20 seconds, all of them alike. It was a big transition. Powertrain viewed Romeo Tractor as a failed plant—but the workers were as good as anywhere. The closing of the tractor plant was an economic thing—the tractors weren't selling. Still, the deal was that we had to get rid of most of the salaried folks and retain most of hourly.

There is simply little to go on in making the transition. Benchmarking visits by the union and management representatives are to auto assembly plants; there are few team-based engine plants to benchmark. More than a decade earlier, in the early 1970s, Volvo had been recognized in the scholarly literature for restructuring the engine building work so one team would assemble an entire engine. The approach had been introduced at a time of low unemployment in Sweden, when it was hard to attract workers to factory jobs. The aim was to make the work more rewarding than just repeating a set of tasks on an assembly line. In Jamestown, New York, a Cummins Engine plant was also known for this type of job enrichment that integrated social and technical systems (the sociotechnical or semi-autonomous team model is discussed in more detail in the next pivotal event in this chapter, "Continuous Improvement and FPS Rollout"). By the time the Romeo Engine Plant is launched, however, these experimental job design initiatives have shifted back to higher-volume approaches, though still retaining some of the team-based elements.

At the time, Ford does have two team-based plants in Mexico—one in Hermosillo and one in Altec. Ford's Tulsa glass plant also has some experimental use of teams, and about a third of the Sharonville Transmission Plant operates with a team-based work system (the E40D lines). But no clear model emerges from the benchmarking visits to these locations, or to the GM/Toyota New United Motors Manufacturing, Inc. (NUMMI) plant in Fremont, California. As Sanborn recalls:

All [the plants we visited] had different team models. Everyone says, "My plant is unique—we have different issues." In fact, engine plants have more machining than assembly plants. There was no model of an engine plant, so we had to make inferences based on what we saw. It was good to have the union on the benchmarking team because they would see things from a different perspective on what would or would not work with the UAW workforce. They were pragmatic. They were clear they wanted this to be successful—all of us wanted this to work.

Piccini works with Sanborn to define the new work system, and recounts their experience.

We sat down together and created a book [called a "white paper"] to help people get to a team-empowered workforce. Though this process, one of the most important things I said was that there was no such thing as a completely empowered work force. You are not empowering people to make every decision. They can't violate company policy or the international agreement or spend the money they want to spend. There was a point with five people in one area deciding who was going to take a day off—you can't get paid for five people and only have four at work. It was the same with a group that wanted to start at 6:00 am instead of 7:00 a.m. The groups ahead or behind them on the line were not coming in at 6:00 a.m. We said, "You need to put up rules." Say what people can work on.

We had to develop that piece and it was all captured in a white paper we wrote. We also decided as company and union leadership that we needed to meet every week during this process.

These weekly one-hour team meetings focus on ideas for improvement in their work areas, and are made mandatory. Making them mandatory raises questions about the idea of empowerment.

"They said, 'How can you do that when you are empowering people?,'" recalls Piccini. "I said you can't change work without people being in the room. You can't force anyone to talk, but if you are talking about changing their job they will say something."

To prepare people to work in these new ways, training is provided. This includes classes on Productivity, Finance and Business Metrics, Quality, Teams, Union Awareness, and Engine Build (where employees actually assembled the engine). Importantly, these courses are taught by members of the plant operating committee and the union bargaining committee. For example, the plant manager taught the Productivity course almost every Friday for the first couple of years. As Sanborn comments, "Having plant leadership teach courses establishes a communications link between workers and leadership that would be important as the launch progressed." Altogether, assembly workers receive about 40 hours of classroom training, machinists and skilled trades about 60 hours, and team leaders about 80 hours—all in addition to "on-the-job" training.

A key feature of the Romeo system is that team leaders can work on the equipment, providing relief when people are on breaks or otherwise as needed. Every aspect of the new work system is negotiated with the local union.

"This had to all be negotiated," notes Sanborn. "The union wanted to make sure we didn't do stuff that was real stupid. There were a lot of issues around whether the union and management could trust each other. On many issues we didn't know what to do at first, and had to figure it out as we rolled out the process."

Although many aspects of the operation are based on ability, seniority still plays a role in the plant. The allocation of overtime, for example, is based on seniority.

Team size is a new issue. These semi-autonomous teams tend to be larger in size than the smaller lean manufacturing teams observed in the benchmarking visits. "On team size," recalls Sanborn, "we saw some facilities with smaller teams of 8 to 10 people. We had teams as big as 50 on the block line or the cylinder head line. They would have meetings once a week. Skilled trades, leaders, superintendent, committeemen all met together. So, we had 50 people in a meeting. It was pretty democratic and well orchestrated. The hourly people were listened to."

Ultimately, the benchmarking, initial negotiations, work design, training, and other factors all pay off. The plant begins production in 1990. A formal reopening features the governor and mayor. The first product to roll off the line is the V-8 engine (4.6 liters, 2 valves per cylinder) for the Lincoln Town car.

As Lee Sanborn recalls:

The plant launched at 35 defects per 1,000 "opportunities"—no other plants were less than 100 at the time. So, the quality was outstanding. This was seen as a raging success. We were the most efficient 8-cylinder plant in the world at launch (with the exception of one highly automated plant in Japan). The entire success was due to two things that were new: work teams and simultaneous engineering.

For the simultaneous engineering, the product people worked with us on a continuing basis and the manufacturing engineers who were designing the equipment were also responsible for production—both the design and operation of the engine block line. In the old days you buy the equipment; I operate it. We blame each other—either you for bad design or me for being too stupid to run it.

We had no supervisors—we had team leaders doing supervisors tasks. We liked the supervisors personally, but they were a communications barrier, only facing upwards. There were three things a team leader couldn't do—discipline people, pay people, and give direct orders.

[To deal with these three things,] we always had an engineer on site and the team leader could call the engineer over and say, "The station isn't manned."

Then the engineer would say, "Is it mechanical?"

The team leader would then say, "No, the person isn't here."

Then the engineer could respond as appropriate with discipline. The same was the case with a pay card signed by the superintendent. Direct orders were just suggestions, but it was possible to bring in the engineer to sort it out if there was a disagreement.

By and large, [the team leader model] worked out better than we hoped. We had to do selection tests. They had mechanical competence, mathematics, problem solving, and other items—with several people in the room observing. We would grade them as they worked on it—union and management rating them. People were not just in it for the money—not enough for that.

Overall, the team structure at Romeo is organized around the major production areas illustrated in figure 5.3.

Over time, Romeo encounters an issue other locations also end up facing: how to *deselect* team leaders. "You had to have 66 percent of people voting someone out," recalls Sanborn. "Then there was a month or six weeks to change behavior. Three were voted out in the first year: one resigned; the other two both survived the second vote. Later the plant shifted to performance as the measure for staying in the role—with a six-month probation period before removing anyone."

The GM-Toyota NUMMI joint venture in Fremont, California, is the first unionized U.S. auto facility to develop a deselection model, and Romeo models its process along the NUMMI lines.

Within the UAW the role of an area committeeperson expands to include working in partnership with the engineer on operational decisions in that area of the plant. While a great deal of attention was given to the roles of team leaders, much less was given to the roles of engineers and others in management—an issue that would not be fully addressed for more than a decade in the Ford-UAW system.

In the years that follow the launch, challenges arise because of the differences between Romeo and Powertrain facilities. As Lee Sanborn recalls, the handling of corporate-imposed headcount reductions—what is called the annual "task"—was a major challenge:

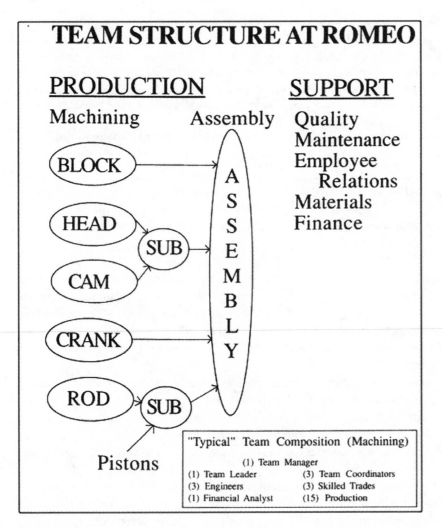

Figure 5.3
Team Structure for the Romeo Engine Plant. *Source:* UAW-Ford National Joint Programs.

The labor and overhead budget was a huge enemy of teams. The norm was to launch with extra people (and then reduce over time to meet the budget), but that wasn't the case here. When we launched, the process was already lean. We began with understanding that there would be no [corporate-imposed] "efficiencies" for five years to avoid turmoil. The deal was to do it as the most efficient plant in the world from the start.

After a couple of years, the Powertrain division has an 8-percent task. All other plants had to take 8 percent, and then if Romeo didn't it would be more for the others [to meet the combined task for the Powertrain division].

The labor and overhead budget approach undermines good teams. A bad system will beat good people every time. If you are only tracking hits and errors and the game is about runs, you will not do as well you might.

Piccini sums up the collaboration this way. "We represent people; Ford represents a profit. We will never do some things that the company wants from a business perspective. It is like the seams on a baseball—they don't ever intersect. Still, we are working together and we can expand the space in the middle."

✳✳✳

In 1991, the Romeo plant received the American Society for Training and Development (ASTD) award for the top training program nationally (for manufacturing). In subsequent years, the plant would be among the first Ford facilities to achieve the ISO 9000 standard for quality and the ISO 14001 standard for environmental efficiency. In 2002, the plant earned the Shingo Prize for excellence in manufacturing. In 2009, the plant celebrated producing its 10 millionth engine.

Today, the Romeo Engine Plant produces engines for a wide range of Ford products, including the F-150 truck, Mustang, Shelby GT 500, and Explorer. The plant makes about 3,000 engines a day, some on its high-volume line and others on its lower-volume niche line, such as the hand-built supercharged 5.4 liter 4-valve engine for the Shelby. The engines produced in Romeo are supplied to about a dozen assembly facilities in the United States and Canada.

As the first UAW-Ford plant with an entirely team-based work system, the Romeo Plant was pivotal. It featured the first integrated set of agreements in the UAW-Ford system on all aspects of how a team-based work system would operate. In later years, different types of team-based systems would emerge in assembly and stamping plants and, ultimately, an approach to work groups would become a central element of the Ford Production System.

Perhaps most striking about the Romeo story is just how much was unknown when the transformation was first undertaken, and the degree to which the model developed was a product of intensive union-management collaboration.

Continuous Improvement and FPS Rollout, 1996–1999

Initiating the transition to team-based work systems and an integrated production system sparks considerable debate within both Ford and the UAW. It is a pivotal event involving a number of years in development, with many twists and turns. By the time the move is made to create the umbrella called the Ford Production System, there is wide variation across divisions and plants in the relevant practices.

The roots of continuous improvement and the Ford Production System go back to 1979, when the UAW and Ford first agree to contract language encouraging what Ford calls Employee Involvement (EI) across manufacturing operations. As we discuss in chapter 1, this parallels a 1973 agreement between General Motors and the UAW on improving the Quality of Working Life (QWL). In Michigan, Ohio, and many other states and communities, there are QWL and related labor-management initiatives dedicated to increasing worker involvement in decisions affecting work. UAW leaders Irving Bluestone and Don Ephlin, along with Ford leaders Ernie Savoie and Paul Banas and General Motors leaders Al Warren and Dutch Landon, earn national reputations for advancing employee involvement and improved quality of working life.

The early experience with EI and QWL remains influential (and complicated) nearly two decades later in three ways. First, worker participation in problem-solving groups is established as voluntary, which becomes a very strong norm—to the point that it is a barrier to instituting teams wall-to-wall. Second, worker participation is established (as separate from collective bargaining) with appointed union and management coordinators who support EI rather than elected union representatives, whose primary focus is on the collective bargaining agreement. This, too, proves to be a barrier when new work systems begin to intersect with collective bargaining in many ways, and because politically appointed EI coordinators are not prepared to drive continuous improvement in operations. Third, worker participation is established as a joint program, distinct from management rights in running production operations. This is complicated by the union's interest in ensuring successful business operation and management's recognition of the value of union input.

Building on the early experience with EI is a second development in which the hourly workforce is connected to a key quality principle, Statistical Process Control (SPC), which is foundational for the Ford Production System. This is introduced to Ford through a series of seminars provided by the quality expert W. Edwards Deming (also discussed in chapter 8). At one of the sessions, in 1985, an hourly worker in the Wayne Assembly Plant, Harold Pagel, is able to attend. This is all new, as he recalls: "I had no idea what SPC was. I always took classes in what was new. The hourly seats were offered on the basis of seniority. Others turned it down, so it came to me. It was Joe Reilly from the international union who enabled this. This was one of the first times that hourly people were able to attend a session like this."

It is a five-day session. Though Deming is limited to a wheelchair at this time, he is still a commanding presence. "There were no questions without raising your hand and god help you if you were late coming back from a break or lunch," Pagel recalls.

Along with a salaried counterpart, Mike Folks, Pagel is charged with implementing what he had learned about SPC.

There was not a lot of understanding in the plant of what we had been trained to do. No one told the layout inspectors, for example. Once we had a plan, many felt intimidated and possibly fearful for their jobs. We were telling people to do things based on the data. The engineers were "shimologists." We would say the data doesn't support this. We had two books to do the upper and lower control limits with a calculator. They resented an hourly person telling them what to do. The books disappeared a few times."

Statistical process control involves calculating the normal distribution on quality, defining upper and lower bounds on acceptable quality, training operators to use gauges or other methods of assessing quality through periodic sampling by the operator rather than a quality inspector, and generating operator suggestions on work redesign, based on the data, to achieve continuous improvement in quality. Pagel helped to implement SPC principles and, in 1989, he was appointed as the hourly SPC coordinator for the plant and put in the office with the layout inspectors. By this time he was an accepted part of presentations with engineers and layout inspectors. "Initially," he reports, "other hourly workers had no clue what I was doing and accused me of being a suck-up." Once they saw what was actually taking place, he adds, and "saw that one of our people had some power in making decisions, they would say, 'this is pretty cool' and would ask me to come and make some measurements. They would see that, hey, management does want us to be involved."

It is the mid-1990s, and the various aspects that keep EI separate from management rights and collective bargaining are becoming problematic, while the worker engagement in SPC is becoming more essential—as the Toyota Production System (TPS) and the idea of "lean" production emerges as a powerful model. It is a model that involves *mandatory* participation by all workers in teams. Unions in Japan and in the unionized NUMMI joint venture in California (between GM, Toyota, and the UAW) are full partners in supporting continuous improvement through the team-based system. There is no strict separation with respect to collective bargaining, no formal designation as a "joint program," and no sharp divide around "management rights." Operating in these more integrated ways involves a different set of operating assumptions then is common in the Ford-UAW system at the time.

Ford and the UAW are using many different team models.[6] In some locations, such as the Romeo Engine Plant, the entire plant is team-based by the mid-1990s, with a model in which each team is semi-autonomous. Sometimes referred to as the sociotechnical systems (STS) model—pioneered at Volvo, Cummins Engine, and Proctor and Gamble in the 1970s and 1980s—in which teams operate without direct supervisors and the work is either highly automated (such as in machining centers) or there are substantial inventory buffers between teams. These factors make it possible for teams to meet without interrupting production and make their own decisions about the way work is done.

The STS model is in tension with the lean manufacturing model, a central tenet of which is reduced in-process inventory (i.e., operating on what is termed a just-in-time basis). This means that inventory buffers between teams are being reduced. Under this model teams cannot operate semi-autonomously. None of the Ford plants have wall-to-wall lean manufacturing teams at this time, but some have what are termed initial application areas, with pilot efforts involving lean manufacturing teams. In one case—the Wayne Integrated Stamping and Assembly Plant—half the facility has a Modern Operating Agreement (MOA) with a team-based work system and the other operates as a traditional assembly plant (discussed more fully in chapter 6). There is also a joint Ford-UAW program focused on preventative and predictive maintenance, called Ford Total Productive Maintenance (FTPM), that involves problem-solving groups of skilled trades workers (tool and die makers, electricians, machine repair, and others). So, the Ford landscape includes EI groups, various types of production teams, and skilled trades teams, all of varying in size, how leaders are selected, how team meetings are conducted, when team meetings are held, and other factors. The powertrain plants (engine, axle, and gear facilities) are the most advanced and have begun to refer to their approach as the Powertrain Production System.

This is the landscape in which Hank Lennox is given lead responsibility to develop the Ford Production System (FPS). As initially defined, FPS has eleven elements:

- SHARP (Ford's Safety and Health Assessment Review Process): safety and ergonomics
- Work Groups: team involvement
- Managing: cultural transformation
- SMF (Synchronous Material Flow): materials and inventory management
- FTPM: Ford's Total Production Maintenance
- IM: Industrial Materials Management
- ME: Manufacturing Engineering
- Environment: includes ISO 14000 certification
- ISPC: In-Station Process Control and Visual Factory
- Quality: includes ISO 9000
- Training: supports all elements

At the heart of the FPS vision is the notion of "inverting" the triangle. Jim Solberg, who was the executive director of Powertrain Operations from 1998 to 2002, developed an initial version of the "rolled triangle," which is presented below in figure 5.4, with the SQDCME metrics (in use at the time) and with teamwork at the top of the triangle. Additional elements of the Powertrain Operating System are included in the triangle.

A subsequent illustration developed in 2001 and presented in figure 5.5 shows the triangles rolling with five layers of management in a typical plant (plant manager and operating committee, area managers, superintendents, supervisors, and frontline workers). The triangle on the left has the plant manager and operating committee singled out as leading continuous improvement while the inverted one on the right has the teams and team leaders highlighted as the "engine" driving continuous improvement. There is a "pull" from customers, workforce, shareholders, and society that motivates the inverting of the triangle.

Of course, drawing the inverted triangle is not the same as addressing all the implications within management and within the union associated with such as change. There are many embedded operating assumptions that need to change.

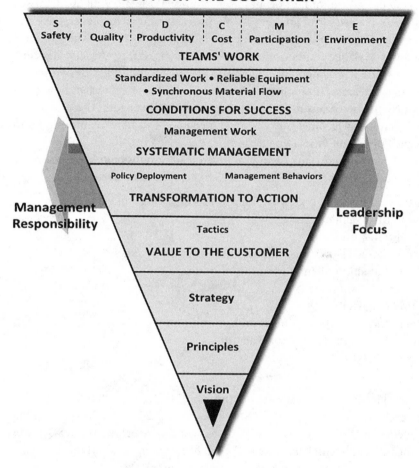

ROLLED TRIANGLE
SUPPORT THE CUSTOMER

S Safety	Q Quality	D Productivity	C Cost	M Participation	E Environment

TEAMS' WORK

Standardized Work • Reliable Equipment
• Synchronous Material Flow

CONDITIONS FOR SUCCESS

Management Work

SYSTEMATIC MANAGEMENT

Policy Deployment   Management Behaviors

TRANSFORMATION TO ACTION

**Management
Responsibility**

Tactics

VALUE TO THE CUSTOMER

**Leadership
Focus**

Strategy

Principles

Vision

Figure 5.4
Powertrain Operations Rolled Triangle. *Source:* Ford Motor Company.

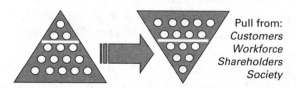

Pull from:
*Customers
Workforce
Shareholders
Society*

Figure 5.5
Inverting the Triangle. *Source:* Ford Motor Company and WorkMatters, LLC.

John Allen, a former HR leader in Toyota's Georgetown location, is brought in as a consultant on the FPS initiative. "We were told that we needed to meet with Joe Gafa, UAW servicing representative for Powertrain, and all the plant managers to talk about this thing called the Powertrain Production System," he recalls. "Jim Poe said [developing the Ford Production System] would be a two-week exercise. Nine months later we had done it. The issue was the managers in the circle who had a lot of resistance. It was hard for people to say that this can't work, but there was resistance. There were turf battles. I know that the management had come to the conclusion that team-based organizations had to be promoted through the Ford Production System. The real issue was that few management people were prepared to operate in that system. They were mostly [focused on] facilitating work and advancing their careers."

At the time, Dan Brooks is on a special assignment from the UAW to work with Al Ver in the advanced manufacturing group and is representing the UAW in the FTPM discussions. "I was going down a hallway and there was a meeting going on involving Hank Lennox and others," Brooks recounts. "I went in and found they were discussing the elements of what would become the Ford Production System. One of the elements was "work groups." I knew there was a parallel effort being led by Pete Piccini, Ben Storemski, and others around what they were calling Continuous Improvement Work Groups (CIWGs). They visited NUMMI and other locations and ended up drawing heavily on the team model in a portion of the Wayne Integrated Stamping and Assembly Plant (ISA)."

For a while, the FPS Work Group element continues to be developed in parallel with the Continuous Improvement Work Group effort. Brooks and others on the UAW team press the issue within the FPS group, and a decision is made to adopt the CIWG approach for North American operations and use the FPS Work Group model elsewhere. This is an important validation of the UAW's influence on a key element of FPS, though there are different views within the UAW on the entire discussion. A group within the UAW that had opposed the 1982 concessions and challenged the union leadership on other matters, called New Directions, opposes participative management and labor-management cooperation, which are seen as a form of work intensification and a sign of union weakness. Additionally, even though the union joins as a full partner in FTPM, some locations fail to follow through on promised training commitments and promised time for preventative or predictive maintenance. "Promises made, promises broken"—is the phrase repeated by the UAW, even at the highest levels.

The FTPM experience, and pressures from within the union, leads UAW vice president Ernie Lofton to make a strategic choice. In the 1997 National Joint Programs meeting, he declares that too often Ford asks the union to support new initiatives and then, when support for the initiative within management dries up, the union is left, in effect, holding the bag. This is one time, he continues, that the union is going to sit in the back of the bus and watch to see what management does. If management gets off the bus, the union will follow. As a black union leader, announcing that the union would continue to sit in the back of the bus represents a complicated pulling back in comparison to the joint support of employee involvement. As a result, while Joe Gafa, Dan Brooks, Jerry Young, and Chuck Browning continue to contribute to the FPS process, the union is also continually monitoring whether management is maintaining its commitment.

Within management, the battles are largely between the major business units in North American manufacturing. Most of the Powertrain plants are further along in moving to team-based work systems than stamping and assembly plants. Moreover, the teams in the Powertrain plants are generally closer to the STS model rather than the lean model. Thus, when the FPS group embraces the CIWG approach, which is a lean approach, the head of Powertrain Operations rejects it. As a result, the initial rollout of FPS is focused in the stamping and assembly plants; Chicago becomes the first assembly plant to pilot FPS in initial application areas. The FPS rollout includes eight hours of CIWG training.

The consultant John Allen, contrasting between the choice of semi-autonomous or lean manufacturing model for FPS, discusses the associated tensions. "[The FPS team model was] not a direct link to Romeo. They had eliminated supervisors, but engineers had become supervisors. The team structure in Romeo was more semi-autonomous. The teams were in competition with each other; it was not system-wide. In eliminating supervisors they substituted engineers to perform the same functions. The team structure lacked the leadership to make lean become a reality."

The broad strategic tensions associated with the FPS approach surface in plant training sessions. During the initial CIWG training in Kansas City, two individuals deliberately sit with their backs to the trainers even though the trainers are from their own plant. At a certain point, they spin around in their chairs and challenge the trainers, declaring all of the materials are "bullshit." Dan Brooks, there to observe the session, recalls, "There was supposed to be a member of management at each session so that the trainers would not have to handle disruptions. In this case, there was not a member of management in the room. The trainers looked to me as a representative from FPS and I indicated that they should just continue. As it happens, six months later these two individuals both ended up as team leaders and were strong drivers of FPS."

In continuing with the training and in the ultimate engagement of these two individuals, the union is playing a key role in driving the implementation of the new production system.

In the Twin Cities Assembly Plant, the rollout doesn't happen as scheduled. Bill Norton and another management FPS representative fly in, along with Dan Brooks, and meet with the plant manager and the HR manager, Jack Halverson. The local UAW chairman, Ted Lavale, enters the room and asked Dan Brooks to come with him. Dan knows Lavale as a traditional union leader who is sympathetic to some of the New Directions arguments.

The two walk to Lavale's office and after Brooks sits down, the other members of the local bargaining committee enter and stand in a half circle behind him. Lavale then asks Brooks, "Do you know when FPS will be introduced to the plant?"

"No, tell me," replies Brooks.

"I *will* tell you," Lavale says. He takes a calendar off the wall and flips through several months to a particular day—and points.

"This is when FPS will be launched here. Do you know what day this is?"

Brooks says no and asks why that particular day.

"It's the day I retire!"

Brooks gets up, walks out of the room, and heads to the room where the two management FPS representatives are waiting. He tells them they're leaving the plant. The two management representatives at first protest—three days of launch events are scheduled.

Lavale catches up and asks Brooks why he's leaving.

"I am not here sell you a bill of goods," Brooks answers. "I am just here to explain our union's role in FPS." The implication is clear—it is up to local union leadership to step forward if the new production system is going to be implemented.

The three men leave for the airport, canceling the three-day launch visit.

Walking out, Brooks later says, "ended up giving credibility to the UAW team responsible for FPS within the UAW sub-council." It is clear that the UAW is not providing unquestioning support for a managerial program, but checking to ensure local union support.

The importance of union support for FPS is further reinforced as UAW representatives work with management counterparts to assess FPS progress, and to coach plant leaders. Joe Gafa, one of the key UAW representatives involved in assessments and coaching, recalls:

I learned a long time ago you didn't want your boss in the union getting calls on the work you were doing. FPS touched so much—health and safety, quality, daily relationships on the floor. I know we couldn't go out and be bothering the servicing people [from the international union]. We invited them [to join us] and we stayed out of contractual issues. We respected the health and safety and the quality departments. Even though we were making more headway than they were, we let them take the credit. At one point, we had nine hourly people working with us—traveling with a coach to the plants. But you didn't go into a plant without communicating with the local elected union leaders first—to ensure there were not surprises. We would constantly put the local leadership on the top of our ladder.

Despite the initial caution by the UAW with respect to FPS, the representatives engaged in the process take on a proactive role.

"I can remember one time when we were not keeping up in production," Gafa says. "I went to a guy in labor relations who had been there five years and I said, 'Can you tell me the first operation that a spindle went through?' He couldn't. Today people know a whole lot more about the whole process."

As a partner in the FPS implementation, the union brings important insights into the culture of different locations. By this time (the late 1990s), Harold Pagel has left Wayne and is providing training support for FPS. He comments, "I thought each plant would be the same; each plant has the Ford logo and every local has the UAW logo. I had to learn that each had its own DNA...and that you had to learn the DNA before going in...I would talk with international UAW people and find out what the factions were in the local. I would try to understand the reasons why there might be negative views. I would find out who had expressed concerns. I would not try to convince them, but would explain what it was and indicate the opportunities provided through FPS.

✳ ✳ ✳

The codification of 11 elements into a single production system, with work groups as a central element driving continuous improvement, was a pivotal event in the Ford-UAW transformation. It did not happen easily or quickly, however. There were multiple models of teams. Management and the UAW had internal splits over the program—at the strategic level, at the plant level, and in front-line operations. In the end, however, the eight hours of CIWG training, combined with training on the other elements and the initial assessments and coaching, provided an essential foundation for the subsequent success with the integrated operating systems (presented in chapter 8).

In some respects, the case for change was clear—Toyota was enjoying considerable business success with the Toyota Production System. In other respects, though, there was no so-called burning platform. In the mid to late 1990s, after all, Ford was profitable—even if the company didn't lead with respect to quality, fuel efficiency, or product innovation.

In the 1999 national negotiations between the UAW and Ford, a letter of agreement is developed on FPS that reads:

October 9, 1999
Subject: Continuous Improvement Initiatives
Dear Mr. Gettelfinger:

During these negotiations, the parties discussed the importance of those initiatives which enable Ford employees to contribute to continuous improvement in the elements of the manufacturing business. Furthermore, the parties recognized the necessity of continuous improvement to support a focus on the consumer, to deliver products and services with improved customer satisfaction and quality, with great value, and at an affordable cost.

The parties recognize that, in order to achieve and maintain global competitiveness, Ford must remain on the cutting edge of new and emerging organizational, technological and process trends. For example, the Ford Production System (FPS) is a key, business driven foundation process, able to evolve over time as business dictates; and the application of the principles of Appendix I—Continuous Improvement to the manufacturing process is critical to meet customer expectations. The parties also discussed the importance of linking, as appropriate, all Joint Programs to continuous improvement efforts.

The following elements are linked in order to realize fully the vision of FPS:

- SHARP
- Continuous Improvement Work Groups (CIWG)
- Ford Total Productive Maintenance (FTPM)
- In-Station Process Control (ISPC)
- Synchronous Material Flow (SMF)

- Industrial Materials (IM)
- Manufacturing Engineering (ME)
- Environmental
- Quality Process System
- Leadership

During the course of these discussions the parties recognized how improving the Company's operating processes can enhance the work environment and improve competitiveness and job security. The UAW and Ford have achieved significant progress together, and the parties reaffirm their commitment to maximize management and Union support to Continuous Improvement. To ensure continuity, and to recognize the benefits Continuous Improvement provides to all parties, these initiatives should not be suspended and/or otherwise impacted as a consequence of internal differences or unrelated disputes. In addition, to achieve their mutual goals to improve job security and operational competitiveness, the parties recognize the relationship between Continuous Improvement and these other processes/ programs noted above; the need to continue efforts to align Continuous Improvement and the other processes/programs; and to involve all organization components and levels with people working to- gether to achieve common goals.

Consistent with these objectives, the parties reaffirmed their commitment to support and encourage our Continuous Improvement Plant Steering Committees, the National Continuous Improvement Committee and the Senior Advisory

Very truly yours,
PHILLIP A. DUBENSKY, Director U. S. Union Affairs Office
Labor Affairs

Team Start and Stop Designations, 1999

As Ford and the UAW come to understand that work groups or teams were integral to the Ford Production System, a fundamental question surfaces. What is the optimal team size? There is a temptation, of course, to set a standard size for a team to ensure consistency across the operation. Initially, the CIWG model includes a standard for the leader-to-worker ratio. However, Vehicle Operations (the assembly plants) finds it unmanageable on a consistent basis across all parts of a plant. As a result, Ford ends up taking a very different approach.

As Roman Krygier, Vice President of Powertrain Operations in 1999, explains, decisions on team size ended up being driven by the work itself. "In manufacturing, the most important factor was getting the workforce where they could contribute to quality," he recalls. "That centered on how we could organize the workforce into an effective work group environment. We looked at how the processes functioned in each area of a plant. We broke the process into start and stop points so that a group of people would control the elements in the part of the process where they worked. It might be 6, or 8, or 12 people in a work group. The number was less important than the appropriate start and stop points of the process in order to allow a smooth transition to work group designations—minimizing disruptions of the workforce."

This decision is pivotal because the work group size is based on a close look at what jobs are closely related to one another—where one set of work tasks starts and where that bundle of tasks stops. This is particularly important because each work group has a pull cord in its area, connected to a set of red, yellow, and green lights. Under normal operations, the green light is lit. If there is a threat to quality, one pull on the cord turns on the yellow light and brings assistance to the area. Two pulls on the cord turns on the red light and stops the assembly line. Thus, the start and stop designations indicate that space within which workers are responsible for safety, quality, and other matters.

Combined with the work group start and stop designations, notes Krygier, the pull cord is a highly significant change.

A pivotal event was to empower workers to stop the line. That was not a popular decision for many people, but if you let the defect go you then have rework later. It was difficult for people to believe that they could do this. It was a given—sacrosanct—that you don't stop a production line. The focus at the time was entirely on making the production requirements...but production has to meet the expectations of the customer. The aim is for the vehicle to go through the processes the first time without defects.

It took time. When visiting plants, I would ask how many times did you stop the line. The key is not only stopping the line, but getting the reaction team in place to respond quickly. We had to put the discipline behind it. There were team leaders, skilled trades and others who could join in when the line is stopped. That was the pressure point for the whole workforce to be involved in all of our operations—assembly, engines, transmissions, castings, and components.

✳ ✳ ✳

Thus, the simple act of designating start and stop points in each plant was pivotal in then determining the size of the work groups which, in turn, were given the authority and the responsibility to seek help and, if needed, stop the line rather than pass along a defect. Ultimately, it would take a few more pivotal events—including the quality charters discussed in chapter 7, the QOS coordinators discussed in chapter 8, and the targeted training also discussed in chapter 8—before the full potential of the start and stop designations are realized. Once realized, however, Ford's quality would move from near last to best in class.

UAW Glass Plants, 2002

Ford's Visteon Glass Division was established in 1999 as part of a larger plan for a number of different component operations to be divested by Ford. It was also with the understanding that it would not be as rapid or unilateral a divestiture as had been taking place in General Motors with the spinoff of the Delphi operations. Still, in 2002, Ford makes the difficult but expected business decision: sell two plants that manufacture glass for automobiles and other purposes. The Nashville, Tennessee, plant makes curved glass for windshields. The Tulsa, Oklahoma, plant makes flat glass, used in side windows in cars and in residential and commercial building construction.

Around the same time, Ron Gettelfinger, UAW vice president and director of the Ford Department, instructs Joe Gafa and the other individuals involved in FPS to "stand down" due to the lack of agreement on total cost (discussed in chapter 4). Unofficially, the four lead UAW FPS experts indicate to their Ford counterparts and external consultants that the UAW decision should not be interpreted to mean Ford's work on FPS should stop in any way. At the same time, because they are "standing down" from FPS, they have capacity that can no longer be focused within Ford. Further, even though these individuals all have experience supporting FPS implementation in various locations, none has been in the role of an outside consultant guiding an entire lean transformation.

It is in this context that an unusual agreement is reached. The UAW FPS experts will provide technical assistance on lean principles to the two glass plants. The goal is to increase the ability of the plants to find a new owner who will value the work and the union in the operations.

In the end, the UAW representatives' eight-month engagement with the two glass plants is pivotal in two ways. First, it helps improve the circumstances for the Nashville and Tulsa workforces—more so for Nashville because of external marketplace reasons (stronger demand) rather than internal operations. Second, and more consequential for the Ford-UAW transformation, it takes the expertise within the union to a level comparable to that of leading external consultants and beyond that of a number of Ford's own internal company experts. Thus, the glass plant experience is a pivotal event for knowledge-driven expertise within the union.

Gerald Bantom, then the UAW vice president responsible for the Visteon Division, comments at the time, "With the companies under so much pressure, we have got to do things a little bit differently these days."[7]

Gafa reflects back on the experience as "a burning platform for Ron Gettelfinger."

He was concerned to see what we could do for the business. It was not that it could be saved, but it was going to be better for a sale that would benefit the workforce. It took us seven to eight months. We had great chairmen in the locations and we really turned it around.

First, we took teams from both plants to visit Saturn. Then we came back and put together joint leadership processes and governance. In Nashville we focused on the gravity line and turned it around— that was for the production of windshields. Tulsa was different. They produced flat glass and side body glass. At the time the commercial glass business was still good, but furnaces needed to be rebuilt. They were far more lean when it came to skilled trades, but it was what happened in the market place after 2007 that had everything to do with the fate of that plant.

Marty Mulloy was directly involved in the sale of the two plants on behalf of the Ford Motor Company. "The work Joe did was important in the sale of Nashville," he says today. "It helped us find a good buyer who would continue the relationship with the UAW and build on the process improvements they had made."

Mulloy adds, "Tulsa was regrettable. The plant did an outstanding job of improving the operation, but [it was] a victim of circumstances. We had a number of potential buyers of the plant, but none would even meet with the UAW. The company held firm on that as a condition of sale and then there was the downturn in commercial construction. Ultimately that resulted in our having to close that facility."

✳ ✳ ✳

The experience of the UAW being the outside experts on lean principles and wrestling with the business proposition for the future of the plants was pivotal—both for the successful sale of the Nashville plant and for the deeper level of expertise that it represented for the UAW as a partner with Ford. When the UAW representatives returned to their internal support role within the Ford-UAW system they did so with deeper expertise, perhaps greater than that within any U.S. union.

Hourly Six Sigma Black Belts, 2003–2007

The Six Sigma approach to quality emerges as a concept at Motorola in 1986, when a statistician proposes using up to six standard deviations (a standard deviation is one sigma) from the norm as the target for process capability. At six sigma, there is confidence of 99.99966-percent precision in the operation (that is, only 3.4 defects per million). At the time, some of Motorola's products are at only at three-sigma levels of quality (99.7%) or worse.

Soon, Six Sigma becomes an umbrella for a wide range of quality and process improvement tools, each with the sigma level of quality for an operation as a key internal metric. The primary improvement model uses data to drive an improvement cycle: Define, Measure, Analyze, Improve, and Control (DMAIC).

By the mid 1990s, GE embraces the concept and a wide range of organizations follow. Mastering progressive levels of the tools and methods, demonstrated by leading improvement efforts of increasing scope and impact, result in designated capability levels: "green belt," "black belt," "master black belt," and others. Figure 5.6 is a Six Sigma symbol used in Ford briefings.

Beginning in the late 1990s, salaried Ford employees lead process improvement efforts using Six Sigma tools. Frontline UAW workers are often involved in process-improvement efforts, and some begin to earn green belts for their efforts. Attaining black belt status is a substantial leap from green: it involves leadership responsibility for a project at the level of $1 million or more in improvements. So, by the early 2000s, a consequential issue arises inside Ford: whether hourly workers can earn a Six Sigma black belt. In a few cases, plants have allowed hourly workers to lead improvement projects that have resulted in their earning black belts, but there is no formal policy on whether this can happen for others.

The issue is raised formally in the 2003 quality negotiations by Dan Brooks, leading the negotiations for the UAW. Louise Goeser, Ford's head of Quality, rejects the proposed policy enabling hourly employees to lead projects through which they could earn black belts. Language on employee engagement does make it into a letter of agreement, but it is relatively limited in scope:

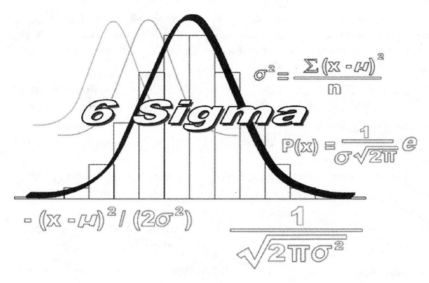

Figure 5.6
Symbol for Six Sigma. *Source:* Ford Motor Company.

During these negotiations, the parties discussed lean principles and opportunities to seek continuous improvement through employee and team engagement. It is recognized that employees and teams have the greatest understanding of how to organize work and eliminate waste. The parties discussed the importance of utilizing workforce input and the positive impact it has on competitiveness and employee morale. In this regard, the parties agreed to support employee or team driven efforts to continuously eliminate waste, improve quality, address health and safety and ergonomic concerns as well as the effective and efficient allocation of work elements. Communications and implementation of employee suggestions will be in accordance with local practices.

Except in the limited application of this letter, its provisions are not intended to conflict with existing language regarding work allocations in assembly plants.[8]

Following the negotiation, many hourly employees earn green belts, but they receive no formal support for leading any projects to earn their black belts. This continues until 2007, when Wilhelmina Allen, a Ford engineering manager, is asked by the co-chairs of the UAW-Ford National Quality Committee (NQC) to champion allowing hourly employees to play the major leadership roles in quality improvement efforts. Dan Brooks, representing the NQC, and Gary Johnson for Ford then take the proposal on the issue to Ken Macfarlane, a director of manufacturing in Vehicle Operations—who is the manufacturing element champion for Quality (each of the directors is assigned a different focus, or element—safety, quality, cost, delivery, etc.). Macfarlane is very supportive.

Wilhelmina Allen recalls the process:

We had been experiencing a huge downturn in the business. Lots of people were leaving the company and many were salaried black belts.... The proposal was that there would be selection criteria just as we had used for the hourly Quality Operating System Coordinators. We joined with the Six Sigma office to do the proposal for the selection process. We reached an agreement on how many there could be per facility. The first candidates took it on as a challenge and something new. Getting the company to agree to have hourly black belts was certainly a pivotal event.

The selection criteria build on the approach to selection for Quality Operating System Coordinators (QOSCs), and the first cohort to enter the program are primarily QOSCs (see chapter 8). This change happens outside the scope of collective bargaining, which is unusual; collective bargaining is the typical vehicle for creating a new role in the hourly workforce.

"This was an important change," notes Dan Brooks. "Instead of having to wait and then bargain for the role, it was just a matter of convincing the company that it was the right thing to do."

Allen makes an important personal commitment in her role as an advocate for hourly workers to go through the Six Sigma black belt training: she decides to do it herself.

I went through the training and could see what they were feeling. The first groups that we put through the training had very few problems. It was a one-and-a-half to two-year training process. They were still working as QOSCs while going through the training.

My background is engineering—so I already had similar training. Also, I had worked at the Dearborn Stamping Plant, which was important. One of the perspectives was that this training would be no different whether it was for hourly or salaried.

Each black belt candidate needs to be assigned a project to lead, and finding projects for Ford hourly employees to lead is essential (as are other forms of support). Recalls Allen:

This first group needed support to participate. There were 35 of them and they needed to be able to come to the class. Also, they needed the right tools and materials, including having a computer. So they needed to have the support from their plant.

In the beginning, black belts need a project and in this case it needed to be with a charter provided by an individual's plant leadership. The project had to be in the system.

It was a culture change. For years we separated hourly and salary. You needed analytical ability, but there also had to be a desire.

The assigned projects are equivalent to the kind of projects assigned for salaried candidates, mostly focusing on reducing process variation. All of the hourly candidates had been green belts, most participating in Vehicle Reduction Teams (VRTs) in their plants. Now they were to lead projects. The hourly work force had been trained in problem-solving tools for years, including what was termed the "8D" model (an eight-step problem-solving model) and the "5 whys" model advanced by the quality expert W. Edwards Deming. Now they needed to be able to apply a much broader range of tools.

Armentha Young, a Quality Operating System Coordinator introduced in chapter 2, is an example of an hourly worker who was in that first cohort earning a Six Sigma black belt. She comments on the process:

One of my greatest achievements during my role as a QOSC was when I successfully completed the Six Sigma Black Belt certification process. I received my certification on October 19, 2010. I along with 5 other QOSCs and some members from the leadership team at Dearborn Truck Plant began this endeavor in March of 2009. This was the first time I had ever jointly attended a training session with salaried people at this level, which made the experience awkward and somewhat intimidating. In addition, I was aware that at one time only salaried personnel were given the opportunity to participate in this particular training....I felt that I would now be able to truly understand why and how decisions are made that affect Quality. The training was usually a four-week process, but due to the launch of the new 2009 F-150, which was a demanding time in the plant, the training had to be broken up into many months. The QOSCs played an integral role in the launch; I had the task of coordinating the Extra-Ordinary Quality Initiative (EQI) inspection stations. These inspection stations were designed to put a 200-percent, sometimes a 300-percent effort toward protecting the customer and the work drew on my Six Sigma training and my experience an hourly quality inspector....

It would be over a year before I took the exam. It was February 26, 2010, at 12:00 p.m.; I remember studying for weeks. I was determined to pass this exam, and I did. But in order to become certified, I needed to complete two projects. This part of the process is where the salaried workforce comes to recognize and appreciate the skills and talents of the hourly workforce. No longer were we management and employee, we were team members pursuing the same goal. This experience doesn't eliminate the notion of salaried versus hourly, but for me personally it demonstrated how much more we as an organization can achieve when titles, classifications, and separation aren't the central focus.

Another member of that first cohort was Rusty Woolum, who had begun as a QOSC in the Sharonville Transmission Plant in 2001. Describing the Six Sigma training, Rusty states, "I am a sponge." Since completing the training, his focus has been on applying the principles to process improvement with respect to a special assignment on supplier relations, which he explains as follows:

I am learning so much about the processes in every supplier. It sounds just like the issues we had in Ford. I wanted to go to the suppliers and listen to the operators. They would find out I was UAW. One supplier said I wasn't welcome. I still showed up and spoke to the quality manager first. I said let's take titles away—let's talk quality. I am not here to organize your plants. I am here to talk quality. After that they would share confidential Dimensional Control Plans (DCPs). We built a trust foundation. You had to build that. For two-and-a-half years that is what I did. We would open up the DCPs. We might be in Georgia and then South Carolina and then back. I will tell you based on the data the next launch was the best in the company and I believe the work we did with suppliers was a big piece of that.

The challenges in driving process improvement with suppliers are not just attitudes toward hourly UAW workers. Sometimes, it is more about conveying crucial frontline information, as this comment from Woolum indicates:

"The beautiful thing about going into the supplier is a focus on what is critical with the parts....I can remember being in the supply base and talking to them about what was critical to our processes in the plant. What they thought was nonfunctional in a part was actually important. They didn't realize our welders used the triangle on the part to locate it for welding. There were issues with the welders with variation in the parts when they were welded together. When I went to the supplier, they initially said that the print didn't call for it—it isn't HIC [a High-Impact Characteristic]. Well, it became HIC quickly.

Reflecting on the overall experience with hourly Six Sigma black belts, Wilhelmina Allen notes, "Everyone was successful in completing the training and being certified with the first group. Since 2008, a total of 137 hourly people have been through the process. The numbers parallel the training of salaried people during this same time period."

Allen adds, "Not everyone completes the training and the implementation of a project (which is needed for certification)." For the hourly workforce, there has been a 23 percent dropout rate. Many of the dropouts are people selected outside the proper criteria, such as those who haven't yet completed green belt training. The dropout rate for salaried employees is not as high, but even there, as Allen notes, "not everyone has the analytical background to be successful."

Looking ahead, Wilhelmina Allen concludes,

The VRT process and the QOSCs have helped management refocus on how to be in tune with what the operator wants—more so than what an engineer would know. Often, the QOSC has worked the operation and may have written the operator instruction sheet.

The journey will be led by the base operator in the future. That is where process leadership will help the operator do the best job for the customer. The hourly black belts are a key part of the infrastructure to support this process.

***

The training and utilization of hourly Six Sigma black belts has been pivotal in at least three ways. First, and most important, it represents an investment in and appreciation of the capability of the frontline workforce by management at all levels. It builds on and extends the QOSC role.

Second, hourly black belts have been pivotal within the hourly workforce and among suppliers in helping people learn new ways of working with hourly workers as subject matter experts. This has taken initiative and skill on the part of the individuals as they perform in these new roles. It also has required changing assumptions by others.

Finally, the change is pivotal in that it happened on its merits, outside of collective bargaining.

Powertrain Operations Plant of the Future, 2007–2008

By 2008, Ford has invested substantial resources into training the workforce in all elements of the Ford Production System. Most facilities are operating on the basis of lean principles and the operating systems are beginning to show success. A number of leaders in management appreciate the ways in which the hourly workforce is central to continuous improvement in the business, particularly at a time of great economic challenge. Still, there is considerable debate within management leadership around whether enough progress has been made to change long-standing plans to invest in new operations in Mexico.

For the UAW, whose members have been helping drive the improvements in safety, quality, and productivity, new investment in the United States is expected in return.

Kevin Bennett begins to explore new ways of utilizing the talents of the hourly and skilled workforce. He is newly appointed as director of New Programs, having been executive director of Powertrain Operations for two years and, before that, Powertrain's director of engineering for eight years.

Bennett focuses on the mechanical skills involved in maintaining uptime in the Powertrain facilities, which includes highly automated, complex equipment. He has an idea: locate skilled trades employees—who have completed full apprenticeships and mastered particular trades—directly on the assembly line, integrated with the production teams. He's not suggesting skilled trades workers do production work, but that they move from the separate areas of plants where they wait for calls to come in requesting help. On the actual line, they will gain a much higher level of understanding about the work in a given area and be able to react much more quickly.

This means a major restructuring of the work of skilled trades employees, who are the most elite members of the workforce (and who have the most transferable skills to other employers and industries). Talent retention has always made management particularly cautious about change involving these workers. The proposed change, though, has the potential for a dramatic improvement in plant efficiency. A typical Powertrain plant faces considerable downtime, with 55-percent efficiency typical at the time. Having the skilled trades workers as members of Integrated Manufacturing Teams (IMTs) affords the potential to increase uptime to around 75 to 80 percent—an efficiency improvement of a third.

Realizing this opportunity requires that skilled trades employees cross the traditional lines of demarcation between the trades: an electrician on the assembly line as part of a team may end up doing some machine repair work, a machine repair worker on the same team may do some electrical work, and both may have to do some work outside of traditional skilled trades functions that are needed to keep the line running, such as replenishing spare part inventories. Clearly, some work across lines of demarcation will require new training and certification, but other aspects of the integrated roles are well within the current capabilities of the associated trades.

Pilot efforts with IMTs have been in operation in the Lima, Ohio, plant since 2004 and the Cleveland Engine 2 Plant shortly thereafter—demonstrating the effectiveness of the approach. The question now is whether it can be broadened across the system, including in Vehicle Operations assembly plants, not just the Powertrain facilities. Historically, Vehicle Operations rejects as "not invented here" any ideas that come from Powertrain. Management faces this challenge.

The union faces a challenge, too. The IMT idea is sure to be controversial with skilled trades workers who have long defended the lines of demarcation between their trades. UAW leaders, though, know IMTs are central to the business case for bringing work back from Mexico.

A number of UAW leaders are discussing the "factory of the future" during the 2007 negotiations. There are divisions within the union. One faction insists on maintaining traditional
skilled trades lines of demarcation and opposes trades taking on nontraditional work. They
believe the current system is adequate and efficiency gains can be achieved through an
enhanced Total Productive Maintenance process.

On the other side are the union's experts in high-performance systems, responsible for
programs on Continuous Improvement, Quality, and Safety. They understand the need for
transformational change and what it will bring. Brett Fox is the coordinator for Continuous
Improvement. Fox recalls:

In 2007, there was interest to increase IMTs across Powertrain. In February 2007, I was in Continuous
Improvement, and the company wanted all Powertrain to sign up and asked how it would fit in Vehicle
Operations and Stamping. We felt some [in the company] were looking to move too quickly—we knew
it doesn't fit well in some settings. Windsor Engine had the Canadian government support and had no
resistance to full IMT, while Lima and Cleveland were at 80–90 percent. Some International union staff
opposed IMTs and scared off other Powertrain plants.

During negotiations, we had dialogue [going] on full-blown across Powertrain and ended up drafting
language to open the door for all plants—and no longer used the term "IMT." We put a letter together
for skilled trades on the same team, but it was more about their serving in a helping-hands role—more
advisory to work groups for FTPM and problem solving.

Following the 2007 negotiations, Bennett and Vice President of Labor Affairs Marty Mulloy
begin a series of meetings within management, initially to develop more fully Bennett's
vision and generate the business case.

Bennett recalls the discussions:

We looked back over the history of America having a lead in volume production, why it lost the lead,
and what it would take to get it back again. The gradual buildup of categories in which work is divided
was a key problem. We asked ourselves, "If we took a pure model of a manufacturing plant, what it
would take to run the plant? How would we structure the teams to support production and keep the
factories running? How would we react to things gone wrong?"

We developed team structures based on exactly what the factory would need—in a team structure to
empower people to make decisions to keep the equipment running. This is what led to the integrated
manufacturing team concept. We found it to be a lot more efficient.

Bennett elaborates further on the process of building support for the idea.

We needed to have the significant stakeholders bought into the need for change. People felt
we were already fairly efficient and we were making improvements every year. But could we do
better? These were quite small meetings for people to engage the information and then provide
the project with direction. We looked at where we were versus the best in the United States and the best
abroad.

Then we looked at the people the UAW represented and at the management leaders at Ford. What
would it take to move this forward? We looked at the way we had negotiated change previously. If we

wanted a plant to be restructured we would attach the change to new work projects. That way, the changes associated with new work could also include the other change in the operations. Sourcing decisions were the way to do this.

Enlisting UAW support for further development of the idea is key. Kevin Bennett is good at teaching the union how world-class manufacturing operates. He educates people about the roles of indirect labor versus direct labor in plant performance. When he meets with UAW president Bob King, Bennett helps King understand the intricacies of the idea.

After meeting with King, Bennett meets with other UAW subject matter experts, including Brett Fox, Chuck Browning, Dan Brooks—together responsible for Continuous Improvement, Safety, and Quality. "We came out of the 2007 negotiations agreeing to explore what Kevin Bennett had been sharing on his powertrain initiative," Brooks recalls. "I was asked by Mary Anderson, a Ford internal organizational development leader, to join her in a meeting with Kevin. We arrived in Kevin's office, and on the white board was his strategy. It was more like being in a classroom than a meeting with a senior Ford leader."

This approach to change is global and it incorporates leading change management principles. As Anderson recalls, Bennett's "goal was to align skilled trades with production teams."

It was initially focused on Mexico and [on] Germany, Sweden, and Belgium. There are different unions for skilled trades in Europe. He was knowledgeable around the structure of the plant and how teams were set up in these different countries. He was keen on developing a new way of operating, with more integrated teams. In reaching out to the UAW in the United States, the idea was that there would be no reason not to bring the work in here if we could do things in new ways.

Kevin was a leader as teacher. He was very inclusive and used compelling data to get stakeholders to shift their thinking. The Vehicle Operations folks were not interested at first, but when you saw the data on productivity you couldn't dismiss it.

He walked around using Kotter's change management principles.[9] We would be in a meeting and would encounter resistance and he would say, "That is okay—we have to go slow to go fast." He knew the importance of getting everyone involved.

It was key to have someone with courage and conviction at a senior level. Vehicle Operations was so quick to dismiss new ideas. We didn't have the One Ford culture fully in place. He slowly introduced the change with transparency of data.

We are still working on the VO-Powertrain relationship, but the idea of best practice sharing is now more the norm. There is nothing like a near-death experience to get leaders thinking we need to align. I am happy to say that we no longer spend the time and energy we used to on [Vehicle Operations] versus [Powertrain Operations].

✳✳✳

While progress has been made more recently in the bridge between Powertrain and Vehicle Operations, there were still divisions within management and the union in 2008 that were a barrier to the integration of skilled trades as part of the plant of the future. Compounding the challenges, all the key players moved into new assignments for which the plant of the future was no longer their central focus. Kevin Bennett retired and returned to his native Britain.

Bob King was elected UAW president and brought on Chuck Browning as a top member of his staff. Dan Brooks retired and Mary Anderson went on to an assignment in Organizational Development. Marty Mulloy remained with the company and did retain the learning from this initiative, which, as we see in the next pivotal event, carried forward into the 2011 negotiations.

The ultimate impact of the Powertrain Plant of the Future remains to be seen. Bennett's vision and the UAW leadership's engagement with the vision were effective in convincing senior leadership in Ford not to build a new engine plant in Mexico and instead split the work between Lima (Ohio) and Cleveland Engine 2, the two facilities that embraced change and worked to implement IMTs. In this regard it was pivotal as a clear demonstration that investment can follow the development and support of an innovative vision.

While the 2011 negotiations did move the idea of integrated teams further forward, the full transformational potential of this approach remains to be realized on a system-wide basis.

Team-Based Agreements, 2011

Beginning in the mid-1980s, Ford and the UAW negotiate team-based work agreements at a number of U.S. plants. These agreements are based on the premise that having hourly employees engage in tasks formerly assigned to salaried employees, such as planning production schedules, quality control, inventory control, and manpower planning within their work operations, will improve the team's output and, thereby, the company's performance. It is an initial move toward a knowledge-driven work system.[10] In the subsequent years, the plant-level initiatives come together under the umbrella of the Ford Production System and the Continuous Improvement Work Group (CIWG) model.

One key aspect of the 2011 UAW-Ford National Bargaining (which is covered in other respects in chapter 6), is the joint effort to design a Team-Based Work Agreement that codifies lessons from three decades of initiatives involving teams and two decades of UAW-Ford Continuous Improvement contract language.

Jim Tetreault, the vice president for North American Manufacturing, continues what is now a tradition of strong line management participation and leadership in collective bargaining. He has returned from an assignment in Europe where FPS has achieved a high level of employee involvement and process standardization across facilities. He comments on what he saw in Europe: "It really was Jim Padilla's vision of the inverted pyramid." Tetreault continues:

The pivotal point for me was when we sat down in 2011 negotiations. It became clear that not everyone understood the vision. I understood it having seen high functioning FPS plants, but not all had seen it. We agreed to send a small team of UAW people to Valencia [Spain] and Cologne [Germany]—hourly to hourly, union official to union official—to hear it from them. We sent a team over and they came back truly the converted. They said, 'That is exactly what we want to do, now we just need to figure out how to do it.'

The negotiations focused on developing the framework to guide top-down leadership, from directors and managers. Tetreault observes, "It is the plant managers' responsibility—they need to be accountable for developing a plan and then working with the local UAW leadership to refine the plan, including tasks for every team leader to take on. This is to be submitted to Ford and the UAW as part of continuous improvement, with the plant leadership signing the document."

The aim is to eliminate plant-to-plant variation. "Every plant had its own unique concoction for how FPS had been implemented," Tetreault comments. "It was important to set the ground rule for this to be led by the leadership. In Europe and Mexico this is how it worked. You have to begin with standardization of roles and operations."

Key elements of the 2011 agreement include language on governance and mission:

• **Governance Structure**—The National Continuous Improvement Forum consisting of Ford: VP Manufacturing, VP Labor Affairs, and Director, Union Relations. From the UAW: VP National Ford Council and UAW Administrative Assistant. This Forum is responsible for overseeing the implementation of work groups/teams and the governance of the joint Continuous Improvement Charter.

• **Mission**—The parties committed to implementing work groups / teams to a consistent standard supporting global manufacturing strategy using standardization and continuous improvement to enable our work groups/teams to deliver "One Manufacturing—Best in the World."[11]

Recognizing that delivery on the mission requires an ongoing process of operational alignment, the parties identify eight domains in which they will implement defined processes:

• **Operational Alignment**—The parties committed to implement the following eight processes:
  1. Aligned and Capable Organization—Work Group / Team Structure
  2. Standard Team Leader Roles and Responsibilities
  3. Standardized Team Leader Selection and De-Selection Process
  4. Team Leader Training
  5. Manufacturing Work Group Technical Skills Competency Training
  6. Work Group / Team Implementation Plan
  7. Existing Team Leader Transition Plan
  8. Charter Change Management Process

In addition, the collective bargaining platform is used to codify a range of agreements and practices on teams and work groups. This includes agreements on the work group/team structure and on team leaders:

- **Work Team / Group Structure**—Manufacturing facilities will have any combination of the following three teams/groups:

    1. *Production Work Groups*—Approximately 20–30 non-skilled production employees and a Team Leader working on an assembly line.

    2. *Manufacturing Work Group*—Approximately 10–20 non-skilled, semi-skilled and skilled trade employees with a Team Leader (Production or Skilled Trades) working with no traditional lines of demarcation and operating and maintaining equipment within their capabilities.

    3. *Mechanical Work Team*—All Skilled Trades teams with a skilled trades Team Leader working within their capabilities with no traditional lines of demarcation.

- **Team Leaders**—The parties spent a great deal of time discussing the roles and responsibilities, the selection process, competency training, and the compensation of the team leaders, as described in the following four items.

    1. *Plant Governance*—the Local Continuous Improvement Forum (LCIF), which consists of the Plant Manager, HR Manager, Plant UAW Chairman, UAW Bargaining Representatives, have responsibility for process oversight.

    2. *Leader Selection Process*—Candidates are scored using a standard set of questions including: experience and versatility (25 pts.), SQDCPME knowledge and work habits (40 pts.), and people/ leadership skills (35 pts.). Interviews and final selections are made by the Superintendent, Team Manager (First Line Supervisor) and designated UAW Bargaining Representative.

    3. *Competency Training*—The parties agreed to jointly develop training curriculum to support standardization and continuous improvement. Existing and newly assigned Team Leaders will participate in the training.

    4. *Team Leader Compensation*—Newly assigned Team Leaders receive an incremental $1.50 and existing Team Leaders receive $.855 over their existing hourly rate of pay.

This is an increment higher than the Leader Rate at GM and Chrysler and represents the value Ford places on the contributions of its team leaders.

Figure 5.7, which comes from briefings on the agreement, summarizes the Work Group / Team structure.

✷✷✷

While the 2011 agreement did not represent a new approach to teams/work groups, it did serve to codify the diverse practices across the UAW-Ford system. It also signaled the central role of teams/work groups in what is termed by the UAW and Ford as an "aligned and capable" organization.

More than a decade and a half earlier, neither the UAW nor Ford was prepared to make the Ford Production System a joint program: Ford wanted to preserve its managerial rights, and the UAW wanted to maintain independence from the complicated issues around efficiency improvement. With this agreement, however, both parties signaled a clear joint responsibility for the knowledge-driven aspects of frontline workplace operations.

Aligned & Capable Organization

In the Desired State, our Manufacturing facilities will have any combination of the following teams:

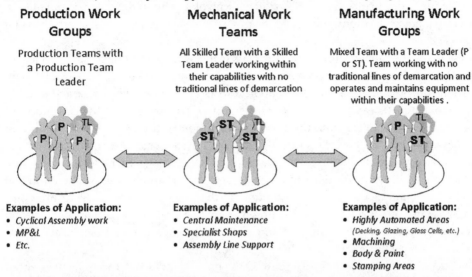

Production Work Groups	Mechanical Work Teams	Manufacturing Work Groups
Production Teams with a Production Team Leader	All Skilled Team with a Skilled Team Leader working within their capabilities with no traditional lines of demarcation	Mixed Team with a Team Leader (P or ST). Team working with no traditional lines of demarcation and operates and maintains equipment within their capabilities .

Examples of Application:
- *Cyclical Assembly work*
- *MP&L*
- *Etc.*

Examples of Application:
- *Central Maintenance*
- *Specialist Shops*
- *Assembly Line Support*

Examples of Application:
- *Highly Automated Areas* (Decking, Glazing, Glass Cells, etc.)
- *Machining*
- *Body & Paint*
- *Stamping Areas*

Each team has skill and capability to run and maintain their area

Work is completed by team members to improve the business against key objectives within their span of control. They are self Managed. They apply Specific processes and methods, make structured improvements, monitor and manage work processes.

Figure 5.7
Presentation on Team-Based Work Systems. *Source:* Ford Motor Company.

Recap: Guiding Principle for Chapter 5—Continuous Improvement

Pairing the idea of *knowledge-driven work* with the idea of *continuous improvement* represents a new mindset. Many employers in the United States and around the world have, for many decades, sought to increase employee involvement—or, as it is now typically called, employee engagement—without making the direct connection to continuous improvement.

As the first pivotal event in this chapter illustrates, leadership at Ford did not initially appreciate this connection. As a result, the total productive maintenance initiative lost more than a decade in the drive to deliver results.

The direct connection between frontline knowledge and continuous improvement was made at Mazda Flat Rock and the Romeo Engine Plant. In both cases, the complexity of moving to a knowledge-driven system, centered on teams, was greater than initially understood. Once achieved, however, there were clear positive results for the business and in the lives of the people working in these organizations.

The integration of the knowledge-driven approach at the enterprise level was the core challenge for the Ford Production System—what was termed "rolling the triangle." This is reflected in the entire architecture of FPS, which is a pivotal event in this chapter, and numerous associated policy decisions, such as the team start and stop designations, another pivotal event.

For the UAW, the support provided to the glass plants was, on the one hand, a product of a more traditional exercise of union power: the stand down on "total cost" covered in chapter 4. On the other hand, it was a unique opportunity to build internal expertise and credibility around a complete lean production implementation. The expertise of the UAW was not just in the senior appointees from the international union contributing to FPS, but also in the development of hourly workers earning Six Sigma black belts. This is an aspect of the union that is not generally known externally and that is still fragile; it remains an open question whether successive generations of union leaders will continue to value these internal skills and capabilities. Also an open question is the degree to which the continuous-improvement mindset will transform the union as an organization. It has happened clearly in a number of local unions, but the UAW International is a large, complex organization with transformational challenges comparable to those Ford itself faces.

The concluding two pivotal events point to the opportunities and the challenges ahead with respect to knowledge-driven work. On the one hand, the Powertrain Plant of the Future embodies great innovation, but its full potential has yet to be realized on a system-wide basis. Similarly, the team-based agreements in 2011 codify principles that have been in development for more than two decades, and are a critical foundation for the future. At the same time, the influx of so many new workers into the system, as well as the turnover in the supervisory and management ranks, are potential sources of instability.

Ultimately, however, what is clear is that supporting and reinforcing the direct connection between knowledge-driven work and continuous improvement represents a fundamental transformation in core assumptions guiding Ford, the UAW, and the UAW-Ford relationship.

SUPPORTING MATERIALS

5.1 Sample, Romeo Engine Plant Root Cause Analysis Charts

The following charts are from an illustrative root-cause analysis conducted by a team in the Engine Block Machining Area of the Romeo Engine Plant. Comparable analyses are completed on a regular basis in all Ford facilities. As the first chart illustrates, a series of costs are identified in the operation (note that the dollar values are masked for confidentiality) and the star indicates the decision by the team to focus its Small Group Activity (SGA) on "scrap."

Next is a Pareto chart that identifies, in priority order, the various factors that contribute to scrap. Note that the top three are highlighted for further analysis.

The number-1 identified generator of scrap (in this case, an operation that is "off-location") is further analyzed to identify root causes, which are shown in a pie chart.

Finally, for each root cause, the team has generated an action plan, with specified responsibility, a due date, and a status report. In a knowledge-driven team-based work system, the systematic use of these kinds of problem-solving and continuous-improvement tools show how frontline knowledge is valued.

A

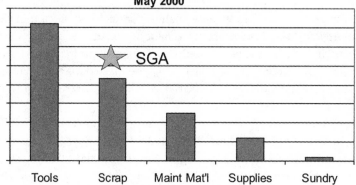

Note: dollar amounts on the vertical axis deleted for confidentiality

B

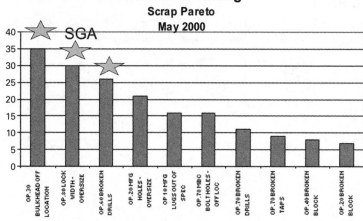

C

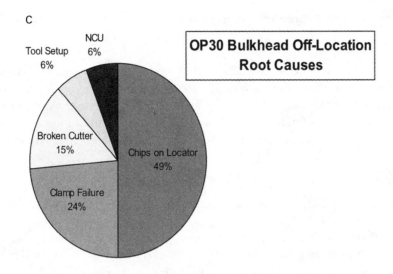

NCU
6%

Tool Setup
6%

OP30 Bulkhead Off-Location Root Causes

Broken Cutter
15%

Chips on Locator
49%

Clamp Failure
24%

D

Action Plans

Item	Description	Action Plan	Responsibility	Due Date	Status
1	Chips on Locator	a) Interim Action - flush chips from station each shift	Operators	6/2/00	Started 6/2/00
		b) Investigate additional flush lines for station	OP30 SGA Team	6/21/00	Preliminary sketch complete
		c) Add chip guards to prevent chip build-up	Millwright	6/29/00	SGA millwright working with group, projected implementation over summer shutdown 7/00
2	Clamp Failure - OP30 Station 7	a) Air switch adjusted to detect cracked clamp arm	Electrician	6/5/00	Complete
		b) Develop DOE to determine appropriate clamp pressure, may be set too high	M. Parus N.VandeGrift	6/29/00	Meeting scheduled to begin discussion
		c) Need vendor support to evaluate clamp design/strength	Ingersoll	7/15/00	Ingersoll evaluating
3	Broken Cutter - OP30 Station 7	a) Investigate tool change frequency	Swanson	6/9/00	Complete
		b) Interim - reduce tool change frequency to 5000 pcs (from 6000 pcs)	M. Parus N.VandeGrift	6/12/00	complete - needs to be re-evaluated after broken clamp arm issue resolved.

Source: UAW-Ford National Joint Programs

5.2 Week in the Life for a Team/Work Group Leader

Introduction

The following is a sample of activities in the typical (and even a bit light) workweek of an "online" work group coordinator/team leader (working on the job and serving as coordinator). It is primarily those activities that involve some degree of empowerment. The sample comes from an actual department in a UAW-Ford components machining and assembly plant around the year 2000. Some details have been changed slightly to make it more broadly applicable.

Tuesday

4:55–5:10	Take inventory
5:20–5:45	Go to office of next Department over to talk with Supervisor about washer flooding in the isle and in our department—put in tickets for Facilities and Scrubber Truck
6:45–6:55	Call to check out why an Operator wasn't paid for Monday
9:40–10:52	Received bad component from Department X—returned it and explained what was wrong
9:50–10:05	Go to General Stores to check out new taps and drills for pedestals
1:12–1:20	Survey Department about reduction in hours
1:20–1:35	Sort and tag scrap tub for removal
2:32–2:55	Line up Tool Crib for afternoons with tooling changes

Wednesday

4:50–6:15	Take inventory; Give schedule for week to the Team; Post weekend schedule; Cover for missing person
6:50–7:25	Informed by Operators that there is no stock to load/unload; Run Raymond hi-lo to get job set-up; Call transportation to ensure hi-low service
7:45–7:55	Contact Facilities/Maintenance and then Skilled Trades Leader about drill bushings for new tooling testing
7:57–8:15	Contact Engineering about new test tooling
9:00–9:35	Direct Team meeting and vote on reduced hours—agreement to work 6 days and 9 hours per day
1:30–2:40	Attend lean Business Unit Steering Committee meeting
2:50–3:10	Sort and tag scrap tub for removal

Thursday

4:50–5:10	Take inventory
5:12–5:35	Search for bike
6:15–6:30	Direct transportation with incoming stock
6:30–6:45	Survey department for weekend work (Sunday)
6:35–6:40	In middle of survey, call Receiving Inspection about contaminated tubs of aluminum caps (bolts mixed in)
7:05–7:20	Show Receiving/Inspection the problem with the aluminum caps
7:25–7:50	Take Engineer through the quality inspection process used as part of a root cause analysis by an internal customer department
8:10–8:25	Prepare for sort of aluminum caps from supplier due to bolts mixed with caps
9:10–9:25	Meet with TPM support person about benchmarking trip to Indianapolis Plant to learn about their process
9:55–10:10	Talk with set-up person from Supplier about aluminum caps
11:45–12:10	Go see Work Group Coordinator in internal customer Department Z about special run parts that will be coming from us
12:30–12:40	Give upper management run-down on cap problem

Friday

4:45–5:05	Take inventory
5:15–5:55	Set up with Internal Customer Department Z to run special parts
6:40–6:55	Sort and tag scrap tub for removal
6:10–6:25	Plan overtime schedule for weekend and also plan coverage for next week
1:40–2:05	Go to Internal Customer Department Z to check about special parts—did not run—will try again on Monday
2:15–2:20	Line up Maintenance and afternoons on finisher Piping work

Saturday

5:45–10:27	Dig through storage area, sort, arrange and consolidate; Separate scrap from other Departments mixed in our area; Separate foundry returns; Get ready for lean "red tagging" exercise

Monday

4:50–5:10	Take inventory
5:30–6:12	Try to arrange coverage for Thursday and Friday
6:20–6:40	Discuss with Facilities and Maintenance supervisor problems with pipe work from the weekend
7:40–8:20	Back to Internal Customer Department Z about special parts (which were returned to us over the weekend and which need to go back to the Department Z staging area (happened twice)
7:05–7:15	Call Inspection Receiving about the amount of parts to be returned to Supplier (foundry scrap)
9:05–9:20	Show Inspection Receiving person location of 18 baskets to be returned to Supplier
11:30–12:10	Review tubs of scrap from nearby department (after weekend sort)
12:30–12:55	Sort and tag two tubs of scrap for removal
1:45–2:10	Discuss possibility of getting a person from nearby department for coverage during hunting season

Additional Comments

Note that the coordinator points out that many activities will be handled by the contact people from the work group:

• For example, it would be typical for the Safety Contact Person to put in tickets for missing guards on the machines.

• Similarly, it would be typical for the Preventative Maintenance, Quality, and other Contact Persons to be working on those issues.

While the week-in-the-life-activities are primarily those associated with the coordinator position, some are additional developmental activities that are independent of the coordinator position:

• For example, it happens that this Coordinator has attended training to earn a Raymond Hi-Lo operator's license.

• As a result, this individual might drive the Raymond to get a new battery and take it through the safety check-sheet—because of the training, not just due to the role as a Coordinator.

Assignment for the "Week in the Life" Data:

Analyze the data from the "week in the life." Work in small groups to answer these questions:

• What impact will these activities have on safety, quality, schedule, cost, morale, capability, and environment performance?

• What will be the impact of improved feedback to this person on each of the performance metrics?

• What would be your priorities if you were serving as a coach or supervisor for this individual?

• To what degree is this a high performance work system?

Source: Ford Motor Company and WorkMatters, LLC

Comments

This "week in the life" training module on the role of a team leader was generated by Joel Cutcher-Gershenfeld after shadowing a particular team leader in a components operation in the year 2000. In some cases, events that took place when Cutcher-Gershenfeld was not present were recorded in a diary and then included in the write-up based on joint dialogue. This has been used in training within the UAW-Ford systems and in university classroom settings to illustrate the dynamics of a role that is in transition to being more knowledge-driven.

6   Negotiated Change

Guiding Principle: Interest-Based Relationships

Negotiated change is central to many of the pivotal events in the Ford-UAW transformation. These negotiations, in most cases, do not follow the traditional, adversarial bargaining model. While a problem-solving approach to negotiation in general may be less common, its roots go back to more than 75 years ago and involve the concept of "integration." In 1933, Mary Parker Follett introduced the concept of "integration" to the management literature and signaled its transformative potential.

There are three ways of settling differences: by domination, by compromise and by integration. Domination, obviously, is a victory of one side over the other. This is not usually successful in the long run for the side that is defeated will simply wait for its chance to dominate. The second way, that of compromise, we understand well, for that is the way we settle most of our controversies—each side gives up a little to have peace. Both of these ways are unsatisfactory. In dominating, only one [side] gets what it wants; in compromise neither side gets what it wants....Is there any other way of dealing with difference?

There is a way beginning now to be recognized at least and sometimes followed, the way of integration....The extraordinarily interesting thing about this is that the third way means progress. In domination, you stay where you are. In compromise likewise you deal with no new values. By integration something new has emerged, the third way, something beyond the either-or.[1]

Richard Walton and Robert McKersie incorporated this idea of "integration" into their landmark 1965 book *Behavioral Theory of Labor Negotiations*, which captures the tension and interdependence between "integrative" and "distributive" bargaining (sometimes referred to as the "creating" and "claiming" aspects of bargaining) as well as other aspects of negotiation.[2] Later, using integration as a negotiation process was the central building block for Roger Fisher and Bill Ury in *Getting to Yes*, which highlights the importance of focusing on interests, rather than positions, to achieve the full, integrative potential.[3]

In this chapter, we expand on the idea of interest-based bargaining and identify what we call interest-based relationships, in which the interest-based approach to bargaining bridges over to characterize ongoing relationships, not just negotiations.

The focus in this chapter is mostly on formal collective bargaining negotiations, but in each case there are informal underlying relationships before and after negotiations that are rooted in an appreciation of interests. The events presented involve substantive agreements, process innovations, and underlying relationships—all of which were pivotal.

Taken together, these pivotal events present a very different picture of collective bargaining than is typically perceived. Collective bargaining is often viewed as an old institutional arrangement that impedes innovation. This chapter, however, reveals collective bargaining as powerful mechanism for innovation, in two ways. First, in some cases—such as in the 2003 negotiation on quality—the bargaining process recognizes innovative practices that are then codified and extended more broadly. This was true with respect to the formalization of QOS Coordinators, including an agreement to use competence-based criteria in the selection of these hourly workers. There had been islands of innovation preceding the negotiation, but 2003 made it a system-wide practice.

Second, in other cases, new ideas are developed at the bargaining table specifically aimed at initiating innovation, such as happened with the 2007 VEBA as a new approach to retiree health care that simultaneously increased worker security around that issue at a time when the risk of Ford going bankrupt faced all concerned, and helped Ford stock move from junk bond status to investment grade, enabling future product investment. These dual roles of collective bargaining, codifying existing innovation and launching new innovation, are central to the pivots in this chapter.

Nine pivotal events are presented:

Chapter 6

Pivotal Events	Overview	Type, Level
Vehicle Operations Modern Operating Agreements, 1990–1995	Negotiating Modern Operating Agreements (MOAs) makes explicit the connection between the economic performance of the business and the work rules with the union. But this piecemeal approach to change is incomplete in important respects.	Planned, Plant Level
Automotive Components Holdings (ACH), 2000–2013	A series of negotiations concerning the Automotive Components Holdings (ACH) reflects an industry-wide set of moves to focus on the "core" business, selling components plants and contracting out key engineering and design responsibilities.	Planned, Enterprise Level
National Negotiation— Quality, 2003	Most aspects of this negotiation are traditional, but an interest-based approach to quality enables labor-management partnership on this issue and proves a precursor for the 2007 negotiation.	Planned, Enterprise Level

Chapter 6

Pivotal Events	Overview	Type, Level
Action America, 2005	There is an unprecedented level of information sharing between top UAW and Ford leaders in the regular Action America meetings, which are pivotal in the subsequent economic downturn.	Planned, Enterprise Level
Bargaining Over How to Bargain, 2006	Building on the 2003 quality experience and seeing the economic storm clouds on the horizon, both the UAW and Ford enter into a comprehensive restructuring of the collective bargaining process—matching a problem-solving approach to bargaining with a challenging agenda.	Planned, Enterprise Level
National Negotiation—VEBA, Entry Wage, 2007	With the very future of the enterprise on the table, the parties reach agreements that break in important ways from pattern bargaining (an echo of the 1982 negotiation) and that are central to Ford not taking federal bailout money.	Planned, Enterprise Level
National Negotiation—Pattern for Crisis Negotiation, 2009	With the federal government driving negotiations at GM and Chrysler, the UAW-Ford negotiation is a strategic move for both parties.	Planned, Enterprise Level
National Negotiation—Health Care, Profit Sharing, 2011	A national negotiation serves as a platform for innovative approaches to health care, and an improving economy (and new formula) make possible 2012 profit-sharing checks of $8,800 per employee.	Planned, Enterprise Level
Entry-Wage Team Leaders at Chicago Assembly, 2012–2013	Team leaders hired at the new entry wage at the Chicago Assembly plant are integrated with higher-seniority team leaders earning the traditional wage—a story still unfolding. The plant has among the largest number of new entry-wage workers in the system, many in jobs that would not have existed in the United States were it not for the lower wage, but that still raise complicated issues.	Unplanned, Plant Level

Vehicle Operations Modern Operating Agreements, 1990–1995

Between 1990 and 1995, a series of plant-level negotiations in Ford's assembly plants use the leverage of new investment to achieve more flexible work practices and improved productivity in operations. Codified in what are termed Modern Operating Agreements (MOAs), these agreements do not have the coherence and coordination of the 2006–2007 Competitive Operating Agreements (COAs) discussed in chapter 2. Instead of the enterprise-wide strategy associated with the COAs, each MOA is a pivotal event for the particular plant, and the cumulative impact is complicated. The principle of linking flexible work practices with investment is clearly established, but the dynamic of pitting one plant against another (or parts of one plant against other parts of the same plant) is controversial within the UAW. These agreements also create a diversity of practices across plants that add to the variability among production operations. We focus on just some of the MOAs negotiated during this time.

Joe Reilly is the administrative assistant from the UAW Ford Department responsible for supporting local union leaders in the Ford assembly plants. He comes out of the tough Mahwah, New Jersey, plant and has a reputation as an aggressive bargaining unit chairman. Don Ephlin, the UAW vice president who leads the negotiation of the 1982 mutual growth agreement, appoints Reilly as assistant and mentors him on the principles of worker empowerment. Reilly then supports Ford plants promoting Employee Involvement (EI) meetings in the frontline operations. Subsequently, however, when Steve Yokich becomes the UAW vice president responsible for the Ford relationship, the emphasis on employee involvement is reduced and Reilly is more limited in what he can do.

By 1990, a new UAW vice president responsible for the Ford relationship, Ernie Lofton, is on board. He appoints a number of people to key roles leading change around new work systems, but does not advance a national agenda on these issues. As a result throughout the 1990s, management is the moving party and it does so, in part, through MOAs.

The first MOA challenge comes in 1990 and concerns a potential new investment at the Wayne Integrated Stamping and Assembly (ISA) Plant. Before bargaining begins, support is needed from the UAW's regional council. The council votes down the idea of an MOA negotiation. The chairman from the plant counters with the idea that the changes should be made only in part of the plant, which will become a separate bargaining unit.

"We agreed to have two bargaining units in the plant," recalls Reilly, "with teams just in the assembly part of the plant. We may have regretted it."

Selling the agreement to the local workforce is challenging. "You had to use some pressure to get people to do what was really better for them in the long run," Reilly notes. "The split plant was a compromise based on traditional bargaining. Management wanted a full, team-based agreement in exchange for the product placement decision and the new investment, while the union countered that only some of the new jobs would be based on the team structure."

Reilly makes the case to the membership for the team-based agreements with an appeal to worker empowerment. "I said, 'We are all smart people and we want to do a good job. We didn't come in to be abused by a supervisor.' The line I used was, 'Maybe we could get rid of these supervisors.'"

While this is an important consideration for the workforce, the actual model management is pursuing does not necessarily center on worker empowerment. Rather, the primary value for management is seen in consolidating job classifications, eliminating production standards and piecework agreements, and establishing what are so-called bell-to-bell operations (in which workers in a given area are prohibited from leaving the plant early once they've achieved their day's production goal, a practice in some locations). Even though the Wayne facility does have experience with employee involvement and hourly engagement in Statistical Process Control (SPC), these experiences are not the dominant feature of the change. Harold Pagel, who as we saw in chapter 5 was the plant's hourly SPC coordinator, is selected to be the first of four hourly training coordinators under the MOA. The selection process involves labor and management both submitting lists of names, and Harold is on both lists. He is selected in part because of his expertise with SPC and also because both hourly and salaried leaders know of his success as a hockey coach. Despite his expertise and that of others involved in the process, there are larger dynamics as a result of the split approach.

As part of the MOA, a new stamping plant is built, which is then integrated with the assembly plant. This new plant has the team concept, a single job classification, and uniforms for all the workers, even as other parts of the integrated operation run traditionally. Pagel recalls:

There was lots of jealousy. As part of the implementation team, we were allowed to park in the salaried lot because it was closer to the new facility—the hourly lot was a quarter mile away. There are four of us wearing uniforms and all the others in management in civilian clothes. The new building had a 700-foot bridge to the rest of the operation, which came to be called the Mason-Dixon line. If you crossed that bridge with a uniform on you would be ridiculed. At one point it become so bad that I went to the union leadership and handed in my cards. The union did respond by introducing some perks on the traditional side, including uniforms that were a different color.

The dynamics around being a partial team-based system swamp the knowledge-based principles.

The next MOA concerns the 1995 investment in the Villager/Quest product at the Avon Lake Assembly Plant in Ohio. Again, it results in a negotiated agreement to launch the 1996 product with a team-based work system in a third of the plant, with other products made along traditional lines. Concurrently, the F150 axle assembly operation in the Sterling Axle Plant is also carved out as a team-based pilot area within the plant. In each case, MOAs are negotiated based on the leverage associated with launching new products. The Sterling negotiation is particularly challenging since the investment commitment has already been announced and the negotiations is now after the fact.

The next MOA is in the Kentucky truck assembly plant. "We went down there," says Reilly, "and there was a strong chairman. He said, 'We won't stop you, but we are not going to do a damn thing to help you.' We went to a membership meeting and they did vote for it."

The Ohio Assembly Plant is another case where new work leads to an agreement for half the plant to be team-based and half to be traditional.

Even after agreements are reached, achieving the full potential proves difficult. Tensions and jealousies emerge between people working in the team-based parts of the plants and the traditional parts of the plants. Where there are separate bargaining units, competing local union representatives each advocate for the value of the approach in their areas.

Dan Brooks represents the UAW in developing the principles around team-based work systems. "Many of the managers in the MOA plants," he remembers, "didn't understand lean principles and some did not agree at all with the idea of participative management. There were traditionalists on both sides. For example, they didn't know how to manage a versatility matrix to make the reduced classifications work."

Joe Reilly also notes that challenges exist within frontline management as well as within the workforce. "The frontline supervisors were a barrier. [There was] almost an unholy alliance between the workforce and the supervisors against change from the outside."

✳ ✳ ✳

The Modern Operating Agreements reached during the early 1990s were pivotal in making the connection in the assembly plants between new investment and increased flexibility in operations. They represent an incomplete pivot, however, because they led to a "split the baby" compromise rather than a fully integrative solution like that advocated by Mary Parker Follett (quoted at the beginning of this chapter). Forces within labor and management drove the compromise agreements, and the legacy of these partial innovations continues to this day—with dual bargaining units continuing in these plants even after they have implemented teams throughout.

Reflecting on this series of MOAs, Reilly acknowledges that the partial agreements were not optimal, but argues that they were the best that could be achieved at the time.

"It was the only way to get it done," he says. "You are facing a solid wall and you have to look for some way forward."

Automotive Components Holdings (ACH), 2000–2013

Ford pioneered the vertically integrated enterprise and organized the parts or components operations in various ways over the years. As we saw in chapter 4, for example, a number of facilities operated as the Plastic and Trim Products Division in the 1990s. Other facilities, such as the Sharonville Plant (producing gears and transmissions) and the Sterling Plant (producing gears and axles), are part of the Powertrain Division (and are mentioned in other chapters). In 2000, the company seeks to sell off most of its components operations, and a new independent supplier organization is created—Visteon Corporation.

Ford conducts internal management negotiations around what and who will be part of the new Visteon. U.S. labor law limits the UAW from negotiating on the actual business decision to establish Visteon Corporation, but does require Ford to negotiate on the impact of the decision on the hourly workforce. These negotiations are followed in most cases (but not all) by a third negotiation with the outside companies acquiring the operations. At stake is the survival of the individual operations and Ford as a whole. How they handle this negotiation will have implications for the reputations of Ford and the union. Meanwhile, at competitor GM, the component operations are being spun off into the Delphi Corporation, which provides an important counterpoint for this set of pivotal events.

In 2000, 17 plants are grouped together under the banner of the newly established Visteon Corporation. Motivating the move is the strategic decision that only stamping, engine, assembly, and a few other operations are core to the business. The average wages in competitive operations for glass, seats, plastics, engine components, and other parts are well below the wages and benefits provided under Ford's master agreement with the UAW. In many cases, the gap exceeds $30 per hour (taking into account fully fringed benefits)—nearly half the total hourly cost within Ford.

Thus, this change is challenging on many fronts. Managers are allocated to Visteon or Ford—sometimes voluntarily and sometimes with no choice—and all the branding changes. Ford signs and logos come down, replaced by Visteon signs and logos. All the new Visteon employees have to adjust; they are no longer part of the Ford family. And as the Visteon Corporation is created, many other suppliers are asked to take on increased responsibility for the design and engineering of components.

By January 2005, Visteon's North American operations have revenues of $8 billion, with 17 plants and slightly more than 18,000 UAW hourly employees. It struggles to be profitable; the preceding fourth quarter of 2004 fell short of expectations and first quarter forecasts are far below market expectations. The financial crisis deepens, and by the end of the first quarter of 2005, Visteon loses $160 million. Banks are threating to deny credit, which is essential for ongoing operations.

At the same time, Delphi Automotive Systems, General Motor's counterpart to Visteon, a spinoff beginning in 1997 and completed in 1999, is undergoing similar challenges. Both must address uncompetitive work practices and uncompetitive hourly wage rates. Declining volumes at Ford and GM result in less revenue for these suppliers, both of which depend almost exclusively on their former parent companies for survival. As Ford and GM struggle to remain profitable, they reduce the margins they pay on their parts from Visteon and Delphi, which deteriorates the financial performance of both suppliers. By October 2005, Delphi files for bankruptcy and threatens to void the UAW-Delphi Agreement—with the potential to shut down General Motors. Visteon is on the brink of filing for bankruptcy as well.

The responses to these dire business situations are very different. Delhi CEO Steve Miller opts to fight it out with the UAW, using threats and intimidation. Ford's senior management team decides to engage the UAW leadership in a dialogue, promoting joint problem solving to achieve mutual shared interest. These paths lead to very different outcomes.

Don Leclair, Ford's chief financial officer, consults with bankruptcy experts and concludes that a Visteon bankruptcy has potentially disastrous consequences for Ford Motor Company. Visteon is by far Ford's largest supplier, providing critical components across Ford's entire product line. Most of its automotive components would take months and potentially years to replace. For example, if Sterling Axle Plant ceases production, every North American assembly plant that produces rear wheel drive trucks and SUVs will be forced to shut down.

What are Ford's options? The first is not to intervene, and instead let Visteon sort out its own financial crisis—which will, in all probability, result in a free-fall bankruptcy. But this will be self-destructive. Visteon has already dropped three credit rating levels and its creditors are threatening to shut off the supply of parts from Tier 2 suppliers. Bankruptcy will lead hedge funds to pick apart the company, leaving Ford in dire straits.

Another option is to purchase Visteon and reabsorb the entire corporation back into Ford. But this would put Ford in a worse position than before the spinoff. Not only is it a failure to address Ford's North American automotive parts cost issues, it forces the company to assume responsibility for Visteon's global supplier relationships—and Ford lacks the financial resources and technical skills to support such a move.

The third option is to create a temporary LLC, take back Visteon's North American plants, and then negotiate an agreement with the UAW to address the plants' uncompetitive work practices and compensation levels. This avoids Visteon going bankrupt and ensures that parts shipments to Ford will continue. The challenge, though, will be to negotiate an agreement with the UAW to turn around Visteon's fundamental weakness—uncompetitive work practices and unsustainable labor costs. Only by doing so can Ford transform the Visteon facilities into ones attractive to potential buyers or close them and reabsorb Visteon employees with Ford service back into Ford plants.

Negotiation between the UAW and Ford commences in late February 2005. UAW president Ron Gettelfinger, Gerald Bantom, vice president of the UAW's National Ford Department and UAW legal counsel Dan Sherrick represent the UAW. CFO Don Leclair, Marty Mulloy, Labor Affairs vice president, and Ford attorney Steve Kulp represent the company.

Ford's primary interest in the negotiation is to ensure an uninterrupted supply of parts and components, and to address the fundamental issues that make these U.S. plants uncompetitive. Ford also wants to retain a workforce skilled in manufacturing operations while being able to sell operations that are not core to the company's ongoing business. The UAW wants to secure continued employment for the workers in these facilities, achieve transfer rights and other related rights in the larger Ford system, and have as much of the work as possible remain in UAW-represented operations. After intense negotiation, the UAW and Ford leadership agree to implement the third option.

Still, though, the UAW needs to open up the Master Agreement, which requires ratification by the membership (only once since 1941, during the 1982 crisis negotiation discussed in chapter 1, has the UAW agreed to open up the Master Agreement during the term of a contract). In May, only days before impending Visteon bankruptcy, Bantom announces that UAW rank-and-file members have ratified the agreement and Ford establishes Automotive Components Holdings LLC (known as ACH) to restructure 14 plants with 18,000 hourly employees.

The agreement has several key elements:

• 12 Visteon U.S.-UAW facilities will be transferred to ACH as a subsidiary to Ford Motor Company (two Visteon plants are reabsorbed into Ford).
• ACH employees who formerly worked for Ford Motor will be offered an opportunity to flow back to Ford as positions open.
• ACH employees will be offered buyout packages in 2006.
• Newly hired ACH production employees will be hired at a competitive rate within the supplier industry—approximately $25 per hour, with full fringe benefits.
• All ACH plants will eventually be sold if buyers can be found, or closed.
• ACH plant management and local unions will begin negotiation on structuring competitive local agreements to improve plant efficiency.

Al Ver, Ford's vice president for Business Development and Manufacturing Engineering, assumes responsibility as ACH's CEO in the fourth quarter of 2005. A highly innovative executive with a reputation for establishing trust and accountability among his staff, he visits every ACH plant with Chuck Browning, his UAW counterpart, to deliver a clear message to plant management and local UAW bargaining committees: "Come together and negotiate a competitive Modern Operating Agreement (MOA) and place your plant in a position to be purchased by another supplier in the industry you compete in." Ver promises he will deliver the management resources and capital to turn the plants around.

True to his word, Ver is tenacious in acquiring resources for ACH and building a high-performance management leadership team. Over the course of one year, all the ACH plants negotiate MOAs that dramatically increase operating efficiencies and plant morale, improving the plants' prospects for acquisition.

The union's conclusion that it can best serve its members by helping to fix each business to sell to another company is based on its top priority—preserving the jobs. The UAW has to analyze what work practices would put the locations in a better position to be sold, building on what they had learned in the earlier efforts to improve and sell the glass plants (discussed in chapter 5).

In his role representing the UAW's membership at Ford, Browning recalls,

The original focus was on making the businesses successful and keeping them. The company shared financial data with us. They were extremely transparent with all the business metrics. It became obvious to us that it would put the job security of all members in danger if something wasn't done.

Initially, we would go in under existing contracts to make positive changes as best we could. We made some great gains in error proofing, safety, and so on. There were other areas, such as work practices, that were not as easy because there was contract language based on a mass production environment but that no longer applied with the flexibility needed in a lean environment. The contract language became the bottleneck. The key to educating the local chairman was sharing data. We were fortunate to have almost all experienced chairmen, bargaining committees, and servicing representatives. It became obvious that without change, the businesses would not survive.

Workforce issues are complex and central to success. A major issue was ensuring that people who were "blue" had a soft landing. For workers to have a stake, there were several things needed. First, there had to be work—product brought in. Commitments of investment and work were key. Then, as efficiencies were achieved on the floor, the question became what to do with excess workers. A portion could be redeployed with new work coming in the plant. A portion was able to transfer to other plants. And a portion was offered buyout incentives to retire. As Browning explains, "If I had a desire to stay in the building, the work was important. If I was looking for something different, but wanted to stay with the company, I could transfer. If I was looking to retire or do something very different, the buyout was appealing. We insisted that everyone have a soft landing." He adds, "This was pretty unique. In the past and in many other cases, the company just focused on the business and the union just focused on the people. In this case, we both focused in both areas."

Over the next nine years, Ford and the UAW "clean up" the uncompetitive work practices to prepare the plants for sale. Ford's Purchasing Operation, led by Tony Brown and Bert Jordan, identify potential buyers for the facilities, which all the while maintain best-in-class safety, quality, delivery, and cost.

Of the 12 U.S. UAW facilities transferred to ACH, six are sold (and remain UAW organized), four are consolidated into existing ACH plants, and two are closed, their products sourced to UAW-organized suppliers. Meanwhile, ACH opens two new components facilities in economically disadvantaged area devastated by the 2008 recession: Detroit Manufacturing Systems (DMS) in the vacated Gateway Industrial Center in Southwest Detroit creates 500 UAW jobs; Detroit Thermal Systems (DTS) in Romulus Michigan creates an additional 350 UAW jobs.

Over the course of nine years, by 2013, Ford manages to improve its automotive parts cost structure by more than $750 million per year from 2005 levels. ACH parts are shipped to Ford without interruption, incoming parts achieve dramatically improved quality levels, and thousands of employees return to Ford—protecting their job security. Any employee wanting to retire or quit is offered a buyout packages that are the same as others in the UAW-Ford system (discussed in chapter 3).

✳ ✳ ✳

In times of crisis, it is easy for unions and management to resort to accusations and threats. Ford and the UAW instead decided to work toward understanding each other's interests and find a collaborative solution that achieves each party's objectives under some of the most adverse financial circumstances imaginable—literally, the brink of bankruptcy. All parties were winners: Ford, the UAW and its members, and the communities where plants are located.

General Motors took a very different path. Delphi was eventually purchased by a group of investors that included Cerberus Capital Management, Appaloosa Management LP, Harbinger Capital Partners, Merrill Lynch, and UBS Securities. The fully accounted cost GM incurred to resolve the Delphi bankruptcy amounted to more than $1 billion dollars, and GM had to reintegrate four Delphi plants. By 2009, the burden of the Delphi bankruptcy became one of the many straws that broke the back of America's largest automaker and forced GM itself to file bankruptcy. While Delphi has since returned from bankruptcy and improved its profitability as a business, the transaction costs were considerable.

The ACH negotiation is pivotal in illustrating the use of an integrative, negotiated approach to the management of a portion of the operations found to be outside the core business and uncompetitive. The workforce had options that took into account their various interests, and the plants were either reintegrated into Ford, consolidated with other components facilities, or sold to companies that maintained them with UAW representation for the workers. While wages in these facilities are lower than in Ford assembly plants, they are consistent with wages in comparable union-represented supply plants. Bankruptcy would have put the jobs, pensions, and other benefits of every worker at risk.

Navigating this process involved transparency with operating data, high levels of collaborative engagement between the UAW and Ford, alignment across the management structure (purchasing, engineering, operations, labor relations, finance, etc.), and a shared resolve to find an appropriate path forward—a resolve that would be needed across the entire enterprise in the 2007 negotiation.

National Negotiation—Quality, 2003

Ford's overall quality numbers in 2001 are lower than nearly all its major competitors. In advance of the 2003 auto negotiation, both the UAW and Ford begin to grapple with the challenge of improving these numbers, and by the time the collective bargaining quality subcommittee is formed, there is some evidence of results. This negotiation becomes pivotal to providing an opportunity to codify the gains and extend the efforts. It will require, though, a fundamental change in the way both parties address product quality. The leaders of the collective bargaining quality subcommittee, which is established for the six months of national negotiations, are drawn from the UAW-Ford National Quality Committee (NQC)—a standing joint forum first established in 1982.

Dean Blythe, Ford chair of the NQC, recalls:

If I look at the early efforts of the National Joint Quality programs, it was more along the lines of awareness—quality is important and here is where we stand relative to the competition. There were lots of people walking around with the view that Ford was world class, but that was not the case.

The UAW-Ford National Quality Committee developed communication programs to raise awareness and a series of training programs in error proofing, preventing recurrence, and so forth. The training was generic and good, but it was taught to people on a somewhat random basis and was not job specific. This all happened during the late 1980s through the 1990s; then there was a pause.

At this point, in 2003, we were pondering where we go from here, that's when Dan Brooks showed up.

The pause results from leadership priorities within both Ford and the UAW. On the Ford side, CEO Jacques Nasser in the late 1990s shifts the company's focus to acquiring brands (Land Rover and Volvo) and "business adjacencies" to grow the company. Under President Steve Yokich from 1994 to 2002, the UAW's orientation is traditional labor-management relations. Work on the Ford Production System and other elements of a transformation continue during this period, but it not one of the union's strategic priorities.

By 2003, however, Jim Padilla is Ford's president and chief operating officer, and Gerald Bantom serves as the UAW vice president responsible for Ford. Bantom asks Dan Brooks to take the skill sets he learned beginning in the 1990s in various lean initiatives and apply them to Quality. Brooks takes over as UAW co-chair of the NQC in December 2002 and immediately has everything removed everything from the NQC office.

"I clearly understood the objective Gerald had given me," he recalls. "Ford was last in quality, and for our own survival we had to make sure we were doing everything in our power to improve. I wanted to start with a clean slate."

In their first meeting, Blythe assures Brooks that they will work as a team to achieve a shared vision on quality, but he does not offer a specific plan for the joint quality program. Brooks already has a good understanding of Ford's business model, and asks that they meet with Adrian Vido—director of Quality for Vehicle Operations—so they can learn the corporate business plan for Quality.

In the meeting, Vido reviews the plan. Then Brooks proposes that the NQC assist in making the business plan successful, using existing contractual language. "We knew we needed to standardize our approach and document what we were doing in a way the company and union leadership could support," says Vido. "Quality had to become a 'value add' to the company and not just an inspection activity that was working outside the business plan."

During the first part of 2003, Brooks, Blythe, and Vido together visit quite a few facilities to learn the elements of the Quality Operating System and observe how it is being implemented. Brooks and Blythe make similar trips with Vido's counterparts in Powertrain, Visteon, and Ford Customer Parts and Service Division. They observe that while quality is a central element of the Ford Production System, it is not fully integrated into FPS, and that because of this certain aspects of how Quality is managed are not well known at the enterprise level.

As the year progresses, and as is traditionally the case in a bargaining year, the focus shifts to preparing for the national negotiation. Blythe and Brooks see the upcoming negotiation as an opportunity to make a difference.

In preparation for negotiation, the company requests a two-day training session on interest-based bargaining facilitated by Joel Cutcher-Gershenfeld. It is designed as joint training, and Marty Mulloy approaches Gerald Bantom with an invitation for the UAW to participate—something that has not ever happened in the auto industry. The UAW declines the offer, but indicates no opposition to the company utilizing training that involves more of a problem-solving approach to bargaining. Deane Blythe attends the training and shares the training materials and his lessons from the training with Brooks, who knows of Cutcher-Gershenfeld's work on FTPM chartering (discussed in chapter 7) and on other Ford issues. Brooks likes the approach and brings the idea to Joe Gafa, his assistant director, who indicates it would be a good idea for the UAW collective bargaining subcommittee on Quality to try the interest-based bargaining approach.

No formal training takes place, but Brooks shares the principles with his team. Each session focuses on a given issue, for which the interests of both parties are explored and options are identified.

"There was a timetable," recalls Blythe, "and the question was how to use the time effectively to talk about the issues—so that everyone understood the issues and the priorities—not just the final package and the way things would be implemented. We had almost an issue per meeting so that when we got to September everyone understood where we were. There were no surprises and we were the first committee to settle."

Despite consistent progress, Brooks finds himself frustrated with the way the company side hangs on to old positions and only has one person speaking for their side. Brooks recalls, "I guess I shouldn't have been surprised by the fact that there was still the traditional habits at play. Clearly, not everyone's ideas were allowed to be expressed, which was frustrating. In fact, some of these habits remained at play even during the 2007 negotiation, where all subcommittees used the IBB [Interest-Based Bargaining] approach, and it really didn't change until the advent of the Business Plan Reviews."

The end result of this process is an agreement on a standardized approach to Quality across all Ford divisions, with adherence to process as a key element. This includes what is termed "hourly free-effort" of Quality Operating System Coordinators (QOSCs) to be devoted specifically to quality. Their role is formalized, with responsibility to teach, mentor, and enforce the QOS. The parties agree to a targeted-training method to make certain the right people get the right training at the right time. Chartering of quality forums (discussed in chapter 7) is embraced as a way to make certain everyone knows their roles and responsibilities.

Following the preliminary agreement within the subcommittee, calibration is needed with the main table. When Deane Blythe returns from those meetings, however, the UAW is shocked by what it thought would be the final language of an agreement.

"I looked at the package and nothing of what we agreed to was on the paper," remembers Brooks. "I looked to my left, then to my right, stood up, and took my team from the room. Needless to say, we were extremely upset. When I got to my desk, the phone was ringing. It was Blythe, who asked what the problem was. I told him that the package submitted was not what we agreed to. He then told me, 'Dan, you know I have to do the obligatory three-pass.' It now seems funny but at the time it sure wasn't."

As Blythe explains, "You pass paper on Monday and plan to bring in subcommittees by Friday. The exchanges of paper were part of the established way of doing this. It was part of the tradition that remained at that time. We knew way back early what the final package would look like."

Having a traditional "three-pass"—a power-related approach—occur after the intensive interest-based problem solving violates the trust and openness that has been established. At the same time, the three-pass is a longstanding norm and not adhering to it would violate expectations of people at the main table who are not part of the problem-solving process. As we will see in the pivotal event (later in this chapter) on "bargaining over how to bargain," it is essential to discuss the bargaining process in advance to avoid such missteps.

The UAW and Ford agree to historic language and initiatives—an agreement that connects the joint Quality and Employee Involvement programs. It includes the following language:[4]

The long-term success of the Company, and the job satisfaction and job security that can result from "best-in-class" quality frequently require an integrated relationship between UAW-Ford Employee Involvement and the "Best-In- Class" Quality Program, as well as coordination with the other joint programs, especially on a local level. Achieving total quality excellence in every aspect of our manufacturing, assembly and parts distribution operations is possible only when all workers are involved fully in the effort.

The Union and the Company are committed to providing a work environment which allows each worker to contribute fully to the quality of Ford products and services. In this regard, it frequently will serve our broad interests if the personnel assigned to the UAW-Ford Employee Involvement and "Best-In-Class" Quality Program efforts are used on complementary special projects. This would include assisting in local training and other initiatives that benefit the workplace. When relevant, and as approved by the Joint Governing Body, combined national conferences and training would be held. Similarly, these activities may be conducted on a divisional or operations basis as determined by the parties.

The parties also agree to conduct a study that bridges the innovations between Powertrain and Vehicle Operations around the Quality Operating System support, stating, in part:

Following the effective date of this agreement, the Vehicle Operations Quality Office, in conjunction with the UAW-Ford National Quality Committee, will conduct a detailed study to determine the potential application of the Powertrain Operations Quality Operating System Support Process Model to Vehicle Operations facilities covered by this agreement.

The review will include an analysis of the existing Vehicle Operations employee roles and responsibilities around the Quality Operating System, determine the degree of correlation to the PTO QOS Model, and develop recommendations for more effective utilization of current personnel to enforce the QOS Process.

***

As we discuss more fully in the presentation of the Quality Operating System (QOS) in chapter 8, the shift from quality being an "add-on" joint program to an integrated commitment centered on the business plan for quality was a pivotal move. It set the stage for the full-on blitz in the following years to attain "Best-In-Class" Quality, achieved in 2010. The use of an interest-based approach on this issue enables the innovation, but it is complicated since the balance of the bargaining still takes place in traditional ways.

Action America, 2005

Since Ford's 1941 recognition of the UAW, meetings between UAW leaders and senior Ford management had generally been reserved for formal occasions. Ford's CEO, CFO, and president would be present to kick off the national negotiation and for photo opportunities when a contract settlement was reached. They would join with UAW leaders at other ceremonial events. The lack of direct contact wasn't about animosity between the company and the UAW at the highest levels; it just reflected a common practice among many companies to minimize the exposure of senior and operating management to organized labor representatives. Labor relations professionals either would see senior leaders' time as too important to be devoted to meetings with union leaders, or that such meetings might unintentionally lead to suboptimal decisions. In these cases, labor relations managers are essentially protecting the union relationship as their turf.

By the mid-2000s, though, it is clear that the challenges Ford faces from international competition require new strategies for joint dialogue and action at the highest levels—not just union dialogue with the labor relations managers. The decision by senior Ford management and UAW leadership in 2005 to establish a monthly meeting titled "Action America" to exchange information and discuss issues of mutual interest formalizes an interest-based approach to relationships that proves pivotal for both parties. While negotiated change is usually centered at the collective bargaining level or at the workplace level, Action America is a formalization of negotiated change at the strategic level.

What is important about the forum is the high level of the officials involved, frequency of the meetings, and candor and transparency of the tone. Beyond that, the overarching orientation transcends the UAW and Ford: the parties decide to call the meeting "Action America" because the success of Ford's manufacturing operations in the United States benefits not only the UAW and Ford, but also the country. Both see the future of manufacturing and middle-class jobs in the country as dependent on achieving world-class quality and cost levels, and these issues, along with broader community concerns, are the focus of the forum.

The initial Action America meeting takes place on September 9, 2005. In attendance for Ford are Mark Fields, president of the Americas; Joe Hinrichs, vice president for Manufacturing; Marty Mulloy, vice president for Labor Affairs and Joe Haymon, group vice president for Human Resources. UAW leaders at the meeting include Ron Gettelfinger, the International president, and Bob King, then vice president for the National Ford Department.

Fields recalls:

I remember Marty saying we needed to amp up the relationship. We decided to meet on a monthly basis. I wanted to establish a relationship with Bob King. We knew we needed to look at the business environment and both know where we stand on a competitive basis. If you are not sharing with your partners, they will only see things as our asking for more.

To establish the relationship and build trust, we would share with the union the same briefings we would give to the board. There were even times that we would share the slides before the board saw

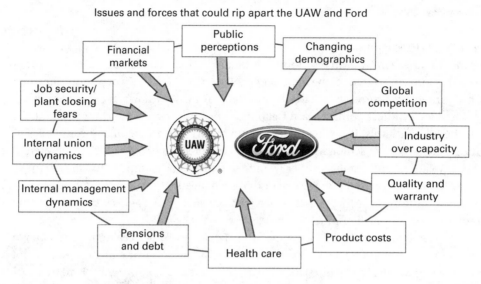

Figure 6.1
Motivation for Action America.
Source: Ford Motor Company and WorkMatters, LLC

them. As a result, when we came to negotiations, we were spending more time on the problem solving and less debating the data. It was also a chance for the union to bring its issues directly to the line managers and not just go through labor relations.

Bob King participates in Action America first as the UAW vice president responsible for the Ford relationship and later as UAW president. Reflecting on the meetings, he recalls,

Action America had been key during a time of rapid change. It started in 2005. The monthly meetings were critical. It kept Ron Gettelfinger connected to what was happening at Ford. The other two companies [General Motors and Chrysler] haven't done that. We would see the quarterly earnings reports and the board presentations. We found that if you give everyone the same facts and give them time to absorb the information, they will come to similar conclusions.

In launching the Action America process, the image in figure 6.1 is used as part of the motivation for working together in new ways.

The monthly Action America meetings follow the same agenda they did at their inception. The typical agenda includes the following:

1. **Business Update**: The president of the Americas covers the "state of the business," safety performance, financial metrics, market share, cost performance, and quality issues in detail.
2. **Operational Issues**: Topics covered include the status of plant launches, specific plant productivity and/or quality challenges, competitiveness of operations, relationship challenges, in selected plants, and so forth.

3. **Government Affairs**: Issues of mutual interest are discussed and subject matter experts from the UAW and Ford are invited to provide insights.

4. **Union Issues:** The president of the UAW present issues of national scope while the vice president, National Ford Department covers specific UAW-Ford labor issues (manpower planning, contract interpretation, safety initiatives, quality issues, etc.).

5. **Community Initiatives:** Numerous Joint UAW-Ford initiatives that reach out to the community are discussed and supported (e.g., assisting Detroit schools, Make-a-Wish Foundation, ramp building in homes for the disabled, United Way, March of Dimes).

Marty Mulloy notes a maturing over time in these meetings that adds to their value for both Ford and the UAW:

The quality of the dialogue in the Action America meetings improved over the years. As the meeting participants became more comfortable, dialogue became more collaborative and the parties became more appreciative of one another's perspectives. Rather than state a position and wait for a response (in the early days it would be more accurate to say "wait for the bomb to go off"), both parties began explaining their interests and patiently waited for a response before "selling their solution." It was not uncommon for the parties to walk away with a better solution than what they walked into the meeting attempting to achieve.

✳✳✳

The value of the Action America meeting led the company to expand its engagement strategy with the UAW. From Bill Ford, executive chairman of the board, and CEO Alan Mulally all the way down to the labor-management relationship in each of the plants, the company recognized the value of transparency in sharing information and establishing a cadence of meetings. Moreover, value was placed on the importance of listening and building a relationship based on trust. Indeed, negotiation at this level is primarily around relationships and trust. The UAW reciprocated with its appreciation for the engagement, placing particular value on the relationships built with line managers and executives.

As Mulloy concluded, "When times get tough it is our natural instinct to push our demands even harder. What Ford and the UAW learned is that when times get tough we need to understand one another even more. The odds for success are far greater working together than battling one another. Action America established a foundation of relationships on which we could draw in tough times."

Bargaining Over How to Bargain, 2006

At a time of accelerated change in markets, technology, and society, the bargaining process can itself become a subject of negotiation. If the process being used is not well matched to the issues, change is needed. Any change in "the rules of the game," though, can be challenging. All parties have to agree that the risk of continuing with the current process may be greater than entertaining discussion about changes in the process—a form of negotiation known as "bargaining over how to bargain."[5]

In 2006, the UAW and Ford formally begin bargaining over how to bargain, something that has never been done on a formal basis. To grasp the significance, it is important to understand the highly structured and scripted nature of national auto negotiations.

Some of the planning for the national auto negotiations begins on both sides as soon as the previous negotiations conclude—with unresolved issues noted, implementation planning matrices developed, and internal long-range strategy dialogue begun. Within the UAW, these preparations are crystalized almost a year before the opening of negotiations with a National Collective Bargaining Convention, during which priorities identified from among the members and local unions are formalized as bargaining demands. Within Ford and the other auto companies, working groups are established more than a year in advance to analyze issues that will likely be on the table during negotiations. The actual bargaining process involves more than 250 people serving on 20 to 25 subcommittees, as well as at a main table where the final economic package is negotiated and non-economic issues resolved in the subcommittees are formally reviewed and approved.

In fall 2006, the leadership in both the UAW and Ford are concerned that the deteriorating economic environment may require rethinking the bargaining process. Meeting at a Catholic retreat and seminary outside Detroit, four representatives from the company (led by Vice President for Labor Affairs Marty Mulloy) and five from the union (led by Bob King, the vice president for the UAW's Ford Department) invite Joel Cutcher-Gershenfeld to discuss the principles of strategic negotiation and interest-based bargaining. Both King and Mulloy state at the outset that the company and the union are facing dramatic challenges likely to require both sides to bargain in new ways.

Bill Dirksen, then Ford's U.S. Labor Affairs executive director, comments later on the challenges. "This much was clear," he says. "If we went through the same old processes that we used in the past, it was not going to yield us a different outcome.... We talked about the definition of insanity being doing the same thing over and over again and yet expecting different results. Well, we didn't want to fall into that trap."[6]

In the following months, labor and management develop a plan to conduct a series of offsite joint training sessions with lead negotiators from both sides. Staff members from the UAW and Ford are assigned to design the session. Initially, the members set forth a very cautious design that limits experiments with the bargaining process to selected subcommittees. The two chief negotiators reject this. The entire bargaining process, they insist, has to be "on the table" as the parties bargain over how to bargain.

The plan involves two two-day sessions, both at a conference facility in northern Ohio, with Cutcher-Gershenfeld as the session facilitator. The first session involves about 100 people, including the co-chairs of the 24 subcommittees to be established for this negotiation, the main table bargaining teams, and other key local leadership. The second session includes many more key local managers and union leaders.

At the first session, Mulloy signals an important shift within management. "Traditionally," he explains, "labor affairs has led negotiations and then shared the results with manufacturing. That has changed; manufacturing will be deeply engaged."

Joe Hinrichs, then Ford vice president of North American Manufacturing, also speaks at the first joint session. "The UAW National Ford Department isn't much good without Ford," he says, "and Ford isn't much good without the UAW and the workforce. Let's recognize that from the get go."

Hinrichs continues, "People have been frustrated about the bargaining process in the past. We have people's time and we need to have a process that respects and utilizes their time. We have difficult issues to get through and different perspectives to get through on these issues—to find solutions that work for everyone."

The visible leadership of manufacturing executives, not just labor relations staff, is a crucial feature at this session and throughout the 2007 negotiation. Hinrichs and other manufacturing leaders bring additional credibility and problem-solving capability to discussions on the overall economic challenges facing the company and on specific business matters such as sourcing work or the Quality Operating System. Additionally, they bring a highly pragmatic view, matching the bargaining process and the efforts of the participants to the issues that must be resolved.

At the session, the hopes of the entire assembled group for the 2007 bargaining process are expressed, including:

• Open minds, open communication, and open discussions.
• Both parties make it clear what they need and what their expectations are at the beginning of the negotiation.
• Negotiate an agreement that will position the company to compete while maintaining the standard of living of the union members.
• Successfully ratify a fair agreement that includes reinvestment in North America.
• The people who negotiate the agreements are around to help implement the agreements.
• Serve as an example of what companies and unions can do together.

The parties also identify the fears they have going in to the bargaining process. These include:

• The process will not be sufficient to address the issues.
• Anger shuts down the process.
• Ford won't get up off the core/noncore bull crap [referencing Visteon, discussed earlier in this chapter].
• Special or individual interests dominate instead of the overall interests of both parties.
• We don't get this thing right.
• We negotiate a destructive agreement for one or the other side.

- Failure to implement.
- Day-to-day operational issues will sidetrack us.
- There are people who are not in the room who will not support the process.
- Bankruptcy.

By the end of the first session, the parties develop a standardized, structured seven-step process to be followed by each of the 24 subcommittees. The actual give and take of negotiation doesn't begin until Step 5. The steps are as follows:

1. *Opening and Shared Vision:* Each side will make opening statements on an issue (including the formal presentation of UAW demands as per the UAW Constitution) that are designed to be constructive, and both will engage in a joint brainstorming process to identify those aspects of the issue on which there is a shared vision of success.

2. *Joint Data Collection:* Where appropriate, both sides are empowered to conduct joint data collection on the issue.

3. *Analyze Underlying Interests:* Both sides will engage in the joint identification of underlying interests that each has with respect to the issue—collected in separate lists of union interests and management interest—facilitated by the co-chairs or by internal facilitators available on request.

4. *Generate Options:* Both sides will engage in full brainstorming of options on each issue, which includes the opening demands from the UAW as well as additional options based on the interests identified and the data collected—again with facilitation available on request.

5. *Negotiate Agreements:* Having discussed the elements of a shared vision, data, interests, and options, the parties will then engage in the bargaining toward agreement on each issue.

6. *Main Table Calibration:* While the major economic issues are reserved for the main table, most of the rest of the bargaining is distributed over subcommittees that will periodically update the main table on their efforts.

7. *Anticipate Implementation:* When agreements are reached on issues, the parties will also set in place clear action plans for implementation, specifying the who, what, when, where, why, and how needed to implement the agreement.

In this process, hard bargaining is still anticipated on many issues, but not until step 5, where it can be informed by the dialogue on the elements of a shared vision, any joint data collection that has taken place, the analysis of underlying interests, and brainstorming on options.

One dilemma the parties face is how to present formal demands from the UAW Collective Bargaining Convention without immediately triggering a counter demand from the company and then ending up in a traditional, positional bargaining process. The UAW Collective Bargaining Convention, which had taken place in the summer of 2006 and where the platform for negotiations with Ford, Chrysler, and GM had been established, set an overriding theme tied to the discontent of the workforce ("promises made, promises broken" was the refrain coming out of the convention). Taking this into account, it is decided by participants in the bargaining over how to bargain session that the UAW will present its opening demands consistent with the mandate from the convention but that there will be no counter demands from the company until after the overall vision, the underlying interests, and relevant data have been fully explored. Similarly, the union will not respond with counter demands to opening issues raised by the company until after the joint visioning, analysis of interests, and joint data collection.

For the second session, training is developed around the skills associated with each step in the process. Bridgette Morehouse, one of the lead Ford managers responsible for the joint training sessions, describes the process of bargaining over how to bargain this way:

We had 300 negotiators and 24 subcommittees.... We had several offsites with the joint subcommittee leadership—both sides together in the room. It's the first time we'd done this in history. Typically, each side would train their teams separately and come together at the negotiating table. Instead, we gave the teams specific tools to address the negotiations from the interest-based perspective....

We actually made big posters that we put in all the conference rooms around world headquarters when we were doing the negotiating to remind the teams the process steps that we trained them in.... And they really focused on how to lay out what are the issues that each side had, to discuss those, to figure out ways to collect data that they needed jointly,... generate options together, and periodically review progress with the main table.

An additional process decision is to use internal facilitators. Morehouse explains:

We also trained several internal UAW and Ford facilitators who were seen as neutral to the bargaining approach.... Within the 24 subcommittees, we had a lot of people who were very experienced in the traditional way of bargaining and in the traditional approach. So when you're getting into a stressful discussion or getting into some new ground, it's easy for people to go back to their way of doing things historically.... We had the facilitators who were trained, who could come in and kind of recalibrate the subcommittees if needed.

While the agreement is to follow a comprehensive process, the parties reserve the right to revert to traditional negotiations.

"There was so much anger in the system," recalls Bob King. "After a lot of internal discussion with our local union leadership and our staff, we decided to try an interest-based approach. We were always clear on both sides. We were going to try this and, if it worked, great. If it didn't work, then we'd fall back on a traditional approach."

***

As we will see in the next pivotal event presenting the 2007 negotiation, the parties did not have to revert back to the traditional approach and the problem-solving process was instrumental to breakthrough outcomes. The bargaining over how to bargain was an unprecedented break from the traditional process for the entire negotiation and signaled a key principle going forward—matching the bargaining process to the issues being negotiated.

National Negotiation—VEBA, Entry Wage, 2007

The 2007 national negotiation is pivotal: the future of the enterprise is at stake. Not only is an agreement reached that sets the stage for Ford's survival and resurgence following the Great Recession, but the transformation of both Ford and UAW is extended.

In advance of the 2007 negotiation, both the bargaining in 2006 of the plant-by-plant Competitive Operating Agreements (discussed in chapter 2) and the bargaining over how to bargain (discussed earlier in this chapter) signal that this is going to be a unique and challenging negotiation. The negotiation features echoes of the 1982 negotiation, when the Mutual Growth Program was forged in the face of dramatic business losses and massive layoffs (discussed in chapter 1).

Lead negotiators at General Motors do not want a repeat of their collapsed lead in the 1982, which gave Ford a competitive advantage. The actual decision as to which employer will be the target is in the hands of the UAW, and the decision will not be made until the end of August. This reverses the historical pattern, in which a wage increase negotiated at the strongest employer is imposed on the rest of the industry. Now, it is a case of the union seeking the minimum concessions from the most vulnerable employer. At the time, the "Big Three" are all suffering declining market share and Chrysler's ownership by outside equity capital is an unknown variable. In important ways, the different circumstances in each company are placing the future of pattern bargaining in the industry "on the table" in this negotiation.

Within the UAW-Ford relationship, each party sounds highly contrasting themes. Bob King is the UAW vice president responsible for Ford, and the union's chief negotiator; he represents the UAW's theme "promises made; promises broken."[7] A number of factors are responsible, including the fact that some of the most productive plants, where the union has actively partnered with management to implement new work systems, are slated for closure. These include Ford plants in Atlanta, Georgia; Batavia, Ohio; Norfolk, Virginia; and Wixom, Michigan. Further, the company has invested billions in cash and resourcs over the past decade to acquire and manage four European brands (Aston Martin, Jaguar, Land Rover, and Volvo) that a majority equity interest in Mazda. Union members feel these acquisitions represent investments diverted from U.S. operations.

At the same time, Ford sounds a theme of economic crisis. "The company was facing the very real possibility of bankruptcy," says Ford's chief negotiator, Marty Mulloy, vice president responsible for global labor affairs. The company argues that it needs the union to work with it to prevent a downward spiral.

The union has to determine how much of this is traditional pre-bargaining rhetoric and how much is about a genuine crisis for the company and the industry. "I was elected at the 2006 UAW convention," recalls Bob King. "I had the independent parts suppliers and organizing. I was given the new assignment of Ford. When I came in, Ford immediately started talking to me about their difficult financial situation. Having been in a lot of negotiations, I was immediately skeptical, thinking about negotiations a year from now, this is all preparing me for what they want to accomplish in negotiations."

Wendy Fields-Jacobs, the UAW's special assistant to the vice president and international representative, recalls the challenges facing the UAW going into the negotiation,

From our perspective, we had to crystallize the key interests of our members. This negotiation was about protecting retiree benefits, ensuring jobs and investment, and securing a greater voice in the business. We believed that our jobs are too important to be left to management alone. We were also aware that what we did would impact communities and others as well. At the end of the day, this had to be an agreement that could be ratified and implemented on the ground.

Bill Dirksen, then Ford's executive director for U.S. labor affairs, outlines the challenges facing management.

You really can't understand the choices we made unless you understand the challenges that the union and the company [were] facing.... From a business standpoint, we needed to fundamentally change our business model, and that included our cost model. Our cost and our structure was [based on a] 25 percent share of the [market], and we [were] at a 16- or 15-percent share. So, we had to fundamentally and dramatically change our business model. And at the same time, UAW was also under siege. Among other things, they wanted to secure their future and the future of their members through investment in the United States. So, you can kind of look at these things and say, well, they were pulling in opposite directions. Well, our challenge was to make those things pull in the same direction.

Compounding the substantive challenge, the parties face process challenges. Chuck Browning, in his role in the UAW's Ford Department, explains that they run counter to the typical position in which the union found itself.

Traditionally the UAW often had to be in a reactive mode. The company would do certain things and we'd react to them. That worked very well for a long time....

The majority of the time is not trying to understand each other's position; it's trying to convince the other group that you're right in how you want to resolve it. At times, this approach creates idle time. When you're not discussing the problem, you start discussing the person across the table from you, and things get personal, and things get antagonistic. And a lot of time is wasted too. But, again, it's a process through the years, you know.

Sometimes there's clarification—we want to clarify what we're asking you to do, but we really don't want to have a lot of discussion. This goes on, and eventually you go through this clarification and arguing. Then, as you get close to the deadline, that's kind of the driver to get discussions going. You end up doing a lot of work in a short amount of time because the urgency of avoiding a strike is what sets the pace in the traditional contract. You end up with a lot of win–lose type scenarios. "We got what we want at the expense of you," and vice versa.

Thus, going into the negotiation, powerful forces are at work with the potential to pull the parties apart, including shrinking market share, perceived broken promises, and an ingrained habit of traditional, adversarial bargaining styles—the same forces that motivated Action America (as illustrated in figure 6.1). But other forces have the potential to enable the parties to work together, including a history of joint programs and a shared need for survival—the foundation of pivotal events on which the negotiation rested.

Despite the overall market shift away from trucks, which has been Ford's most profitable and successful market segment, and Ford's publicly visible decline in market share, the company knows that the UAW will need a detailed understanding of the state of the business before entering the 2007 negotiation. Beginning in early 2006, Ford's top executives decide to put all the cards on the table, approaching the negotiation with an unprecedented level of transparency (as presented in chapter 2).

Ford's chief negotiator Mulloy explains:

We'd lost $12 billion the year before—$12 billion! Talk about the loss of market share! We had been consistently a 25-percent share company from the early 1980s all the way into about 1997, when we started really losing share. . . . We made 4.3 million vehicles in about 2000 and we're making 2.5 million vehicles now. . . . So, you can imagine what happens to your whole infrastructure of your plants. You have to make reductions. . . . We had nearly 100,000 hourly employees going into negotiations, but the market share really only required about 50,000 employees, somewhere in that range. We were in deep, deep trouble.

I give Bob [King] a lot of credit. When Bob came, he brought an energy level to his position and to the engagement of what the challenges are facing Ford Motor Company. I recall a meeting with Bill Ford [executive chair of the board of directors] and he said that effectively the future of Ford Motor Company as an institution hinged on the outcome of these negotiations. So, as a senior management team we had to figure out our game plan.

The first thing we decided on is utter transparency and information sharing with the UAW. As bad as it is and as difficult as it is, we decided to share the information and have the union understand the business financials just as well as we do. That started at Bob's level and went all the way through to the plants. We told plant management, "Have discussions with your local chairman, bargaining committee, so you will all understand the challenges to the company going forward."

As part of this process, the union is invited to bring in its own financial analysts to examine the company's finances and operations. UAW chief negotiator King explains:

We had an outstanding individual, Eric Perkins, who had spent a number of years on Wall Street, and who went in and did a deep dive into Ford's financial and business situation. To Ford's credit, they really opened things up.

Eric was pretty harsh on Ford in a lot of the interviews and the meetings he did. At first I think they didn't like him very much, but they began to find out that this guy really knew the business, and the questions he was asking could help them in some of their management strategies. It set a different tone for us.

Even the company's cycle plan for new products, the most secret of business information, is shared with the union—for the first time.

The results of the analysis are sobering. As Eric Perkins recalls, "People thought the company was saying it was worse than it was. For a long time Ford had been the most profitable of the big three—up to 2001. By this time, GM was buying components for less and was eroding market share in many areas. The engines had fallen behind. You can't close a plant and solve a problem like this. Ford was behind on fuel economy and performance. I told the UAW it was worse than they said." A series of briefings are then held for regional and local union leaders, with Perkins attending and taking questions from the floor. Reflecting on the process, King says, "No company has been as open as Ford has been and that makes a substantial difference."

"There may not be a company in the world that would share the kind of information that we shared with the UAW in terms of our finances, our product plans, and access to our senior leaders," Mulloy says. "At the end of the day, it came down to the fact that we trusted these guys—we are really in it together."

The willingness of both sides to operate with a standardized process across all subcommittees and the main table reflects their joint experience with standardized, structured processes in quality, safety, and other aspects of business operations. At the same time, both sides have some concerns given the substantial changes in the process. So, to build capability with the new process and demonstrate its effectiveness, UAW and Ford agree to have four of the subcommittees—safety, quality, sourcing, and grievances/discipline—begin bargaining a month before the official opening of negotiation—using the new process. This, says Bill Dirksen, "sounds like a small thing, but actually it was very important."

It was unprecedented starting committees before the opening day, but we did it to get a start on interest-based bargaining. It was a way to put the training into practice on a small scale so that the leadership would stay close to it and make sure it stayed on the rails.

We also picked committees that we felt would be able to put what they learned into practice and kind of set the right tone.

Because the four initial subcommittees operate constructively, the parties bring the full process forward for the entire national negotiation. Every meeting room has a poster on the wall with the agreed-upon steps in the bargaining over how to bargain process (see figure 6.2).

When bargaining officially opens on July 23, 2007, UAW president Ron Gettelfinger frames the negotiation as important not only for the UAW, but for good jobs in America. "Last time around," he says, "we talked about bargaining for families. This time around we are talking about bargaining for the country as a whole....This is not just about us; these negotiations are about everybody."

Not all the bargaining is between labor and management across the table. An old adage in industrial relations says that it takes three agreements to get one—an agreement *within* labor, an agreement *within* management, and an agreement *between* labor and management. This intraorganizational or internal bargaining[8] shifts significantly on the management side during the negotiation. As Ford's Marty Mulloy comments:

There's as much negotiating going on at the management table among senior management as there is within the union. An absolute key is to be aligned with your CEO. That is always the case, but, in the

Start Up: Confirm sub-committee
membership, meeting logistics and
establish simplified Charter

Scope: Use Charter to identify issues to be
addressed by the sub-committee – what
is and is not "in scope"

Standardized process:
1. Shared vision for success
2. Joint data collection
3. Analysis of underlying interests
4. Brainstorming of options
5. Identifying potential language/elements
   of agreements (as appropriate)
6. Anticipate implementation, including
   recommended communication and training

Calibration: Schedule periodic main table reports

Figure 6.2
UAW-Ford Subcommittee Bargaining Process. *Source:* Ford Motor Company and WorkMatters, LLC.

past, labor affairs acted in practice like it's our business, let us do it, and we'll tell you what the outcome is.

[In 2007], we made a philosophical and a strategic decision that we were going to break from that way of doing business. We started meetings very early with our [chief financial officer]....The VP in charge of manufacturing operations, Joe Hinrichs, was absolutely key to the successful negotiations. We viewed it as a team sport. We had to make sure our product development people were on board. We had to make sure our purchasing people were on board. So, when we're sitting across the table with the UAW, we had a play that we could execute.

The expanded role of line managers in the negotiation is seen in the local talks on the competitive operating agreements, where plant managers and the number-2 line manager (referred to in Ford at the time as the Lean Manufacturing Manager) play key roles. The process is helped by the fact that all the North American plant HR managers and Lean Manufacturing Managers had been meeting on a quarterly basis since 2002 as part of the accelerated implementation of "lean" and "Six Sigma" practices for quality and effective operations and team-based work systems in production operations—a process co-led by senior line manufacturing executives and top HR executives (discussed in chapter 4). Thus, there has already been substantial integration between manufacturing and staff leading up to the negotiation.

Within the UAW at the national level, the same internal functions do not need to be bridged in the same way, but there is tension because the paid staff of the union has been down-sized as dues-paying members have been lost.

The 24 national subcommittees cover a broad range of topics, including attendance, benefits, health and safety, health care, job security, overall economics, quality, pensions, skilled trades, sourcing, supplementary unemployment, training, and other topics. Although many of these issues involve both common and conflicting interests, the parties hold to the collaborative process, jointly collecting data, asking questions, and exploring options. In some cases, issues are highly distributive (with many conflicting interests) and more intensive process support is needed. For example, the subcommittee on sourcing (outsourcing and insourcing of work) reaches a point where Bill Dirksen and Wendy Fields-Jacobs meet separately with the co-chairs to keep the process on track. In other cases, facilitation assistance is called in. However, some subcommittees addressing highly contentious issues, such as skilled trades, function much more smoothly than historically has been the case.

Typically, tensions overwhelm the process in at least some of the subcommittees. "None of the groups became stuck or fell apart," recalls Dan Brooks.

Henry Ford III, great-great grandson of Henry Ford, had been working as a schoolteacher after graduating from college and has recently joined Ford in the Labor Affairs staff. He is assigned to work on one of the subcommittees. He comments:

The amount of work that goes into the contract negotiations on both sides is staggering. The amount of data crunching and discussions—the huge number of hours that go into a contract is not appreciated on the outside.

I was impressed on both sides with the level of transparency. It was no secret that the company was in dire straits; the union was also in a difficult situation with the lost membership. Both sides had to take a hard look. One of the reasons we were able to come to a pivotal agreement was that there were no secrets. That was essential in getting everyone to understand the issues.

The work of the UAW-Ford subcommittees and the main table continues through the summer, as do negotiations at GM and Chrysler. During this time, there are preliminary signals sent by the UAW that the lead target employer for the 2007 negotiation will be GM—a decision formally announced at the end of August. In the GM negotiation, important elements of an agreement are coming together by the end of the summer, but a settlement proves elusive. On September 24, 2007, 73,000 UAW workers at GM are called out on strike for two days before the full package is finalized. On October 10, 2007, a five-and-a-half-hour strike takes place at Chrysler before they accept an agreement similar to the one the UAW had reached with GM. The UAW and Ford, by contrast, reach agreement without a work stoppage and with some important modifications in the agreement.

Bill Dirksen reflects on the bargaining process:

Going into the negotiations, we were clear that interest-based bargaining was not a silver bullet that would solve all of our problems. It would not make the issues any easier or the bargaining any smoother. We knew that it was going to be a very difficult bargaining session, and it was. And we didn't want false expectations, but we did believe it would be a key enabler to help us find solutions and solve problems that we wouldn't have solved otherwise—find solutions that we never would have found in the past because we were in our own positional foxholes and not wanting to come out, just protecting our position. We encouraged people to get out of those foxholes and explore together creative solutions to problems that we share. And in many cases that worked for us.

The 2007 UAW-Ford negotiation has challenging issues on the table for labor and manage-ment, including rising labor costs. Ford uses what the company calls a "penny sheet" to cal-culate labor costs. In 2007, says Marty Mulloy, the penny sheet was $72 an hour.

That's all in. That's everything. Wages are about a quarter of that, but you've got benefits, past service costs, and other costs. If we had another carryover agreement, we were looking at $110 an hour by 2011. You just can't invest at $110 on a penny sheet. Instead, the agreement that we reached with the UAW helped save jobs. We were going to close a number of facilities that we ended up being able to keep open. We were going to source products outside of the United States that we decided to keep within the United States. And it was because of the results of the bargaining—the creative problem solving with the UAW—that we were able to make some tradeoffs.

Perhaps the most dramatic change to come out of the negotiation involves the voluntary employee benefits association (VEBA). Both labor and management in this industry and oth-ers have faced significant challenges over legacy pension and health care benefits for retirees. The VEBA involves taking the retiree health benefit costs off the company books and a $13.6 billion financing arrangement (involving cash and equity) in which the union hires the management team to administer these retiree health benefits going forward.

"The VEBA was historic for the Ford Motor Company and in the industry," says Mulloy. "First of all, it placed retirees in a much better position going forward. As well, the VEBA places us in a much more competitive position so that we can invest in product within the United States. In my view, it was win-win."

Wendy Fields-Jacobs echoes this from the UAW's perspective. "Our first goal was protect-ing retirees," she says. "The best way to do this turned out to be through the VEBA....But it was not just finding the right agreement, but also explaining it to all of our members. This is a major departure from what is traditional."

In the 2008 panel presentation following the negotiation, Bob King concludes:

The full transfer doesn't happen until 2010. So, we're in the process now of selecting our trustees, hiring the professionals for benefit management and investment management, and working these issues through the legal system. Then, we will be able to take on full responsibility for the health care of retir-ees. We view it as a major win-win because if these costs had stayed on the company's books, under federal accounting standards, it was a huge detriment to the company staying financially viable. If any company goes into bankruptcy (and in the parts sector we have seen a lot of bankruptcies), retirees are often lucky to get 20 cents on the dollar. With this VEBA set up, if any of the Big Three went into bank-ruptcy, which we are working hard to avoid but is still possible in this economy, then those retirees are protected. They would not be if we did not have a VEBA.

While GM is in the lead in the negotiation and thus helps produce the initial language on the VEBA, many of the incorporated ideas come from what the UAW had learned from the brainstorming over the summer in the UAW-Ford negotiation. Moreover, as we will see, subse-quent modifications in the VEBA in 2009 are first negotiated by the UAW with Ford, building on the foundation of mutual understanding established through the interest-based process.

The negotiations also involve discussions of difficult sourcing decisions—issues around plant closings and new product placements. In a number of cases, the union is able to reverse decisions, including bringing work back from Mexico to the United States. As Dan Brooks notes, "It was clear in the sourcing decisions that the company did understand the union's situation."

"It is a partnership," Joe Hinrichs elaborates. "We knew we needed solutions that would work for everyone. We wanted to have a balanced story to tell. We were waiting to finish the VEBA and I came down to the presentation on the operating agreement. At that point, it was the right time to indicate exactly where we were on the cycle plan—plant by plant. When we were done, Jeff Washington [of the UAW] started a standing ovation."

Dan Brooks adds, "After all the hard work, it was mind blowing. What was presented was beyond the expectation of any of the bargainers—not just the decisions, but the level of detail and the underlying understanding of the business."

The VEBA is immediately highlighted by the media as an important breakthrough, and saving the plants is big news in their respective communities. But the agreements on what the parties term an "entry wage" are at first interpreted by critics and some in the media as a two-tier wage package.

In fact, two-tier wage systems negotiated in the 1980s and 1990s had proven unstable once a majority of the workforce came under the lower wage tier, and thus had fallen out of wide use.[9] In the 2007 auto negotiation, the parties construct an arrangement that involves a lower starting wage for certain new workers, but still provides opportunities to move up into the full wage and benefit package. The result is a continued ability to attract new workers, a lower average wage cost across the workforce, a mechanism to increase union membership, and the preservation of good jobs (even if it takes longer to achieve the full set of wages and benefits).

The entry wage arrangement established by GM (and then adopted by Chrysler) is different in some respects from the one the UAW-Ford subcommittee develops. The GM-UAW and Chrysler-UAW language spells out a fixed formula with the lower wage tied to certain offline positions. The Ford-UAW subcommittee's more flexible arrangement enables both parties to utilize the entry wage better, across a wide range of positions.

Bill Dirksen credits interest-based bargaining for the flexibility of Ford's entry-level agreement. This wage and benefit structure, says Dirksen, "offered a more cost-dependent entry labor rate and an opportunity to go into a higher rate of pay over time." He adds:

We took the agreement that came out of the General Motors-UAW settlement, but we didn't just simply follow the pattern and get on with life. Because we laid a foundation of an interest-based bargaining approach, we improved it in a way that actually was a much better version of that system for Ford Motor Company. This approach allows us to implement it much faster and I think more fairly. For the UAW, it protects some of their key interests, such as seniority rights tied to the jobs. I believe that if we had been taking a traditional approach, we never would have found that solution.

Chuck Browning elaborates:

GM and Chrysler identified specific jobs at lower rates—jobs driving lift trucks to deliver materials to the production line, warehouse work, inspection work, and so on. The problem [as] we saw . . . was that those jobs were performed by the highest seniority people—they were the most desirable jobs. Based on the COA experience, our leadership nationally and locally said that that agreement will create huge problems in the plants. It would have created an environment that was the opposite of what we had done historically in the plants. We said that all those jobs amount to 20 percent of the workforce—so we said keep the structure in place and not identify a job, but pay based on seniority hired in the plant. Chrysler almost voted down the agreement because of the initial language—they went through hell on that.

We also saw this as not conducive to lean operations.

We broke pattern and then they opened agreements and followed suit. The downside is that people are doing the same work at different levels of pay, but this was a huge improvement over what it would have been.

I give credit to Gettelfinger on being open to this. It had to be hard to do. It says he listened to the members and was humble enough to say it was a better solution.

The entry wage represents a break from the pattern bargaining model—even if the issue is the same at Ford as at GM, the UAW-Ford approach draws on the interest-based problem-solving dialogue and is more fully matched to the interests of both parties. Subsequently, both the GM-UAW and the Chrysler-UAW negotiators revisit the issue and make some adjustments for implementation that incorporate ideas that come out of the UAW-Ford negotiations. Given the general reluctance of negotiators to revisit agreements once settled, and the historic forces of pattern bargaining, this adjustment by the other auto negotiators is important evidence that the UAW-Ford process produces more mutual gains.

For the UAW, the entry-wage agreement is part of a larger shift toward deeper influence in business decisions. Says Fields-Jacobs of the UAW:

It was about securing a greater voice in the business, not just having a voice in bargaining, with more transparency and understanding but finding ways so that our members locally—the local president, chairpersons, and others—could have a voice on the business that's ongoing.

We had to ensure their greater understanding of what happens in their four walls, how that impacts on what vehicles are produced in their plants, and what happens going forward. It can't be that they are just walking away from the table after bargaining, but that they have an ongoing voice.

Additional elements of the agreement build on the specific plant-by-plant competitive operating agreements, with agreements on sourcing decisions and product placements. This includes commitments from Ford to build five new flexible body shops in UAW-Ford assembly plants, and to make specific investments in new technology in Stamping and Powertrain Operations. Moreover, certain Ford manufacturing facilities previously identified for closure by the company are able to remain open.

An important additional element of the process established in the "bargaining over how to bargain" phase involves an agreement to anticipate implementation during the negotiations. Ford labor relations manager Jack Halverson explains:

We had a history of broken promises and we knew our plant leadership needed to be key and core in implementing the agreement going forward. So, we all knew early on in the process that implementation was going to be something that needed to be considered. The first joint session that we had in February, the concerns about broken promises came out loud and clear to both sides. In the second joint session, where we had all the company and the union co-chairs of the subcommittees, implementation planning for the 2007 agreement started at that time, before we ever went to negotiations.

One key tool provided to help with implementation involves placing the negotiated agreements into a format called the "Five Ws & How," which specifies the what, why, who, when, where, and how for implementation. By having implementation dialogue during the negotiations, the parties explore various "what-if" scenarios. In the process, additional insights surface that lead to more robust agreements.

Halverson describes that process:

As we were bargaining and exploring potential solutions, we talked about how we would be able to implement these solutions. Sometimes we talked about what we thought might have been a good agreement, but we couldn't come up with a method that would be workable for implementation. And the best agreement in the whole world isn't worth anything if it either doesn't get or can't be implemented....

Coming out of negotiations, there are probably more changes with this agreement than I've seen in any of the agreements in my history with Ford. And there are many, many provisions that need to be implemented.

Implementation is an ongoing process. It requires constant communications. It requires checking and adjusting your plan when you're not getting the results that you're expecting.

A handshake photo (see figure 6.3) is traditional at the end of negotiations, though this one conveys a level of enthusiasm more than a traditional handshake.

✳ ✳ ✳

Reflecting on the process and the results, Chuck Browning of the UAW says, "I hope that, as people look back on what the UAW did at this time, they will conclude that we helped save the domestic automakers here in the United States."

The contract was ratified by more than 80 percent of the UAW-Ford workforce—a sign both of the membership's knowledge of the competitive context and the degree to which the union workers saw the agreement as an acceptable response to the competitive pressures.

National Negotiation—Pattern for Crisis Negotiations, 2009

The 2009 auto industry negotiations involve an unprecedented role for the U.S. government—a product of the Great Recession and the bankruptcy of General Motors and Chrysler. Ford avoids bankruptcy, thereby sparing America's taxpayers from underwriting what some see as management incompetence. This means, though, that Ford does not have the same leverage with the UAW granted to GM and Chrysler by the bailout conditions. By not seeking a government bailout, Ford is at risk of being uncompetitive. Navigating these challenges will be a major test of the relationship between the UAW and Ford.

Figure 6.3
Handshake at the Conclusion of Negotiations. From left to right: Bob King, Ron Gettelfinger, Bill Ford, and Alan Mulally. *Source:* UAW-Ford National Joint Programs.

The story unfolds with Ford's outlook at the beginning of 2008, which is very positive. By the end of the first quarter, Alan Mulally's restructuring plan is well under way. Ford is making substantial progress in turning around the company. The $12 billion loss in 2006 gives way to a net profit of $100 million in the first quarter of 2008, with a full return to profitability forecast by year's end. Ford's labor agreement of 2007 had decreased fully fringed labor cost from $72 per hour in 2007 to $56 per hour, thus reducing the company's uncompetitive position to the foreign transplants from $25 to $8 per hour. The company is in a position to improve dramatically its 80-percent capacity utilization thanks to the $6 billion reduction in total hourly labor cost and the closure of five assembly plants. (Indeed, by 2014 capacity utilization exceeds 120 percent with overtime.)

In the second quarter of 2008, though, Lehman Brothers' subprime financial crisis results in a loss of $2.8 billion. That September, Lehman Brothers files for Chapter 11 bankruptcy and, by the end of the year, 15 U.S. banks have failed. Several others are saved only through government intervention or acquisition by other banks.

Meanwhile, the Dow Jones Industrial Average is declining; by March 2009, it has dropped 54 percent over a 17-month time span. Key sectors of the U.S. economy such as building and construction are devastated and consumer confidence drops by about half. The impact on the American automotive industry is dramatic: the North American Seasonally Adjusted Annual Rate (SAAR) of sales declines from 17.2 million vehicles in 2006 to 13.5 million vehicles by the end of 2008 and to 12 million by 2009. For a capital-intensive industry such as automotive manufacturing, this is catastrophic.

By the fourth quarter of 2008, General Motors acknowledges it will run out of cash by mid-2009 without a combination of government funding, a merger, or a sale of assets. In February 2009, President Obama forms an Auto Industry Task Force to make recommendations regarding restructuring and GM and Chrysler's request for a bailout. The Task Force incorporates the December 2008 term sheet that lists four changes that must be made to the GM and Chrysler's labor contract with the UAW before either company can qualify for bailout money:

1. Competitive labor rates with the foreign transplants (Toyota, Honda, etc.)
2. Competitive work practices with the foreign transplants
3. Competitive termination and layoff provisions with the foreign transplants
4. Half of the VEBA debt to the UAW VEBA Trust converted from debt to equity

Bankruptcy enables GM and Chrysler to wipe clean billions of dollars of debt. It also provides both companies with the opportunity to leverage these government demands for contract concessions and to renegotiate a more competitive agreement with the UAW. Immediately GM and Chrysler approach the UAW to discuss amending the contract to comply with the term sheet. Because of its sheer size and scope, GM leads these discussions.

The first three Task Force items, as complex and painful as they have been for the parties historically, are within the scope of the UAW and GM to carve out an agreement that will satisfy the government. Converting half the VEBA debt to equity, though, is a stumbling block. This poses an enormous problem for GM and the UAW VEBA Trust. The most critical issue negotiated in the 2007 agreement had been the establishment of the UAW VEBA Trust. GM's Other Post Employment Benefits (OPEB) obligation is approximately three times Ford's $25 billion OPEB obligation. GM had transferred $10 billion from its existing company VEBA to the UAW VEBA Trust and had negotiated to fund the remaining obligation at approximately 60 cents on the dollar. Independent actuaries had estimated the plan would last 80 years—more than enough time to cover present retirees and the vast majority of active employees.

The Task Force's requirement that half of GM's debt to the UAW Trust be converted to GM stock places the UAW VEBA Trust in the dangerous position of being significantly underfunded. Hundreds of thousands of fixed-income retirees are poised to lose their health care benefits. This issue is the proverbial "show stopper," halting progress even as the March 31, 2009, deadline to report back to the Auto Industry Task Force looms.

On November 18, 2008, the CEOs of the Big Three automakers petition Congress for $25 billion in emergency loans. Then, on December 5, they return to the House Committee on

Financial Services seeking another $38 million in emergency loans. Ford testifies in support of the loans, but stands out among the three since it does not ask for bailout assistance. Ford's strategy is instead to concentrate on the core business and deal with the financial crisis internally to avoid needing federal assistance. Mulally testifies in favor of the bailout in part out of fear that if GM and Chrysler go bankrupt, it will bring down nearly all of the automotive suppliers and shut down Ford as well—leading to Ford's own bankruptcy.

Eventually, GM and Chrysler appeal directly to the White House. On December 12, the U.S. Treasury Department agrees to $700 million in emergency loans for GM and Chrysler, taking the money from the Troubled Asset Relief Program (TARP) fund that had been established to bail out financial institutions. Between the United States and Canadian taxpayers, GM and GMAC receive $77 billion and Chrysler and Chrysler Financial receive $18 billion.

Ford's plan is to wait until GM, Chrysler, and the UAW cut a deal with the government and follow quickly with pattern bargaining for the same contractual provisions.

By mid-January 2009, it becomes apparent that the UAW and GM are nowhere close to coming to an agreement to satisfy the Task Force. If no agreement is reached, the parties have two options: accept the terms dictated by the Task Force or refuse and liquidate both GM and Chrysler. UAW members at GM and Chrysler will lose their jobs, retirees will lose their health care benefits in a couple of years, and pensions will be in serious jeopardy.

In January 2009, Joe Hinrichs, Ford's group vice president, Manufacturing, concludes it is too dangerous to sit idly by while GM and the UAW failed to make progress. He and Marty Mulloy drive down to UAW's Detroit headquarters, Solidarity House, and propose to Ron Gettelfinger and Bob King that Ford and the UAW strike a deal that can be used as a pattern for the eventual UAW/GM/Chrysler negotiations in Washington with the Task Force.

Gettelfinger had already been quietly exploring this option. As a result, he is receptive. After meeting for three hours, Gettelfinger calls his Executive Council together to consider the Ford offer. Bob King calls Marty Mulloy later that evening to inform him that the Executive Council agrees to have Ford lead negotiations going forward.

It is important to note that the trust built between Ford and the UAW is the key enabler bringing the parties together for a quick decision to move forward. The meeting at Solidarity House lacks all the characteristic bravado of traditional bargaining. Instead, the parties discuss their common interests and develop options to construct an agreement that will serve the needs of the UAW, Ford, and the domestic industry.

In early February 2009, the UAW's National Ford Department (NFD) and Ford meet to construct an agreement that will eventually serve as the blueprint for the upcoming negotiations involving GM/Chrysler/UAW and the Task Force. It takes just over one week, and the agreement is put before the UAW membership for ratification. It is the first concessionary agreement the UAW has taken to the rank-in-file in more in 25 years, and it wins ratification with 59 percent voting in favor.

The agreement includes changes to the National Agreement that save Ford $500 to $700 million:

- Elimination of Guaranteed Employment Numbers (GEN) or Job Banks
- Suspension of COLA (Cost of Living Allowance tracking inflation)
- Suspension of lump sum increases
- Competitive overtime and relief time provisions
- Flexibility to schedule production work patterns

The parties also agree that if the eventual UAW agreement with GM and Chrysler brokered by the Task Force embodies elements that place Ford in an uncompetitive position, they will sit down again.

The U.S. government has some consternation about the UAW-Ford terms and conditions, but the pattern is set.

Ford's Joe Hinrichs reflects on the negotiation and the complexity of the deal:

[Negotiation in] 2009 went as well as it did because of the competitive operating agreements in 2006 and the 2007 national negotiations. GM and Chrysler were under the gun. We stepped in and said we had a way to get there. GM and Chrysler were being more aggressive than the government required. We went to Solidarity House for a private meeting with the UAW. We told them we could do the VEBA as 50 percent stock to free up cash and then offer the bondholders around 30 cents on the dollar. We signaled to the UAW what we wanted to happen.

I said to Ron [Gettelfinger] we could do this... without relying on government money. The UAW was the target of some in the government and the media. So here was a way they could be seen as reasonable in doing what Congress expected—but with Ford so we could chart our own path forward without government money. Both parties trusted each other. We did an agreement in a week—with seven people sitting around the table in my office in World Headquarters—from Monday to Sunday. It was all based on the relationships we had established.

We couldn't guarantee that the bondholders would accept the deal—it was voluntary. In fact, it worked out as we thought it would.

The UAW's Chuck Browning observes:

Ford had an advantage on plant efficiency and being able to get money when they still could. One advantage was that they were not reliant on government loans. On the other hand, Chrysler and GM had a huge cost advantage going through bankruptcy. Ford was not going to be in the negotiations with the government, so the company had some smart executives and a close relationship with the UAW. The UAW was experiencing GM and Chrysler pushing for changes. So Ford offered the chance to make reasonable cost changes to set the pattern.

We went into the 2009 negotiations and were able to come to solutions without our backs against the wall that would help the company and that addressed concerns we had with the language.

GM and Chrysler conclude negotiations consistent with the UAW-Ford agreement, but the government insists on additional terms. In September 2009, the UAW and Ford reopen negotiation around the additional provisions. It is difficult: Ford's financial picture is improving (from February to November 2009, Ford's stock increases from approximately $2 to $8 per share, and the company's capital value increases from approximately $7 billion to $30 billion) and the UAW expresses reservations about its ability to win ratification of further concessions. Within a few weeks, the parties reach a settlement that adds provisions from the UAW agreements with GM and Chrysler:

- Elimination of Skilled Trades Lines of Demarcation
- Entry Level Employees are placed in a separate hourly retirement plan
- Provisions on the percentage and wage levels of entry-level employees
- No Strike and Lockout Clause—Arbitration to be used as a potential final remedy

The tentative agreement is taken to the membership and, on November 2, the UAW announces it has been overwhelmingly defeated. Ford's hourly employees feel they have sacrificed enough and that the company is safe from bankruptcy. The elements that had placed Ford in a less competitive position than GM and Chrysler will become issues to be negotiated in 2011 national bargaining.

"One thing we learned in all of this is durability," notes Marty Mulloy. "Just because the second negotiations didn't work out, doesn't mean you quit. You dust yourself off and continue to try to do the right thing."

✳ ✳ ✳

Ford's decision to lead 2009 negotiations with the UAW and not wait for a pattern settlement to emerge from GM and Chrysler was a strategic move for Ford and the UAW. This made it possible for Ford to negotiate the most important elements that needed to change in the Master Agreement and the UAW was able to achieve the most favorable terms in a difficult situation. Given the defeat of the second set of modifications, there is a high probability Ford might not have been able to achieve any concessions had it waited, which would have placed the company in an even more extreme uncompetitive position going forward and set a dangerous precedent leading into 2011 national bargaining.

The 2009 concessions set the pattern going forward, eliminating economic escalators such as COLA and general wage increases in future contracts. Instead, compensation was based on lump-sum increases and profit sharing that varied with the company's fortunes.

Immediately after the first set of concessions in the first quarter of 2009, the company offered an opportunity to financial institutions holding Ford debt to accept a cash settlement at a percentage less than the full debt level. A number of banks and other financial institutions, fearing a Ford bankruptcy in the future (the GM and Chrysler bankruptcies had heightened the level of fear) accepted the offer. The result of this transaction fundamentally changed the financial trajectory of the company. Ford had eliminated approximately $10 billion of debt and lowered the annual cash interest payment by more than $500 million. In less than two years, the company's $10.8 billion cash net loss in 2008 became a surplus of $1.4 billion in 2010, a turn around of more than $12 billion.

The UAW also gained a great deal from Ford's success. An agreement in the revised 2009 VEBA settlement provided the UAW with 362 million warrants to purchase Ford stock at

$9.20 per share. At the time of the agreement, Ford stock was trading at approximately $2 per share. By March 2010, Ford stock was over $12, and each warrant was valued at $4.83 per share. The UAW VEBA Trust realized a gain of $1.78 billion, and the proceeds were used to support benefit payments to nearly 200,000 Ford retirees and beneficiaries—providing an additional level of security as the UAW became the nation's largest purchaser of health benefits.

National Negotiations—Jobs, Health Care, and Profit Sharing, 2011

Whereas the 2007 national negotiations illustrate crisis negotiations and the 2009 negotiations add the U.S. government to the picture, 2011 is a very different context for negotiations. It is pivotal in that the company has returned to profitability but is determined to reach an agreement that allows for sustained success. The union is equally determined to make improvements in a number of key areas, including the entry-wage pay level, pay for team leaders, and the profit-sharing formula. Both parties are committed to containing health care costs. The situation is also unique in that the VEBA provides the UAW with stock ownership of GM and Chrysler even as it is negotiating with Ford—most likely the first time a union in the United States is engaged in collective bargaining with a company while having a stock position with its competitors.

In comparison to 2006, when Ford lost $12 billion, or the near collapse into bankruptcy in 2009, the turnaround for the company going into the 2011 negotiation is remarkable. In 2010, Ford's North America Automotive profits are $5.4 billion and vehicle sales increase from 1.9 million units in 2009 to 2.4 million units in 2010. Ford's performance also carries over to improvements in vehicle quality, capacity utilization, and manufacturing efficiency. Ford has experienced a rebirth, and people wanted to be a part of Ford.

By mid-2011, weeks prior to the opening day of national bargaining, Ford stock stands at $12 a share, quite a rise from its low of $2 in 2009, and the company's market capitalization has increased to $40 billion. By not filing for bankruptcy and accepting taxpayers bailout money, the company's reputation has improved dramatically. Consumers who once would not even consider a Ford are now visiting Ford dealership showrooms and are impressed with the company's new fuel-efficient product lineup.

Figure 6.4 reviews the key events in 2006–2007, 2008, and 2009 that affected the 2011 negotiations.

Several key figures of past negotiations have moved on as the 2011 national bargaining negotiations open. The changes are significant. Bob King has replaced Ron Gettelfinger as UAW president, and Jimmy Settles has replaced Bob as vice president responsible for the UAW's National Ford Department (NFD). Within Ford, Joe Hinrichs has become global vice president for Asia Pacific Operations, replaced as executive vice president for Global Manufacturing by John Fleming. Other key leaders and the core staff supporting both the UAW and the company remain intact to carry over the institutional learning's from prior efforts

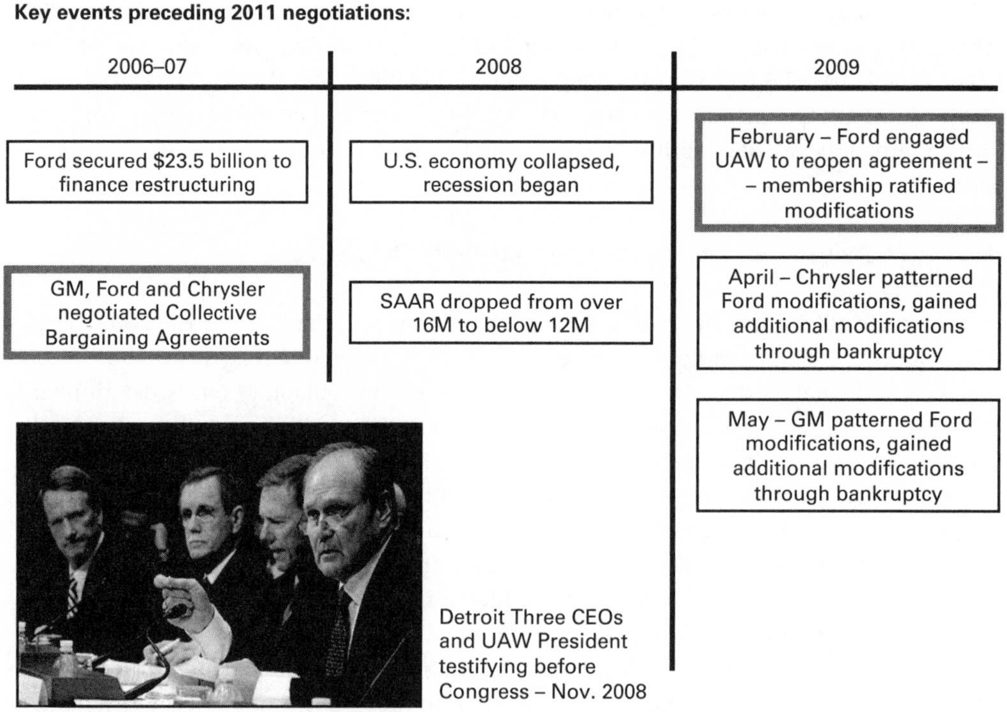

Key events preceding 2011 negotiations:

2006–07	2008	2009
Ford secured $23.5 billion to finance restructuring	U.S. economy collapsed, recession began	February – Ford engaged UAW to reopen agreement – – membership ratified modifications
GM, Ford and Chrysler negotiated Collective Bargaining Agreements	SAAR dropped from over 16M to below 12M	April – Chrysler patterned Ford modifications, gained additional modifications through bankruptcy
		May – GM patterned Ford modifications, gained additional modifications through bankruptcy

Detroit Three CEOs and UAW President testifying before Congress – Nov. 2008

Figure 6.4
Key Events Preceding 2011 Auto Negotiations. *Source:* Ford Motor Company.

working together. Figure 6.5 is the official photo of the national negotiations teams for the UAW and Ford (consistent with the spirit of this book, some of the work behind the scenes is also evident in the photo).

The financial crisis of 2005–2009 teaches Ford senior leadership the importance of sharing information with the UAW. Without the cooperation of the UAW during the restructuring of North American Operations, the company would not have survived. Ford's senior leaders make a point to open up their calendars for candid discussions with King, Settles, and his senior NFD staff. Bill Ford, the board executive chairman; CEO Alan Mulally; Mark Fields, the president of the Americas; CFO Lewis Booth; Fleming, the executive vice president Global Manufacturing; Jim Tetreault, vice president, Manufacturing; and other senior-level operating management "open the books" and exchange data transparently with the UAW. As a consequence of these discussions, senior management comes to understand and respect the UAW's interests more fully. A commitment to working toward mutually beneficial solutions builds. Ford and the UAW have learned they have much more in common than they once thought, and that their common enemy is, in fact, the competition.

Figure 6.5
2011 UAW-Ford National Negotiations Teams. *Source:* Ford Motor Company.

Within management, Ford develops seven distinct work streams to plan for the 2011 negotiation: Economics, Product Investment, Communications, Government Affairs, Manufacturing Priorities, Contingency Planning, and Employee Benefits. Senior management gets monthly updates on each of them, which serves several useful purposes:

- Early identification and response to UAW interests
  This is particularly important for planning items with long lead times—such as product development projects—that dictate sourcing and determined employment levels.
- No surprises
  Key company stakeholders are all engaged and talk through various options—no hidden agendas allowed.
- Collaborative dialogue
  Higher-level solutions are achieved by pooling intellectual talent and experience.
- Comprehensive labor strategy
  Diverse functional leaders work with the Labor Affairs Office to develop and execute a comprehensive, holistic strategy.

The cadence of these meetings within management increases after negotiation begins. As the deadline approaches, the meetings shift to involve senior management in making trade-offs in the final days before settlement.

In the weeks prior to the deadline for the 2011 agreement, John Fleming and Jim Tetreault invite Jimmy Settles and his NFD team to the Product Investment Strategy Room. This is the "Holy of Holies" of Ford, where product investment and sourcing information is "kept"—something every original equipment manufacturer (OEM) carefully guards from its competitors. To the UAW, this room embodies jobs for their members and revenue for their business operations. Being invited into this room signals trust and mutuality at the highest level.

Sourcing for each product and its impact on every plant is discussed in detail. Since Ford and the UAW engage in continual discussions throughout the year, there are few surprises. However, seeing the data in the strategy room demonstrates how diligently the company has worked on trying to make a business case to source jobs in America.

Ford clearly understands that there is nothing more important to the UAW than job security for its members. It takes planning to develop a business case that works for the UAW and for Ford. It is a process of continually working with product investment alternatives and engaging in ongoing dialogue.

Still, even with the strong relationship between the union and the company, there are substantive issues in which each party presents competing data. Ford emphasizes the "gap to transplant" in hourly wages. At the same time, the UAW develops an analysis of the declining wage premium afforded to its members (figure 6.6)—as a contrast with the Ford's "gap to transplant" data.

Historically, the Big Three follow pattern bargaining that results in very similar contracts at Ford, GM, and Chrysler. National issues such as wages and benefits are almost identical (local contract issues may vary greatly). The UAW's philosophy has long been to have domestic wage parity among GM, Ford, and Chrysler: by treating all three companies equally, they compete in issues other than hourly compensation. It is a strategy that worked well within North American until the arrival of the transplants in the early 1980s.

The GM and Chrysler bankruptcies, though, create the possibility that Ford will lose wage parity among the three. This becomes a key issue going into 2011 national bargaining with the UAW. After the rejection of the October 2009 tentative agreement, which would have leveled the playing field between Ford and GM/Chrysler, NFD works with Ford to resolve three of the four non-pattern open issues before 2011 bargaining begins. The one issue that remains is the no-strike, no-lockout clause that substitutes arbitration as the remedy if the parties fail to negotiate an agreement on all open issues.

President Obama's appointee to the U.S. government's Auto Industry Task Force, Ron Bloom, drafts the language imposed on the UAW. Dynamics between the Task Force and the industry executives are sometimes conflictual and sometimes border on cooptation. In this case, at the insistence of Chrysler's CEO Sergio Machionne, arbitration is included in the 2009 UAW GM and Chrysler Agreements. Machionne is concerned that without the

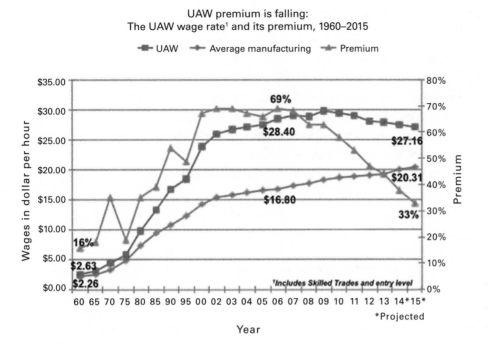

Figure 6.6
UAW Wage Premium Analysis. *Source:* UAW.

protection of arbitration, the UAW will return in 2011 to bargain for the same uncompetitive provisions that resulted in Chrysler's bankruptcy. Figure 6.7 shows the language Bloom constructs, as presented on an internal Ford briefing slide.

The language does not specify the type of arbitration that will be used or the process that will be followed. These issues are debated between GM, Chrysler, and the UAW. The bottom line is that Ford is the only company among the three that can be struck by the UAW, which places Ford in a clear competitive disadvantage—especially considering that the UAW's strike fund exceeds $750 million, and would be used against Ford alone. Strike benefits of $500 per week for each Ford employee would finance a strike for more than eight months—at which point the company would run out of cash. Even a strike of a relatively short duration could seriously compromise the company's product programs and investment.

Ford's positive relationship with the UAW reduces the risk of a strike, but it is still a contingency that must be considered.

Further complicating the situation, the UAW VEBA Trust owns 55 percent of Chrysler and 17.5 percent of GM. Again, no union in the United States engaged in collective bargaining has ever held an ownership position with the competitors of the company across the table.

GM MEMORANDUM OF UNDERSTANDING
RE: BINDING ARBITRATION

Upon expiration of the 2007 Agreement, the parties will enter into a new National Collective Bargaining Agreement which will continue in full force and effect until September 14, 2015. <u>Unresolved issues remaining at the end of negotiations on the 2011 renewal of the 2007 Agreement shall be resolved through binding arbitration</u>[1] with <u>wage and benefit improvements</u>[2] to be based on General Motors/Chrysler maintaining an all-in hourly labor cost <u>comparable to its U.S. competitors, including transplant automotive manufacturers</u>[3].

••

Notes/Analysis:

1. All "4 walls" of the agreement are covered
2. Improvements noted, meaning that wage and benefit elements will likely not regress
3. Expands comparator base beyond Toyota and Honda

Figure 6.7
GM Memorandum of Understanding on Binding Arbitration. *Source:* Ford Motor Company.

Ford's success in turning around the company spurs some union employees to advocate for a return to the "good old days" of cost-of-living adjustments (COLA) and base wage increases. This poses an enormous problem for Ford, whose total compensation of $58 per hour is still $8 above the transplants. Furthermore, none of the transplants have COLA as a provision in their compensation.

Ford's strategy is to achieve a competitive agreement without the arbitration language. A realistic set of internal goals is identified that takes into account the UAW's interests as expressed in the regular strategic forums.

• Jobs: As the only real job security for employees (as opposed to former Job Banks), jobs are what most employees are concerned about coming out of the recession.
• Ratification Bonus: Upfront money appeals to most employees and helps in ratification.
• Profit Sharing: Revise the present plan to make it more relevant to employees and deliver a high level of income opportunity.
• Footprint: Rationalize manufacturing operations and offer new jobs to anyone adversely affected.
• Automotive Components Holding (ACH): Continue selling remaining plants and offer existing employees entry-level jobs in Ford.
• Competitive Work Practices: Expand the use of flexible work teams and incremental pay for team leaders.

• Health Care: Implement an enhanced care program to concentrate on helping the 20 percent of employees that constitute 80 percent of health care costs.
• Increase Utilization of Assets: Use alternative flexible work schedules to produce more products and, as a result, create more jobs in the community.

Ford's profitability (higher than GM) and the need to get the contract ratified without a strike means Ford will pay an incremental amount above GM. However, it is Ford's goal to have the amount minimized so that it will not become an ongoing cost disadvantage. The company sends a consistent message to UAW president Bob King: Ford should not be disadvantaged to GM because Ford has been proven more capable in managing its company, thereby avoiding bankruptcy and government assistance.

"To Bob King's credit," comments Marty Mulloy, "he worked hard to make sure Ford was not disadvantaged because it avoided bankruptcy. Furthermore, Jimmy Settles and his NFD team conducted themselves with the highest level of integrity and bargained hard to leverage jobs for his UAW constituents and an improved profit sharing formula for his members."

The UAW selects GM as its strike target and proceeds to complete negotiations without having to take any issues through arbitration. This means Ford will follow GM's pattern agreement, minimizing the potential of being severely disadvantaged relative to GM. On October 4, 2011, Ford reaches a tentative agreement with the UAW that is beneficial to the union, the company, and the nation. Ford commits to $6.2 million in plant-related investment and the creation of 12,000 hourly jobs (figure 6.8). This investment in the Midwest creates middle-class manufacturing jobs in communities hit the hardest by the recession.

The contract is taken to ratification and initial returns from a few locations are not favorable, leading the union to ramp up its efforts to inform its members about the key features of the agreement. Once fully understood, the agreement wins ratification, with 63 percent of the membership approving the settlement—a testament to the leadership of Jimmy Settles and his team.

By 2014, Ford exceeds its original forecast and creates a projected 18,000 hourly jobs. The economic multiplier effect of an automotive assembly is approximately 1:9. Thus, with the multiplier, Ford—working with the UAW—creates for its communities more than 150,000 new jobs. This level of job creation is unprecedented over the last three decades in the domestic automotive industry.

The economic outcome of the agreement proves to be a winning formula for the UAW and Ford. The company avoids COLA and general wage increases that escalate active labor rates far beyond the foreign transplants and adversely affect product investment in the United States (Ford's labor cost remains at approximately $60 per hour). Hourly employees receive an annual $1,750 lump-sum payment (equivalent to 3-percent increase), and a revised profit-sharing plan pays out $1 for every $1 million of North American profit when profits exceed $1.25 million (a ceiling is set at $12,000 per person).

2011 CBA jobs and investment

• Investment, Jobs and Footprint
  – $16 billion investment, including $6.2 billion in U.S. plants
  – Plan to create 12,000 new jobs in the U.S.

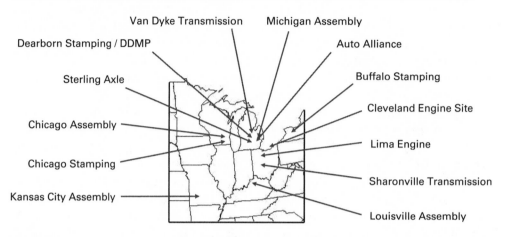

Figure 6.8
Collective Bargaining Agreement, Jobs and Investment. *Source:* Ford Motor Company.

Ford's former profit sharing plan had been so complex that it literally took a roomful of CPAs to explain the intricacies of the formula. With the new transparent formula, employees can easily estimate their potential payout after each quarterly earnings statement. Employees can now translate how their plant's performance directly affects the company's bottom line and their own pocketbooks.

"For profit sharing," Settles notes, "the issue was that the person on the floor needs to understand what it means."

I was always skeptical about profit sharing. No one could explain the formula. We spent thousands to this accounting firm to see if it was done right. It started in the 1980s and I always wanted to do this in a way that was understandable to the person on the floor.

We finally got to a formula based on the work with Ford. Even if GM went first in the negotiations, we still focused on what made sense with Ford. Each worker gets $1,000 per billion in profits. There is a cap at $12 billion. It does a lot for morale and for quality. People understand that they are part of the business—they don't want things that they can control to have a negative impact on profit sharing. People used to think there were two or three books, but this is transparent.

The UAW's decision to change its compensation philosophy from economic escalators to sharing in the rewards of success in the marketplace has major ramifications for job creation. In the last few years, Ford directs more investment to the United States than in previous decades, and the payoff for the hourly employees from the profit sharing plan is extraordinary: since the 2011 agreement, payouts average $8,300 in 2012 and $8,800 in 2013—equivalent to a 14 percent lump sum increase. Coupled with the guaranteed $1,750 lump sum, the average Ford hourly employee receives lump sum payments of $10,300, or 17 percent annually. This is a tangible follow-through on Alan Mulally's philosophy of "profitable growth for all."

Ford also provides a signing bonus of $6,000 and advances $3,750 of 2011's profit sharing payout of $6,200, which is normally paid in March of 2012, to coincide with the ratification bonus payment. This provides employees a total lump sum of almost $10,000 upon ratification.

Finally, agreements on health care in 2011 represented tangible progress on one of the most challenging employment-relations issues in the U.S. context. "In 2011," notes Jimmy Settles, "we reached an agreement on a program to reach out to the people who are most sick. Twenty percent of the people account for 80 percent of the cost. We call it the "enhanced care program.... We both felt we had to do something to reverse the rising costs. Health care costs are rising faster than inflation. Too often we defer dealing with hard issues—in this case we said we would do something."

∗∗∗

Agreements on profit sharing in 2011 make the principle "mutual growth" tangible and understandable in new ways. Language on team leaders (discussed in chapter 5) codifies past innovation and sets the stage looking ahead. Agreements on health care enable both parties to contain health care costs while providing increased health services to workers with chronic diseases.

Reflecting on the bargaining process in 2001, Ford CEO Mark Fields comments, "Because we had a process of internal alignment and because we had Action America we spent majority of time on problem solving."

The next national negotiations are in 2015. There will be many new faces on both sides of the table. They will be building on a strong relationship between the parties and a pattern of negotiated change that is increasingly distinct between each of the three major U.S. auto companies.

Entry-Wage Team Leaders at Chicago Assembly, 2012–2013

This pivotal event centers on a mid-contract negotiation of the incremental pay premium paid to team leaders hired in at the new "entry wage." The Chicago Assembly Plant plays a central role in this process.

The Chicago Assembly plant produces the Ford Taurus, Explorer, Police Interceptor & Utility, and Lincoln MKS—products so popular that the plant runs a three-shift operation for all of 2012 and 2013. The upsurge in sales had begun earlier and, based on commitments to the UAW, Ford expands production in this aging plant rather than in other facilities—as initially indicated in the Way Forward plan. The Chicago plant's importance transcends the specific

UAW-Ford context. President Obama has visited the plant to highlight the need for growing good-paying manufacturing jobs in the United States.

First established in 2007, the entry wage in 2012 is $16/hour; the average hourly wage for workers hired before 2007 is $28. Some 58 percent of the Chicago plant workforce, 2,250 workers, began at the entry wage. This includes a large number of individuals who were hired in at the lower entry wage and who have made it through the selection process to become team leaders.

The entry wage is controversial. Following the 1982 and 1992 recessions, successive waves of two-tier wage agreements become a way to ratchet down average wages over time while minimizing the burden on the current workforce. The experience with these earlier arrangements teaches two key lessons: such agreements become unstable when a majority of the workforce is at the lower wage, and that instability can be tempered if there is a mechanism for lower-tier workers to move to the upper tier over time.[10] As is noted earlier in this chapter, the 2007 UAW-Ford agreement included a commitment to cap the entry-wage workforce at 20 percent of the total hourly U.S. UAW-Ford workforce (with some exceptions, such as insourced jobs and preexisting Tier 2 positions), after which first-hired entry-wage workers—in this case, workers in Chicago—will move up to the traditional wage.

We focus here on team leaders hired at the entry wage who work alongside team leaders earning the traditional wage. The quotes come from confidential "vertical slice" focus group sessions with team leaders, supervisors, superintendents, and other top union and management leaders, facilitated by Joel Cutcher-Gershenfeld on all three shifts in the plant in January and February 2013.

Initially, entry-wage team leaders in this plant and others receive no pay premium for their work as a team leader, while the team leaders in the traditional classifications were awarded a premium of $1.50 per hour. Just before the focus groups,[11] Ford decides to provide a pay premium for the entry-wage team leaders. The 90-cent premium corresponds to their wage rate, which is 60 percent of the traditional pay. It is rare for an upward pay adjustment such as this to be made outside of national negotiations, but this reflects a shared recognition by labor and management that some form of premium should be associated with the work of a team leader.

In many ways, the entry-wage and traditional team leaders view the operations similarly. In the focus groups, entry-wage and traditional team leaders alike share an appreciation for the strengths of the current operations. Many consider the "pride in seeing when you build a quality product" to be a particular strength of the plant.

"We have a good workforce," says one team leader, "smart people and good workers—management and hourly."

Another notes, "We have a reputation—Ford—that is positive, including not taking the government loans."

Many others make similar statements. And they cite other strengths. The plant "improved on downtime from where we were from the start of C crew" (the plant's third shift, with the lowest seniority). Team leaders show they've taken on responsibility for quality and cost when they "QR [quick response code] vendors [which] generates money back to the plant general fund."

"There is a special type of attitude required here," a team leader notes. "We push harder than Chrysler and GM." Statements like these indicate that team leaders—whether traditional or entry wage—are proud of the work they do and the products they build.

Still, the team leaders express concern that not all newly hired workers value the work to the degree that the team leaders believe new workers should. "It's a big deal to get a job like this," says one, "but it doesn't [always] seem that it's seen that way." Another team leader points to the need for greater "appreciation for having a good job—not taking the job for granted—not walking past a box that needs to be picked up."

The entry-wage team leaders do have concerns about the two-tier system: "The training comes with the team leader role, but not the pay," notes one. Another comments, "When you have entry employees doing jobs that seniority employees don't want to do, such as team leader, there should be the same dollar increment or whatever goes with a classified job."

A third acknowledges that "at least [we get some] some recognition," but adds that because being a team leader is not termed a "classified" position in the plant, there is no associated pay increment. The entry-wage team leaders do benefit from training and recognition, but don't have the additional opportunities associated with classified positions.

These issues of morale and fairness have internal implications for the union, as well as for management. "The entry-level folks don't feel equal—they say, 'your' union hall," notes one union leader, who also acknowledges, "Some senior people act like they are better."

It is an issue that works both ways. An entry-wage team leader's comments, "The union doesn't treat the second-tier employees the same as a seniority employee—at least that's how it seems."

Based in part on the data from these focus group sessions, senior corporate management and international union leaders see that even the adjustment to 90 cents an hour for entry wage team leaders still risks low morale among these team leaders and a continuing divide with traditional team leaders. The entry wage itself is seen as essential to new job creation, but the savings associated with maintaining this gap for team leaders may be far less than the costs. Remarkably, after considerable dialogue, the parties agree that all entry-wage team leaders in the system will be given the full $1.50/hour provided to traditional-wage team leaders. Further, entry-wage workers in other hourly leadership roles for which they were receiving no pay premiums are granted the same premiums as the traditional workers in these roles.

✳ ✳ ✳

The adjustments at Ford directly addressed the pay-premium issues among team leaders—an unanticipated implication of the original entry wage agreement. Were it not for the entry wage, fewer jobs would have been created in the Chicago Assembly Plant and in other U.S.

locations—a total projected to be over 18,000 by the end of 2014. As we discuss earlier in this chapter, the 2011 negotiations included a strategic choice to increase the base wages of the entry-wage workforce. Initially, this involved positional bargaining. The union indicated an interest in parity in 2011. Management offered to move all the workers to the same wage, but only if total compensation remained constant—which would have involved decreasing the wages of workers at the traditional wage. Predictably, the union indicated that was a non-starter. Increasing the entry base wage and proving all workers with lump sum increases was the resulting negotiated agreement. All workers continued to benefit equally from the profit sharing agreement, which generated checks of more than $8,300 for all hourly workers in 2012 (entry level receiving the same amount as traditional employees). The mid-contract agreement documented here represents a mutual recognition of an issue much like the profit sharing, where the signal sent by equal treatment overrides the economic necessity of keeping overall compensation competitive.

Mid-contract upward pay adjustments are rare events in the UAW-Ford history. Neither GM nor Chrysler made comparable adjustments for their team leaders—a further break from pattern bargaining. This pivotal event indicates a capacity for negotiated change outside of formal collective bargaining. It is the product of an interest-based relationship, not just interest-based bargaining. There may not be many future pay issues on which there is equally clear data and agreement on the need for a mid-contract change, but even occurring in this case is testament to a transformed relationship.

Recap: Guiding Principle for Chapter 6—Interest-Based Relationships

Interest-based bargaining is a problem-solving alternative to positional negotiations. The sequence of pivotal events involving formal negotiations reveal the importance of moving to this greater degree of problem solving during bargaining. Indeed, the guiding principle is one of interest-based relationships that precede negotiations and then continue forward into the implementation of the negotiated agreements.

The first pivotal event was actually a series of potential pivots: each time a Modern Operating Agreement (MOA) was negotiated in a Vehicle Operations (assembly) plant. While these negotiations had transformational potential, putting team-based work practices on the table, labor and management alike approached them in a "divide the baby" way—parts of a plant associated with a new product would involve new ways of working and parts would remain traditional. Where the new work was implemented, it was not a full knowledge-driven system. There were reduced numbers of job classifications, for example, but not robust mechanisms to support continuous improvement in the operations. Work and relationships were changed only partly and the results were also incomplete.

The Automotive Components Holdings (ACH) negotiations around Visteon also had a strong instrumental focus. The aim was not the transformation of Ford or the UAW, but the resolution of a business challenge around component parts plants that were not core to the business. In fact, however, the decision to bring the plants back under the Ford umbrella and avoid a bankruptcy was not just a business decision. It also involved enabling the employees to reenter the UAW-Ford system and have access to, for example, early retirement and voluntary separation packages that far exceeded anything Visteon would have been able to do (or that any other U.S. employer was providing during the recession). The problem solving on the part of the lead negotiators was through constructive relationships, rather than through a formal change in the negotiations process.

The process for the 2003 negotiation on the one issue of quality shifted to an interest-based approach. Based on this approach, the parties reached an agreement that standardized key aspects of quality across the systems and established the role of an hourly Quality Operating System Coordinator (QOSC). In this way, collective bargaining was not just a vehicle for a compromise or imposed agreement, but for an integrative solution that exceeded what either side might have anticipated going in—illustrating the principles first articulated more than 75 years ago by Mary Parker Follet.

The Action America information sharing "amped up" the relationship between Ford and the union—see Mark Fields on this subject in this chapter and in chapter 9—through regular meetings at the highest levels of Ford and UAW. The result was not just a softening of attitudes before bargaining, but a combination of interpersonal relationships and open information sharing that built mutual respect and understanding. In 2005, the parties would not have had any conception of the challenges that would soon face the industry, but the investment in these relationships proved pivotal to their success in surviving the crisis.

By contrast, the bargaining over how to bargain in 2006 was a product of increased awareness of an economic crisis and represented a pivot that built on the 2003 approach to quality—extending it to the entire negotiation process. Even though Ford was not the lead in the national auto negotiation in 2007, the bargaining process involved agreements on the two most important issues—the VEBA and the entry wage—that were more comprehensive and reflective of all interests than in the GM and Chrysler agreements. This is reflected in the fact that GM and Chrysler made the unprecedented move of reopening their agreements to adjust them in ways more aligned with the UAW-Ford agreement on these issues.

The 2009 negotiation (and events in 2008 leading to them) represented a case where it was in the interest of both the UAW and Ford to control their own destinies rather than have the auto industry pattern come through GM and Chrysler, with the U.S. government also at the table as part of the bailout and bankruptcy process. The result was an agreement that involved enough concessions to save the industry, but no more. By contrast, the proposals being advanced by GM and Chrysler would have involved more extensive concessions and what would have likely been much greater pressure from the union to reverse the concessions fully as the economy recovered—a less stable dynamic driven by positional bargaining rather than interest-based bargaining. At the core of the UAW-Ford approach were, of course, the personal relationships that had been developed long in advance of the 2009 negotiation.

By 2011, that pattern was well established—a more problem-solving approach to bargaining as well as a foundation of relationships based on interests more than positions. This resulted in innovative approaches to health care, ACH, and insourcing UAW middle class jobs—three issues of importance in the UAW-Ford relationship and more broadly in society.

The mid-contract adjustment in the increment provided to team leaders who where hired at the entry wage represents the product of an interest-based relationship—where both parties agreed to an adjustment in pay that would normally have been reserved for collective bargaining.

The 2015 negotiations are sure to present new challenges. Sustaining a transformation will involve new events with the potential to be pivotal in positive or negative ways for all the parties.

SUPPORTING MATERIALS

6.1 Appendix S Language

Appendix S (2003 National Negotiations)

UAW-Ford Memorandum of Understanding for the Health and Safety of Employees

The UAW and Ford are proud of their accomplishments and long standing dedication to the resolution of employee health and safety concerns. This Memorandum of Understanding reflects the concern of the UAW and the Company for the health and safety of employees in the workplace. Jointly, the parties will continue to strive for a healthier and safer workplace through the involvement of all employees.

In order to foster a culture and environment that embraces every aspect of workplace safety as a way of life and overriding value in everyday activities, management representatives from all areas of the Company, along with the UAW, formed a Safety Leadership Initiative. This initiative focuses on leadership commitment and management involvement and accountability at all levels and builds upon the long standing commitments of the UAW and Ford to health and safety and best-in-class joint training programs.

With a goal of zero fatalities and serious injuries, the leadership of the UAW and Ford will continue jointly to sponsor activities to support a relentless daily focus on safety that protects employees, prevents accidents and injuries, and provides a safe workplace. Initiatives will continue to focus on: enforcing and complying with health and safety programs, procedures, and safe work practices; supporting effective and efficient NJCHS training; expanding upstream pro-active design for health and safety; conducting effective Safety Process Review Boards; exploring methods to enhance safe pedestrian movement in aisles; inspecting and maintaining combustion equipment; energy control and power lockout emphasis; walking and working surface safety; expanding the involvement of employees, team leaders/coordinators, supervisors, and work teams in the overall safety process; and ensuring joint health and safety audits of all plants and facilities to achieve continuous improvement.

Accordingly, the Company shall have the obligation to continue to make reasonable provisions for the health and safety of its employees during the hours of their employment. The Union shall cooperate with the Company's efforts to carry out its obligations. Therefore, the following Memorandum of Understanding for the Health and Safety of Employees is adopted.

I. National Joint Committee on Health and Safety

The parties recognize that efforts directed toward a safe and healthy workplace must represent a fully joint commitment. Therefore, the National Joint Committee on Health and Safety (NJCHS) was established as a mechanism to guide health and safety concerns in the appropriate direction. The National Joint Committee shall continue to be comprised of equal numbers of representatives from the Union and the Company. Union representatives of the Committee will be appointed by the Director of the National Ford Department. Each party will appoint to the Committee at least one member who has professional training in industrial hygiene or safety. Among those matters that would continue to be appropriate for discussion by the NJCHS would be significant developments of a mutual interest in the health and safety fields, changes in the Company's health and safety programs due to legal requirements or Company policy revisions, review of the meaningful injury and illness experience of the Company's plants, and procedures to minimize employee exposure to known harmful physical agents or chemicals.

In the course of NJCHS discussions, the Company will continue to disclose the identity of any known harmful physical agents or chemicals to which employees are exposed. In addition, the Company will continue to arrange for surveys of specific plants at the request of the National Ford Department. Results of such surveys, as well as regular plant surveys conducted will be provided to the International Union through its representatives on the NJCHS.

Past arrangements will continue to be made through the NJCHS for professional health and safety representatives of the International Union to visit Company plants in connection with particular health and safety problems.

The NJCHS has access to plant data required on OSHA Form 300A("Summary of Occupational Injuries and Illnesses"), or any successor document, the total manhours worked and the incident rate for each plant for the comparable period. Also, the Company will continue to provide to the International Union through the NJCHS prompt notification of fatalities and serious injuries resulting from work-related accidents.

National Joint Committee functions are as follows:

• **Sponsor joint conferences that provide training and education, and stimulate interest in health and safety programs and procedures.**

Conferences/meetings sponsored by the NJCHS for Company and Union Health and Safety Representatives will be held no less than annually or as deemed necessary by the NJCHS to provide required training and education and to stimulate renewed interest in health and safety programs and procedures to further improve the workplace for all employees. Conference expenses, including wage payments for lost time, will be paid with joint funds. Joint funds will pay for lost time (eight hours per day base rate plus COLA) for Unit Health and Safety Representatives who participate in these conferences. The Company will recognize and compensate properly appointed alternates when the Unit Health and Safety Representative is out of the plant to attend such training. The NJCHS will consider appropriate requests to provide financial support for periodic Operations meetings of safety professionals to share best practices and receive current health and safety information.

• **Oversee joint training and education.**

The Company will continue to provide additional joint health and safety training to enhance safety awareness, hazard recognition, and technical skills of employees covered under the terms of this agreement. To provide for consistency and uniformity, the NJCHS will continue to consider joint funding requests from the plants to enable them to design training programs to meet local needs (for example, specialized training to address unique health and safety concerns of foundry employees). After submission to the NJCHS for review, funding requests covering projects which are consistent with NJCHS objectives will be referred to the Joint Governing Body of the Education, Development and Training Program for approval.

• **Evaluate health and safety research needs and recommend appropriate research projects.**

The parties recognize that certain health and safety matters require thorough study and appropriate analysis and research to identify and address the issues. The NJCHS will continue to evaluate health and safety research needs, recommend appropriate research projects and communicate the findings to affected employees. The NJCHS will make recommendations to the Joint Governing Body for funding of the specific project(s) under consideration as described in Section III of this Appendix S. The results of research conducted within Company facilities will only be used for purposes specifically authorized by the NJCHS.

• **Participate in operations—Safety Process Review Boards (SPRB).**

A Safety Process Review Board, co-chaired by a senior member of Operations management and a member of the National Ford Department Health and Safety Staff (or other similar arrangement approved by the Company and the UAW National Ford Department) has been established in each Operation having employees covered by this agreement. The NJCHS will continue to participate in activities of these SPR Boards which are expected to meet monthly or otherwise by mutual agreement to review and resolve health and safety issues and to disseminate corrective actions and information throughout their respective Operations.

• **Conduct joint health and safety reviews of plant facilities.**

The NJCHS will continue to sponsor and oversee a national joint team of Company and Union representatives to review Company facilities and activities with regard to NJCHS programs, federal and state regulations and Company health and safety policies and procedures. The NJCHS will develop specific training requirements for review-team members. The team's principal functions will continue to be to encourage Local Union and Management cooperation concerning continuous improvement in health and safety matters, and to highlight strengths and assist in identifying areas where improvements are needed. Joint reviews will be conducted as deemed necessary by the NJCHS, but in no case less frequently than once every 18 months for manufacturing, assembly, and parts distribution units. The NJCHS joint audit process will include both scheduled and unscheduled facility audits. In addition, facilities are required to conduct quarterly self assessments using the Company's Safety and Health Assessment Review Process. Joint Leadership at the facility are responsible for ensuring the accuracy of the facility's self-assessment. Results, action plans, and status are to be reviewed quarterly at the Plant Safety Process Review Board Meetings. As part of our overall efforts for continuous improvement, the Union and Company agree to the joint selection and appropriate use of third parties for certain aspects of joint health and safety audits.

II. Existing Provisions

The following separate contractual provisions are reaffirmed as being in full force and effect in conjunction with this Memorandum of Understanding.

- Article VI, Section 8;
  Unit Health and Safety Representative
- Article VII, Section 23(b);
  Special Procedures—Health and Safety
- Article X, Section 4;
  Health and Safety
- Letters of Understanding:
  The following letters of understanding are unpublished.
  — Additional Health and Safety Representatives (10–31–73)
  — Limitations on the Addition of a Health and Safety Representative and Benefits Representative for Units between 600 and 1,000 Employees Already Having Such Representation (10–4–79)

III. Ongoing Research

Present Research Projects

The parties will continue to meet regularly to discuss the progress and results of the following special studies, which were initiated during previous agreements:

- Lung Cancer Study
- EST research

Both projects are to be completed by year-end 2007.

Potential Research Projects

The Company and Union agree to examine and conduct research projects on subjects that address immediate health and safety needs such as ergonomics or serious acute injury prevention. The NJCHS, where appropriate, will meet, share information and coordinate research agendas with UAW-General Motors and UAW-Chrysler with respect to future projects.

IV. Training and Education

The parties recognize the desirability of wide dissemination of information concerning the causes of illness and accidents and preventive measures which can be implemented and, therefore, are continuing to address the need for health and safety education and training through ongoing programs and projects listed below. Evaluation of training programs, including monitoring training awareness and understanding, will be conducted as determined by the NJCHS.

- Hazard Communications (HazCom)
- Energy Control and Power Lockout (ECPL)
- Guidelines, Responsibilities, and Safe Practices (GRASP)
- Skilled Trades and Apprenticeship Training
- Air Sampling/Industrial Hygiene Workshops
- Powered Material Handling Vehicle (PMHV)
- Confined Space Entry (CSE)
- Shiftwork
- Safety Talks
- Health and Safety Training for Supervisors and Committeepersons
- Teleconferences
- Representative Training
- Train-The-Trainer Sessions
- Orientation for new Unit Health and Safety Representatives, Alternates and Company Safety Engineers
- Training for Health and Safety Representatives/Safety Engineers

V. Other Important Matters

- Hazardous Materials and Environmental Control
- Review of Technology
- Ergonomics (Fitting Jobs to People)
- No Hands in Dies
- Communications
- Preventive and Environmental Maintenance and Plant Housekeeping
- Industrial Hygiene/Occupational Health
- Noise Control and Hearing Conservation
- Radon Gas
- Tasks in Isolated Locations
- Tag Procedures
- Plant Safety Process Review Boards
- Safety/Work Teams
- Emergency Response and Notification

Source: UAW-Ford Collective Bargaining Agreement, 2003

Comments:

The contract language on health and safety illustrates the way in which collective bargaining can codify existing innovations and set the stage for future innovation. Note that language such as this is not the product of hard bargaining and then waiting to see who gives in at the deadline. It is the product of give and take, but it also reflects problem-solving dialogue based on a mutual interest in workplace safety.

6.2 Letter on "Best Options for the Auto Industry Crisis"

Best Options for the Auto Industry Crisis

November 20, 2008

Authors:

Susan Helper
Research Associate, International Motor Vehicle Program (IMVP)
Research Associate, National Bureau of Economic Research
AT&T Professor of Economics
Weatherhead School of Management, Case Western Reserve University
susan.helper@case.edu; 1-216-368-5541

John Paul MacDuffie
Co-Director, International Motor Vehicle Program (IMVP)
Associate Professor of Management
Wharton School, University of Pennsylvania
macduffie@wharton.upenn.edu; 1-215-898-2588

Joel Cutcher-Gershenfeld
Dean and Professor
School of Labor & Employment Relations, University of Illinois
joelcg@illinois.edu; 1-217-333-1454

Teresa Ghilarducci
Director, Schwartz Center for Economic Policy Analysis
The New School for Social Research
ghilardt@newschool.edu; 1-212-229-5901 x4911

Thomas Kochan
George Maverick Bunker Professor of Management
Sloan School of Management, Massachusetts Institute of Technology
tkochan@mit.edu; 1-617-253-6689

IMVP (http://www.imvpnet.org)
The International Motor Vehicle Program (IMVP), founded in 1979 and headquartered at MIT, is an international network of professors and graduate students who do collaborative research aimed at understanding the strategic and competitive challenges facing the global automotive industry.

The views expressed in this paper are solely those of the authors and not those of their universities or any other programs or groups with which they are affiliated.

Best Options for the Auto Industry Crisis

Executive Summary

This memo builds on evidence and knowledge gained from 20 years of research and active involvement in the auto industry, much of it carried out under auspices of the International Motor Vehicle Program (IMVP), a research network headquartered at MIT and funded by the Alfred P. Sloan Foundation.

Based on our work we believe the extraordinary crisis facing the Detroit 3 automakers (GM, Ford, Chrysler) compels Congress to take actions that:

- Avoid the economic and human impact of potentially losing 1.5 to 3 million jobs;

- Enhance long term industry competitiveness;

- Accelerate improvements in fuel efficiency and development of energy-saving vehicles;

- Hold the industry and all its stakeholders — unions, suppliers, dealers — jointly accountable for reducing costs and improving quality and responsiveness to customers;

- Minimize the human costs of transforming the industry by fully implementing health care, pension, and workforce adjustment reforms from recent labor contract negotiations; and

- Minimize the government's financial exposure and provide appropriate monitoring of progress toward these goals.

Our view is that what the Detroit 3 needs is **not** what Chapter 11 bankruptcy provides best -- the ability to break contracts and lower costs unilaterally. Suppliers are already operating on near-zero margins and in bankruptcy themselves, and progress made on labor/pension/health care costs just needs the opportunity for full implementation. Rather we urge continued pressure and incentives to improve operational performance, reduce waste, make smarter strategic decisions, learn and collaborate better. To achieve these goals:

- The government should provide access to the equivalent of Debtor-in-Possession (DIP) financing to make continued operations possible without filing for bankruptcy.

- Any company requesting funds should present restructuring plans that include:
  - Aggressive and achievable targets for improved fuel efficiency, beyond those currently required by law, and development of alternative energy vehicles.
  - Clear milestones for working with suppliers, the union, dealers, and other stakeholders to accelerate the pace of improvements in quality, productivity, responsiveness to customers, and other appropriate performance metrics.
  - Joint union-management plans to minimize the human costs and to aid adjustment to workers, engineers, and managers displaced by industry restructuring.
  - Implementation of the recently negotiated VEBA plans that restructure and control the costs of retiree health care.
  - Foregoing dividends and setting executive compensation levels to be no higher than the average for automakers selling cars in the US.

- An oversight commission should be created with the power to accept, reject, or request modifications in submitted plans and to monitor progress in achieving these goals.

- Congress should commit to coordinated, complementary changes in health care and energy policy.

Analysis and Detailed Plan

Since the problems facing the Detroit 3 are partly of their own making, any government aid should require conditions that do not allow a continuation of the status quo but instead advance national policy interests vis-à-vis energy independence, long term competitiveness, innovative capabilities, and economic and human development. Still, the current crisis is not entirely attributable to company and/or union failures to attend to these past problems. The devastating impact of the financial crisis on consumer confidence and access to credit, combined with an unprecedented spike in fuel prices, has caused automotive sales to drop from 15 million/year to 10 million/year. This is not a permanent shift in demand but a temporary shock (of unknown duration).

The Detroit 3 have already taken major steps towards strengthening their long-term competitiveness, including negotiating pathbreaking contracts with the UAW that dramatically reduce health care and pension costs for existing employees and retirees and decrease salaries and benefits for new employees; developing a product portfolio much better matched to current demand conditions; and achieving impressive improvements in quality, reliability, and productivity that have substantially closed the gap with competitors.[1] The popular media still reports on "gold plated" benefits, "uncompetitive" work rules, and earlier job security provisions such as the "jobs bank" – all of which have been adjusted in substantial ways under the current labor agreements and operating practices. The financial crisis has struck at a time when these initiatives are still being implemented, hence their benefits are not yet fully visible — and there is a distinct lag in public perception. Allowing one or more of the companies to fall into bankruptcy would abort these efforts. This positive trajectory should have a chance to continue.

In this context, Chapter 11 bankruptcy would exacerbate the problems facing the industry and impose substantial costs on society. What a Chapter 11 bankruptcy provides best -- the ability to break contracts and lower costs unilaterally is not what is needed. Suppliers are already operating on near-zero margins and in bankruptcy themselves, and progress made on labor/pension/health care costs need to be fully implemented. Rather we urge continued pressure and incentives to improve operational performance, reduce waste, make smarter strategic decisions, learn and collaborate better.

The auto industry contains valuable capabilities — related to technological innovation, national security, energy independence, and new solutions to mobility problems — whose loss should not be taken lightly. After a bankruptcy, the human capital embodied in some individual engineers would be redeployed at foreign automakers and new U.S.-owned start-ups, but the social capital developed among teams of engineers working in collaboration at automakers and suppliers would be lost. In particular, the financial crisis has caused automakers to postpone the launch of potentially game-changing models, such as GM's plug-in hybrid (the Volt), and the Cruze, which gets 45 miles per gallon with a turbocharged conventional engine.

While further cuts in employment at the Detroit 3 are certain to happen — in all job categories and across supplier and dealer networks — government aid can minimize the dramatic impact of an

---

[1] For example, a 1990 International Motor Vehicle Program study, *The Machine That Changed the World* (1990) found that Toyota made "cars with one-third the defects, built in half the factory space, using half the man hours" of US producers. Today, the Toyota advantage on these factors is either non-existent or very small. For example, at GM overall performance in the J.D. Power Initial Quality Survey has improved 25 percent in the last five years; GM has also cut its warranty expenditure in half since 2002. Ford's gains in quality and warranty costs exceed those of GM. And the Detroit 3 have innovated--they gave us the minivan and the SUV. Not the innovations that environmentalists would have liked, but ones that maximized profits given the (mis-quided) public policy around gas prices at the time.

immediate bankruptcy and soften the negative impact on the already weakened economy. Conservative estimates place that impact at 1 to 1.5 million jobs lost in 2009 alone. Some estimate the ripple effect of job loss could reach 3 million or higher. This is an immense number; only 1.2 million jobs nationwide, across the entire economy, have been lost so far in what is already a very severe recession.

We see bankruptcy as an overly blunt tool to deal with the complex problems of this highly integrated industry, one which cannot easily be broken up into chunks of assets that can be redeployed efficiently elsewhere. Furthermore, handling something as huge and complex as the bankruptcy of GM would tie up private and public financial and human resources in complex legal proceedings that would last for years. It would also be difficult for management in bankruptcy to undertake major new initiatives, since their focus is very much on what is going on in bankruptcy court. Meanwhile, huge costs would fall on federal, state, and local governments in the form of growing unemployment benefits, health care costs, and pension terminations — at amounts likely to far exceed the amounts of aid under consideration. Unlike with air travel, which has continued even as airlines have entered bankruptcy, consumers contemplating the purchase of a vehicle from a bankrupt company will face economic concerns (can I get this car serviced?) and, more significantly, psychological barriers (what are my risks with this company's products?). If, as many predict, bankruptcy led to Chapter 7 liquidation rather than Chapter 11 restructuring, this would involve a multi-year adjustment process as plant capacity is adjusted under new owners, with massive workforce displacement during the transition. Finally, the bankruptcy process is not designed to give public policy considerations any priority; it exists solely to protect creditors and their financial interest.

Thus any government aid must be structured to address the full short term and long term dimensions of this complex problem by:

- Avoiding economic devastation from failure of the Detroit 3 that will be felt nationwide;

- Allowing the important restructuring steps undertaken by these companies and the UAW to come to fruition;

- Insuring that the Detroit 3's worst status quo tendencies, deeply entrenched in their corporate cultures, are met with strong conditions, imposed from a position of deep understanding of how the industry actually operates;

- Facilitating a transition to a smaller but competitively viable U.S.-owned auto industry by avoiding abrupt jolts via a more phased trajectory; and

- Advancing vital U.S. policy objectives in which the auto industry can play a central role.

We believe that the government aid must be conditioned on the Detroit 3 and all its stakeholders — suppliers, dealers, unions — developing the capabilities that have led companies like Toyota and Southwest Airlines to dominate their industries. These firms excel at managing a *knowledge-driven* organization, based on disciplined problem-solving and improvement processes, cognitive contributions from every organizational member, and effective coordination on complex interdependent tasks (such as changing the die in a stamping press in seven minutes, or turning around a plane at the gate in 20 minutes) that is grounded in long-lasting, respectful, and trust-building relationships.

Where the Detroit 3 have made big improvements in recent years, it is because they have begun to learn — after a long fallow period of "not getting it" — the lessons of continuous learning in the factory and in the product development process. Indeed, all three automakers now have some locations that are true knowledge-driven workplaces, delivering world class performance on safety, quality, cost, and other indicators. The 2007 UAW contract negotiations also provided dramatic evidence of a new approach to complex problem-solving among parties more accustomed to adversarial locking of horns.

But despite signs of forward motion, the Detroit 3 have been plagued by difficulties perpetuated by old habits and mindsets in such areas as supplier relations and dealer relations.

Consider, for example, vehicle quality, an outcome resulting from complex interactions between product design, supplier capability and reliability, and assembly plant capability and shop floor teamwork that promotes continuous improvement. We see impressive improvements over the past few years for the Detroit 3 in assembly plant quality. A variety of indicators now show quite small differences between US and Japanese producers. Product development changes have also contributed to quality, both in improved design-for-manufacturability and in enhanced "look and feel" that signals quality to consumers. These gains are already providing substantial savings in warranty costs. For example, Ford reported over $1 billion in warranty savings in 2007.

Progress in union-management efforts to promote team work and flexibility has been made, though there is still work to be done. Some plants continue to be slow in adopting modern productivity and quality enhancing work systems and cooperative relationships. The pace of transforming union-management relations to achieve world class performance levels needs to be accelerated and union and management need to be held accountable for fostering and achieving continued improvements. The contract at the GM-Toyota joint venture (NUMMI) signals the sort of labor agreement that complements a knowledge-driven work system and there are other local and national agreements throughout the industry that provide helpful models.

The parties did take aggressive action in their last contract negotiations to lower future wage and benefit costs. The UAW agreed to establish a health care trust fund (VEBA) to take retiree health care costs off the companies' books, producing an estimated $2,000 savings per car. Workers will pay approximately 25% of the costs of the fund by diverting future wages into the trust. New employees will be enrolled in a hybrid defined contribution/defined benefit plan (a cash balance account) which reduces and stabilizes future benefit costs. Wages for new workers are lower and all workers pay more in deductibles and co-pays. Innovative joint initiatives to improve worker health and increase access to lower cost nurse practitioners and physician assistants were also introduced. As we noted earlier, "bloated wages" and "gold-plated benefits" — popular characterizations of the source of Detroit 3 problems — are simply not accurate statements about true causes of this industry crisis. Calls for shared sacrifice are appropriate given the urgency of this moment, but need to take these recent advances into full account.

Suppliers are a crucial determinant of the performance of a car. Purchased parts account for far more than half of the costs of making a car. (In contrast, wages and benefits paid to UAW assemblers — the focus of much attention — account for less than 10%.) These parts also account for an important part of automotive performance.

Unfortunately, the Detroit 3 lag behind Japanese firms in the quality of supplier relations. Annual surveys by Planning Perspectives, Inc. calculate a Working Relations Index, based on a supplier's rankings of its automaker customers. From 2002 to 2008, on a scale from 0 to 500 (where 0-250 indicates poor supplier relations and 350-500 indicates very good supplier relations), the range of scores for Toyota was 314 to 415; the same range for Honda was 297 to 384. In contrast, the range for GM was 114 to 174; Ford's range was 162 to 191; and Chrysler's range was 161 to 218.

Why are relations so poor? US automakers continue to try to reduce component prices using competitive bidding. This mechanism pits suppliers against each other, assuring that margins remain slim. However, this mechanism does not yield the lowest system cost. The true cost of a component includes not just its per-unit cost, but the cost of installing it, the quickness of a supplier's response to unanticipated problems, and warranty costs. A car is a highly complex product, with 5000 parts that must come together with tolerances as low as 1/1000 of an inch, and where a fault in quality or delivery can shut down an assembly plant, costing up to $10,000 per minute. Most sub-assembled components are designed especially for a particular product; finding the best design requires input from both the supplier and the automaker. For example, a lighter-weight latch assembly is cheaper, but may not withstand the force that will be placed on it in a particular application—something that is often determined only when the design of all surrounding parts is known.

The Detroit 3 have insisted that suppliers do more of the design of their products (usually without additional compensation) and imposed 3 to 5 per cent annual price cuts without any shared effort to find pragmatic ways to reduce costs. The impact of these actions is to squeeze supplier margins, leading many of them to the edge of bankruptcy even before the current crisis.

An alternative way of relating to suppliers is shown by Toyota and Honda. These automakers also push suppliers extremely hard—but in ways that improve quality, develop products that consumers want to buy, and yield profits that sustain suppliers through the business cycle. The process starts with a rigorous joint examination of each step in the production process, whether it is necessary and whether it could be done more cheaply. This exercise is carried out both at the design stage and after the part has gone into production. The information that surfaces during this process yields far greater savings than does multiple rounds of competitive bidding.

Delphi introduced this process — learned from managers it hired from Honda and Toyota — with its long-time suppliers in 2003 and achieved cost reductions of 20-30%, both by improving suppliers' processes and being willing to make changes in its own designs (e.g. reducing the number of variations of a product; simplifying attachment points). Unfortunately this process ended when Delphi filed for bankruptcy.

Bankruptcy is particularly damaging to organizations that are pursuing continuous learning both within their boundaries and in their relations across firms. In bankruptcy, contracts can be torn up, with terms renegotiated at lower prices. In the auto industry, excessive payments are not the main cause of the industry's distress. Many suppliers are already close to bankruptcy and the UAW has made substantial concessions. Instead, the various groups involved in the industry need to work together very differently than in the past, reviving and accelerating initiatives already under way, in pursuit of knowledge-driven work systems.

What bankruptcy court is good for is to get people to do the same things, only cheaper. What we believe, in contrast, is that the savings in the auto industry will come largely from doing different things (e.g., systematically studying costs and eliminating waste, increasing the ability to assemble multiple types of cars in a single plant). There is not a large payoff for the first option. The stock price is already close to zero (meaning shareholders have little equity left); many suppliers are themselves in or close to bankruptcy, and the UAW has already taken pay cuts, to the point that they will soon make less than their transplant counterparts. (In any case; active UAW employees account for at most $800 per car.) It is possible that management, bondholders, and dealers could be paid less, but we think there are better ways to do this, as described below.

The airline industry is often cited as an example of an industry that continued function in bankruptcy. However, there is a key difference. In the airline case, airlines continued operating as usual – flights landed and took off as before. The airlines did not make major changes to their operations --as we are suggesting is required to create a viable auto industry.

What is the alternative to bankruptcy? While the U.S. government could nationalize a company like GM simply by purchasing 51% of the available equity (a bargain at present, at less than $1 billion), this would be a contentious outcome given our nation's historic allegiance to private enterprise A more achievable alternative would be a process that preserves the best while avoiding the worst of what a normal Chapter 11 bankruptcy provides, while building on the successful lessons of past government intervention in supporting firms in troubled industries.

Based on these goals, we advocate a process that includes:

- The government should provide access to the equivalent of Debtor-in-Possession financing to make continued operations possible without filing for bankruptcy.

- Any company requesting funds should be required to present restructuring plans that include at a minimum:
  o Aggressive and achievable targets for improved fuel efficiency and development of alternative energy vehicles.
  o Clear milestones for working with suppliers, the union, and other stakeholders to accelerate the pace of improvements in cost, quality, productivity, customer responsiveness, and other appropriate metrics related to supplier and dealer performance.
  o Joint union-management plans to minimize the human costs and aid adjustment to workers, engineers, and managers displaced by industry restructuring.
  o Implementation of the recently negotiated VEBA plans that restructure and control the costs of retiree health care.

- An oversight commission should be created with the power to accept, reject, or request modifications in submitted plans and to monitor progress in achieving these goals.

- Congress should commit to working toward health care and Medicare reforms that provide universal access to quality, cost-efficient care, and towards energy policy that creates ongoing incentives for consumers to shift towards fuel-efficient vehicles.

Note that this is not a full plan, but a set of potential elements in a framework. Our aim to suggest a viable path, but to refrain from mapping it out in detail since many inputs are needed from diverse stakeholders before anything could be codified.

Evaluation of other plans

Above we contrasted our proposal to the alternatives of Chapter 11 and Chapter 7 bankruptcy. In recent days, other proposals have been made; in this section we compare our plan above to these various alternatives. In each case, we try to examine likely outcomes, not idealized ones.

Alternative 1: companies file for Chapter 11 bankruptcy, and the government provides "Debtor-in-Possession" financing

This option seeks to restructure but runs the considerable risk of one or more of the firms ending up in liquidation if consumers worry about future service, warranties, or resale values. Liquidation would in turn lead to huge losses in capabilities and jobs. Moreover this option retains the problems of Chapter 11 bankruptcy (consumer uncertainty, no representation of social interests, focus on cutting margins on tasks done already, rather than fact-based collaboration to identify waste and opportunities for improvement).

Alternative 2: Companies are liquidated, and the government provides aid to workers and communities.

This is a vastly more expensive option than a $25 billion loan, plus it disrupts valuable social networks for advanced engineering. If, for example, GM was liquidated, in the short run we would see a minimum of 500,000 jobs lost. (This number assumes that only 60% of workers at GM and its suppliers are actually unemployed, the others find jobs at other automakers and suppliers.) This number is unrealistically low, but even if we paid each of them $50,000 for a year, that's an outright expenditure of $25 billion, without including their health care, or retiree pensions, or lost tax revenue or the possibility that a GM bankruptcy drives other suppliers down. A year is nowhere near long enough to rebuild the economies of Michigan, Ohio, and Indiana from the loss. In contrast a $25 billion loan that is the first liability to be paid off is much, much cheaper.

Alternative 3: Sen. Levin and Rep. Frank bills

These bills have many good provisions. They provide for $25 billion in loans, which companies can access if their proposal is approved by an oversight board. The loans come with warrants that allow the government to take an equity position, and prohibitions on paying bonuses to executives making over $250,000 ($200,000 in the Frank bill), offering golden parachutes, or paying dividends while loans from the government are outstanding. All other obligations would be subordinate to the loan from the taxpayers, yielding a high likelihood that it would be paid back.

To get the money, the automakers must submit both a Short-term Operating Plan by December 1, and then a Long-Term Restructuring Plan by March 31, 2009. The long term plan must be "an acceptable restructuring plan for long-term viability and international competitiveness, including meeting enhanced fuel efficiency standards and for advanced technology vehicle manufacturing, and restructuring of existing debt" to quote from the summary of the Frank bill. The Frank bill also includes an oversight committee to be made up of the secretaries of Labor, Energy, and Transportation and the EPA Administrator. Both bills take the money from the $700 billion banking bill already passed, and maintain the oversight provisions (such as they are) of that bill.

We find both bills promising, though we prefer the Frank bill's oversight panel. We would add two provisions:

1. A commitment to exceed the Corporate Average Fuel Economy requirement of 35 mpg by 2020, by 10% (This requirement could be made contingent on the passage of a bill requiring permits to emit greenhouse gases, to ensure that there is demand for such vehicles.

2. The "Financial Stability Oversight Board" in the Frank bill (described above) should be assisted by a panel of automotive industry experts who would create a set of operational metrics to ensure that the improvement programs we described above are well underway. Because of the interdependencies described above, there is a large payoff to collaborative relations, relations that are not well suited to being judged by conventional financial metrics. These metrics are focused on the short term, and can make it look attractive to (for example) squeeze supplier margins, not taking into account the long-term disadvantages of reduced ability to collaborate to reduce system costs.

We find this approach quite promising. We share the frustration of the public with the past decisions by leaders of the industry, and harbor no illusions that this plan has a 100% chance of producing a viable industry. However, we do not believe such a rigorous standard is necessary to meet to justify public investment in the industry. We believe that providing a well-secured loan to avoid imminent massive job loss in the industry is an intelligent use of public funds.

Conclusion

There is opportunity in this crisis. All stakeholders, amid the painful sacrifices that will be required, must keep this in mind. If the crisis is framed in zero-sum terms, the probability of a destructive scramble for each stakeholder to preserve its own benefits and prerogatives to the exclusion of others will increase dramatically — as will the risk of overwhelming losses for all. The plan outlined here would address the immediate crisis and put the industry on a path toward restoring its long term competitiveness, providing sustainable jobs and helping the nation meet its environmental challenges.

Source: Susan Helper, John Paul MacDuffie, Joel Cutcher-Gershenfeld, Teresa Ghilarducci, and Thomas Kochan.

Comments:

This unsolicited letter was drafted during the weekend following the televised auto industry hearings in which it was clear to the coauthors and many other experts on the auto industry that the U.S. government had no understanding of the scale and scope of the challenge or the relevant recent history in the industry. The letter represents a time-bound white paper on the industry and reflects the uncertainty of the moment. The letter makes what turned out to be an incorrect assumption—that Chapter 11 bankruptcies with government receivership would be a lengthy and debilitating. Still, the letter does signal pivotal events in the industry that preceded the economic crisis and that are essential for an understanding of what is to be done to avoid a collapse of the industry.

6.3 Briefing Slide on Working Together

Source: Ford Motor Company

Comments:

Marty Mulloy used this slide in many internal and public presentations. In some forums, he was asked whether the fellow on the bottom left was meant to represent him and if the fellow on the right was meant to represent Bob King or Jimmy Settles.

7   Joint Alignment

Guiding Principle: Disciplined, Standardized Processes

In 1797, Albert Gallatin, who later became U.S. secretary of the treasury under Thomas Jefferson and James Madison, introduced a profit-sharing plan in his New Geneva, Pennsylvania, glass factory. As he was reported to have said at the time, "The democratic principle on which this nation was founded should not be restricted to the political process but should be applied to the industrial operation as well."

According to Milton Derber, a noted scholar of industrial relations, this is the first known articulation of the concept "industrial democracy." In his 1970 book *The American Idea of Industrial Democracy, 1865–1965*, Derber defined the concept as including representation, equal rights, right of dissent, due process, responsibility to live up to contractual duties, minimum standards for employment, information sharing, and personal dignity. For Derber, collective bargaining represented the culmination of industrial democracy in America. He praised collective bargaining for its flexibility and adaptability. He concluded with the observation that because collective bargaining "is an idea developed out of pragmatic experience, it has the capacity for change as conditions change."[1]

Contrary to general views of collective bargaining, we saw in chapter 6 that it indeed proved to be an adaptable institutional arrangement for the UAW and Ford. Now we turn to exploring how industrial democracy in the workplace involves ongoing mechanisms for alignment and change in addition to collective bargaining. In particular, we highlight the pivotal events around ensuring robust, adaptable forums for joint dialogue and action at the plant, divisional, and enterprise levels. We also present pivotal events on building change management capability among those involved in developing what we see as the institutional infrastructure of joint forums.

Guiding innovations in the institutional infrastructure is the key principle of "disciplined, standardized processes." This is a foundational principle in lean and Six Sigma systems, usually applied to the work process and technical systems. Here we see that a disciplined, standardized approach to institutional forums (social systems) has been just as important in the Ford-UAW transformation.

The initial reaction of some union and management leaders to the idea of disciplined, standardized processes for meetings is a concern with bureaucracy and too many meetings. Underlying the concern is an appreciation for a harsh reality of organizational life: that any new institutional arrangement, even one set up with a worthy purpose, becomes focused on ensuring its survival more than its original purpose. Union and management leaders may not know that the idea dates back to a 1911 book by Robert Michels, or that he calls this "the iron law of oligarchy,"[2] but in many organizational settings there is an instinctive sense that new meetings will lead to added bureaucracy without sufficient added benefits. Thus there is a tension between the ideal of industrial democracy and the reality of bureaucratic arrangements, which are more focused on their continued existence than the original idealistic goal.

Peter Drucker's 1946 book *Concept of the Corporation*[3] celebrated the importance of disciplined, standardized processes as foundational for the success of General Motors at the time. He recommended, however, that GM move in the direction of "federal decentralization" (comparable to the structure of the United States) and which was roundly rejected within General Motors.[4] What Drucker envisioned was a productive, dynamic tension between centrally driven standardization and locally generated innovation. In fact, in the case of GM and at Ford, the corporate model evolved to be more rigid, with the business successes of the 1990s masking a static tension between internal fiefdoms and central authority. We saw management's effort to wrestle with this tension in chapter 4, in the case of Ford 2000.

During the 1970s, socio-technical systems theorists reinforced Drucker's notion of dynamic tension. They argued that when designing new systems it was important to incorporate the minimum critical structure—no more and no less.[5] Using charters to structure joint forums, as we will see in this chapter, is far less complex than a collective bargaining agreement or a corporate statement of policies and procedures, but has more structure than an agreement to meet with a stated vision or purpose. The additional attention to roles and responsibilities and other matters represents the minimum critical structure needed to bring to life Albert Gallatin's vision of industrial democracy in the workplace comparable to the democratic principles valued in society. Indeed, it may be better at delivering results.

This chapter highlights seven pivotal events:

Chapter 7

Pivotal Events	Overview	Type, Level
Atlanta Assembly Plant, FTPM Chartering, 2001	The first use of charters in the UAW-Ford system establishes a formal structure for the Ford Total Productive Maintenance initiative, providing a stable foundation—with union and management leaders' roles and responsibilities aligned.	Planned, Plant Level

Chapter 7

Pivotal Events	Overview	Type, Level
Dearborn Assembly Plant Chartering, 2001–2003	As the Dearborn Assembly Plant changes from a car to a truck plant while accelerating lean principles and establishing a flexible production system, a broad array of charters provides needed social system stability.	Planned, Plant Level
Time and Data Management, 2001–2003	The lean implementation process demands a more stable and consistent social infrastructure, including standardized scheduling of meetings and flow of information—contrary to an individualistic "cowboy" culture that can still be found in management.	Planned, Enterprise Level
Quality Chartering, 2004	The development of charters for the UAW-Ford National Quality Committee and divisional quality committees is a pivot away from these supplementary communication channels being integral to achieving best-in-class quality.	Planned, Enterprise Level
UAW-Ford National Joint Program Conference, 2006	The National Joint Program Conference shifts from a celebratory event to a launching pad to close the gap on quality with the competition.	Planned, Enterprise Level
Safety Chartering, 2008	The lessons from quality chartering extend to safety, providing a key foundation for safety to shift from a loosely connected set of practices to an integrated operating system.	Planned, Enterprise Level
UAW-HR Change Agents and HR OD Institute, 2009–2010	The increasing focus on building the capability to sustain the change marks maturation in the transformation process and shift toward the management of continuous change.	Planned, Enterprise Level

Atlanta Assembly Plant FTPM Chartering, 2001

It is 2001, and Ford's Atlanta Assembly Plant is already experiencing some success implementing elements of the Ford Production System (FPS). Anthony Hoskins is the newly appointed Lean Manufacturing Manager (LMM), a role established to replace the assistant plant manager role. As chapter 4 presents, the plant manager's job is to run "today's plant," while the LMM has lead responsibility for transitioning to "tomorrow's plant."

The Ford Total Productive Maintenance (FTPM), one of Hoskins' first areas of focus, aims at improving equipment uptime (and, ultimately, productivity) through preventative and predictive maintenance. There are strong UAW appointees in both the FPS coordinator role and the FTPM coordinator role. While they do see some targeted improvements in machine-

uptime and other metrics, they are concerned that they are not seeing evidence of continuous improvement.

Hoskins learns from the UAW's Joe Gafa of a new idea that may help advance the joint
work on FTPM: establish a charter for the joint activity. Roger Komer, a retired UAW expert
in organizational development working with Joel Cutcher-Gershenfeld to help the UAW and
Ford accelerate the implementation of FPS principles, conceives of the charter as something
less formal than a collective bargaining agreement, but more structured than the existing
joint understandings on FTPM between the union and the company.

Cutcher-Gershenfeld works with Komer to generate a draft template for an FTPM charter.
Gafa arranges with Hoskins for a three-hour chartering session—called "reenergizing FTPM"—
with the full Ford management operating committee and the full UAW local bargaining committee to review the draft.

At the session, Gafa talks about the important contributions skilled trades employees can
make to FTPM and Hoskins talks about the importance of FTPM to overall plant performance. Cutcher-Gershenfeld projects the elements of the draft charter on a large screen.

The "preamble" draft reads, "This is a living document that may only be changed by a
consensus of local UAW-Ford leaders." This sparks immediate discussion: everyone understands how to operate by consensus, but what is meant by "leaders"? The group agrees on a
change: "This is a living document that may only be changed by the Plant Manager in consensus with the Plant Chairman, Atlanta Assembly Plant."

The mission statement reads, "Re-energize FTPM in manufacturing plants utilizing coaching principles, Six Sigma, and management behaviors to establish a process for FTPM, including a process for FTPM budgets." A draft statement of purpose, which employs many lean
and Six Sigma principles, follows this mission statement. It is reshaped in places through
group discussion. Ultimately the draft included the following five goals:

1. Complete needs analysis based on current state—includes constraint management, value stream development, level of CIWG implementation, status of 7 steps of FTPM, PM Planning process and failure
reporting methods.
2. Begin Define, Measure, Analyze, Improve and Control (DMAIC) Process.
3. Prepare detailed Master Schedule and A3s. Include the following areas:
   a. System Development, Implementation and Improvement.
   b. Process Development Implementation and Improvement.
   c. Operational Transformation.
   d. Cultural Transformation.
4. Develop FTPM Scorecard Metrics.
5. Form Plant (FTPM) Vertical Steering Committee.

The statement of purpose makes clear that the goal in reenergizing FTPM is for all parties
to better understand the current state, including mapping of the plant's value streams. This
is a key aspect of the technical system. The continuous improvement work groups (CIWGs)
are a key aspect of the social system. The DMAIC process (Define, Measure, Analyze, Improve,

Control) is part of Six Sigma, and A3s are a lean tool (specifically, one-page overviews of continuous improvement projects).

Other key parts of the charter include the logistics for meetings, including a relatively long discussion on whether alternates can be send to FTPM steering committee meetings. While some in the room indicate they would like to be able to send alternates, both the plant manager and the chair of the union bargaining committee send a clear message: no alternates, and attendance is mandatory.

Following the session, copies of the new draft charter are distributed to all participants and they are given a week to suggest edits. A week later, at the first jointly chartered FTPM meeting, all present sign the document—with the top two signature lines reserved for the Ford plant manager and the UAW bargaining chair. All present are literally charter members of the FTPM forum, which becomes a living document.

A year later, at a meeting of the Lean Implementation Network (see chapter 4), Hoskins presents the FPTM chartering process as a leading practice for others to consider. "Atlanta was already a stable environment when I arrived," he states, "but charters added further stability and structure." He indicates that the plant is seeing tangible improvements in machine uptime and concludes, "We have been needing something like this for a long time."

While the FTPM charter was beneficial in Atlanta for a while, changes in local union leadership and larger dynamics around the UAW's engagement with FPS (discussed in chapter 3) limited the charter's long-term use in this location. Despite the infrastructure for sharing innovations provided by the Lean Implementation Network, there was not a senior level corporate champion for the FTPM chartering, and FTPM chartering did not diffuse to other FTPM efforts.

Although Harbour Consulting rated the Atlanta Assembly Plant in 2006 as the most efficient auto plant in North America, its distance from suppliers was a cost barrier that could not be overcome. The plant ended up closing shortly after 2006 under the Way Forward plan that consolidated operations in the face of declining market share. The innovations with FTPM, including the use of a charter, traveled with Hoskins as he became plant manager at the Chicago Assembly Plant and then as a director of Manufacturing. Recently, in reflecting on the experience, Hoskins points out how the charter was connected to the continuous improvement process:

✳ ✳ ✳

We did value stream mapping in Atlanta and saw that FTPM was key to getting throughput in a plant that is running fairly well. The value stream mapping then helped in teaching at the team leader level what the opportunities were, including the preventative and predictive maintenance opportunities. When you can sit and talk jointly with the people who are doing the work and they see that the union and management are joining together that makes a difference. Under the charter it is clear that you have all the people rowing in the same direction.

While the FTPM charter was a valuable document, as Hoskins indicates, the chartering *process* was more important. Through it, the leadership literally got on the same page around the governance of the FTPM initiative. Further, with each change in the leadership of the plant—union or management—the charter provided a way of reducing the instability during the change. The new leader would be introduced to the charter (adding a baseline understanding for how things work) and the arrival of fresh eyes was an occasion to see whether the charter needed adjustment in any way.

The use of charters is the first pivot toward a systematic approach to institutional infrastructure for quality, safety, and what the UAW and Ford term "time and data management" (presented later in this chapter).

Dearborn Assembly Plant Chartering, 2001–2003

The 2001 revitalization of the Rouge complex centers on transition: the existing Dearborn Assembly Plant (producing Mustangs) changes its production focus to become the Dearborn Truck Plant (producing the F150 and other associated products) along with its integration as an engine and a stamping plant. It is an externally recognized showcase as the most environmentally advanced auto plant in the world (see chapter 4). It is also designed to lead the way with platform-based production that will accommodate up to six different models interspersed on the assembly line—allowing great flexibility in responding to market demand. But the internal structure and operations are not nearly as modern as the new facility or the new technology. A Modern Operating Agreement (MOA) is negotiated along with the new investment—providing for a small number of job classifications for assembly and skilled trades work, was well as other flexibility in operations. This, however, represents a major culture change for the workforce, which will be working with the most flexible production system in a U.S. Ford facility. In this context, the operating roles of managers and the representational roles of the union are not entirely clear.

The key players have varying degrees of experience with the kind of system being implemented. Jay Richardson has led the revitalization of the Rouge and has delivered on Bill Ford's environmental vision. Dennis Profitt is brought in as the site manager; he has just returned from assignment in Europe overseeing team-based operations more flexible than is typical in the United States. Jeff Faistenhammer had been HR manager in Cleveland Engine Plant 2 and so is also used to operating with team-based work systems; he comes on as HR manager at the Rouge. Jerry Sullivan is the president of UAW Local 600; his experience is in a more traditional plant, but he is willing to negotiate the MOA in exchange for the new investment and new products in the site. Sullivan is willing to trade flexibility for job security.

Production operations must be launched without the luxury of time to get the new social system in place. There is also ongoing tension in the air from the Rouge explosion two years earlier. "There were several times where people walked off the job after the Rouge explosion," Faistenhammer notes. "Smells would come through and couldn't be identified. People were scared."

Profitt assigns Doug Mertz to be an internal Ford change agent and brings on Roger Komer, an external consultant who is a retired UAW organizational change agent and Joel Cutcher-Gershenfeld, an external consultant working with Komer, to bring structure and discipline to the social system while the ramp-up and launch is taking place. The three worked together at the Ford Sterling Axle Plant.

"This started the trend of chartering at the plant level," Mertz notes. "My job in the Rouge was to set up the joint infrastructure."

To prepare, Mertz and Komer consult organization design documents from the Cleveland Engine Plant 1 and other plants operating under the principles of a team-based system. Komer sets up an office area in the Rouge complex with extensive resource materials, field-tested from the Sterling Axle Plant. Faistenhammer recalls;

Roger was there every day and every night. He was constantly talking to the union and the company. Both sides didn't understand the new system. He brought real tools in that people could use. Tracking tools on a computer, single point lessons, charters. His office at the Rouge was amazing.

He would present to the union on new work systems and how work happened. He would present on how to lay out the budget in an area so people could do something about it. He would help foreman to give stump speeches when they needed to speak to an issue. The union came to trust him; he was not just seen as an outsider. I am convinced that Roger's presence and how hard he worked was pivotal.

The plant is running "pre-builds"—prototypes built just prior to what is called "job 1" with the F150. The F150 is selling well in the marketplace and there is corporate pressure to bring products to market, even if it is at the expense of building lean capability. Mertz notes:

We had made the transition from Dearborn Assembly to Dearborn Truck, but there were issues with the new layout of the line. It was a lean layout with just-in-time delivery of materials. We where shifting from Mustangs to F150s. When we started to ramp-up production, we were struggling with getting to the needed jobs per hour. There was a ton of pressure on [Dennis Profitt].

If you look at it using a force field analysis, you see that they are trying for reinforce lean principles, but at the same time they are being pushed increasingly hard for volume. It is very difficult to reinforce the new principles and to run the truck plant at full volume. [Profitt] was in a hard spot.

The joint leadership instructs Mertz to begin chartering the regular meetings in the various areas of the plant, such as meetings on quality, safety, FTPM, and other topics. The reception to chartering is lukewarm. "I never spent so much time alone in a conference room," Mertz recalls. "We would announce a chartering session, but initially people didn't show up. Dennis Profitt was fully supportive of the chartering and said that he expected his people to participate. But they were running production and did not see value in sitting in a room."

Mertz adds that the UAW leaders were not clear on their role in the process. This is what chartering was designed to address, but first people had to know enough to show up for the session.

There is high-level sponsorship for the chartering from Profitt, the UAW Local 600 president Sullivan, and Faistenhammer, the HR manager, but challenges persist. "The sponsorship by the leaders is critical," says Mertz, "but it is not enough. The plant leadership wanted to charter all these other forums, but initially they were not focused on themselves. It was only after they chartered themselves that they really saw the value."

The FPS Leadership Planning Forum, the first charter developed, involves all the top union and management leaders and serves to reinforce the implementation of lean principles concurrent with the new product launch. Signed by all plant leaders on February 19, 2001, the charter makes clear the purpose of the forum, which includes identifying and resolving issues that might inhibit the effective implementation of the Ford Production System, as well as designing policies, procedures, practices, and processes to sustain the FPS initiative. It signals the importance of aligning the physical plant, operational assumptions, and human/cultural elements. A plant "book" of standardized aspects of the social infrastructure is highlighted, along with a focus on SQDCME and FPS metrics. Box 7.1 is the full text of the charter (note that this text is from a 2002 update of the charter, which is a living document; changes are visible, such as change from assistant plant manager to lean manufacturing manager).

Box 7.1
FPS Leadership Planning Forum Charter

(Physicals, Operational Assumptions, Human/Cultural Alignment)

Preamble
This is a living document and can be changed by consensus of the FPS Leadership Planning Forum Active Members.

Mission
FPS Leadership Planning Forum is a joint team from DAP Ford management and UAW Leadership members that is focused on, but not limited to, implementing and implementing FPS in DAP/DTP.

Purpose
1. To identify and resolve issues that inhibit effectively implementing and sustaining FPS implementation and culture change at DAP/DTP to meet annual level goals. Level 7 for DTP launch.
2. To design and develop effective policies, procedures, practices and processes that foster implementation implementing and sustaining of FPS initiatives.
3. To ensure alignment of physicals, operational assumptions, human/cultural elements in the implementation process of implementing and sustaining.
4. Build a social infrastructure plant book to standardize and formalize the process.
5. To develop and ensure implementation of policies related to FPS are implemented and sustained.
6. Will act as the FPS Steering Committee and guide implementation.
7. Ensure that Policy Deployment is communicated and implemented plant-wide to focus on SQDCME and FPS Measurables.

Box 7.1 (continued)

Active Members

When an active member is unable to attend they may send a replacement who will act as a resource member. The replacement will not be counted when determining quorum or participate in decision making.

Manufacturing Manager Lean Mfg Mgr	UAW Chairpersons
Final Area Manager	Bargaining Committeeperson
MP&L Manager	Bargaining Committeeperson
Planning Manager	Employee Resource Coordinator
FPS Salaried Coordinator	FPS Hourly Coordinator
Quality Manager	ERC—M&C unit
Body Area Manager	UAW Quality Rep
Paint Area Manager	FTPM Coordinator
	Job Security Representative

Resource Members

Plant Manager	Launch Training Representative
DAP\DTP	Transitional Coordinators Site HR Manager
Site Manager	FPS V.O. Coach

Third Party Facilitators

Training Development Leader—DAP

Facilitator resources as needed

Roles and Responsibilities

Active Members

1. Attend all meetings and arrive on time.
2. Constructive participation.
3. Respect all opinions.
4. Discuss issues not personal conflicts.
5. Follow-up on action items.
6. Follow agreed upon forum procedures.

Resource Members

1. Attend meetings as required. Resources members listed on the charter have an open invitation. Other resource members will be invited as needed.
2. Provide information for discussion and participate constructively when requested.

Third Party Faciliator(S)

1. Facilitate forum activities.
2. Update tracking matrix.
3. Prepare and distribute agenda.
4. Issue meeting minutes.
5. Maintain files.

Box 7.1 (continued)

6. Meeting timekeeper and scribe.
7. Enforce charter.
8. Coaching and counseling members who consistently violate the forum charter.

Procedures

1. Meetings
   • Forum meeting held every Monday from 1-2:30 pm 12:30 – 2 pm in the E.I. Center. Whenever possible the meeting will be held to 1 hour.
   • Additional meetings and rescheduling must be done by consensus.
   • Each meeting will follow established agenda.

2. Agenda
   • Agreement or revisions to the agenda.
   • Housekeeping Issues.
   • Special topics or reports
   • Matrix Issues.
   • Discussion of following meetings agenda.
   • Element reports.
   • Agreement on communication.

3. Decisions
   • Made by consensus. (Can everyone live with this decision?)
   • Must have a quorum to reach consensus.
   • Quorum is a minimum of 3 active union and 4 management representatives with at least 2 Bargaining Committee Members.

4. Managing the Meeting
   • Active Members have the right, by consensus, to request that a resource member be excused from the meeting for confidential discussions.

5. Managing the matrix
   • The Standard Tracking Matrix will be used to track issues.
   • Standard criteria for prioritizing and adding issues to the Matrix.
     ✓ Is it FPS Related?
     ✓ Is it a policy making issue?
     ✓ Is there somebody else already addressing this issue?
     ✓ Can this issue be resolved immediately in the current meeting? (still added to the matrix as a resolved issue.
   • When an issue is added to the matrix it must be clearly defined, have an initial report date established, have a responsible party identified and be prioritized.
   • Reassigning and identifying appropriate forum to address current matrix issues and new issues.

6. Communication
   • Communication required between meetings will be distributed via email. Matrixes, agendas and other Forum material can be read by members listed on the charter at W:\FPS Leadership Planning Forum

Box 7.1 (continued)

7. Discussion
   • Issues will be discussed using Current State/Desired State Gap Analysis methodology, and will be structured by the 5W's and How model.
   • All discussion must be data driven.
   • Discussion may be halted to address housekeeping issues upon request of an Active Member.
8. Other
   • Radios must be off. Pagers and cell phones must be on vibrate mode.
   • Meeting interruptions should be limited to the extent possible.
   • Refrain from participating in side conversations including use of pagers to communicate to other attendees.

Agreement Date: September 30, 2002
Agreement by:

Title	Signature
UAW Chairmen	
Bargaining Committeeperson	
Bargaining Committeeperson	
Bargaining Committeeperson	
Job Security Representative	
FPS Hourly Coordinator	
Employee Resource Coordinator	
Employee Resource	
Coordinator – M&C	
UAW Quality Rep	
FTPM Coordinator	
Manufacturing Manager	
Final Area Manager	
MP&L Manager	
Planning Manager	
FPS Salaried Coordinator	
Quality Manager	
Body Area Manager	
Paint Area Manager	

Source: UAW-Ford National Joint Programs.

Next is the Good and Welfare Mutual Growth Forum Charter, which combines the idea of a "good and welfare" meeting of union and plant management leadership with the idea of a "Mutual Growth Forum" as originally established in the 1982 negotiations. Thus, the forum combines informal top-level dialogue with formal discussions on the plant products, investment, and jobs. Box 7.2 presents the initial sections of the Mutual Growth Forum Charter.

While most of the charters correspond to elements of the Ford Production System or the UAW-Ford national joint programs, one of the early charters builds on the new product launch process. New product launches include an engineering process called "manage-the-change," designed to ensure alignment among all parties affected by any engineering design change. The process distinguishes Level 1, Level 2, and Level 3 changes. While at the Sterling Axle Plant, Komer had adapted the process for social as well as technical changes; it is creative move, capitalizing on the familiarity of all parties with the process and the underlying principles around alignment in support of change, but using it to ensure alignment of frontline workers before there are changes in how they do their job.

Komer suggests setting up a "manage-the-change" forum at the Rouge, with the appropriate charter. Mertz is tasked with chartering the forum, as he explains.

One part of the Quality Operating System is the manage-the-change process, which is mostly focused on engineering changes and workload allocation. For this forum, we got the appropriate union representation and appropriate company representation involved and set out a vision to more clearly define and align how we handle Level 1, 2, and 3 changes, each with a different depth and type communication. A change may be minor, but you can't have operators coming in on a Monday and have their workstation changed without first getting their input.

Mertz adds, "We turned manage-the-change into a more robust process to ensure that the leadership received feedback from the operators on changes."

Box 7.3 is the "Mission" and "Purpose" section of this charter.

Ultimately, all joint forums and teams for the Dearborn Assembly Plant are chartered, including many central to the launch of the new work system. Even some management meetings that don't formally involve the UAW are chartered, including the Leadership Forum, which is the plant management operating committee. In total, over 30 forums are chartered, including:

Environmental Systems Team
Equal Application Committee
Error Proofing Element Team
FPS Element Champions
FTPM Team
Good and Welfare Mutual Growth Forum
Joint Continuous Improvement Committee
FPS Leadership Planning Forum
Industrial Materials Element Team

Box 7.2
Good & Welfare Mutual Growth Forum Charter (Excerpts)

Preamble
This is a living document that may only be changed by consensus of the Good & Welfare Mutual Growth Forum's active members

Mission
The Good & Welfare Mutual Growth Forum is a joint union and management team that is focused on, but not limited to, promoting cooperation between the union and the company through better communication, systematic fact finding, and addressing as early as possible issues affecting the interests of employees, the union, and management

Purpose
1. To communicate and resolve current local union concerns on a timely basis
2. To communicate and resolve current management concerns on a timely basis
3. To communicate current competitive challenges/realities that could affect the long term viability of the plant
4. To ensure flawless execution of policy deployment

Active Members
Individuals holding the following positions are *active members* of the Good & Welfare Mutual Growth Forum:

Manufacturing Manager	UAW Chairman
Lean Transitional Manufacturing Manager	UAW V.P./Barg. Comm. Rep.
HR Manager	UAW Bargaining Comm. Rep.
Labor Relations Supervisor	UAW Bargaining Comm. Rep.

Resource Members
Individuals holding the following positions are considered *resource members* of the Good & Welfare Mutual Growth Forum:

Resources will be asked to attend on an "as needed" basis only by consensus of the Good & Welfare Mutual Growth Forum's Active Members

Third Party Facilitator(s):
Individual(s) holding the following position(s) are the *third party facilitator(s)* for the Good & Welfare Mutual Growth Forum:

A third party facilitator will not be used

[Additional elements of the charter follow.]

Source: UAW-Ford National Joint Programs.

Box 7.3

Dearborn Truck Plant "Mission" and "Purpose" from the Manage-the-Change Charter

---

Mission

The MTC Communication Flow Process Subgroup is a team from the Dearborn Assembly Plant that is focused on, but not limited to, improve internal and external customer satisfaction through the elimination of change-related outcomes

Purpose

1. To develop and implement a manage the change communication flow process that will ensure people affected by change are notified in advance and provided the opportunity for input and feedback
2. To serve as a clearing house for all Level 1, 2, and 3 changes
3. To coach change initiators through the manage the change communication flow process
4. To track and maintain documentation for all Level 1, 2, and 3 changes
5. To monitor compliance with the manage the change communication flow procedures

---

Source: UAW-Ford National Joint Programs.

Job Security and Operational Effectiveness Committee
Leadership Team
Measurables Team
Mechanical Engineering Element Team
Medical Placement Committee
Quality Operating System Element Team
Quick Change Element Team
Safety Process Review Board
SHARP Element Team
Superintendent Forum Charter
Team Leaders' Meeting
Training Element Team
UAW Issues Meeting
Visual Factory Element Team
Work Group Element Team

Area teams and committees are also chartered, including the Body Area Implementation Team, Final Area Implementation Team, and Paint Area Implementation Team.

"I have always believed that the process for joint alignment and implementation is critical," says Mertz. "People think they have the required infrastructure in many cases, but they don't. So much is dependent on the personalities. We are trying to get a system in place that is bigger than any one person, but to start it is key to have support from the union chairman, the plant manager, and the HR manager."

In addition to the chartered forums, there are also regular team meetings. All these meetings in total come to be seen as the social infrastructure for a lean production system.

Dennis Profitt shows skill in orchestrating the process. One evening around 7:00, Joel Cutcher-Gershenfeld is walking by Profitt's office and is invited in. Profitt says he's reading the meeting minutes from a sample of the frontline team meetings that week. He identifies issues they are working on so he can then make sure that the appropriate plant-level forums are aligned and ready to support the teams. This also lets him test whether the system is surfacing and addressing the issues on a timely basis.

Profitt's review of team meeting minutes is one of various formal and informal feedback loops that help keep the system functioning effectively as the social infrastructure of the Dearborn Assembly Plant.

✳ ✳ ✳

An overly bureaucratic structure: that was the initial characterization by many in the UAW and Ford organizations to the chartering of so many teams and forums in the Dearborn Assembly Plant. The increased levels of support needed for a lean, team-based work system, however, require a stable, robust set of forums on all the key issues. There must be a flow of data, based on performance metrics, into each forum that—as we will see in the next pivotal event—will ultimately lead to the embrace of "time and data management" on a system-wide basis.

The chartering of the many Dearborn Assembly Plant forums reflected institutional creativity. For example, connecting the "Good and Welfare" meetings with the Mutual Growth Forum combined informal relationship building and problem solving with formal dialogue on the business of the plant. Similarly, adapting the engineering "manage-the-change" process to include a central role for frontline operators instantiated underlying operating assumptions that valued frontline work.

Innovation in social systems, as much as innovation in technical systems, is foundational for the UAW-Ford transformation.

Time and Data Management, 2001–2003

In the Ford plant culture, the more traditional managers are known as "cowboys" or "Marlboro men" for their individualist approach to driving performance results. In 2001, a newly appointed plant manager at one of Ford's assembly plants even boasts to Joel Cutcher-Gershenfeld that he changed all the standing meetings when he arrived at the plant just to show everyone who's in charge. Clearly, a system moving toward greater reliance on coordinated continuous improvement across all facilities and increased appreciation of knowledge at all levels of the organization cannot function in this way.

Indeed, lean production principles—which center on eliminating all forms of waste in an organization—characterize that plant manager's action in changing all the meetings as a form of waste (defining *waste* as anything that does not add value to the end product). Lean principles highlight eight common sources of waste: overproduction, waiting, inventory, transportation, over-processing, motion, defects, and inefficiency in managing the workforce. The Ford initiative around time and data management is designed to address the latter form of waste directly.

At a 2001 meeting of the Lean Implementation Network, Al Ver, the vice president of Manufacturing Engineering and Business Planning, and Roman Krygier, the vice president of Manufacturing, engage in a dialogue with the group of approximately 150 lean manufacturing managers, HR managers, and change agents on how efficiently Ford manages its workforce. The consensus is that a great deal of time is wasted each day because calendars are not aligned and customer priority issues too often get set aside when people run out of time. The participants all agree that time is their most precious resource, and that the greatest leverage to serve the customer is in aligning the talents of the workforce to address priority customer issues.

Obviously, Ford needs to "work smarter," but Ver and Krygier know that simply spouting such clichés will be not deliver results. They want to change the process and help the plants' operating committees (the plant manager and those direct reporting to him or her) better manage their workforces.

Why is there insufficient time (which everyone agrees is the most precious resource)? Meeting participants point to demands coming from many different corporate functions—all claiming to be top priority—as a constant disruption and a source of waste in the system. To improve how time is used to meet objectives, the group adopts an initiative to *prioritize* their objectives; *identify key stakeholders and meeting participants*; and *allocate time and frequency for meetings* to address each objective. This is implemented as a matrix tool with the day of the week as the horizontal axis and time as the vertical axis. Each minute of every day is allocated: work to be completed at an assigned time slot. For example, Health and Safety meetings between the plant union chairman and the plant manager are given a time allocation, and calendars are coordinated and locked into the schedule. The same process is followed with each FPS objective (Safety, Quality, Delivery, Cost, People, Maintenance, and Environment) and for other key issues.

The Time and Data Management initiative involves all plants in North and South America.

It is one thing, however, to write down meeting times on a calendar. Getting people to respect the schedule is an entirely different matter. So, Ver and Krygier, the management champions of the initiative, commit to respect the calendars of their subordinates and protect them from staff interruptions. The timing of plant visits and corporate phone calls are carefully constructed to avoid disrupting the flow of the plants' time and data management calendars.

Getting the "cowboys" on board proves even more challenging. By 2002, though, all plants are told they have no choice but to implement the Time and Data Management initiative. Still, it takes a full year before all the plants are on the schedule, with a few plant managers who resist embracing the change moved out of their role, which sends a very strong signal to all.

Adrian Vido leads Quality in Manufacturing and in 2003 incorporates "time and data management" as one of the four core pillars in the Ford Quality Operating System (all of which are presented in chapter 8). "Now a director of Manufacturing knows exactly when to call the plant on a given issue," he notes, "with all the right people in the room at that time."

"If everything is important," Vido adds, "then nothing is important. Time and data management forces prioritization—it forces people into regular meetings on the right issues and places limits on corporate's ability to pull people out of the plant."

When the hourly black belts are launched in 2007 (see chapter 5), Wilhelmina Allen notes that time and data management is key, enabling what she refers to as "tremendous integration in their jobs." The hourly black belts can all map their improvement efforts onto the standardized structure of meetings, each with standardized information.

Commenting on the connection between charters and time and data management is Anthony Hoskins, one of Ford's directors of Manufacturing and the LLM in the Atlanta FTPM pivotal event earlier in this chapter:

Chartering is engrained into the fabric of the company—it is central to time and data management system. All meetings should have a purpose, under the chartering format, with the right stakeholders. We may not always use the term "charter," but the principle is key. Being clear on who are the stakeholders, what decisions can be made, what is a quorum, etcetera. This is a fundamental process for running the plants. Now that we are on a three-crew, seven-day operation this is even more important. The leadership has to be even more efficient with how we manage time and make decisions.

***

Establishing time and data management as one of the four pillars in the Quality Operating System is an indication of the importance of standardizing operations. Time and data management has proven foundational in furthering the alignment of labor and management across the different levels of the relationship—workplace, collective bargaining/institutional, and strategic. Today, as a vice president of Manufacturing manages his or her plants and a union vice president leads his or her membership, both know exactly what issues are being worked on at each plant across the world at each hour on each day of the week.

Quality Chartering, 2004

The interest-based approach to quality signals the alignment of labor and management on quality in the 2003 National UAW-Ford negotiations. There are now hourly Quality Operating System Coordinators in every plant, selected based on their expertise with quality principles. Based on the SQDCME balanced scorecard, there are standardized measures of quality in every plant at the work group, area, plant, divisional, and corporate levels. Time and data management adds standardized weekly union-management meetings on quality, using standardized quality data. The goal of "best-in-class quality" is shared between labor and management leaders.

Even with the strategic alignment, Dan Brooks as the labor co-chair of the UAW-Ford National Quality Committee has a basic question for his executive counterparts responsible for quality at the Ford Motor Company: "What is my role and what is the role of this committee in helping Ford achieve best-in-class quality?"

There is no clear or consistent answer. For the most part, management sees the UAW as a means of communicating to the workforce the importance of quality. That falls far short of the potential role that the union and joint quality forums can play. Brooks, who followed the experience in Atlanta with the FTPM chartering, suggests to Dean Blythe, his management co-chair on the UAW-Ford National Quality Committee (NQC), that Joel Cutcher-Gershenfeld be asked to do the same thing for quality.

Brooks and Blythe are aware of how chartering helped clarify and standardize roles at Atlanta, and they are also aware of the limited diffusion of the idea when starting at the plant level. They meet with Cutcher-Gershenfeld and specify that the chartering should begin at the highest level, with the NQC and the Divisional Quality Committees, and the parties should then live with the charters for a year before attempting a system-wide diffusion.

Adrian Vido, who leads Quality for Ford's Vehicle Operations, responds positively to the idea of a charter for the NQC and the diffusion plan.

We knew we needed to standardize our approach and document what we were doing in a way the company and union leadership could support. Dan came to us with the chartering idea. We had embraced the message from Ann Stevens on bad quality, "don't take it, don't make it, don't pass it along."

Chartering resonated with all of us, but not all leaders were there. We said we are going to put this puppy in a charter. A charter is a grant of authority and we were granting the authority to the membership at large to execute in the specified manner—with clear roles and responsibilities.

On January 14, 2004, the members of the NQC gather for an offsite meeting in northern Ohio, joined by other Ford leaders of Quality and executives, including the vice president of North American Vehicle Operations, directors of Manufacturing from Ford's three main divisions (Vehicle Operations, Powertrain, and Stamping), and representatives from the Visteon Division and Ford Customer Service Division (FCSD), which includes parts warehouses. Cutcher-Gershenfeld facilitates. The goal of the two-day event is better alignment between the UAW and Ford to achieve best-in-class quality and increase the effectiveness of the NQC. Some UAW and Ford leaders are positive about the session, but others are skeptical. Attendance is mandatory.

Everyone recognizes how rare it is for top union leaders to be at an offsite such as this with senior operating executives. Seating assignments at round tables of six or seven people deliberately intermix the participants.

The session begins with a review of the goals and an overview on chartering, along with current problems motivating the gathering:

• Joint forums (such as the plant joint steering committee) are disrupted every time there is a new leader from union or management.

• The agenda in joint forums is taken over by whatever issue is "hot"—even if it doesn't belong in that forum.
• The roles and responsibilities in joint forums are not clear.
• The meeting process is not as effective as it could be.
• The number of pressing issues requiring joint attention is increasing.

The people at each table discuss their own expectations for the session and then report to the full group. Some of the key expectations are:

• Learn more about the inner workings of the National Quality Committee, the divisional committees and the Quality Operating System.
• Align as a full group—around direction and approach for what is to follow as next steps—beginning immediately on Friday when we return—in a standardized way.
• Develop an understanding of the intent with the new negotiated [quality] language.
• Create a meaningful charter for National Quality Committee and respective divisions—with clear linkage to internal customers (local quality committees and others) and external customers—making a difference in the marketplace.
• Anticipate how we will deliver this message on the charter—cascade, catch-ball to the plants—follow-on charter with internal customers (local quality committees).
• Aligned vision and effective deployment of the tools—but be mindful that the shadow we cast is aligned with what the employees need—we are their support system—without alignment, there will be a disconnect.
• Ensure that tools are a value-add—a pull, not a push.
• Improve quality and employee participation across Ford and Visteon.
• Make certain that charters have clearly defined roles and responsibilities so that when new leaders come in it will be an effective learning tool—the structure and method of the charter is an enabler for improving quality.

The elements of a charter are summarized, incorporating lessons from the FTPM chartering and the Rouge charters:

Preamble
  • For example, stating that it is a living document
Mission
  • Overall statement of what the forum seeks to do
Purpose
  • Specific role of the forum—sometimes in relation to other forums
Active Members
  • Positions represented as active members of the forum
Resource Members
  • Additional positions held by individuals serving as a resource to the forum
Roles and Responsibilities
  • Specific roles and responsibilities of different members of the forum

Procedures and Operations
   • Meeting frequency and operating procedures
   • Additional operating agreements, such as the use of an "Issue Tracking Matrix"
Signatures
   • Current and future members of forum sign to indicate agreement with the provisions of
   the Charter

The participants then break out into separate groups for the NQC and the Divisional Quality Committees. They are asked to brainstorm lists of what they see as the best and worst aspects of the committees. In priority order, national-level "best" items are:

• Everyone here wants to make quality better
• Good in a crisis
• Joint delivery of a message
• Attempt to engage plant floor workers (QLI)
• Provides communication channel that otherwise wouldn't exist
• Training development
• Quality hotline effectiveness

While being good in a crisis is a plus, the participants discuss that the aim is to standardize quality to avoid crises. The Quality Leadership Initiative (QLI), presented in chapter 8, shows up on the "best" list as an "attempt" to engage the frontline workforce, but it also appears at the top of the "worst" list (here in priority order as well):

• QLI is not effective.
• How do we measure the effectiveness of NQC?
• We don't use the tools that are on the shelf.
• Engaging employees to implement and sustain quality (garner operations support).
• Fail to openly communicate.
• We don't delegate well.
• Measure training effectiveness.
• Quality concern resolution process (leadership/evidence) and tracking of it

As we will see in chapter 8, the QLI is a largely top-down reengineering approach to quality that falls short of its potential as a pivot. In additional to the QLI, the "worst" list signals the importance of increased frontline engagement in driving quality.

The lists at the divisional level are similar, but with more emphasis on alignment across levels. The "best" list at the divisional level includes (in priority order):

• Manage to work through differences to resolution.
• Movement toward a standardized process.
• Motivated and knowledgeable people.
• In general—common goals and common vision.
• Genuine appreciation for what quality means to the success of the business.

- Best-In-Class—a living document that affects everyone.
- Framework of processes exist—hot line, QOS.
- Openness, willing to share.
- Accountability, responsibility (but just firefighting).

The list emphasizes the common goals and vision in various ways. The "worst" list highlights process issues, including these items (in priority order):

- Lack of effective meetings.
- Have them to have them; lack of substance; unclear what purpose of each meeting is to have.
- Poor communications—Division to Plants; lack of agreement on best way to communicate.
- Poor alignment—Local to Operations to National.
- Objectives, Communications, Measuring, Acceptance.
- Lack of accountability/responsibility.
- Results are highly variable.

With this preparation, the parties are ready for the chartering process. A draft is prepared in advance, copies are distributed to all participants, and each section is reviewed and edited by the entire group on a big screen. Box 7.4 is the final version.

Finally, the group creates a written shared vision of success that focuses on the In-Station Process Control (ISPC) and the Quality Operating System. They use Roger Komer's " Five Ws & How" format (figure 7.1) to specify a list of stakeholders ("who"), the focus ("what"), key milestones ("when"), locational factors ("where"), an elevator speech on the change ("why"), and guiding principles ("how").

The session generates a draft national charter, with an agreement to reflect on it and reconvene back in northern Ohio a month later to develop divisional charters for Vehicle Operations, Powertrain, Stamping, Visteon, and Ford's Customer Service Division (FCSD). True to the original plan, they live with the charters for a year and then begin chartering plant quality committees.

"The chartering process really brought standardization to the local quality committees—some of which were effective and some of which before chartering were just paper programs in name only," Dean Blythe comments. "The chartering made it clear that everyone had a commitment to make it work."

✱✱✱

The charters developed during the NQC and Divisional Quality Committee session went beyond a focus on ensuring a stable and effective process. They also codified substantive roles and responsibilities, including those derived from contract language. On the one hand, this made them more complete. On the other hand, it meant they had to be kept up to date as tasks were completed and priorities changed—consistent with the preamble that states they are living documents.

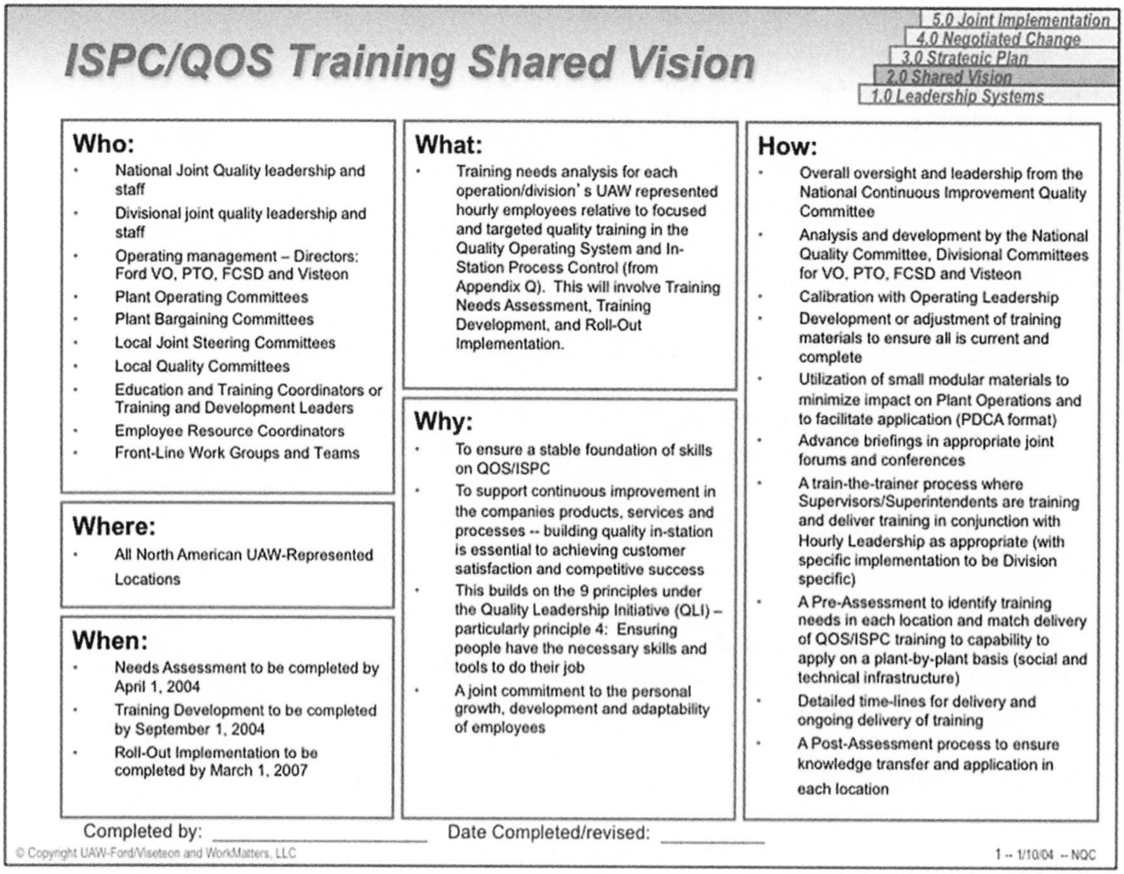

ISPC/QOS Training Shared Vision

5.0 Joint Implementation
4.0 Negotiated Change
3.0 Strategic Plan
2.0 Shared Vision
1.0 Leadership Systems

Who:

- National Joint Quality leadership and staff
- Divisional joint quality leadership and staff
- Operating management – Directors: Ford VO, PTO, FCSD and Visteon
- Plant Operating Committees
- Plant Bargaining Committees
- Local Joint Steering Committees
- Local Quality Committees
- Education and Training Coordinators or Training and Development Leaders
- Employee Resource Coordinators
- Front-Line Work Groups and Teams

Where:

- All North American UAW-Represented Locations

When:

- Needs Assessment to be completed by April 1, 2004
- Training Development to be completed by September 1, 2004
- Roll-Out Implementation to be completed by March 1, 2007

What:

- Training needs analysis for each operation/division's UAW represented hourly employees relative to focused and targeted quality training in the Quality Operating System and In-Station Process Control (from Appendix Q). This will involve Training Needs Assessment, Training Development, and Roll-Out Implementation.

Why:

- To ensure a stable foundation of skills on QOS/ISPC
- To support continuous improvement in the companies products, services and processes -- building quality in-station is essential to achieving customer satisfaction and competitive success
- This builds on the 9 principles under the Quality Leadership Initiative (QLI) – particularly principle 4: Ensuring people have the necessary skills and tools to do their job
- A joint commitment to the personal growth, development and adaptability of employees

How:

- Overall oversight and leadership from the National Continuous Improvement Quality Committee
- Analysis and development by the National Quality Committee, Divisional Committees for VO, PTO, FCSD and Visteon
- Calibration with Operating Leadership
- Development or adjustment of training materials to ensure all is current and complete
- Utilization of small modular materials to minimize impact on Plant Operations and to facilitate application (PDCA format)
- Advance briefings in appropriate joint forums and conferences
- A train-the-trainer process where Supervisors/Superintendents are training and deliver training in conjunction with Hourly Leadership as appropriate (with specific implementation to be Division specific)
- A Pre-Assessment to identify training needs in each location and match delivery of QOS/ISPC training to capability to apply on a plant-by-plant basis (social and technical infrastructure)
- Detailed time-lines for delivery and ongoing delivery of training
- A Post-Assessment process to ensure knowledge transfer and application in each location

Completed by: _____   Date Completed/revised: _____

1 -- 1/10/04 -- NQC

Figure 7.1
Five Ws & How for In-Station Process Control and Quality Operating System. *Source:* Ford Motor Company and WorkMatters, LLC.

Box 7.4
Joint Governance Structure: UAW-Ford National Quality Committee (NQC) Charter

Preamble

This is a living document that may only be changed by consensus of the National Quality Committee's active members, with guidance and direction from the UAW-Ford Quality Improvement Steering Committee. This charter has a companion charter in the form of the UAW-Visteon "National Quality Working Committee" (NQWC) Charter.

Box 7.4 (continued)

Mission

The UAW-Ford National Quality Committee is committed to driving "Best-In-Class" quality through the joint efforts of the UAW and Ford. We will partner with and support front-line operations in their quest to deliver World Class quality to our customers by:

- Supporting Divisional and Local joint quality efforts
- Helping to institute quality principles and practices across the business
- Ensuring a climate of fairness and respect

These elements will help to sustain and grow the business, while enabling the personal growth, development and adaptability of the workforce.

Purpose

1. To implement the provisions of the UAW-Ford "Best-In-Class" Quality Program
2. To develop and recommend programs and provide feedback to the UAW-Ford Quality Improvement Steering Committee
3. To participate on and support the operation of the UAW-Ford Divisional Quality Committees and help them in assisting Local Quality Committees
4. To promote personal growth and development of all Ford employees in the understanding and use of quality principles and practices

Active Members

Individuals holding the following positions are active members of the National Quality Committee:

UAW NQC Co-Chair	Ford NQC Co-Chair
UAW Reps—Servicing Ford	Management Reps—Ford

Resource Members

Subject Matter Experts, as Appropriate
Program Assistant II, Secretary, Word Processor

Overall Governance Structure

UAW-Ford Quality Improvement Steering Committee

UAW-Ford National Quality Committee

UAW-Ford Vehicle Operations Quality Committee	UAW-Ford Powertrain Operations Quality Committee	UAW-Ford Customer Service Division Quality Committee

UAW-Ford Local Quality Committees

Box 7.4 (continued)

Roles and Responsibilities

Roles and Responsibilities with Respect to the Quality Improvement Steering Committee:

• Overall responsibility to implement and support the "Best-in-Class" Quality Program as listed in Appendix Q, through the Divisional and Local Committees

• Provide input and feedback to the Quality Improvement Steering Committee—and to be responsive to strategic direction from the Quality Improvement Steering Committee

Roles and Responsibilities of the Co-Chairs:

• Follow and implement the UAW-Ford National Quality Committee charter

• Strategically plan for future training programs for the workforce to support ongoing "Best-in-Class" Quality Program initiatives

Roles and Responsibilities of the Active Members:

• Follow and implement the UAW-Ford National Quality Committee charter

Roles and Responsibilities with Respect Overall Contract Language and Committee Operations:

• Coordinate the Dealer Panel and Vehicle Concern Resolution Process, including receiving and ensuring appropriate responses to identified Customer Concerns from consumers or employees

• Plan and execute conference and forum activities, including the National Joint Conference

• Promote UAW-Ford "Best-in-Class" Quality Program internally and externally

• Provide appropriate joint input and support in the establishment and accomplishment of joint quality performance business metrics

• Support quality reward and recognition programs, including RISE Awards, President's Quality Awards, and others

• Administer Quality Concern Resolution Process and Quality hotline

• Lead Quality Leadership Initiative or Quality Excellence Program, as it applies

• Work with Supplier Technical Assistance, as appropriate

• Ensure compliance to all contractual commitments and NQC procedures

• Review quarterly divisional quality training reports

• Facilitate communications between Ford and Visteon with respect to Quality

• Maintain Dealer Panel/VSCRP and Quality websites

Roles and Responsibilities with Respect to the UAW-Ford Divisional Quality Committees:

• Overall responsibility to implement and support the "Best-in-Class" Quality Program as listed in Appendix Q, through the Divisional and Local Committees

• Communicate quality objectives and strategies under the "Best-in-Class" Quality Program to Divisional levels

• Provide tools, coaching and other support, as appropriate, to enable the implementation of quality objectives and strategies at Divisional levels

• Serve as a resource to Divisions in meeting quality goals and objectives

• Provide reward and recognition as appropriate

Box 7.4 (continued)

Roles and Responsibilities with Respect to the Facility Quality Committees:
- Overall responsibility to implement and support the "Best-in-Class" Quality Program as listed in Appendix Q, through the Divisional and Facility Committees
- Communicate quality objectives and strategies under the "Best-in-Class" Quality Program through the Divisional Committees to Facility levels
- Provide tools, coaching and other support, as appropriate, to enable the implementation of quality objectives and strategies through Divisional Committees to Facility levels
- Coach Local/Facility compliance to the Local Quality Committee (LQC) Effectiveness Assessment
- Serve as a resource to Facilities, through Divisions in meeting quality goals and objectives
- Certify Facility level local UAW Quality Representatives
- Identify leading quality best practices—internally and externally
- Provide existing NQC training as requested
- Provide reward and recognition as appropriate

Resource Members:
- Serve as subject matter experts, bringing expertise from Local, Division or National levels
- Fulfill job responsibilities as specified under relevant contracts and policies
- Support the Committee activities by updating the issue tracking matrix, preparing and distributing agenda, issuing all meeting minutes and maintaining all files

Procedures and Operations
- Staff assignments will be aligned by Divisions/Operations—UAW and Ford (including all operations covered by the master agreement)
- A monthly meeting will be held for the National Quality Committee
  - The meeting dates for the upcoming year will be established by the end of December the prior year
  - Decisions will be made by consensus, unless otherwise indicated (Can everyone live with the decision?)
  - Meetings will begin and end on time
  - Rescheduling of meetings and additional meetings will be handled by the Co-Chairs
  - Each meeting will follow a pre-established agenda
  - Radios must be off, cell phones and pagers must be on vibrate mode
  - Expectations for the next meeting will be communicated at the end of each meeting
  - Discussion that is considered confidential will not leave the room unless specifically agreed upon by the members
  - Each meeting will be facilitated by the Committee Co-Chairs
  - All meeting minutes will be typed and maintained by the appropriate resource member
  - All communication during the meeting will be honest, open and without regard to 'titles'
  - All active members are expected to report out during the meeting on status relative to the Master Initiatives Matrix

Box 7.4 (continued)

- A Master Initiatives Matrix will be maintained, providing the status of activities
  - Standard criteria for prioritizing and adding issues to the matrix are as follows:
    - Is it related to a UAW/Ford Joint Quality Program?
    - Is it a policy making issue?
    - Is someone else/another group already addressing the issue. If so, is the issue being addressed properly?
    - Can this issue be resolved immediately in this meeting (still added to the matrix as a resolved issue)?
  - When an issue is added to the matrix it must be clearly defined, have an initial report date established, a responsible party identified and an interim report out date or appropriate due date assigned
  - An accomplishments list will be constructed on a rolling basis as activities are completed on the Master Initiatives Matrix
- Participate in and support Division/Operations Quality meetings and efforts
  - VO Quality Meeting
  - PTO Quality Meeting
  - FCSD Quality Meeting
- Ensure capability to provide tools and coaching support
  - Develop and implement personal skill development plans for relevant national staff
  - Track progress to personal skill development plans for relevant national staff
- Systematically track performance of joint quality metrics and review progress toward "Best-in-Class" standards through the Division/Operations and Facility Committees
- Major initiatives will be discussed using Current State, Desired State, and Gap Analysis methodology and an action plan will be developed for each open issue
- All announcements, decisions, and policies will be disseminated using policy deployment methodology.
- Ensure effective leadership and staff transitions
  - Review National Committee Charter and other relevant documents to minimize instability associated with leadership and staff transitions
- The National Quality Committee Charter will be reviewed no less than once per year during the fourth quarter.
- The Joint Governing Body (JGB) process will be followed for all funding requirements/requests.
- All committee communications to the field will be in the required call letter format (including the appropriate and correct usage of multiple logo letterhead) maintained by appropriate resource members. These communications will be forwarded to all NQC active members via electronic files prior to mailings.
- All external communications and committee support materials will be completed by the appropriate resource member.
- All active committee members will follow the established procedure for notifying the committee Co-Chairs or another designated representative of their daily schedules including travel, plant visits and offsite meetings.
- All committee active members are expected to be accessible via pager during business hours.

Box 7.4 (continued)

Signatures

Barb Scott	Joe Gafa
Matt DeMars	Marty Mulloy
H. T. Procter, Jr.	Adrian Vido
Stan Gilchrist	Steve Opaleski
Colleen Moynihan	Jim Firlit
Robert O'Donnell	Claudia Anderson
Clarence Whitfield	Janet Horvat
Ed Roginski	Linda Miller
Ken Macfarlane	Paul Kosaian

Source: UAW-Ford National Joint Programs.

The principle of stable, effective forums is embodied in the charters. The charters have sufficient specificity to enable joint governance in the complex setting of the auto industry, while not having so much detail as to add unneeded bureaucracy.

The Quality charters were a pivot away from "add on" joint communication meetings and a pivot toward forums that are integral to how the company achieves best-in-class quality. The charters held union leaders accountable for business results on quality and management accountable for approaching quality in a way that includes the union and its members. As we will see in chapter 8, the principle of disciplined, effective forums became a key building block for all of the operating systems in the Ford Production System.

UAW-Ford National Joint Program Conference, 2006

The initial 1982 language on Mutual Growth Forums leads to yearly meetings between the UAW and Ford on the status and progress of the joint programs negotiated over the years. These conferences, usually held in Las Vegas, gather together UAW and Ford senior leadership, staff representatives responsible for the joint programs from the union and company, division leaders, and HR staff, along with UAW and Ford leaders and appointed representative from UAW local unions and plant managers—all of whom network and build relationships. One feature of the meetings is awards for outstanding joint programs and innovations in quality, safety, and other topics. As with the Cleveland Engine Plant 1 pivotal event (and Windsor Engine before that), awards can be a factor in keeping open a plant at risk of closing.

Many in the UAW and Ford are critical of these meetings for being too superficial. Some UAW members contend that difficult issues like sourcing are not surfaced or addressed adequately. Within Ford, critics note the cost of running a conference for a thousand people or so, and bemoan the insufficient attention given to business fundamentals.

The 2003 conference illustrates the scale and the resources devoted to these meetings. There, Ford's 100th anniversary makes for a highly celebratory event. It is also the centennial of Harley-Davidson, another iconic American brand also known for innovative labor-management relations. The conference features a keynote address by the vice president of Harley-Davidson's Powertrain Division and celebration of the Harley edition of the Ford F150 pickup (also brought to market in 2003). There is a special retirement reception for a top UAW official and other celebratory activities.

The 2006 conference, in contrast, begins on a far more somber note. There is tension on the faces of senior Ford leaders who have already seen the bottom fall out of auto sales at the beginning of the year. The UAW leaders are braced for what may be major layoffs.

The entire second day of the conference is devoted to quality. The National Quality Committee's report includes an update on the chartering process that has cascaded to local plants (discussed earlier in this chapter), the completion and roll out of the Quality Targeted Training Process (discussed in chapter 8), and that the Quality Operating System coordinators have been selected, trained, and are on the job (also discussed in chapter 8). Ford's quality is improving, but not as rapidly as desired.

Union and management leaders hear from Anne Stevens, North American vice president of Manufacturing, who stresses the importance of individuals taking responsibility for not passing on bad quality. She repeats her by now well-known phrase: "Don't take it, don't make it, don't pass it along." Ken MacFarlane, the director of Manufacturing for Vehicle Operations, follows her, challenging the audience to approach quality as if it is World War III. He points to a map to indicate where Ford is relative to the competition. The data he shares, some of it highly confidential, reveals how wide the Ford gap still is. The company is acknowledging that quality is still at risk.

There are breakout sessions, organized by division. The Vehicle Operations session is the highest profile and the one with the most at stake: the assembly plants are the biggest part of Ford's economic engine, and their culture has been hardest to change. For Joe Hinrichs, the newly appointed vice president for Vehicle Operations who has come from GM (where he was a plant manager), a Powertrain plant, and service as CEO of Ford of Canada, this is chance to influence the thinking of all the union leaders, including some who have not fully embraced the Ford Production System, and the plant managers, including some who still see him as an outsider in Ford and an outsider in Vehicle Operations.

Hinrichs presents competitive data on quality, some far more detailed than any competitive data most of the UAW leaders have seen. He is blunt: plants must be competitive to be rewarded with new products. As Hinrichs explains:

We were very concerned with the whole situation. Having just come back from Ford of Canada...I wanted to make a difference on the competitiveness of our business. I took the approach to go product-by-product, plant-by-plant, on safety, quality, cost, QRS surveys, intelligence, and Harbour efficiency data. The high-level intent was to get people thinking differently about where we were on a competitive basis and to foster dialogue.

We were doing the same thing over and over and getting the same result. ... The business needed a different result.

Hinrichs's data is comprehensive and alarming. Nearly all plants trail the competition. Senior UAW leaders consulted in advance of the briefing had supported him laying out the full picture. Now Hinrichs concludes by asking each plant manager and each UAW chairman to develop a road map for what they can do to improve over the next 30 to 60 days.

The presentation is galvanizing. Clearly, things have to change in every facility to secure future work. But one UAW chairman attacks Hinrichs, partly calling his presentation into question but also making note that he had come from GM. Another UAW chairman counters: "We are ready to talk about this—the data is what it is." Hallway conversations are highly energized.

It is a complete contrast from the celebratory tone of past conferences and accelerates the joint focus on ensuring business success in an increasingly competitive market.

Following the conference, the plant-by-plant negotiation of Competitive Operating Agreements begins (presented in chapter 2).

✳ ✳ ✳

Although there has been a long history of UAW-Ford National Joint Conferences, the 2006 conference is pivotal in how it breaks from the past celebratory tone and instead focuses on business realities. That sets the stage for a fundamental shift in the relationship between the UAW and Ford. Although the concept of mutual growth has long been a theme at these conferences, the tone in 2006 reinforces and extends the orientation during the 2003 chartering of the National Quality Council—shifting the joint programs from serving as a communications vehicle and into forums for dialogue and action on the future of the business itself.

Safety Chartering, 2008

Safety has a long history between Ford and the UAW. The first UAW-Ford Collective Bargaining Agreement in 1941 contains a health and safety provision. Safety and apprenticeships are the first UAW-Ford joint programs. The first appointed roles for UAW members (that is, not elected union positions) are as safety representatives—chosen locally and certified by the National Joint Committee on Health and Safety (NJCHS). Joint health and safety conferences are held annually beginning in 1974, are expanded to twice a year in 1984, and a third annual conference on ergonomics is added a few years later. This longstanding joint program is a source of pride for all associated with it.

Unfortunately, no record of continuous improvement in safety performance matches that pride. The system-wide focus on safety that follows the Rouge explosion lasts only lasts a few years. By the early 2000s, safety is still on the agenda—but the attention is not well focused. Most plants have internal management meetings on safety, internal union meetings on safety, joint meetings of top union and management leaders on safety, meetings of designated UAW and Ford health and safety representatives on safety, area meetings on safety, and team meetings on safety. There are corporate safety audits and government safety inspections. Safety is certainly not ignored, but the many safety efforts are not necessarily well coordinated, let alone tightly integrated. In most plants, slips, falls, and near misses are still major problems. There continue to be regular violations of power lockout procedures (cutting of electricity during repair work). While the long-term trend is one of improvement, there are continued high-consequence events buried in the data—like amputations. Most tragic are the fatalities: two in 2003, two in 2004, one in 2006, and two again in 2007.

When Dan Brooks takes on responsibility for the joint UAW-Ford safety program in early 2008, he recommends reorienting the various elements of the safety program into a full Safety Operating System comparable to the Quality Operating System (presented in chapter 8). Gregory Stone, a physician and corporate leader for safety, has been mining the safety data and sees the persistence of high-consequence events. He embraces the idea of a more tightly integrated approach to safety, comparable to what Ford and the UAW have achieved with quality. Chartering, both agree, is a key first step in this process.

On July 23, 2008, Frederick Todd of UAW Local 387, a die setter in the Woodhaven Stamping Plant, dies on the job. The discussions on the Safety Operating System and chartering take on a new urgency. A joint meeting of UAW and Ford health and safety representatives is convened on August 26, 2008, with the topic for discussion "Learning from Catastrophic Accidents and Near Misses: Improving the UAW-Ford Safety Operating System." UAW vice president Bob King opens the session:[6]

Today's event is because we are unsatisfied collectively with the health and safety record. The Woodhaven fatality shook me up. There is something wrong with our system if fatalities like that happen.

My first reaction was to take an immediate and strong action. Then I stopped and asked what do I need to do to address the underlying culture—rather than just take an immediate action. We decided to take a deeper approach.

King urges the participants to work within the system and, if needed, to reach beyond the regular system with any safety issue. He is calling for a change in the culture—not just the surface behaviors. He concludes his opening remarks:

We need to redefine the roles and responsibilities of safety and health representatives. Then we will be tough on accountability. If you are feeling burnt out and not up doing this, do us a favor and step aside. We all have to be committed to creating safe workplaces. We are the best in the world in quality and we are committed to nothing less on safety.

Although the fatality has put safety on everyone's mind, there is an undertone of skepticism about importing ideas from Quality. Dan Brooks is seen as an outsider on safety issues. He does get people's attention, though, when he brings up a politically sensitive issue: that addressing safety will require the union to address the behavior of its members.

The tone shifts further when participants are provided with actual accident reports and near-miss reports from Ford-UAW locations (with identifying information removed). They are asked to break into small groups and identify evidence of the system functioning as it should and where there are potential disconnects. Building on insights from the case examples (see supporting materials in chapter 8 on "near misses" for one of the examples used) and their own experience, participants identify four aspects of safety, such as the Safety and Health Audit Review Process (SHARP) review, that are standardized to a reasonably good degree. A much longer list of 19 aspects of safety, such as daily safety talks or pre-task analysis, are seen as highly variable in the system. There is a general understanding that any improvement efforts attempted on a variable basis are likely to do little more than produce greater variation (islands of success, rather than consistent improvement across the system).

In addition to near-miss incident reports, the group reviews plant-level near-miss data. In small groups and as a whole, participants discuss ways improve the use of near-miss data to build a stronger culture of prevention in the plants.

Implications for a plant-level Safety Operating System are identified at the end of the meeting:

- A major focus on ergonomics
- Being more proactive in prevention—time on the floor, finding root causes (including the use of data, such as near misses)
- A huge barrier in communications—union with management (and even within the union) on us all communicating on safety issues
- A "fresh eyes" approach—with cross-plant visits that are reciprocal—jointly walking in each other's plants
- Work with the work teams—safety audits by safety reps on the work teams—the idea of distributed safety representatives tied to small group activity
- More consistency in the safety rules and processes—how they are implemented and operated
- Self accountability—among union brothers and sisters so we are not protecting people for doing what they shouldn't be doing (dates back to some of our experiences as elected representatives)
- Being able to work with labor relations and get consistent and appropriate responses—hourly and salaried
- Training for new UAW chairpersons or new plant managers so they can maintain the process

Intensive work on the Safety Operating System and a set of draft safety charters follow after the meeting.

In November 2008, all union and management health and safety representatives are brought together (most had been at the August session), along with other senior union and management leaders. Three overall goals are identified, each associated with a different dimension of alignment (or misalignment) in a complex system (behavior, structure, and culture):

- Goal 1 (behavior): Standardize distributed safety knowledge and capability
- Goal 2 (structure): Standardize supporting safety infrastructure

• Goal 3 (culture): Change the overall safety culture to promote transparency, standardization, problem-solving, and continuous improvement

The specific objectives for the session are:

• Build a shared vision for health and safety in UAW-Ford operations
• Review and adjust draft charters for the Manufacturing Safety Council & the Nation Joint Committee on Health and Safety
• Identify and plan next steps

Bob King opens the session on behalf of the UAW. "These are tumultuous times," he says. "Recent fatalities and serious injuries show that we need to do more with Safety. The use of charters and standardized methods from Quality will help us in Safety. The UAW-Ford relationship is one of the greatest assets that we have and we will be applying it to Safety to take it to a higher level in these efforts."

On behalf of Ford, Marty Mulloy echoes the same themes and also signals the larger societal context. "The chartering process began in quality," states Mulloy. "At first it seemed like a lot of tedious details, but it became clear that laying out roles and responsibilities clearly does deliver results. These are challenging times—the views of at least half of the United States suggest that they don't like the UAW or the U.S. auto industry—which means that we need to educate Americans on the good things we are doing. People should be able to look at us with admiration—they should be able to say that they were wrong—the UAW and Ford are producing great value, great quality, and great safety."

Gregory Stone then introduces and explains the first draft of a global occupational health and safety management system (figure 7.2; discussed in more detail in chapter 8). It is a central element in what becomes the Safety Operating System.

Stone points out that most plants go right to the part of the chart with the SHARP and think of that as their Safety Operating System. The audit, he says, is an important part of the process, but it is not the entire process—it is only one source of feedback in the process.

After the opening remarks from senior leaders, the participants are asked what would constitute success for the session. Participants express interest in learning about the idea of an operating system and indicate their desire for genuine dialogue.

• Start to all see the operating system in the same way
• Focus our attention on supporting the facilities/plants
• Identify what structural changes are required to have a quicker and more aggressive way of eliminating fatalities and serious injuries
• Put the "moose heads" on the table—talking about the barriers to improving safety
• Gain a better understanding of the safety operating system
• Produce two charters—NJC and Manufacturing Safety Council
• Return to the overall governance and system slide to identify potential adjustments in that representation

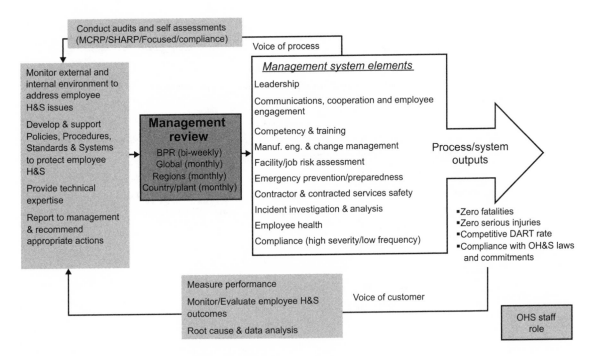

Figure 7.2
Global Occupational Health and Safety Management System. *Source:* Ford Motor Company.

The analysis of the safety incidents and other safety data from the August session is reviewed with the full group. Participants are then introduced to the text for two draft safety charters—one for the UAW-Ford National Joint Committee on Health and Safety and one for the UAW-Ford Manufacturing Safety Council. As with the quality chartering sessions, the draft text is projected on a large screen, and each section is reviewed by small groups and the entire group. Small edits are made in real time; notes on more complex adjustments are taken for subsequent action. Before moving on from a section, group consensus is achieved.

During the review of the draft charter for the Manufacturing Safety Council, a senior Ford manager makes a key suggestion: incorporate the Six Sigma DMAIC model (Define, Measure, Analyze, Improve, Control) directly in the charter (though the terms are adjusted in some ways to match the safety context).

Box 7.5 is the text of the charter that results from the review.

Finalized in December 2008, the charter is distributed to all North American locations. The UAW-Ford health and safety reps are given a draft template for a local plant safety charter and charged with conducting plant chartering sessions—a task made relatively easy in nearly all locations by the fact that local union and management officials have all been operating under the local quality charters for at least two or three years.

Box 7.5
UAW-Ford Manufacturing Safety Council Governance Structure

Preamble

This is a living document that may only be changed by consensus of the Manufacturing Safety Council.

Mission

The mission of the Manufacturing Safety Council is to define and drive the Safety Operating System to deliver world-class safety results.

Purpose

The purpose of the Manufacturing Safety Council is to Define, Monitor, Measure, Analyze, and Improve Continuously (DMAIC) the Safety Operating System (SOS), including:

- Define System/standards
- Measure results
- Analyze data
- Measure conformance
- Continuously improve
- Control the Safety Operating System

Active Members

VP North America Manufacturing
Manufacturing Director, Car Assembly
Manufacturing Director, Stamping
Manufacturing Director, Engine
CAW H&S Coordinator, FOC
Company Co-Chair, NJCHS
Managers, Occupational Health & Safety
Executive Engineer, PTO Manufacturing Engineering
Manufacturing Director, ACH
Manufacturing Director, Truck Assembly
Manufacturing Director, Transmission
UAW Co-Chair, NJCHS
Labour Affairs Planning Manager, FOC
Director, Occupational Health & Safety
Director, VO Manufacturing Engineering
Director, MP&L

Resource Members

Subject Matter Experts, as appropriate
Regional Safety & Security Managers
UAW International Representatives, NJCHS
Ford Safety Engineers, NJCHS
Ford Land

Box 7.5 (continued)

Research & Engineering (R&E)
Ford Customer Service Division (FCSD)
UAW International Representatives, Servicing

Overall Governance Structure

Manufacturing Operating Committee—Monthly		
Manufacturing Safety Council—Monthly		
UAW-Ford NJCHS—Monthly	ACH-LLC SPRB—Quarterly	CAW Master Health & Safety Committee
Local Facility Operating Committees—Daily		
Local facility Safety Process Review Boards—Monthly		

Roles and Responsibilities

Roles and Responsibilities with Respect to the Manufacturing Safety Council:

• Overall responsibility to implement and support strategies and objectives to reduce employee injuries and illnesses in North America.

• Assist in the communication of health and safety objectives and strategies.

• Provide tools, coaching and other support as appropriate to enable the implementation of Health and Safety objectives and strategies.

• Serve as a resource in meeting Health and Safety goals and objectives.

• Drive joint NJCHS.

• Ensure adequate resources in the manufacturing operations to implement the strategies and objectives agreed upon in the Manufacturing Safety Council.

• Agree on strategies and timing for improvement actions in the manufacturing operations.

• Monitor the performance of the manufacturing operations and the implementation of strategies and improvement plans

• Review and direct the analyses of data for formulation of health and safety strategies and timing.

Roles and Responsibilities of the Manufacturing Directors:

• Generate alignment within all manufacturing groups with the agreed upon strategies and objectives.

• DOM interventions, post-incident.

Box 7.5 (continued)

Roles and Responsibilities of the Joint Members:

- Review for concurrence and timing respective UAW and CAW contractual commitments, work plans supporting health and safety strategies.
- Monitor and support UAW and CAW Health & Safety Representatives and Company Safety Engineers at the local level.

Roles and Responsibilities of the Manufacturing Engineering Representatives:

- Follow up and monitoring for engineering-led or assisted corrective actions and strategies to improve health and safety.
- Develop strategies for improvement of health and safety performance with respect to new model programs and launches.
- Provide input into new or modified standards for production and facility equipment.
- Monitor the performance of construction contractors and the implementation of strategies and improvement plans to prevent contractor injuries and illnesses while working on Ford projects.

Roles and Responsibilities of Occupational Health and Safety:

The OH&S Office is responsible for:

- Monitoring and evaluating employee health and safety issues.
- Staying abreast of technical developments and governmental activities.
- Developing policies, procedures, standards and systems to protect employee health and safety for review/approval by the Council.
- Providing technical expertise; conducting audits, measuring performance, reporting to management, and the Manufacturing Safety Council.
- Recommending appropriate actions as needed for sustainable improvement in health and safety.

Resource Members:

- Serve as subject matter experts, bringing expertise from staff or local levels
- Fulfill job responsibilities as specified under relevant contracts and policies
- Create and distribute meeting minutes and agendas

Procedures and Operations

- *One meeting* per month will be held by the Manufacturing Safety Council
  - **A small group strategy meeting will be held in addition to the monthly meeting at the direction of the MSC.+**
  - The meeting dates for the upcoming year will be established by the end of December of the prior year.
  - Decision making in the Council meetings.
  - Meetings will begin and end on time.
  - Each meeting will follow a pre-established agenda.
  - All electronic communication devices must be on vibrate mode. Members receiving calls are to leave the meeting during the call.

Box 7.5 (continued)

    o All meeting minutes will be typed and maintained by the appropriate resource member.

    o All active members are expected to attend and report out during the meeting on status relative to the Manufacturing Safety Council work plan and any initiative or issue matrices used.

    o Meetings will be conducted using Webex for participants who cannot attend in person.

    o Meeting documents will be posted in a Team Connect site for viewing prior to the meeting.

• A Manufacturing Safety Council work plan matrix will be maintained, providing the status of activities.

    o The basis for the work plan is the strategies and objectives agreed upon

    o Other assignments will be documented in issue matrices as directed by the Safety Champions

    o An accomplishment list will be constructed on a rolling basis and maintained by the appropriate resource member.

• Systematically track performance of joint health and safety metrics and review progress toward objectives.

• All announcements, decisions and policies will be disseminated using policy deployment methodology.

• The Manufacturing Safety Council Charter will be reviewed annually during the fourth quarter.

We, the undersigned, agree to follow this charter dated January, 2010, with respect to the operation of the Manufacturing Safety Council:

J. P. Tetreault, Vice President NA Manufacturing	Jose Islas, Manufacturing Director Car Assembly
W. P. Russo, Manufacturing Director Engine	J. C. Wood, Manufacturing Director Truck Assembly
P. P. Kosaian, Manufacturing Director Stamping	K. Williams, Manufacturing Director Auto Transmission
N. A Broggi, Manufacturing Director ACH	D. G. Brooks, Assistant Director National Ford Department, UAW
CAW National H&S Coordinator Ford of Canada	R. A. Cook, Labour Affairs Manager Ford of Canada
C. D. Petersen, Ford Co-Chair NJCHS	G. M. Stone, Director OHS
H. M. Tarrant, Manager OHS	D. C. Brecht, Manager OHS

Box 7.5 (continued)

M. S. Jones, Manager OHS	L. G. Cash, Director VO Manufacturing Engineering
S. B. Carl, Executive Engineer PTO Manufacturing Engineering	P. Stec, Director MP & L, North America

Source: Ford Moter Company

Dr. Stone, reflecting on the safety chartering and the overall impact of charters, comments that it "goes back to clarifying roles and responsibilities, getting people engaged, and engaging them in the process....Time and data management provides a cadence for safety that builds on the charters."

Chartering, Stone notes further, has "morphed into every FPS meeting now having a charter—it is now a common standard."

✳✳✳

Union and management leaders needed to have a context for the chartering: how it fits into the larger safety system and why it is important to do. As was the case with quality, the actual charter is important, but the chartering process is more important. It is a process where participants literally get on the same page with key aspects of their vision, mission, roles, responsibilities, and logistics. Implicit in the process is a transformation of safety from a subject addressed separately by the union, management, and the joint program into a subject in which all safety activities are under a single umbrella—benefiting from the unified efforts of all involved.

UAW-HR Change Agents and HR OD Institute, 2009–2010

The auto industry is still engaged in complex negotiations with the federal government in 2009. Within Ford, however, there are early signs of success in the marketplace—reflecting, in part, the decision not to take the bailout money as well as the new Ford and Lincoln products that are the company's focus after selling off various brands. In the past, Ford might have become complacent after making such great strides in a crisis; that is the company's past pattern. This time, though, the focus within Ford and the UAW shifts to building capability to sustain the changes that have enabled success.

After years of benchmarking and sustained implementation of lean and Six Sigma principles, senior union and management leaders in Ford and UAW clearly see the value of a team-based, knowledge-driven, flexible work system with a stable, effective social infrastructure (including aligned support functions such as finance, HR, engineering, and others), all oriented around a "pull" from customers. Increasingly, it is also understood that sustaining the change requires new skills within labor and management.

Mary Anderson, a manager of Organization Development (OD), observes, "It takes someone of courage and conviction at a senior level to sponsor change." She speaks not just of the decision to *initiate* change, but the responsibility of a sponsor to follow through with the change and address system barriers as they emerge—barriers brought to their attention by the facilitators of change.

Increasingly, Anderson's job is to ensure appropriate professional development for these individuals. Within the UAW, a group of internal change agents is emerging, some in the long-standing role of appointed Employee Resource Coordinators (ERCs) and some in nontraditional roles, such as organizational development specialists (like Roger Komer, mentioned earlier in this chapter, and John Nahornyj, mentioned in chapter 2). Some earn Six Sigma black belts (as we saw in chapter 5). Within management, naming change agents for each plant in 2001 as part of the Lean Implementation Network (chapter 4) and the managers earning Six Sigma black belts constitutes another group of internal change agents. There are both union and management FPS coordinators who also serve as change agents.

A one-day joint conference titled "Driving Change from Within: Appreciating Internal Change Agents" is held for change agents throughout the system on June 19, 2009. Joel Cutcher-Gershenfeld, the session facilitator, defines four domains in which the session aims to leverage knowledge: the role of an internal change agent; transformation and change within labor unions; transformation and change within management hierarchies; transformation and change within society.

On behalf of the UAW, Dan Brooks indicates that the session is honoring the memory of Roger Komer and celebrating the work of internal change agents. Komer, a UAW change agent who was one of the pioneers of this role in the UAW, has recently passed away. Marty Mulloy then begins with some recollections.[7] He had been the HR manager in the Sterling Axle Plant when Komer was an Employee Resource Coordinator (ERC), and yet to be formally designated as a union change agent.

I recall many years ago—I was just a kid—a teacher told me that the difference between who you are today and the person you become will be the books you read and the people you meet. In 1992, I met this guy Roger Komer—he changed my life....

We had the F150 axle line—we were told we had to go in and get a MOA on this line. The work was already committed to the plant, so it was not an easy negotiation. Still, we hammered out a deal. Then I get a call from Roger. It is Martin Luther King Day—a company holiday—and he says I have to get in the plant. We have work to do.

[When I arrive at the plant], Roger has a flip chart with a drawing of a bus—the SS Sterling—going off a cliff. There is this little bald guy driving the bus.

He said, "That is you."

He saw in me the ability to be more than a typical HR manager and was challenging me to lead the change in a different way—to not drive the bus off the cliff. In the negotiations, we had changed 250 jobs out of 2,000 people in the plant, which was typical of the MOAs at the time. Roger challenged me and said it had to be the whole plant....

What makes a person a genius—it is not the education—it is the ability to see insights that others couldn't see. This guy has the right vision and the right insight. We are now at an inflection point for the Ford Motor Company. I wish with all my heart we could sit down with Roger and ask how we could take advantage of this opportunity.

Dan Brooks then shares his own experience as a union change agent participating in the corporation's Quality Operating Committee, observing that the union has considerable power and influence within the company. "The union's influence is a source of strength for Ford," he notes, "which is a story that should be better told."

The discussion of internal change agents, the first domain for the session from which to leverage knowledge, focuses on seven specific roles of change agents (highlighted here in italics), and participants offer examples and observations that illustrate them. Discussing the more specific role of *expert in new work systems* leads to a discussion about implementing alternative work schedules for skilled trades workers in one location, expanding the role of the ERC in another, and jointly utilizing W. Edward Deming's "Plan, Do, Check, Adjust" (PDCA)[8] cycle in another location. With respect to *sounding board and moral compass for leaders*, people in the room share their experiences working with top union and management leaders in their locations to develop "win-win" implementation plans for newly negotiated contract language. The discussion of *advocate for the front-line workforce* focuses on supporting team leaders in their roles, documenting the gains from small group activity in the plants, and ensuring fair treatment in the context of a facility that was closing. One participant comments that he "was just at a retirement and we were talking about the old way of inspecting in quality—running around like chickens with our heads cut off. Now…we have COAs and team agreements. We have teams with a designated quality leader."

Participants discuss the more specific role of *designer of learning events and developer of learning materials* and talk of developing training for people coming back from long-term disability leave and training people in the operation of daily shift start meetings. The role of *partner with external resources* raises an example in which supporting external resources conducted a "fresh eyes safety walk" followed not by the typical lecture but with real engagement of the workforce to solicit ideas on improvement. Under *contributor to external communities of practice*, participants emphasize the value of reaching out to personal networks such as the people at this session. Finally, as a *systems architect*, participants speak of the importance of internal change agents connecting their work to the business metrics and the many operating systems under FPS.

There is similar dialogue on the other three dimensions of the change agent's role—within a union, within management, and in broader society. Thomas Kochan, a professor of work and employment research at the MIT Sloan School of Management, is the keynote speaker, and emphasizes the broader societal role. He discusses the challenges for the auto industry in Washington, D.C., and in the global economy, and concludes by urging the participants to broaden their horizons.

Think about the next problem to be solved on a day-to-day basis, but also challenge yourself to see the larger picture. Be able to challenge the finance and marketing people so they value what you are doing. Educate your constituents and bring those voices to these larger settings. Don't let the old managerial prerogatives or functional distinctions to get in the way. You know how to get things done—make what you are doing visible. Make it public to the nation—so that a year from now or two years from now you can invite the president of the United States to see the auto industry of the future.

Later in 2009, Ford's Organization Development (OD) Institute is launched, dedicated to training HR professionals in change management. The training includes three weeks of in-person learning along with six virtual learning sessions on organizational development between the first and second weeks and between the second and third weeks. Participants write learning journey papers and have a four-hour final exam before graduating.

The process begins with senior Ford managers in the United States and cascades through all of Ford's Global Business Units.

***

Most of the pivotal events presented in this book involve planned change. Some involve unplanned change. This pivotal event signals the recognition that the transformation increasingly involves continuous change. It also signals the importance of change management capability as a valued skill set. One outside observer notes how the event reinforces the degree to which change is being driven by the UAW and Ford on a partnership basis.[9]

The HR function has been central to many of the pivotal events, but it has continued to be defined primarily around traditional HR functions (staffing, compensation, succession planning, training, etc.) and the Labor Affairs role. With the UAW-HR lean staff development and the establishment of the Organizational Development Institute, change management is formally recognized as a key element of the HR function.

Recap: Guiding Principle for Chapter 7—Disciplined, Standardized Processes

In transforming work and relationships to deliver results—for labor and management—disciplined, standardized processes are an essential foundation. Initially seen as potentially too bureaucratic and certainly as a threat to managerial prerogative and union independence, all parties came to see the value in embracing this degree of structure.

At the Atlanta Assembly Plant, the FTPM charter illustrates the value of plant union and management leaders all being on the same page with respect to total productive maintenance. Beginning at the plant level on a single issue, however, limited the potential for diffusion. In the Dearborn Assembly Plant, the systematic use of charters, still at the plant level, illustrates the flexibility of the format. It is applied to all joint forums, all FPS elements, and even to meetings within management (including the Plant Operating Committee).

The importance of disciplined, standardized processes is in discussion, in parallel, at the enterprise level and becomes formally instantiated as "time and data management" on a system-wide basis. By 2003, this ensures regular meeting times and a regular flow of performance data relevant to all FPS elements. The forums themselves, however, are still variable in their structure and operation. It is the quality chartering in 2004, first at a national and divisional level and then at the plant level, where the appropriate degree of specificity in this system is achieved. In other organizations, there might be a need for more or less structure, but for the UAW and Ford, charters find the sweet spot that enables consistent focused delivery of results.

The 2006 UAW-Ford National Joint Program Conference injects a sense of urgency into the joint processes—with the presentations on competitive realities. Joint programs have been transitioning from "add-on" communications vehicles into "value add" parts of the organization for a long time—dating back to the 1982 articulation of mutual growth as the overarching objective. In a business crisis, the process accelerates around survival and success. In this process, beginning with the 2006–2007 COA negotiations (chapter 2) and extending through the 2007 national negotiations (chapter 6), the UAW is able to advance its interests as well as Ford—illustrating the value of mutual growth as an umbrella framework (and as an alternative to traditional concession bargaining).

The extension of the quality charter approach into Safety illustrates the value of the principle across FPS elements at the enterprise level. Indeed, as is noted at the end of the safety chartering pivotal event, *all* FPS elements now incorporate charters.

Finally, underlying the appreciation of disciplined, standardized processes are the internal change agents who provide the needed facilitation support. This pivot signals a post-transformation shift around sustaining change, not just implementing change. Viewing these union and management individuals as "sustaining agents," not just "change agents," is a pivot that has been signaled, but for which the work is not yet complete. Similarly, transforming the HR function to deliver on change management across the enterprise is on the horizon, but not yet complete. In this regard, and in many others, the Ford-UAW transformation is entering the unending phase of continuous change.

As a vehicle for industrial democracy in America, collective bargaining alone has not fulfilled the potential Milton Derber wrote of half a century ago. The use of charters, connected to time and data management, for joint forums is an important complement to collective bargaining as an institution. It is also an important addition to the concept of a corporation. The charters instantiate a collaborative domain in which the mutual interests of labor and management can be channeled in a structured and disciplined way to deliver results of value to both parties.

Derber may have been overly optimistic about collective bargaining, but he was absolutely correct in the analogy between democracy in society and democracy in the workplace. Both require adaptable institutional arrangements that allow for the governance of collective interests.

SUPPORTING MATERIALS

7.1 Five Ws & How

Revitalizing mutual growth forums:
Five Ws & How shared vision (2005)

Who:

National Level:
- Senior UAW and Ford leadership
- Appropriate support resources and subject matter experts

Divisional Unit Level:
- Appropriate Union and Divisional management leadership
- Divisional strategic business planning resources
- Appropriate support resources and subject matter experts

Local Level:
- Union and management facility leadership, including: UAW Local Bargaining Committees and Ford Facility Operating Committees
- Appropriate support resources associated with employee involvement and continuous improvement in operations, including ERCs

Where:
- Offsite educational and alignment sessions at appropriate locations
- Chartering sessions at individual facilities
- Support resources at UAW-Ford National Programs Center (NPC) and at Divisional/Business Unit Levels

What:
- A UAW-Ford initiative aimed at improving relations ensuring long-term UAW and Ford success – building on National, Divisional and Local Mutual Growth Forums
- Understanding the "gap to transplant" and pursuing mutually acceptable methods for closing the gap
- Mechanisms to ensure that gains in operational effectiveness can be linked with job security though new investments in people, technology and operations

Why:
- UAW and Ford face deep and continuing competitive challenges
- Revitalization of Mutual Growth Forums at National, Divisional and Local levels is essential addressing competitive challenges
- Mechanisms to ensure that gains in operational effectiveness will be rewarded through new investments in people, technology, and the operations

When:

4th Quarter Milestones, 2005
- Initial alignment across UAW National Ford Department; Ford VO, PTO, FCSD, ACH; UAW-Ford National Joint Programs; Ford Labor Affairs, and other key stakeholders
- National & Divisional MGF, and MGF Working Group established
- Initial establishment of implementation support systems
- Initial communications on Mutual Growth Revitalization

1st and 2nd Quarter Milestones, 2006
- Calibration of Facility Chairpersons and Facility Managers
- Training of ERCs and other support resources
- Establishing support systems for flow of information on "gap to transplant" and other relevant data
- Initial revitalization and intensification of efforts at Local, Divisional/Business Unit and National levels
- Calibration at National Joint Programs Conference

3rd and 4th Quarter and Ongoing Milestones, 2006
- Continued revitalization efforts at Local, Divisional/Business Unit and National levels
- Periodic review and adjustment at all levels

How:
- Coordination across National, Divisional and Local Levels
- Joint education at all levels on competitive realities
- Stable and effective Mutual Growth Forums at all levels, coordinated with other joint forums and initiatives as appropriate
- Standardized processes for joint alignment and implementation, with associate support systems
- Aligned with SQDCME Manufacturing Councils, Time and Data Management, Lean Implementation Network, and other initiatives
- Structure process for periodic review and adjustment

Comment:

The Five Ws & How is a concise format for joint alignment and implementation on a change initiative. This example was used for the revitalization of the Mutual Growth Forums.

7.2 JAI Model

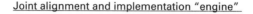

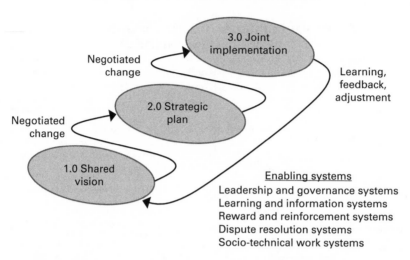

Source: WorkMatters, LLC

Comment:

The Joint Alignment and Implementation Model adds a continuous change model to the chartering process, involving a Shared Vision (1.0), a Strategic Plan (2.0), and Joint Implementation (3.0) for each issue. Chartering is part of the enabling system for leadership and governance. This model was developed by Joel Cutcher-Gershenfeld and Roger Komer through interactions with Dan Brooks, Marty Mulloy, and others in the UAW-Ford system.

7.3 Joint Safety Simulation Exercise

Note: The following simulation exercise was prepared for use in the UAW-Ford National Joint Safety Chartering Workshop as a "table-top" exercise. It is designed to be read and discussed in small groups and then in the full group to bring to the forefront insights into ensuring a robust social infrastructure for joint safety efforts.

The Role Conflict

It looks like it is going to be another grueling day for the plant health and safety team.

First, the Plant Manager called the Safety Engineer and came down like a ton of bricks because of a rise in last quarter's First Time Visits to the Medical Office. Even though this should have been anticipated given the increased attention to prevention being given throughout the plant, the Plant Manager didn't want any safety measurable to be increasing. The Director of Manufacturing is going to react to the rise in First Time Visits and not know the story behind it. What is worse, the Plant Manager specifically told the Safety Engineer to go talk to the Medical Office about this without involving the union. The specific message was, "this is our Medical Office and we need to make sure we have our ducks in a row before placing it on the agenda in a joint meeting. I don't want this getting out and having a life of its own before we understand the problem!" Now what should be done? The management Safety Engineer and the union Health and Safety Rep always work together on everything, so going to the Plant Medical Office without a head's up the union Rep would be a serious break from the regular way of working together.

Second, the Plant Chairperson is being challenged in the next local election by the current Skilled Trades Representative. Moreover, this person has let it be known that he has his own person who he wants to appoint as the union Health and Safety Rep once he is elected. So what happens? This same Skilled Trade Rep learns that one of the afternoon shift Supervisors has looked the other way when people are running their machines without the proper guards in place. Instead of coming to the Health and Safety Rep or the current Chairperson with this information, this fellow prints up flyers saying that the current Chairperson and Health and Safety Rep are also looking the other way on safety!

Third, both the management Safety Engineer and the union Health and Safety Rep have been very proud of their "near miss" data, which they took as evidence of a growing culture of prevention. However, one of the Area Managers stopped by and privately suggested that the safety team take a close look at the data. She said that she couldn't speak up on this publicly without getting pressure from the other Area Managers, but she had real worries about data integrity. After a relatively quick look it was found that more than half of the "near miss" incidents are real and they have triggered good learning on prevention in those work areas. On the other hand, it looks like there are quite a few cases that either involve actual minor injuries (that should have been OSHA recordable incidents) or there are cases that are not really "near misses" at all. These look to be entries by team leaders and supervisors who know that having "near miss" data was important and they have really stretched the meaning of the term. It may be that this was done with the support of Superintendents and even some Area Managers—it is not clear. There is a major safety audit coming up and the question is: How to handle the "near miss" data?

It is not even lunchtime and already that day is a mess. What should the management Safety Engineer and the union Health and Safety Rep do?

Guiding Principle: Align and Stabilize, then Integrate

The rise of the industrial revolution replaced craft production with mass production—both of which, as integrated operating systems, have intertwined assumptions, practices, and technologies. Each also has its own logic. The Ford Motor Company was, of course, a leading exemplar in mass production. In Europe and certain scholarly fields, mass production is still referred to as "Fordism."

To Westerners, the Toyota Production System at first seemed to be just a variation on the mass production system, but it came to be seen as embodying "lean" principles with their own distinct logic and underlying operating assumptions.[1] Indeed, Eiji Toyoda, cousin of the Toyota Motor Company founder Kiichiro Toyoda, and later the Toyota president and managing director, developed this approach with the textile efficiency expert Taiichi Ohno after being awed by the productive capability of Ford's River Rouge complex in a visit just after World War II (the visit was personally hosted by Henry Ford). In adapting the idea of an integrated manufacturing operation to Japan, where land was more limited, just-in-time supply arrangements were needed, which then required higher levels of worker involvement in every stage of the process and a need for continuous improvement. Nearly two decades later, Eiji Toyoda returned to the United States to visit the Rouge complex, nervous to see how it had advanced compared to more than a decade of continuous improvement in Japan. He was stunned to see that the Rouge complex was virtually unchanged.[2] Lean principles have since been applied more broadly in service as well as manufacturing operations, and across entire enterprises. In particular, the knowledge-driven aspects of lean principles and the concept of customer "pull" distinguish this integrated operating system from craft and mass production.

It is somewhat ironic that the Ford-UAW transformation, which includes lean principles for work operations and also features partnership principles for union-management relations, means that Ford is now departing from "Fordism." It is rare that the progenitor of one system (in this case, mass production) helps point the way to a new system; typically, the originator—once eclipsed—doesn't regain leadership.[3] Nevertheless, Ford has survived the end of "Fordism" and today is helping write the book on the transformation to a new "post-industrial system"—the name of which will ultimately be settled by history (candidates include "flexible specialization,"[4] "lean production"[5] or "lean enterprise,"[6] "service science,"[7] "knowledge-driven work,"[8] and others). Here we add to the discussion the idea of "integrated operating systems."

While the postindustrial model is a fundamental departure from traditional mass production, there are still some foundational aspects of the mass production model that continue to be relevant. For example, in his 1926 book, *Today and Tomorrow*, Henry Ford stated, "Today's standardization...is the necessary foundation on which tomorrow's improvement will be based. If you think of 'standardization' as the best you know today, but which is to be improved tomorrow—you get somewhere. But if you think of standards as confining, then progress stops."[9] A key feature of the integrated operating systems involves standardization, such as time and data management, charters, and other aspects of social and technical stability.

This still-emerging alternative to mass production also involves new operating assumptions that have many roots. Particularly important are ideas about statistical quality control advanced by W. Edwards Deming and based on his work with Walter Shewhart at Bell Labs during World War II. Although Deming and Shewhart had successfully applied these ideas in industry during the war, there was little interest in U.S. industry to continue with them after the war, in part because the ideas involved empowering all workers with knowledge and key roles in working with the statistical data, as well as focusing on the system as a whole. There were some deep assumptions embedded in the ideas for which U.S. industry was not ready. Deming, however, did find an enthusiastic audience for these ideas during the postwar years in Japan.

At the core of Deming's work was a simple, yet radical notion—improving quality required new ways of organizing the *system* of work, rather than a focus on the efforts of individuals within the system. Frontline work was of central importance, based on the knowledge of frontline workers as they monitored their own quality.

To this day, Japan honors this continuous-improvement, systems approach with the annual Deming award for quality.

Although Ford was ahead of most U.S. companies in reaching out to Deming in 1983 for advice on quality, managers at Ford were not prepared at the time for Deming's focus on the company's culture and management approach. They preferred to focus on quality tools and methods. At the time, his seminars at Ford were primarily used to reinforce the use of statistical quality control by quality engineers—not as a fundamental change in the operating system. During the next decade (up to his death in December 1993), this dynamic was repeated in many U.S. companies.

To address head on the lack of take-up in the United States, Deming formulated 14 principles of management,[10] four of which are particularly relevant here (listed with their original number from his full list):

1. Create constancy of purpose toward improvement of product and service, with the aim to become competitive and to stay in business, and to provide jobs.

9. Break down barriers between departments. People in research, design, sales, and production must work as a team, to foresee problems of production and in use that may be encountered with the product or service.

10. Eliminate slogans, exhortations, and targets for the work force asking for zero defects and new levels of productivity. Such exhortations only create adversarial relationships, as the bulk of the causes of low quality and low productivity belong to the system and thus lie beyond the power of the work force.

14. Put everybody in the company to work to accomplish the transformation. The transformation is everybody's job.

Today, Deming is also honored in the United States for his pioneering role. The ideas are now widely acknowledged, although application of the ideas is still inconsistent. Too often, lean and Six Sigma tools (which build on Deming principles) are applied piecemeal rather than as part of a systematic transformation. If the more fully integrated systemic approach represents a better model, why has the actual application of the ideas in U.S. industry been so mixed?

A key underlying factor becomes evident when we consider the assumption embedded in Deming's injunction that "the transformation is everybody's job." This statement incorporates the assumption that all (or at least the vast majority) of workers genuinely want to do a good job and contribute to a transformation.[11] This may seem contrary to many models of change management, which begin with the assumptions of resistance to change and a limited number of champions.[12] Deming's point is that that transformation encompasses and is enabled by the knowledge and capability of the entire workforce. He is not saying that there will be no issues or concerns, or no need to make the case for change, but he begins with an assumption that everyone can and will make transformation their business (if enabled to do so).

Disciplined and structured processes are essential to achieving change on this scale. As we saw in chapter 6, new approaches to collective bargaining (converting it into more of a problem-solving process) require new forms of discipline and structure. Similarly, the charters and "time and data management" we discuss in chapter 7 center on bringing structure and discipline to joint activities. So, a fundamentally different assumption about people is combined with structure and discipline that is consistent with that assumption.

In this chapter, we present pivotal events that add up to integrated operating systems for quality, safety, and other key issues. In doing so, we draw on Deming's approach to variation and integrate it with the process of organizational transformation. It is a fundamental principle that variation in a system must be reduced before trying to generate improvements. The pivotal events in this chapter illustrate the importance of this principle of reducing variation in social as well as technical systems.

Figure 8.1 (with some explanation) illustrates the importance of reducing variation to enable system improvement. By now, the concept is almost conventional wisdom for

Figure 8.1

Hypothetical Dart Game Illustrating Importance of Reducing Variation before Improving. *Source:* Work-Matters, LLC.

technical systems, but it is just as relevant for social systems. The figure was developed by Joel Cutcher-Gershenfeld and has been used in various Ford-UAW briefings.

The figure shows the results of two players in a hypothetical dart game in which points are awarded based on how close the darts are to the bullseye. Clearly, the player on the left has won more points, but that player hasn't hit the bullseye, so there's room for improvement.

Imagine you're a coach for dart players, and your job is to improve the performance of these two players. Though it may seem in principle that it would be easier to coach a higher-scoring player, coaching the player on the right would actually be the easier task. Telling the player on the left to aim a bit to the left or right or higher or lower would likely generate even more variation than was apparent in this round on the dart board. By contrast, where the player on the right needs to aim is much more obvious—you know exactly what to suggest to improve. This illustrates the risk of trying to improve a highly variable system and the value of stability before improvement.

This chapter features six pivotal events centered on moving beyond piecemeal change (highly variable) to integrated operating systems. To Deming's admonition to stabilize before improvement, we add a pre-condition: "alignment." This could be alignment of the UAW and Ford, alignment of functions within Ford, alignment of elected and appointed representatives or local and national representatives within the UAW, and other instances of stakeholder alignment. Thus, the guiding principle for the chapter is "Align and Stabilize, then Integrate."

Chapter 8

Pivotal Events	Overview	Type, Level
✓ Q1, 1980s, 1998, and 2002	A supplier certification initiative instituted in 1982 transitions from a one-time inspection program to a partnership as part of an emerging Quality Operating System.	Planned, Enterprise Level
✓ Quality Leadership Initiative, 2002	A top-down reengineering of the change process in response to a "burning platform" on quality falls short as a transformational pivot, because it is not sufficiently systematic as a strategy and it is rooted in a narrow, re-engineering logic.	Planned, Enterprise Level
Fresh Eyes Auditors and QOS Coordinators, 2000–2004	A restructuring of Quality embodies the key elements in a quality strategy that redefines the work of the frontline workforce.	Planned, Enterprise Level
Quality Operating System, 2003	A focus on four underlying pillars that represent structured discipline in the social systems transforms a list of elements of a Quality Operating System into the central driver for continuous improvement.	Planned, Enterprise Level
Targeted Training, 2003–2007	Skills and abilities are inconsistent across the enterprise, but the resources to address the problem—particularly time off the job—are highly constrained. Targeted training provides a way to build capability within operating constraints.	Planned, Enterprise Level
Safety Operating System, 2008	A second domain shifts from separate elements into an integrated systems approach to continuous improvement—a key additional element that points to system-wide transformation.	Planned, Enterprise Level

Q1, 1980s, 1998, and 2002

When the Ford Motor Company invites W. Edwards Deming to present his ideas in 1983, quality is already the focus of a 1982 strategic initiative by the company, which it calls Q1. Ford may not be ready to hear Deming's advice about the management of the enterprise as an integrated system, but Statistical Process Control (SPC) tools and methods are being advanced more broadly under the Q1 banner. The program is applied to Ford's assembly, engine & transmission, stamping, and components plants, as well as to external organizations designated as "preferred suppliers." Organizations must be invited by Ford to apply; they can't independently seek Q1 status. The process is intensive—a series of notebooks must be assembled documenting the quality performance of every aspect of the operation, which is followed by a multiday site visit in which the claims in the notebooks are verified.

Among UAW members in Ford facilities, the reaction to Q1 is mixed. There is certainly pride in quality. When a plant achieves Q1 status, the award is given to both the UAW chair and the plant manager, together on stage with the full plant workforce in attendance. It is the first time most workers—hourly and salaried—see the union and management leadership recognized together for any plant accomplishment. As we noted in chapter 4 in the Quality Leadership Team pivot, pride in quality can also be seen in the new ad campaign by Ford, "Quality is Job 1," which features frontline workers with both the Ford and UAW logos on their uniforms giving a big "thumbs up" on quality. These are reportedly among the most successful ads Ford has produced.[13] Workers throughout the system appreciate hourly employees being featured in the ads.

At the same time, though, UAW members are concerned that the new statistical process methods may result in fewer quality inspection jobs. They also resent what they see as Japanese management practices. The parking lot at UAW headquarters (Solidarity House) in Detroit has new sign that greets visitors: "You can park your Toyota in Tokyo." Indeed, all foreign cars are prohibited from parking there.

Consistent with quality principles, the Q1 process does involve increased input from frontline workers. John Nahornyj recalls the process in the Cleveland Engine Plant (CEP) in the mid-1980s.

Hourly individuals were selected via "temporary job postings" to act as Q1 coordinators representing specific manufacturing areas within the plant. At CEP, 5.0L engine assembly was one such area, as was "Area B," which consisted of four machining areas (Cam, Connecting Rod, Piston, and Exhaust Manifold). The hourly coordinator was responsible for working with area supervision, hourly employees, and quality control personnel assigned to Q1 to utilize and implement Statistical Process Control methods to both understand process capability and to make decisions based on that understanding. Control charts were placed at key operations and maintained daily by both the operator and the Q1 coordinator. Process improvements were made based upon the data from those charts.

Over time, the Q1 standard intensifies. When, in 1987 for example, the International Standards Organization establishes ISO 9000, a new quality management standard, Ford incorporates it into Q1. When published, ISO 9000 is paired with ISO 9001, which provides guidance for organizations seeking to meet the standard.[14] To be invited to become a Q1 supplier, an organization must now first meet the ISO 9000 standard.[15] Still, once an organization achieves Q1 status, a flag is flown outside the facility; maintaining the status only requires passing periodic recertification visits. Q1 features principles that will become central to a Quality Operating System for Ford, but it is primarily a set of practices, not an integrated quality operating system.

The first evidence of Q1 being more than a set of tools and techniques comes with a 1998 update to the Q1 process, in which the quality notebooks produced by the facility must specify that the plant complies with the seven categories of what is termed the Ford Q1 Quality Operating System (QOS): Communication, Teamwork, Management Review, Measureables, Qualifying Tools, Continual Improvement, and Dynamic Process. For example, under "Communication," the facility must demonstrate that "employees at all levels are aware of the FORD Q1 (QOS) process" and that "senior management has communicated clear expectations of the FORD Q1 (QOS) process." Under "Teamwork," the standards include: "A champion is identified for each measurable and is actively involved with teams"; "teams are allocated resources to function effectively"; and "cross-functional problem solving and quality improvement teams have been established to work on opportunities identified by the FORD Q1 (QOS) process." All standards center on demonstrated use of structured problem-solving tools and methods, with associated support.

The 1998 update to Q1 makes the program more systematic. Still, it is structured as a one-time event.

Ford issues the second edition of the Q1 program in 2002. It marks a shift from supplier certification to a partnership with suppliers around continuous improvement. In materials prepared for suppliers,[16] Ford first indicates the value of the Q1 program: "By recognizing quality achievement at the manufacturing site level and by applying consistent, understandable metrics to ensure high quality, Q1 has become a quality brand name trademark, both domestically and around the globe." Then Ford poses the question, "Why change?" and responds: "In the past, Q1 has been seen as a diploma of sorts, a one-time award that didn't need to be renewed. Once the award was achieved, suppliers had limited interaction with Ford. Previous Q1 metrics weren't predictive, so they didn't always assure quality performance. But in a competitive industry, consistent quality and continual improvement are necessary for survival."

The change is signaled in this excerpt from the response to the rhetorical question, "What is Q1 2002?"

It is a set of fundamental quality and manufacturing disciplines that ensure a supplier's success and drive a supplier's continual improvement.... Suppliers are expected to achieve Q1 2002 independently— it is a relationship. Ford stands ready to offer suppliers its expertise and assistance.

✳ ✳ ✳

The 2002 change in Q1 is a key part of the larger transformation within Ford around integrated operating systems (discussed more fully later in this chapter). Given what is at stake on quality—success in the market place, warranty costs, and liability if there are safety issues associated with bad quality—the systematic Q1 process is an essential part of enterprise operations.

Today, the full set of automotive quality standards continues to evolve and encompass topics ranging from the overall product development system to training, document control, prototype approval, fastener durability, heat treat material analysis, and hundreds of other considerations. Some of the standards are unique to Ford; some are common standards shared by Chrysler, Ford, and General Motors; and some are international standards. Ford's suppliers still vie for Q1 status, which today signifies a high level of process control and discipline in the operations, as well as a partnership relationship with Ford.

Quality Leadership Initiative (QLI), 2002

By 2002, quality is a burning platform for Ford. The 2001 recall of the Ford Explorer requires the replacement of 6.5 million faulty tires. At the same time, there is a court-ordered recall of 7.9 million cars and trucks to replace faulty ignition modules.[17] The issue is not whether to transform quality, but how best to do so.

The Ford 2000 initiative is no longer the primary vehicle for change, but its successor, Jacques Nasser's Business Leadership Initiative (BLI), is still a top-down reengineering approach to transformation. With respect to quality, it takes the form of the Quality Leadership Initiative (QLI), led by Louise Goeser, the vice president of Global Quality. Meanwhile, operating in parallel, the Ford Production System (FPS) is an alternative bottom-up process improvement approach. Both are similar in how they embrace the quality standards established by Q1 with suppliers and the time-and-data quality metrics reflected in the SQDCME balanced scorecard. Where BLI and FPS contrast is in their underlying assumptions about the change process for continuous improvement in organizations.

How to address quality is not just an internal management question. The union is also involved. In February 2002, the UAW takes a highly unusual step for a U.S. union. Garry Mason, UAW co-chair of the UAW-Ford National Quality Committee, sends a letter to all UAW regional directors and regional servicing representatives (all key leaders from the international union) on the subject "Quality Crisis." The letter addresses specific quality-performance issues such as the use of the "stop button" that allows hourly workers to call for help or stop the assembly line so that out-of-spec quality production does not leave their area.

February 26, 2002
To: UAW Regional Directors
UAW Regional Servicing Representatives
Subject: **Quality Crisis**

We are in a fight for our jobs. As Vice President, Ron Gettelfinger has said numerous times, "Quality is our job security." We have had you in several meetings over the past couple of years and our message has never changed. We must not insist but demand that the "Stop Button/Stop the Operation" Procedures be fully utilized in your locations. We are still hearing too many instances of employees having a fear to stop their operation for bona fide quality issues.

At the recent Committeeperson/Supervisor training sessions held the last two weeks of January, an audience response session was held. One of the questions asked for Quality was, "How often do employees in your area utilize the Stop Button or Stop the Operation Procedure?" In three different sessions consisting of 76% salary, 24% hourly, the choice of "infrequently" was chosen 44%, 42%, and 47%, respectively. Although design and supplier issues account for the majority (80—85%) of recalls and customer dissatisfaction, those percentages are unacceptable for the 15% to 20% that are plant controllable. Ford Motor Company spent 3.6 billion dollars on warranty last year.

Another question that was asked on the audience survey was "What is the biggest inhibitor to quality/customer satisfaction at your location?" Again, bearing in mind the makeup of the audience

76% salary, 24% hourly, the most chosen answer was "Emphasis on Productivity/Production" at 39%, 36%, and 40%, respectively. Equally disturbing, the second most chosen answer was "Unstable/Incapable Processes" at 20%, 19%, and 26%, respectively. Although productivity is important, to choose it over quality when Ford's market share fell to 20.5% as of February 13, 2002, because the public doesn't want our products is unacceptable. Market share as you have heard before has a direct bearing on our job security. A little over 1% decline in market share could mean closing another assembly plant. There is absolutely no excuse for an unstable/incapable process.

Why do I believe this? Because we have the Concern Resolution Process and not one form has been sent to the National level describing an unstable/incapable process. We just recently received forms from one of the assembly plants dealing with the paint area that named supervision by name. Although those were not properly signed off and have to come back through the system, it is the type of information we want.

You can choose to be part of the solution or choose to be part of the problem. I want names of Management that are not allowing our members to exercise their contractual rights (i.e., Stop the Operation Process). I want names of Management that are signing off on QR's from suppliers that constantly send you poor quality parts. I want names of Management that are pulling tags off rejected material. I want reports on engineering changes, such as the fuel line hose that was changed in Norfolk and other assembly plants (the hose was longer and stiffer and created a kinking problem when it was installed). The decision to change was made after a 20-piece trial 8 or 9 months ago in Dearborn from what we're being told. The Quality Representative at Norfolk reported this immediately and we were able to address it. I want numbers on the UAW people that have been written up for quality-related incidents like the one in Kansas City Assembly for not securing the steering wheel (it was later learned that the supplier did not put enough threads on the shaft to allow the operator to do his job and the discipline was removed). The Quality Representative brought this and some other issues up at the North American Quality Planning and Assistance Meeting and was told by his Plant Manager that every time the Quality Representative opened his mouth the Plant Manager got another assignment. Just the attitude we need to turn around quality.

If you think that you are protecting your plant by keeping these issues in house, you are sadly mistaken. It will cost us jobs unless we can address these issues and let Management know that we will not let their poor decisions erode our membership. Our International Representatives assigned to the National Quality Committee will be visiting your locations and will be walking the floor. If they hear of incidents that you have been made aware of but not being addressed then you are part of the problem and will be dealt with accordingly. In fact, Vice President Ron Gettelfinger has said publicly that if it is necessary to assign the entire Ford Department to Quality, he will to turn this crisis around.

I would like this information no later than March 5, 2002. A lot of you have reported issues that we have been able to address, but not near the number of incidents that Vice President Ron Gettelfinger, or other members of his staff hear when they visit the plants.

Fraternally,
Garry G. Mason
UAW Co-Chair

Note that the UAW is specifically making visible a key operating assumption—"keeping these issues in house"—that doesn't fully get addressed until the launch of CEO Mulally's BPR process (chapter 4).

There are many responses to the quality crisis. The Q1 process is revised to be more than a periodic certification (as we saw earlier in this chapter). QLI is promoted as part of the solution as well, with a three-phased change process. Phase I focuses on the development and deployment of nine QLI principles, which begins in April 2002.

Quality Leadership Initiative (QLI) Principles

1. Quality is Job #1! It is our responsibility, our job security and our future!
2. Zero Defect Mindset—"Don't take it, don't make it, and don't pass it on."
3. Relentless daily focus on quality.
4. Ensure people have the necessary skills and tools to do their jobs.
5. Effective measurement and feedback for continuous improvement.
6. Help suppliers help us succeed.
7. Effective quality leadership at all levels.
8. Changes never compromise quality.
9. The Customer is our shared concern.

Communicating the principles involves an appeal to company employees for support in the quality drive via "Quality Stand Down" presentations in all Vehicle Operations, Powertrain, and Stamping facilities, as well as all Ford Customer Service Division parts depots, and to staff in Product Development and Purchasing.

Phase II involves a strengthened Quality Concern/Suggestion Process. Employees are encouraged to raise concerns when they see quality issues go unresolved. Phase III involves a scorecard to track progress in following up and addressing the quality concerns. Goeser encourages workers to raise concerns, which some managers resent—they see her as disrupting the "Old Boys' Club" by embarrassing people in public. The norm in Ford is that problems aren't made public; despite the UAW letter challenging this norm, managers are expected to take care of their own business.

In June 2002, Garry Mason moves on to a new assignment supporting Ron Gettelfinger as president of the international union. Dan Brooks assumes the role as UAW co-chair of Quality. In his first day on the job, Dean Blythe—his Ford counterpart for Quality—brings him the QLI plan for 2003. To Brooks, it looks more like a "flavor of the month" initiative than a full plan to reverse the quality crisis. He is reminded of Deming's principle to "eliminate slogans, exhortations, and targets," and says so. Still, QLI is a source of feedback in the system and has support from top Ford and UAW leaders. So, Brooks supports the 2003 plan, which follows.

2003 Quality Leadership Initiative Communications Strategy

Early January 2003

• Conduct local employee meetings to provide an update on the status of QLI and additional information on the Quality is Job #1 theme and 2003 QLI Plans.
• Provide plants/depots/operations with 10-minute generic script to be used by Superintendents or higher in natural work group meetings (hourly and salary) during the month of January (arrangements

must be made with all non work group employees either as part of an associated work group or as a group by themselves). Each location would determine its local communications strategy in terms of timing, location, size of meetings, etc.

• Locations would be provided the Blue QLI Principles Card with Principles #1 (Quality is Job #1) and #5 (Effective Measurement and Feedback for Continuous Improvement) highlighted for distribution in employee meetings.

Rollout Plan

• Script outlines and instructions would be distributed before the 2002 Christmas shutdown. Cards would be shipped during the Christmas holidays.

• Beginning in January, Plant/PDC and Operations Managers and Directors would meet with Local Operating Committees and UAW Leadership to customize the message (script) for that location.

• Once the local message was finalized, Union and Company Leadership would meet with District Committeepersons / appropriate appointed representatives and Superintendents to prepare them to deliver the "tailored" message. To the extent possible, meetings should be held by Plant Manager, Chairperson, Bargaining Committee, and Operating Committee.

Topics Covered

• Recap of May Stand Down
• QLI activities since May
  - Hot Line Experience
  - Local Stand Down Items Closed
• Local Quality Performance—Plant/Area/Department
• Explanation of "Quality is Job #1" theme and Principle #5 ("Effective Measurement and Feedback") at XYZ location
• 2003 QLI Communications Plan
• Department/Area Quality Priorities
• Q & A; Employee Comments

February 2003

• Provide locations with materials for a 30-minute employee information meeting around QLI Principles 1 and 5 as well as a complete explanation of the planned QLI Communications Process for 2003. The meeting would also highlight both Corporate and Local Quality objectives for 2003.

• Message would be delivered to Department/Area by Superintendents or higher.

• Locations would be provided:
  - Generic script that would be tailored for local messages.

• Rollout Process would be much like that of January, i.e.:
  - Plant Quality Committees and UAW Bargaining Committees determine local messages to be added to generic scripts.
  - Local leadership meets with District Committeepersons/appropriate appointed representatives and Superintendents to help them prepare to deliver the message.

• Key topics (with heavy local content):
  - Explain QLI Principles #1 and #5 and how they apply to XYZ location.
  - 2003 quality objectives—Ford and XYZ location.
  - 2003 QLI Communications Plan.
  - Other local quality matters of note (provide opportunity for employee feedback).

Strategy for Balance of 2003

- Conduct "Work Group" meetings each quarter.
- Focus of meetings would be one QLI Principle and its application at XYZ location.
- Meetings would also recap XYZ location and area/department quality performance to objectives.

The plan guides the efforts of the National Quality Committee through March 2003 and the National Joint Program's Las Vegas conference. Returning from the joint conference, though, Brooks and Blythe shift their focus to the Quality Operating System (discussed later in this chapter). Preparation also begins for the 2003 national collective bargaining negotiation (presented in chapter 6). While QLI does not figure in the 2003 quality negotiations, Goeser is still driving this initiative. In 2004, she works with Ford's Roman Krygier and the UAW's Gerald Bantom to issue another QLI letter. It states, in part:

With your support, we've done a good job of getting QLI off the ground. We've had QLI communication cascade meetings with our plant employees about once a quarter. We've handed out QLI pocket cards with the nine QLI principles to all our employees twice. We've also implemented a Quality Hot Line process for our people. In short, we've built a solid foundation for QLI to succeed. On the other hand, QLI has come nowhere near reaching its potential. Work group surveys show QLI to be only 36% favorable (on average) across the operations. Focus groups tell us QLI requires significant strengthening in the following areas:

- Leadership engagement
- Consistent/effective delivery of the QLI message to the workforce
- Floor supervisor skills relative to coaching, mentoring and facilitation

This turns out to be the last communication on QLI. Goeser is replaced by Deborah Coleman, who is then replaced by Bennie Fowler as the vice president for Quality. He formally embraces the Quality Operating System and advocates for the QOS as an integral part of the Ford Production System. Quality leadership behaviors are still emphasized, but within the umbrella of an integrated operating system.

✳ ✳ ✳

In the midst of a quality crisis, choices about the change strategy are highly consequential and the best choices are not always clear. QLI is a pivotal event that builds on Ford 2000 and BLI—all top-down reengineering initiatives. While each features some tools and methods that are important in advancing quality, these are not systems change initiatives that involve the full workforce in the transformation. The full workforce receives briefings and is afforded the chance to signal quality concerns, but the way work is done across the enterprise does not change in fundamental ways as a result of QLI. It aspired to be more of a pivot than it ended up being.

Fresh Eyes Auditors and QOS Coordinators, 2000–2004

In Ford's Powertrain Division the mix of different technical operations—machining, heat treat, and batch production, as well as assembly—are more conducive to team meetings than in Vehicle Operations. Plus, the culture and leadership has been more open to innovation. So, Powertrain has more flexibility in instituting high-involvement work practices compared to the assembly plants in Vehicle Operations.

Roman Krygier heads the Powertrain Division in 2000. While the burning platform on quality issues that will galvanize the attention of the entire company is still two years off, there are still serious concerns reflected in warranty repair costs per 1,000 units. Even though Powertrain is well advanced under the Q1 audits in demonstrating that the principles of the Quality Operating System are in place, Krygier suspects that the quality performance is not advancing fast enough because the principles are not being followed in a sufficiently disciplined and structured way in the facilities.

Krygier call on UAW vice president Ron Gettelfinger to discuss this issue and proposes a temporary measure to attempt to instill discipline in the QOS. He shares his plan to put hourly people on the floor—he calls them "fresh eyes auditors"—who will have subject matter expertise in the QOS and monitor daily adherence to the process. As Krygier explains,

The Quality Operating System has [designated roles for] work groups, the skilled trades, and so forth. At the core it is the methods, procedures, and standards for how we do our quality work in the manufacturing environment. Some aspects are simple and some complex, but it is all about how you go about your work in whatever part of the system you work—standardized methods and procedures.

I was not confident enough that the procedures were being followed. So we had to put the discipline in place to ensure the procedures were being followed—and I am talking about the salaried workforce here as much as hourly....

If you can get together with the UAW and get a joint commitment—things start to happen. I thought quality was a great area where things could happen.

Krygier makes clear that what he means by quality standards is distinct from production standards such as the number of cars per hour or work standards in terms of time-and-motion study. Production and work standards are related to productivity and are often points of contention between labor and management. On quality standards, though, there is much more likely to be common cause. Gettelfinger concurs with the idea of putting these "fresh eyes auditors" in place in different areas of the Powertrain plants. The idea is communicated throughout the system, and local officials are empowered to select the auditors and establish their roles and responsibilities.

Rusty Woolum is an hourly employee at the Sharonville Transmission Plant, which produces gears and other drive train components for assembly into transmissions. "I was originally hired on August 9, 1993," he says. "The old approach was 'if it shines, send it down the line.'" Later, "We began working in teams. The meetings began with the Standard Business Agenda."

While this was, he notes, the beginning of a transformation in quality, it was not well disciplined initially. "At these team meetings," he says, "people would sit back and read a paper or magazine. Teams were in their infancy."

Then Woolum hears about the "fresh eyes auditors" initiative and decides to apply for one of the positions. "On August 20, 2001, I was chosen as one of the fresh eyes auditors. We were told it would be a three-year appointment...Ford is known for having good processes, but not necessarily adhering to them. Our role would be to monitor adherence to process." This, he recalls, marked an important shift from what he initially experienced as an hourly employee.

Woolum confirms Krygier's concern that the challenge is as much with the salaried as the hourly workforce. "There was some reluctance from management—people saying you have done things one way for years. Now we need to follow the process—in other words reduce variability in response to the voice of the customer. We had the full backing of the union to be in this role."

Initially, says Woolum, he was seen in a "cop role—someone with a radar gun waiting to catch someone speeding....We had to convince people that we were here to help get from good to great." Still, the role was about structure and discipline, or as he puts it, "holding people accountable once they have been coached or counseled."

By early 2003, there are fresh eyes auditors across Powertrain locations—many given the title "Quality Coordinator." Dan Brooks has been appointed as the union's co-chair for Quality. The UAW's Charlie Castle is the international representative servicing Powertrain locations and he takes Brooks to various locations to meet some of these new appointees. Brooks wonders why they are necessary. Each plant also has hourly UAW Quality Representatives—a longstanding role dating back to the 1982 Mutual Growth agreement. They have Ford quality counterparts, too. Brooks asks what these hourly fresh eyes quality coordinators are doing that the UAW Quality Representatives are not.

Castle explains there is no formal role that allows the UAW Quality Representatives to hold people (hourly or salaried) accountable for adherence to quality standards. Doing so would be controversial, seen as ratting on co-workers or reaching beyond one's role or status. The fresh eyes auditors are making a major break with tradition. They have built up a greater knowledge of the Quality Operating System than the appointed UAW Quality Representatives. At the same time, there is variability in capabilities and impact of the fresh eyes auditors across the various Powertrain locations. This will serve as a touch point in the upcoming 2003 national UAW-Ford negotiations for which Roman Krygier, the global vice president of Manufacturing, would co-lead with the vice president of Labor Affairs, Dennis Cirbes.

When the 2003 national UAW-Ford negotiation opens, Brooks puts as a first point for discussion the continuation of the fresh eyes quality coordinators in Powertrain and proposes it be expanded to Vehicle Operations and Stamping facilities. These individuals are doing great work, Brooks contends, and there is evidence of their positive impact on quality. Brooks also proposes that consistent selection criteria, roles and responsibilities, and training be established at the national level—to address the variability across facilities.

Brooks's counterpart in the joint UAW-Ford quality program, Deane Blythe, represents Ford in the negotiations on quality. He recalls that his role was to represent operating management—not just the labor affairs function within management.

"Roman Krygier had experience with the quality coordinator role in Powertrain and [by 2003] he was the worldwide director of manufacturing," says Blythe. "He was implementing [the Quality Operating System] throughout manufacturing and understood what was required and was a big supporter. I can recall him saying this is something that we want to do—if you get any resistance bring that to me."

In fact, there is resistance to the idea from operating managers in Vehicle Operations and Stamping. Adrian Vido, the head of Quality for Vehicle Operations, remembers the resistance.

Quality Coordinators were in place in Powertrain when I took the Quality position. It was apparent to me and to Roman Krygier, who was a strong supporter, that they improved the bottom line in Quality and were value-add positions. As a result, we wanted Quality Operating System Coordinators in Assembly and Stamping to be a topic in our negotiations. I had difficulty running this idea through the company side.

They saw added manpower/costs but couldn't clearly see the benefits....It required a lot of homework on our part to factually demonstrate their impact and role they play in bridging the supervisor to employee communication gap.

In the end, a Letter of Understanding is reached that continues the quality coordinator role in Powertrain, now termed "Quality Operating System Coordinators (QOSCs), and drops the term "fresh eyes auditors." The letter reads as follows:

POWERTRAIN OPERATIONS QUALITY OPERATING SYSTEM (QOS) SUPPORT PROCESS
September 15, 2003
Mr. Gerald D. Bantom
Vice President and Director
UAW, National Ford Department
8000 East Jefferson Avenue
Detroit, Michigan 48214

Dear Mr. Bantom:
Subject: Powertrain Operations Quality Operating
System (QOS) Support Process

Powertrain Operations will continue to deploy the QOS Support Process as defined in the May 22, 2001, letter from Ron Gettelfinger and Roman Krygier for the term of this agreement. Please be aware that staffing levels to support this process may vary, based on customer demand, production volumes and schedules, shift patterns, and general business conditions.

Very truly yours,
TIM P. HARTMANN, Director
Union Relations
Labor Affairs

A second letter establishes a joint study to determine whether adding QOSCs to Vehicle Operations and Stamping would be of value to the company. The study team includes Ford employees from the Quality offices for Vehicle Operations, Stamping, Powertrain, as well as members of the UAW-Ford National Quality Committee. The letter reads as follows:

QUALITY OPERATING SYSTEM (QOS) SUPPORT PROCESS STUDY
September 15, 2003
Mr. Gerald D. Bantom
Vice President and Director
UAW, National Ford Department
8000 East Jefferson Avenue
Detroit, Michigan 48214

Dear Mr. Bantom:
Subject: Quality Operating System (QOS) Support Process Study

Following the effective date of this agreement, the Vehicle Operations Quality Office, in conjunction with the UAW-Ford National Quality Committee, will conduct a detailed study to determine the potential application of the Powertrain Operations Quality Operating System Support Process Model to Vehicle Operations facilities covered by this agreement. The review will include an analysis of the existing Vehicle Operations employee roles and responsibilities around the Quality Operating System, determine the degree of correlation to the PTO QOS Model, and develop recommendations for more effective utilization of current personnel to enforce the QOS Process. This study will be completed no later than June 30, 2004, and subject findings and recommendations will be presented to the Vehicle Operations Joint Quality Committee and the UAW-Ford Quality Improvement Steering Committee.

Very truly yours,
TIM P. HARTMANN, Director
Union Relations
Labor Affairs
Concur; Gerald D. Bantom

"We made road trips evaluating the role [as it was in Powertrain]—it was sealing the deal," Dean Blythe recalls. "All of that activity was from November to February. It was a busy time, but the implementation afterwards was even more time intensive. The language was the concept, but not the end product. It was not all spelled out in that detail. We just kept going—bringing the specifics together. It was an evolutionary process."

Study team members convene and review the findings once the study is complete. They agree there must be a consensus to move forward with a recommendation to Matt DeMars, the vice president of Vehicle Operations, and his directors. But developing a consensus proposal is challenging.

"It was difficult," Brooks explains. "On the one hand, you're asking the company to add incremental free effort heads (that is, additional people not working on the line) who will become QOSCs. That is a considerable cost. On the other hand, you're asking the union to embrace a process that takes autonomy away from the local elected leaders in how these people will be selected and what their roles will be."

There is precedent, however, for a competency-based selection process for hourly appointees. Such a process had been used in a number of Powertrain locations for work group leaders (as discussed in the Cleveland Engine pivotal event in chapter 2). These arrangements, along with other leading practices observed (such as the Lima Engine selection process), become the model for the selection of QOSCs. A training plan is developed and a formula is established to determine the number of QOSCs that will be assigned to each facility.

By the end of 2004, all UAW-Ford facilities have QOSCs. The results are clear. Increased adherence to the Quality Operating System is beginning to drive year-over-year improvements in quality. As Vido states:

The four pillars of the QOS became better understood. It was not optional....The QOSCs fulfilled a key role in the "infrastructure" pillar of the QOS.

A key part of the QOS is to review "every claim every day" during our daily Quality meeting. This occurs at every plant around the world. The key role the QOSCs play is to share the issue with the employees at the affected workstations. [Their role is to] try to understand how the issue was created...and, more importantly, how can we prevent [the issue from occurring or] error-proof the workstation such that the issue would not repeat. They are our first line of response to issues.

Although the QOS has been integral to the Q1 quality certification process with suppliers for a number of years, it is with QOSCs that additional gains are achieved. Rusty Woolum, a QOSC in Ford's Sharonville Plant, describes how his role expanded to include ensuring adherence to quality standards with suppliers. "As a QOSC I always think, what is the next level? One is training; the other is the supply base. Let me tell you how thankful I am to have experienced the work with suppliers."

As Woolum explains, "In 2001–2004, we had dealt with suppliers on a semi-personal level. If we had a problem with incoming material out of spec, we would set up a sort. This would be led by salaried counterparts. In time they saw that [the hourly workers] were efficient in doing this."

The role of QOSCs with suppliers expanded, Woolum explains. "If I had a problem in my area I wanted to be able to contact the supplier directly with data, to recognize that they knew the part better than we did." So, Woolum begins with the assumption that the suppliers have key knowledge. He is also mindful that the "supply base relationships have been horrible over the years."

In one example (in addition to the example in chapter 5), Woolum says, "I went to a plant in Toronto. The plant manager greeted me. I said I wanted to talk to the entire area associated with a given part—whoever has anything to do with the part....I said that I wanted to show them the data. I believed that they were being told to run bad parts. I wanted to show them data from the customer."

This, of course, was not a common role for an hourly worker. Still, as Woolum recalls, "Fifty people came in. I created a PowerPoint presentation and over the next 30 minutes went over problems with the part. I indicated why micron tolerances were so important to a transmission. The questions kept being fired off in the meeting. It was phenomenal they way they cared."

Woolum concludes that the workers in the plant "needed that voice."

***

By 2006, the success of the QOSCs leads the UAW and Ford to want to bring the UAW Quality Representatives' skills up to a level comparable to the QOSCs. The UAW-Ford National Joint Programs reach out to Dr. Ahmad Ezzeddine, the associate vice president for Educational Outreach and International Programs at Wayne State University, to develop the needed curriculum. He notes that the development process reflected the UAW-Ford partnership. "This was a partnership in the development of the training—a three-way partnership. We served as developers and designers, with the UAW and Ford always guiding and facilitating. We didn't do any section without their full involvement and [always] embracing what they were identifying as the focus."

The training is delivered at annual quality conferences, which were, according to Ezzeddine, "always very collaborative and engaged. We would have the whole UAW and Ford team in the room. All parties were always there in force at delivery—it was not just a UAW program or just a Ford program. . . . It was a genuine collaborative experience. This is not something that we saw with other companies and unions."

Just before retiring in 2010, Dan Brooks makes a final presentation to all of the QOSCs and UAW Quality Representatives at the annual UAW-Ford quality offsite conference. Through a series of charts, he documents the division-by-division and plant-by-plant quality performance since 2003. The results are dramatic. Ford has progressed from the burning platform of a quality crisis to best in class on quality.

Brooks tells the QOSCs how proud he is of their work. Both the UAW and Ford, he says, owe them a debt of gratitude. The feeling is reciprocal—Brooks is told just how much the QOSCs appreciate being able to serve in the role.

Still, the quality gains are not permanent—the increased use of Web-based electronics in cars will raise new quality challenges for Ford.

What is pivotal about the QOSC role is not just the turnaround in quality performance, but the underlying message that everyone is responsible for adherence to the system. Ford has shifted from a company with great processes not always followed to one where hourly workers can hold co-workers accountable and hourly workers can even hold salaried supervisors, manager, or engineers accountable. The UAW doesn't just support quality; it is a full partner in driving the Quality Operating System. Within management, advocates for the systems approach are vindicated. The result is a shift in the culture to one where disciplined, structured adherence to process and data-driven continuous improvement are valued and supported by labor and management.

In 2011, collective bargaining focuses on standardizing the structure and operation of teams throughout the enterprise. One key part of this involves agreements around work team leader selection and de-selection. The QOSC model of selection based on standards for expertise is incorporated—reflecting the broader shift within the union to ensure competency-based appointments.

Quality Operating System, 2003

Transformation that delivers results is rarely achieved through an itemized list of things to do—it takes changes in work and relationships that are more complex. In many ways, the Quality Leadership Initiative (QLI) was a list of things to do—surveys were conducted to identify quality concerns. Supervisors and managers would then be assigned to "chase the complaints" until the issues were "closed." This didn't get at sustained changes in the underlying ways in which the work was done.

Anne Stevens, then vice president of Manufacturing, coins one of the key principles in the QLI: "Don't take it, don't make it, don't pass it along." A former graduate student of Deming,[18] Stevens is a strong proponent of a data-driven, systems approach to quality. While she supports the QLI principles, she worries that the results are not being delivered by this approach. Her concern intensifies with the burning platform on quality. She is also worried about the succession of different programs and initiatives. Her observation is that each new program or initiative excites the frontline workers and supervisors who believe it will address issues they see in the operation, only to disappoint them when it doesn't. What she calls the "hope/heartbreak cycle" is something she thinks people can only go through a few times before they become cynical.

In early 2003, Stevens reaches out to meet with Joe Gafa, the UAW assistant director responsible for Quality, and Dan Brooks, the UAW leader on Quality reporting to Gafa. Brooks has faced off with plant managers and directors of initiatives before, but has not met with a Ford vice president. Stevens begins by expressing her commitment to make good on the "don't take it, don't make it, don't pass it along" principle.

Stevens asks Brooks what he thinks about quality in the plants. He recalls looking at Gafa for guidance; Gafa indicates he should speak his mind. Brooks tells Stevens that the problem is that people are not adhering to the process.

"She asks me, 'What do you mean?' I said there are standardized Operator Instruction Sheets (OIS) for every job in the plant, but in almost every case you can see people missing steps. There is no supervisory control to make sure there is adherence to process. People are out there working but not with adherence to process."

Two things can lead to poor quality, Brooks says: bad design and a lack of adherence to process. In most cases, he notes, the problem is not with the design. "It was apparent," Brooks recalls, "that she was not getting the story from the directors about what is going on in the facilities."

Even though something termed a "Quality Operating System" has been in place since 1998, the lack of adherence to the process means it is not achieving its full potential. Adrian Vido is the quality manager for Ford's Vehicle Operation division in 2003, which includes all the assembly plants in which all the quality issues come together in the final product. The challenge is to have all of these plants operating consistently with this system, as well as with the plants that supply them within and outside of Ford.

Vido describes the QOS as "a disciplined set of rules and guidelines for standardized work. It begins with the work of the plant manager." He notes that the nine principles from the QLI are important, and adds that, "the principles resonated with many employees, but the principles could be carried out in many different ways."

In making the transition from a to-do list to an integrated operating system, the SQDCME balanced scorecard—implemented at all levels in 2001—provides the standardized metrics for Quality (as noted in chapter 4). Complementing SQDCME is the time-and-data-management process, also taking shape in 2002 (detailed in chapter 7).

The burning platform in 2002 provides a sense of urgency on change. The lack of results from the QLI "stand downs" on quality and the QLI quality-concerns resolution process is a further driver. Concurrently, the demonstrated results being achieved by the QOSCs reinforce the overarching importance of adherence to standard—even if the selection process for the QOSCs needs standardization, which is achieved through collective bargaining.

When Dan Brooks meets with Adrian Vido in 2003 and asks to be taken through the business plan for quality, it is the beginning of a very different role for the union (discussed in chapters 4 and 7). Brooks sets the business plan side-by-side with the existing letters of agreement and other contract language on quality. The result is a full partnership between the company and the union around delivering quality results—not just the union serving in an add-on communications role.

Chartering the National Quality Committee and the divisional committees in 2004 is key (detailed in chapter 7). Dan Brooks's push to clarify his role and responsibilities is the initial driver: he turns to the idea of a charter, a tool to which he was first introduced while working with FPS though the FTPM charter. The idea proves to be a powerful vehicle to standardize the social infrastructure for quality.

By early 2004, the Quality Operating System is clarified as having four pillars, each oriented toward sustained change in the way work is done (figure 8.2). The first pillar is *standard information*. As Vido explains it, "The same issue should be defined and discussed in the exact same way in every location."

The second pillar—*standard review of the information*—includes the plant manager and everyone else examining quality information at standardized times in the day. Time-and-data management (discussed in chapter 7) drives this pillar.

The right *infrastructure*—the third pillar—involves standardizing who is responsible for supporting each aspect of quality. As Vido notes, "You don't want a quality manager handling a particular issue in one plant and the plant manager doing so in another. This requires standardized roles and responsibilities."

Initially, notes Vido, the QOSCs were not established in their role on a uniform basis. He says that the early stages of the QOS revealed "a void on infrastructure." There were

Figure 8.2
Pillars of Integrated Operating Systems. *Source:* WorkMatters, LLC.

standardized Operator Instruction Sheets (OISs) for every job, but they were not necessarily being followed. Workers in different plants doing the same job on the same project should be able to switch locations and follow the OIS in identical ways. Charters (discussed in chapter 7) are key in specifying roles and responsibilities above the level of the operator.

Finally, the fourth pillar is *standard processes and tools*—some of which, as Vido notes, come from Six Sigma.

The approach to the four pillars of the QOS contrasts with the traditional approach to quality, with involves union and management auditors inspecting the plant with a check sheet. Brooks notes that "they would try to find issues and then it was a 'gotcha' with a report out later in a conference room. It seemed as though the auditors almost got a thrill out of embarrassing the plant leadership." This contrasts, with the approach of Howard Adams on FTPM (discussed in chapter 5): he would observe inappropriate practices and then provide the needed coaching and mentoring directly to the people doing the work.

An illustration showing the importance of the pillars is provided in figure 8.3, which tracks the performance trend from one of the work areas in the Chicago Stamping Plant. In a stamping plant, the time from the last good "hit" from the press on one run for a given part to the first good "hit" on a new run with a new part is termed "hit to hit" performance. The time in between is all unproductive downtime. Today, many stamping operations have the dies on rollers, making changes in just a few minutes. In 2003, it is still a manual operation

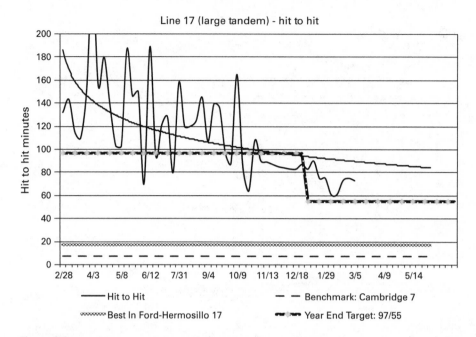

Figure 8.3
Reducing Variation for Continuous Improvement in Stamping Operations. *Source:* Ford Motor Company and WorkMatters, LLC.

and the chart indicates the progress made in decreasing a die change from over three hours to nearly one hour. Most noticeable on the chart is variation, which is large at the beginning of the 15-month time period and reduces considerably concurrently with an increased rate of improvement. When Joel Cutcher-Gershenfeld is in the Chicago Stamping Plant and sees this chart in a work area, he asks the team leader in the area what had happened at the point that the variation was reduced. The response is immediate: "That was when the team leaders and the UAW committeemen began attending the daily shift start meetings." In other words, as all the key stakeholders were working together in a defined forum they were better able to reduce variation and drive continuous improvement—on this productivity measure and on quality measures. The daily shift start meeting is a key part of the infrastructure (pillar three), while having the right stakeholders in the room allows for standardized review of the data (pillar two).

A typical plant visit with Adrian Vido would involve the same coaching and mentoring approach, says Brooks. "Adrian would show up in order to look at the four pillars of QOS. Facilities would set up an agenda for the day—limited to what we call a wide-aisle tour."

The plant would have been preparing these areas for some time for the visit. Adrian would look at the agenda and then set it aside. [He] had the plant's data and would state that he wanted to go to these three areas and talk to the operators on those jobs. It was so amazing. He would go to the person setting up the parts that were causing issues in the system. We would walk up and observe. He might then ask the operator about a key aspect of the work, such as the use of a quality gauge. Invariably, the operator would point to the gauge and explain that he or she was told that it was only needed at the beginning of the shift or something like that. Then Adrian would provide coaching and mentoring on following the quality standard.

It was not a gotcha. That was really impressive.

The coaching and mentoring approach is key for the QOSCs, who have the challenge (noted earlier in this chapter) of holding co-workers accountable for quality performance. Rusty Woolum, a QOSC in Ford's Sharonville Transmission Plant who had served as an elected member of the union's bargaining committee for the plant, recalls one incident.

There was a person with high seniority, now retired, who was trying to do what he thought was right. However, he was not following the process as it was written. The coaching hadn't been to the right level when he first learned the job. Along comes me as the QOSC with all these Powertrain procedures. He was containing, not correcting.

One day, I was on the floor and he saw me coming. He was known for being a little radical. He rose up in this case for what he thought would be a battle with me.

"I thought you were UAW," [he says].

I didn't care to have him question my loyalty.

"Why did you write my area up?" [he asks next].

"You are right," [I said], "it is your area. This is something you should have the utmost care for. There is an internal customer down stream and an external customer. I am here to help you to help others down stream.

"This is not saying you know what to do and didn't do it. I assume you didn't know, but I am here to help."

Years later, on the day that particular worker retires, he comes up to Woolum and says, "Remember the day I asked if you were UAW? Well, I have taken care of my area since that conversation and have learned a lot."

"The story started one way," says Woolum, "and ended up much better."

Summing up the impact of the QOS, Adrian Vido concludes, "The Ford Production System is generating energy off of the Quality Operating System. It is the most mature part of FPS."

✳ ✳ ✳

The pivot here is from a Quality Operating System in name to a QOS in use. The four pillars align different levels and functions within management, between labor and management, and among Ford with its suppliers. Notably, the alignment on "what to do" and "how to do it" happens with coaching and mentoring—not command and control. This sets in motion the cycle reflected in this chapter's guiding principle: "Align and Stabilize, then Integrate." The QOS builds the capability to drive continuous improvement in the operations, delivering results valued by all parties.

In retrospect, aspects of other initiatives, such as the quality concern resolution process set up through QLI and the tools and methods of Six Sigma, do have an important role under the QOS. Both need to be integrated, however, into an appropriately structured and standardized social infrastructure.

Targeted Training, 2003–2007

The 2003 collective bargaining agreement on quality includes a commitment to provide the needed quality training to support the workforce in the accelerated implementation of lean principles. Skills and abilities to support continuous improvement are inconsistent across the various UAW-Ford locations. While there are fresh eyes quality coordinators in the Powertrain locations, new Quality Operating System Coordinators need to be selected and trained in the Vehicle Operations and Stamping divisions.

By 2006, the UAW Quality Representatives begin to be trained at annual joint quality conferences. But that model does not work for others. There are teams and team leaders in many locations, but with great variation in their understanding of quality principles and limitations on how much time off the line can be devoted to training. Even among supervisors and middle managers, there is variation in skills and abilities, including "soft" skills such as how to coach and mentor frontline workers on quality principles.

The UAW and Ford together have extensive experience with training by 2003. The most prominent training has been large system-wide interventions such the 1999 diversity training (an eight-hour module delivered to the full workforce), the 1997–1999 Continuous Improvement Work Group (CIWG) training, and the 1997–1999 Basic Equipment Wellness One and Two training (BEW1 and BEW2). The CIWG training was an eight-hour module that was supposed to be delivered to the full workforce, but that varied in implementation across locations (in some cases, workers doing less-essential work go through the training multiple times to fill the seats designated for other workers who supervisors are unwilling to release from certain key jobs). The BEW1 and BEW2 modules total 12 hours, again designed to be delivered to all workers.

The approach to training in each of these topics comes to be criticized as "peanut butter training," with the same thin layer of training spread across the workforce. What may look consistent on the surface actually has an inconsistent effect, given the underlying variation in knowledge and ability. Some people receive training they already know, while others need much more training than the minimum provided. Further, the training is provided at a single point in time, which isn't always sufficiently close to the time the knowledge and skills need to be applied.

Given the burning platform on quality, implementing the 2003 quality agreements has to be done to ensure the right person has right skills at the right time in the right place, all within tight budget constraints. The budgetary challenge is particularly intense in the Vehicle Operations facilities, where people can't be released from the line for big blocks of training time without substantial cost implications—either training on overtime, backfilling with additional hires, or shutting down the assembly line.

The challenge is approached in a systematic way. The UAW and Ford representatives responsible for developing the quality-training plan first review all the training currently in use in each division for each job classification, and develop a "current state map." They then look at what is needed, again within each division and for each job classification—developing what is termed a "desired state map."

These analyses reveal a deep gap in the information needed for a proper training plan—there is no record of what each individual in each job classification actually knows. The UAW decides to support a break from tradition to address the issue. As Dan Brooks, the UAW's coordinator for the joint UAW-Ford Quality program, recalls:

We decided to conduct assessments before the training to see what knowledge was needed. If people know what is required for them to know, then they didn't have to go through training. We also agreed to do a post-assessment to see if there was a retention of knowledge and if people where now able to apply the knowledge on the job. This was the first time that the union agrees to this kind of post-training assessment. We didn't call it a test, but we knew that retention and application of knowledge was fundamental.

The assessment is to be done in a way that is respectful to the person. A group leader or supervisor would conduct the assessment. If questions are answered wrong then it is up to the facilitator to review what is wrong and make sure that the person learns what we wanted them to learn.

It is also anticipated that some people will have learning disabilities, dyslexia, or even issues around their level of literacy. As a result, facilitators are trained to keep these issues private. Questions are read aloud and if issues are evident, remediation support is to be provided on the side.

It becomes clear that there is a wide variation (by individual) in what people know, as well as wide variation (by classification, and by division) in what they need to know, which makes clear in turn that the "peanut butter" training model will not work. An idea that does exist in the Ford system—the "single-point lesson"—is raised. Although it is not used on a systematic basis, Brooks takes this idea and makes it the centerpiece of the quality training strategy. Dennis O'Connor, an outside training consultant who had assisted with the earlier diversity training, is brought in to help develop the quality training—though the requirements are more restrictive this time. He recalls:

Management had high production quotas and was focused on getting the product out. Labor was saying that technology is changing and we need training. Everyone agreed that training was needed, but how to get it done? The days of the five-hour or eight-hour training sessions were gone.

Dan and his team came up with the concept of single point lessons, which evolved into what we called targeted training modules.

The modules are standardized into 30–45 minute time frames, each with a facilitator's guide and a pre- and post-training assessment. The goal is to make sure people can apply what they learn on the job. O'Connor notes, "The focus on learning outcomes was a major change. It was a shift from 'nice to know' to 'need to know.'"

Complex topics, such as "error proofing" (designing work and products to eliminate the potential for not following a standardized approach) may have five hours of material, which are condensed into five or six 30- or 40-minute modules. Ultimately, the targeted training curriculum grows to include more than 150 modules at the "basic," "knowledge," and "advanced" levels. Says O'Connor:

The idea was not to waste people's time if they already understood what was being taught at a basic level. We were valuing people's time—the workers and the supervisors. The information had to be disseminated, but it had to be on a just-in-time basis at the right level.

The pre- and post-assessments were rocky at the start. The whole concept of being measured was taboo in that environment. But Dan was clear and had support from management that they needed to know what people actually knew.

The assessments didn't use people's names. Keeping the evaluation data anonymous was an important recognition of the culture.

[Still], some people refused to take the pre-test. [But] once people saw that the information wasn't used in punitive ways, it was better.

The post-test is done as a group activity. Everyone reviews the answers as a group and the facilitator helps the entire group to understand the right answers. But there are some in management who resisted the idea of a group post-test. O'Connor says that he, too, "resisted this at first, but this was transformative."

He adds, "The barriers came down as people saw we were interested in teaching them something. People knew we cared about their knowing what the right answers were and it showed up on the job."

All of the targeted-training, single-point lessons are made available through Ford's intranet, which is still a new venue for making training materials available within Ford. Any supervisor or group leader can download and utilize any module, along with the supporting materials. At first, there is resistance to this because of concerns about consistency in delivery. So, to address the concerns, pilot training sessions are conducted.

Dennis O'Connor comments, "We piloted all the models and it was interesting in that some of the naysayers were criticizing our dependence on the supervisors or work group leaders to deliver the training. [But] this was a critical design component—for a national rollout of 150 modules, this was key."

The facilitator's guide that accompanies each module becomes essential. But will that be enough for the supervisors and team leaders to be able to deliver the training? O'Connor reports,

We kept saying it was easy to facilitate. As we were doing the pilots we would meet with a work group leader or supervisor. We would meet them cold on the factory site for 30 minutes to review the single-point lesson, the pre- and post-assessment, and the facilitator's guide. In some cases, that was all the preparation we had. It was pivotal in that it went smoothly. We followed them into the room and they performed admirably. They were not professional instructors. This tool was sufficient to guide them through the process. The light bulb went off—we know this could work across the nation.

Making the training widely available with the ability of frontline leaders to provide the training enables the right person to get the right skills at the right time. O'Connor sums this up:

What we found was that the single point lessons could be introduced just in time—where a supervisor or work group leader observed someone or a few people not using a gauge properly, for example. Then he or she could go to the module on gauging and provide training to that person or a group of people at the next break. It was a just-in-time solution that could be used on a just-in-time basis.

****

In 2007, the Manufacturing Skills Standards Council of Alexandria, Virginia, was invited to assess the training model. "We knew we were onto to something valuable," Dan Brooks says, "but we wanted an independent assessment so it would not just be us saying so."

Measured by people's ability to apply what they know on the job—the ultimate measure of any training—the training was deemed a success. The assessment, though, also identified opportunities for further standardization and improvement, such as in the training delivery by team leaders and supervisors. The evaluation findings include these points from the report's summary:

This report represents an independent, third-party evaluation of Targeted Training, a large-scale quality improvement effort, conducted between 2003 and 2007, that involved all Ford plants, all UAW employees and a large number of salaried employees. A team of experts organized by the Manufacturing Skill Standards Council (MSSC) conducted this evaluation from August through November 2007.

Based upon an approved evaluation framework, the MSSC Team conducted 139, mostly one-on-one, interviews with Ford Division Directors, National Quality Committee leaders, and a cross-section of employees at six plants: Plant Managers, UAW Chairs, Quality Managers, Quality Reps, Trainers, and Trainees.

PRINCIPAL FINDINGS FROM INTERVIEWS

Effectiveness:

• Targeted Training was highly effective in raising awareness and transferring knowledge about quality. *A large majority of workers trained under Targeted Training are still applying knowledge learned.*
• Although Targeted Training improved quality, it did not include quantitative metrics for assessing the direct impact of training on product quality. It also fell short of plans to apply training to individual plant quality improvement needs.

Quality of Curriculum:

• Targeted Training created a *well-respected quality curriculum, based on single point lessons (SPLs),* that is comprehensive, targeted to different levels, and adaptable to individual plant needs. It included a methodology for assessing pre- and post-training impacts on individual knowledge levels.

• At the same time, Targeted Training covered too *many single topics, without sufficient focus on the most important quality improvement methods.* Weekly training was too frequent, with insufficient time to fully grasp and apply training.

Quality of Instruction:

• Team leaders and supervisors were the appropriate instructors, and team meetings provided a good context for instruction and interaction.
• *Team leaders and supervisors, however, had uneven abilities as trainers and, in general, were insufficiently expert on the content of SPLs.*

Efficiency/Cost Benefit:

• Overall, the ROI was positive and resources adequate.
• Large-scale churning and manpower shortages reduced efficiency.

The organizational learning landscape is littered with what are termed "training disconnects"—where the right people are not provided with the right skills at the right time and in the right place. These disconnects often provide valuable insights into how the underlying culture and operation works—which in turn can point the way to more effective organizational learning systems.[19] In this case, the disconnects around the past "peanut butter" training pointed to the development of the targeted training model. By 2009, the success of the new model leads Dennis O'Connor and his associate Penny Drain to publish *Targeted Training,* making the lessons learned with the UAW and Ford available broadly.[20]

Safety Operating System, 2008

A 2007 shift to high-consequence tracking is a key step in transitioning safety from a list of important things to do into a full safety operating system. It represents the beginning of a shift in operating assumptions that will enable continuous improvement by identifying which data are the most important to track. Progress with safety combines with progress on quality and sets the stage for comprehensive use of integrated operating systems for all aspects of manufacturing.

The initial focus on safety metrics is driven by highly visible fatalities and the new insights generated when they are combined with other high-consequence events (such as amputations and lacerations). For example, the data highlight that skilled trades are at greater risk of high-consequence incidents and are in a better position to lead safety awareness. Reporting on "near misses" as well as actual incidents also leads to insights. For example, understanding the ratio of near misses to high-consequence events helps build predictive thinking and point to areas of the plants in which to focus for safety prevention actions. Indeed, predictive thinking is revealed as essential at all levels—at the frontline with teams, in departments, and at the plant, divisional, and enterprise levels.

At the enterprise level, Gregory Stone introduces these more predictive metrics to the Global Manufacturing Business Process Review (BPR). "Every time I report at the BPR," he says, "I put in front of the leadership the ratio of high-potential near misses to incidents." Commenting on the underlying culture change needed, Stone adds, "It has been critical to get people to report that without fear."

However, the move to high-consequence incident tracking does not, in itself, mark the shift to approaching safety as an integrated operating system. The change happens in 2008 when Dan Brooks, who had been leading the advancement of the Quality Operating System (QOS) for the UAW, also assumes responsibility for safety within the UAW-Ford National Joint Programs.

At first, Brooks is apprehensive about the role. Safety is one of the longest-standing joint programs and he does not have deep technical expertise in this domain. Still, he knows the Quality Operating System. His management counterpart, Chris Petersen, is a safety engineer, and sets up a meeting with Harry Tarrant, who heads up Safety for North America (coming out of the Human Resources function) and Stone, the corporate director of Safety.

Brooks asks about the safety operating system at the meeting; this generates a lot of questions about the Quality Operating System. Brooks is taken through the business plan for safety and is told that the Manufacturing Safety Council (MSC) will be meeting the following week.

At the MSC, Brooks again asks about the safety operating system. There are SHARP criteria (the Safety and Health Assessment Review Process), he is told, and he responds that in Quality there are also assessments, but assessments do not make an operating system. He explains that a Safety Operating System begins with the right information, and also includes standardized time-and-data management systems, a supporting infrastructure (including chartered forums), and the tools and methods for continuous improvement.

The management directors and the HR directors understand the question and the answer—they had been working with the Quality Operating System for a number of years. It is just the safety professionals who are new to the idea.

Stone quickly embraces the idea of an operating system. He sees that the safety metrics, the safety audits (SHARP), safety training, and the safety positions (hourly and salaried) must be paired with established and utilized standards for all aspects of the work at every level, as well as mechanisms for continuous improvement. Soon thereafter, Stone develops an initial visual map of the system for North America (figure 8.4).

Discussing the system, Stone comments that it is important for "people to understand what the standard is. If you say you are green—and there is some pressure to report green—then people must really see what is required." The standards for safety build on the SHARP criteria. Elaborating, Stone says, "These are the two critical things: Do you understand what you have to do? Are you doing what you have to do (and helping to improve)?"

There are cultural differences with respect to working to the standard. Stone says, "The key challenge is that it is not part of the DNA in the United States to apply the standard versus people just doing what they think is right." He notes that the continuous improvement aspect of standardization means that it should not be a mindless use of what he terms "brute force" in imposing the standard.

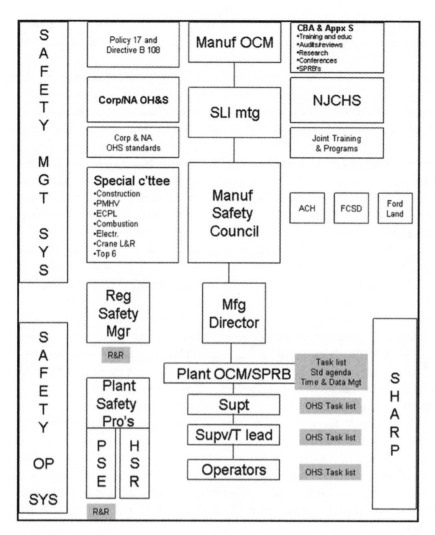

Figure 8.4
North America Occupational Safety and Health System, 2008. *Source:* Ford Motor Company.

"Independent thinking," he states, "is not unhealthy.... [There is a] sweet spot between rigor of standardization and providing room to move for innovation."

As noted in chapter 7, Stone embraces charters as a key way to standardize roles and responsibilities. Joel Cutcher-Gershenfeld is brought in to facilitate enterprise-level chartering. Since the divisions and plants are accustomed to operating under the quality charters, the addition of safety charters in each location happens quickly, building on the enterprise charter. Commenting on the charters, Stone notes, "It has been critical and it is still evolving." He adds that the charters provide "better structure and alignment with what we are doing." It is important that the manufacturing charter links the Safety Operating System with the Six Sigma DMAIC process (Define, Measure, Analyze, Implement, Control)—a set of tools for continuous improvement that are now well established at Ford.

The UAW's Dan Brooks emphasizes focusing on the individual behaviors of the union members. Union leaders usually avoid this individual focus as too controversial, but it is essential for standardization in the operations. There is strong support from line managers. When Jim Tetreault returns from assignment in Europe to serve as Vice President of North American Manufacturing, he partners with the safety support function and the UAW on this issue.

The challenge, as Tetreault notes, is: "How to change mass behavior, while holding people accountable for performance to a standard? How to change the environment to drive the right behaviors?" As Tetreault explains, "The behavior changes are difficult. People need to see something different. We revised the pedestrian safety standard for egress to the plants—with barriers that funnel to doors, only cross lines at designated area. We surveyed every plant for every walking surface hazard. Each plant had things to fix, but there was enormous variation—one plant with 10,000 and one with under 500. That told us the standard wasn't clear—so we refined it with pictures. [The] process took several months and we then had a much more clear standard. Then results were consistent across plants and we began to fix things. Once people saw us fixing things we started working on expectations of behavior. This is what we want you to do to stay safe."

As Tetreault comments further, "You then have to check and audit the results. You have to see how each plant is doing relative to the standard. In the United States and Canada the behavior change is particularly difficult. It goes against the culture for one worker to be telling a co-worker to stop an unsafe behavior. We celebrate individual initiative and adherence to standard runs counter to that. Every operator would say 'I get it, but as soon as I come up with a better way, I will do it that way.' There is a balance between people taking initiative and inventing and having standards. Adherence to standards is more common in other countries. There has to be the appropriate balance between patience and impatience."

The balance is not just for frontline operations. Tetreault comments, "The plant workforce also needs to know that senior leadership is accountable for safety. As the leader of North American manufacturing I had each director work with plants to establish what they would accomplish on safety and other matters. In 90 percent of the cases I pushed the hard on the goals. In 10 percent of the cases I said to back off—it was unrealistic. Getting the objectives correct with appropriate stretch and then holding plant managers accountable is key. This accountability is for directors, plant managers, assistant plant managers, and plant operating committees. If they are not doing that, the plant will stagnate."

Commenting on the role of the UAW in the safety operating system Tetreault states, "The union stepped up in a big way. Without the support of the union it would be difficult to implement. At the beginning of my career I saw limited cooperation on safety between the union and management. By the end we were aligned 100 percent on these issues."

Reflecting on the response to the high-consequence events, Stone observes, "When we have our backs to the wall, we push the BS out of the way." The key point of the integrated operating system is that it applies all the time—not just in a crisis. "It is about embracing the concept of continuous improvement," Stone adds, "[and] it is about alignment. We have shown as a company that once we have alignment we can do amazing things."

✳ ✳ ✳

The vision guiding safety in Ford operations is straightforward: "Our vision is to achieve zero fatalities and no serious injuries, and to protect and continually improve the health of our workforce."[21] As is evident from the safety performance data in figures 8.5 and 8.6, the aim of continuous improvement is being accomplished:

Important as the transition to a Safety Operating System is, what is more important is the broader capability it signals for Ford and the UAW. The addition of the SOS to the QOS sets the stage for a broader transformation to integrated operating systems for all elements of the Ford Production System.

The image of the Ford Production System was introduced in figure 4.2; examine it again to note the use of operating systems for every element. The expansion to the other elements of FPS follows the same pattern as the shift in Safety to the Safety Operating System—it becomes a standardized way of operating across the enterprise.

Recap: Guiding Principle for Chapter 8—Align and Stabilize, then Integrate

The idea of an integrated operating system is not new. Indeed, Ford was using the term "Quality Operating System" in 1998. At the time, however, it would be best to characterize what Ford had as a good list of things to do, not as an integrated operating system. An organizational culture has visible artifacts, but is ultimately defined by deep underlying cultural values and assumptions.[22] Similarly, an integrated operating system will have many visible things to do, but it is ultimately defined by deep underlying operating assumptions.

In the journey to integrated operating systems, the Q1 initiative was a supplier certification program that transitioned from periodic inspections to a more systematic set of partnerships between Ford and its suppliers. The Quality Leadership Initiative complemented Q1 by enabling all employees, hourly and salaried, to raise quality concerns—including in the

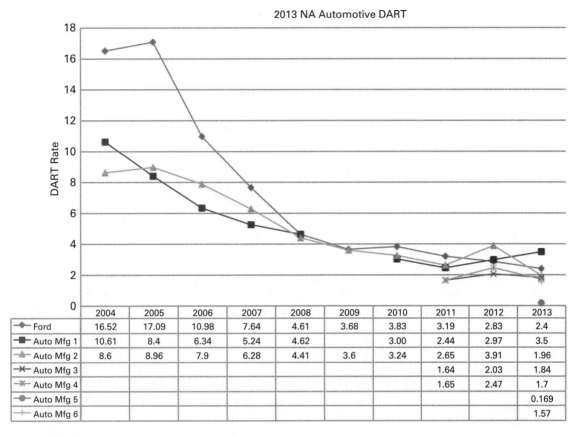

2013 NA Automotive DART

	2004	2005	2006	2007	2008	2009	2010	2011	2012	2013
Ford	16.52	17.09	10.98	7.64	4.61	3.68	3.83	3.19	2.83	2.4
Auto Mfg 1	10.61	8.4	6.34	5.24	4.62		3.00	2.44	2.97	3.5
Auto Mfg 2	8.6	8.96	7.9	6.28	4.41	3.6	3.24	2.65	3.91	1.96
Auto Mfg 3								1.64	2.03	1.84
Auto Mfg 4								1.65	2.47	1.7
Auto Mfg 5										0.169
Auto Mfg 6										1.57

Figure 8.5

Safety Performance Data—DART, 2013. *Note:* DART stands for "days away, restricted, and transferred." It is the measure used by the U.S. Occupational Safety and Health Administration (OSHA) to measure the impact of workplace illness and injury. The results for Ford are indicated. The names of other auto companies are masked. *Source:* Ford Motor Company.

assembly plants that were not subject to Q1. However, QLI was still structured based on the logic of reengineering, rather than on a more broadly integrated continuous improvement approach.

The full pivot toward a quality operating system became clear with the establishment of the hourly "fresh eyes auditors" in Ford's Powertrain Division, the extension in 2003 of what are termed QOS Coordinators across all parts of the North American operations, and the systematic use of charters (as we saw in chapter 7). The four pillars of the Quality Operating System were a full set of tools to align all the parties, stabilize the social system, and integrate continuous improvement in quality across the operations.

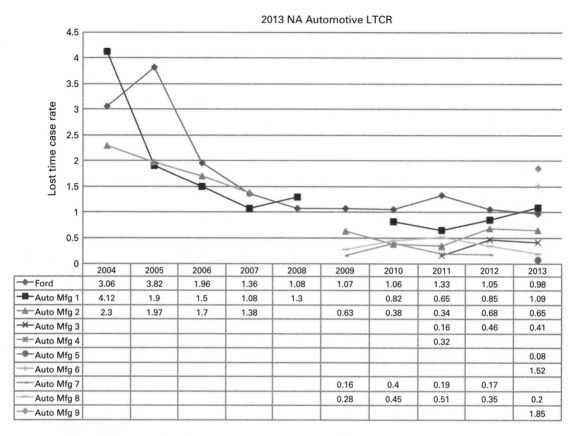

Figure 8.6

Safety Performance Data—LTCR, 2013. *Note:* LTCR stands for "lost time case rate" following an accident or incident. The results for Ford are indicated. The names of other auto companies are masked. *Source:* Ford Motor Company.

	2004	2005	2006	2007	2008	2009	2010	2011	2012	2013
Ford	3.06	3.82	1.96	1.36	1.08	1.07	1.06	1.33	1.05	0.98
Auto Mfg 1	4.12	1.9	1.5	1.08	1.3		0.82	0.65	0.85	1.09
Auto Mfg 2	2.3	1.97	1.7	1.38		0.63	0.38	0.34	0.68	0.65
Auto Mfg 3								0.16	0.46	0.41
Auto Mfg 4								0.32		
Auto Mfg 5										0.08
Auto Mfg 6										1.52
Auto Mfg 7						0.16	0.4	0.19	0.17	
Auto Mfg 8						0.28	0.45	0.51	0.35	0.2
Auto Mfg 9										1.85

Targeted training became the key delivery system for the learning needed to facilitate everyone's contribution to the integrated operating system. Converting materials into single-point lessons enabled the right people to have the right skills at the right time, and in the right place. Under this model, leaders—whether frontline supervisors, team leaders, or higher level managers could really serve as teachers. The Web-accessible single-point lessons, with instructor's guides and assessment tools, made distributed learning a reality—another key element of alignment, stability, and integration.

The extension of the Quality Operating System into the Safety Operating System not only transformed safety, but also marked the beginning of a systems approach to all elements of the production system—Safety, Quality, Delivery, Cost, People, Maintenance, and Environment—each of which has its associated operating system. Today, Ford defines the

Ford Production System in terms of leadership behaviors, operating systems, and common processes: "FPS is a Manufacturing strategic approach that includes the right Leadership Behaviors, Operating Systems, and Key Unifying Processes supported by an Aligned and Capable Organization to deliver Best in World Results." This definition is elaborated as follows:[23]

- **Standardized Global Approach** of Systems, Standards and Processes that is all inclusive
- Model that drives from **process inputs to output metrics** that delivers stability and root cause analysis—linked to **standardized leadership language**
- **Clear Roles and Responsibilities at each level**
- **Model for team types** that ensure ownership of the Process and of Safety, Quality and Flow
- Integrated, Structured Process with Cadenced Activities and Meetings every day through **Time and Data Management at each level**
- Activities and Meetings that structure the interaction to promote ownership, **highlighting of issues and driving Continuous Improvement**
- **Leaders as Teachers**, [a concept] that **engages and motivates people** in the process and achieves sustainability as well as continuous improvement
- [FPS] **Becomes *"The Way"*** we operate our plants to deliver *"Best in World Results"*

This official FPS definition concludes with this observation: "One of the key driving forces of FPS is giving control to the teams and coordinators to initiate changes, eliminating some of the layers of delay and indifference that had plagued previous improvement models."[24]

There are tangible results delivered for the business. In 2009 Ford announces a saving of over $1.2 billion in warranty costs during the prior two years and increases its standard warranty coverage from 3 years and 36,000 miles to 5 years and 50,000 miles.[25] At the same time, the union and the workforce see job growth and work design that values the distributed knowledge and capability of the workforce.

The subtitle of this book is *Pivotal Events in Valuing Work and Delivering Results*. Integrated operating systems represent the rules of the road for how to combine "valuing work" with "delivering results"—honoring W. Edwards Deming's injunction: "Put everybody in the company to work to accomplish the transformation. The transformation is everybody's job."

SUPPORTING MATERIALS

8.1 Operator Instruction Sheet (OIS)

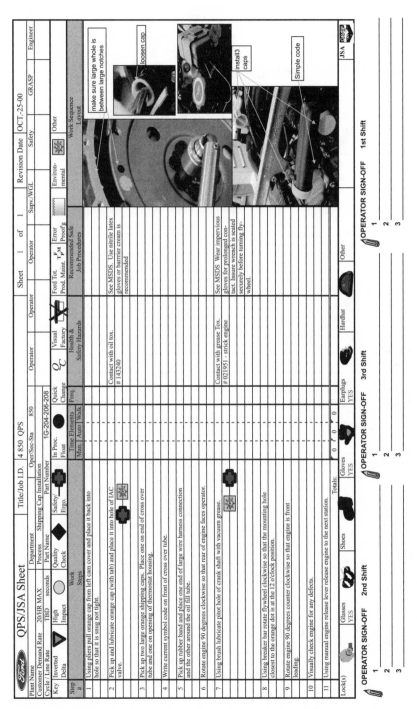

QPS/JSA Sheet	Title/Job I.D.	4 850 QPS					Sheet	1	of	1	Revision Date	OCT.-25-00		Engineer

Source: Ford Motor Company

8.2 Quality Hot Line

QUALITY HOT LINE PROCESS FLOW – FACILITY LOCATIONS   **Q1**

If an employee is either instructed to, or feels pressure to ignore a product concern/quality matter, or has a quality concern that is ongoing or not being addressed by management, the employee may register a complaint by calling the Quality Hot Line at 1-866-723-3937

Employee calls Quality Hot Line (outside agency) available 24 hours/ 7 days per week and may call anonymously

Agency personnel types employee, location, and quality concern information into a pre-programmed screen

Agency personnel calls the employee's facility Security Department with the quality concern information

Local Security notifies appropriate individuals responsible for employee discussion, investigation, and corrective action. Quality Rep., Quality Manager, Plant Chairperson, Plant/Facility Manager, and HR Manager must be notified

Agency sends summary of quality concern case to National Quality Committee Hot Line Administrator, Hot Line Manager, NQC Representatives & NQC Coordinators via e-mail

Within 24 hours, local parties contact employee, implement containment actions, complete 1st page of "Key Information Sheet" and forward to NQC Reps.

Local parties conduct investigation and assure corrective action is taken. When the Quality Representative and Quality Manager agree to close case, they sign off on completed "Key Information Sheet" and forward to their NQC Reps.

NQC Hot Line Administrator screens cases for personal vehicle/dealer concerns (and forwards those calls to CRC) and forwards all other agency e-mails to designated Quality Representative and Quality Manager for that facility (cc to NQC reps), assigns case number, and logs case. NQC reps are also provided a hardcopy of e-mail with Case/Closure Sheet

NQC representatives review adequacy of facility response

If NQC Reps. agree to close case, they complete Case Closure Sheet and return complete file to Hot Line Administrator, who updates log and files case

If NQC reps. agree to keep the case open or refer case back to the facility for handling through their local Quality Concern Resolution Process, they refer it back to the facility for further investigation/response

NQC Reps. may refer special cases to the NQC Co-Chairs for review and closure

Source: UAW-Ford National Joint Programs

Comments:

The Quality Hot Line is intended to:

- Protect the customer
- Detect and fix product quality concerns as soon as possible
- Communicate potential customer concern issues to appropriate stakeholders
- Reinforce our commitment to quality
- Encourage quality behaviors
- Enhance customer satisfaction

8.3 Error Proofing Single-Point Lesson

ERROR PROOFING

Single Point Lesson • **BASIC**

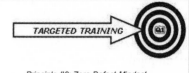

Principle #2: Zero Defect Mindset

September 1, 2004

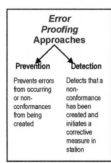

Error Proofing Approaches

Prevention — Prevents errors from occurring or non-conformances from being created

Detection — Detects that a non-conformance has been created and initiates a corrective measure in station

Error Proofing Method:
Use the following method to implement an error proofing device:

1) Locate the non-conformance and isolate the process that created it
2) List all possible errors
3) Determine the most likely error
4) Propose multiple solutions
5) Evaluate each solution
6) Choose the best solution
7) Develop a plan for implementation
8) Measure results/analyze benefits
9) Update documentation affected by EP implementation

To eliminate non-conformances, we must prevent errors from happening!

What is a Non-conformance?

A non-conformance is the result of <u>any deviation from product specification</u> that may lead to customer dissatisfaction.

- Product specifications are set by customer requirements which are translated into design and manufacturing requirements. The phrase "*deviation from product specification*" means the product is not produced according to the manufacturing plan.
- A product must fall into one of three categories to be classified as a non-conformance:
  o Product has deviated from manufacturing or design specifications
  o Product does not meet internal and/or external customer expectations
  o Was made the way it was intended, but still does not work

What is an Error?

An error is any deviation from a specified manufacturing process. Errors can be made by machines or people and can be caused by errors that occurred previously.

- All non-conformances are created by errors.
- This means that if errors can be prevented, no non-conformances will be created.

What is Error Proofing?

Error Proofing is a systematic process improvement tool that is designed to prevent a specific non-conformance from occurring. Error Proofing consists of fail-safe methods of detecting/preventing human or machine error at the source.

- EP locates and eliminates the errors that cause non-conformances.
- EP is also used to locate and prevent new errors.

Error Proofing Example

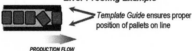

Template Guide ensures proper position of pallets on line

PRODUCTION FLOW

What is Error Proof Verification?

To ensure that the error-proofing device (poke-yoke) is operating properly, a known non-conformance (sometimes called a "rabbit") is put through the process. If the non-conformance is detected, the poke-yoke is working correctly. If it is not detected, the poke-yoke has failed.

Importance of Verification

- Error Proofing only works if we regularly check the error proofing solutions and verify they are doing the job.
- Bypassing safety switches, breaking jigs, or having inoperable switches bypasses Error Proofing and allows for deviation.
- We need to verify that the Error Proofing devices at each work station are operable at the beginning of each shift.

Error Proofing only works when verified <u>every</u> shift!!! We are counting on you.

What are the benefits of Error Proofing?

- Promotes job safety and the prevention of personal injury
- Enforces operational procedures or sequences
- Prevents product and machine damage
- Prevents non-conforming product from being produced or prevents non-conforming product from being passed to the next process
- Increases customer satisfaction with product/company
- To eliminate non-conformances, we must prevent errors from happening.

DOCUMENT: TT19   1   **APPROVED: September 1, 2004**

Source: Ford Motor Company

8.4 Error Proofing Instructor's Guide—Basic

<table>
<tr>
<td>

ERROR PROOFING

Instructor Guide • **BASIC**

</td>
<td>

Principle #2: Zero Defect Mindset

</td>
</tr>
</table>

September 1, 2004

Before the Lesson:
- Review Single Point Lesson
- Understand that the purpose of this lesson is to increase awareness about Error Proofing Concepts
- Develop local examples in everyday life where Error Proofing has been utilized or could have been utilized
- Identify in facility examples of Error Proofing Solutions
- Select one solution and breakdown to each step of method to use as example of structured process

BEST - Presentation Tips:
Incorporate the following bullet points as cornerstones of good presentations:

- Be Prepared!
- Enthusiastic delivery, Emphasize key points, Encourage questions
- Speak clearly, loudly, and confidently
- Tell participants what you're going to tell them (state purpose), then tell them (deliver lesson), then tell them what you told them (summarize).

During The Lesson:
- Introduce the SPL by reviewing with participants the purpose stated in the *Before the Lesson* section, why participants need to know this and what participants need to do with it.
- Explain that the purpose of the assessment is to determine participants' knowledge of the lesson.
- Distribute the pre-assessment tool. Read each assessment question aloud, allowing time for the participants to answer the questions. (Approximately 5 minutes total)
- Collect the pre-assessment tool and then distribute the SPL and allow a few minutes for participants to review. If feasible, review the pre-assessments as participants read the SPL. During instruction, read aloud each section in the SPL where the assessment answers can be found. This helps to emphasize key elements missed in the pre-assessment.
- ASK: *What is a Non-conformance?*
  - o Obtain Participant Responses
  - o Review Definition
- ASK: *What is an Error?*
  - o Obtain Participant Responses
  - o Review Definition
- ASK: *What is the difference between an Error and a Non-conformance?*
  - o Obtain Participant Responses
  - o Error is the action taken by a person or machine that deviates from the specification which results in a non-conformance.

ASK: *Why should we care?*
  - o Obtain Participant Responses
  - o Human error is a natural occurrence. When non-conformances occur on a manufacturing line, there is often a tendency to blame the operator--especially when the error can be traced back to the operator's interaction with the process.
  - o The actual reason for the error, however, is usually a lack of planning or design. In other words, the people who designed the machinery, the layout of the machinery, or the operating procedures did not account for human error during the design phase.
  - o Important facts to realize about human error are:
    - o *Few workers make errors intentionally; most strive to prevent errors.*
    - o *Error is inherent in the nature of humans.*
    - o *Error Proofing alters the work environment to eliminate human errors.*

ERROR PROOFING	
Instructor Guide • **BASIC**	*TARGETED TRAINING*
	Principle #2: Zero Defect Mindset

September 1, 2004

- o When incorporating Error Proofing into the work environment, an understanding of human limitations is essential. Categories of human limitations include:
  - ▪ Vision: People vary in ability to distinguish details, colors, or adjust vision to lighting.
  - ▪ Hearing: Upper and lower thresholds of hearing change when background noise is added.
  - ▪ Repetition Ability: Muscular efficiency and mental tracking decrease as rates of repetition increase.
  - ▪ Review benefits listed. Explore to see if group can add to list.
- • ASK: *What is Error Proofing?*
  - o Obtain Participant Responses
  - o Review Definition
  - o Ask for examples. Follow up with personal examples previously identified or those listed below:

Type	Error	EP Solution
Prevention	Drove off without your gas cap after filling tank	Cap cord
Prevention	Bathtub is left running and water floods onto the floor	Overflow drain
Prevention	Stomping on the brake causes you to lose control of your car and go into a skid	Anti-lock brakes
Prevention	Serious accidents occur from rotating blade of an unattended power mower	Safety Clutch interface
Detection	Resource not machined to specification	Check fixture installed to detect unmilled work
Detection	Two assembly parts are not being aligned properly to allow oil to flow between units	Create check hole in both units to assure proper alignment

- • Review List. Discuss difference between Prevention and Detection solution (Use examples for table above)
- • Review Error Proofing Method by asking one person to read each step. As they do, expand upon the step based upon real time examples in plant.
- • State:
  - • Error Proofing only works if we are all regularly checking the error proofing solutions and verifying that they are doing the job.
  - • Bypassing safety switches, breaking jigs, or having inoperable switches bypasses Error Proofing and allows for deviation.
  - • We need to verify that the Error Proofing devices at each work station are operable at the beginning of each shift.
  - • Only in this manner can we be sure we provide quality product to our customer.

Discussion Questions:
1. What is Error Proofing?
2. What is the difference between an error and a non-conformance?
3. Why is Error Proofing important?
4. Describe the difference between a Prevention and a Detection Solution
5. List the steps of the Error Proofing method
6. What is verification? Why is verification important?
7. How can / will you consistently apply the key points from this lesson on your jobs?

Summary and Assessment
- • Restate the purpose of the Single Point Lesson to summarize.
- • Advise participants that use of the SPL is allowed while taking the post assessment.
- • Distribute the assessment to each participant and give them 5 minutes to complete **INDIVIDUALLY.**
- • After completing the assessment, review **AS A GROUP** to ensure transfer of learning.

Source: Ford Motor Company

8.5 Error Proofing—Assessment—Basic

ERROR PROOFING Assessment • **BASIC**	 Principle #2: Zero Defect Mindset

September 1, 2004

1. Error Proofing is a systematic process improvement tool that is designed to prevent a specific non-conformance from occurring.

            True   False

2. A non-conformance is the result of any deviation from product specifications that may lead to customer dissatisfaction.

            True   False

3. Errors can be created by deviations from a specified manufacturing process.

            True   False

4. All non-conformances are created by errors, but not all errors result in non-conformances.

            True   False

5. By continuously using the Error Proofing Process, errors that cause non-conformances can be located and eliminated.

            True   False

6. Fill in the blanks (in regards to <u>prevention</u> or <u>detection</u>).

_____ errors from occurring or non-conformances from being created.
_____ a non-conformance and initiates a corrective measure in station

7. The following steps describe the _____ _____ _____.
   - Locate non-conformance and isolate the process that created it
   - List all possible errors
   - Propose multiple solutions
   - Evaluate each solution
   - Choose the best solution
   - Develop a plan for implementation
   - Measure results/analyze benefits
   - Update documentation affected by EP implementation

Source: Ford Motor Company

Comment:

This single-point lesson is illustrative of the targeted training materials developed for Ford and the UAW by Dennis O'Connor. It includes a one-page single-point lesson that can be used in a factory setting. The instructor's guide is designed to support team leaders and supervisors providing the training. The evaluation is designed for group dialogue and shared learning.

In this case, the topic is "error proofing"—a key skill and discipline within a quality operating system.

8.6 Sample Safety Near-Miss Report

OH&S - 8 Discipline

8D No.	Problem Title:		Date:	Champion
8327LAP	Near Miss - Rear Suspension Fixture		7/31/08	███████

Plant/Location:	Area/Dpt:	OIS/JSA/Process No.
██████ Assembly Plant	Final Maintenance / 5750	N/A - Toolmaker

D1. Team: Name / Position	D2. Describe the Problem
1. ██████ / ME Manager 2. ██████ / Safety Engineer 3. ██████ / UAW H&S Rep 4. ██████ / UAW H&S Rep	At 11:00 a.m., the east rear suspension setting fixture was being taken off-line to be serviced. This is achieved by placing the fixture in manual, pressing a PV pushbutton to disengage a locking pin, and pulling the fixture out of the frame line conveyor path so it can be worked on. The locking pin stuck, so the toolmaker was rocking the fixture in an attempt to free the pin so it could be serviced. The electrician placed a D018 key into an "emergency locking cylinder bypass" keyswitch and turned the key. The control arm fixture dropped unexpectedly onto a frame. Fortunately, no one was injured as all persons were clear of the fixture when it suddenly dropped.

D3. Interim Containment Action(s):	Date of Implementation	% Completion
1. An investigation in the PLC logic determined why the fixture fell. Upon discovering the condition, the key switch was immediately disabled.	7/31/08	100

D4 Define the Root Cause(s):	% Contribution
1. The D018 key switch disengages the cylinder locks with the fixture in manual without regard for any other logical conditions. The electrician thought that this key switch may be needed to disengage the locking pin for the bridge. With the fixture in the raised position and the cylinder locks disengaged, the fixture fell due to gravity. The key switch is not original equipment with the fixture; it was added sometime after the tooling was delivered.	100

D5 Choose and Verify Corrective Action(s):	% Effectiveness
1. The three other fixtures in the immediate area are of the same design and had the same key switch present. Disabled key switches on other fixtures. 2. Remove the PLC logic from the program.	100

D6 Implement and Validate Corrective Action(s):	Date of Implementation	Validated Date:
1. The three other fixtures in the immediate area are of the same design and had the same key switch present. All were disabled on the same day.	7/31/08	7/31/08
2. Removed the PLC logic from the program.	7/31/08	8/1/08

D7 Actions to Prevent Recurrance:	Closed Date
1. Target complete with PLC and hardwire removals	8/1/08

D8 Recognize and Congratulate the Team:

OH&S - 8 Discipline

Reported by	Revision Date:	Completion Date:
▮▮▮▮▮▮▮		8/14/08

Please use the next pages to attach additional documentation, photos, draws, etc.

Attachments

Source: Ford Motor Company

9   True North: Good Jobs and High Performance

Guiding Principle: Create Value and Mitigate Harm

Integrated operating systems that value the distributed knowledge of the full workforce represent a fundamental transformation from a model rooted in separate domains or "chimneys," with decision making limited to a small number of experts or people with positional authority. It is not that functional domains or hierarchy goes away, but that the underlying operating assumption is one of partnership and broad involvement, with the aim of mutual growth.

Tracing an organizational transformation through a series of more than 50 pivotal events over three decades is not typically done. More often, a few proximate events and decisions are highlighted in stories of organizational transformation, without fully taking into account the combined impacts of the many preceding events that will be relevant in any large organization. Focusing on pivotal events suggests there is no one hero (or villain) in a transformation story and that the process is a continuing one. With each pivot, the transformation is reinforced and extended, or restrained and undercut. Pivots can be negative or positive from a given perspective, but by definition they have the potential for change that is not neutral.

The pivotal events presented in this book have been organized around the themes presented in chapters 2 through 8 (chapter 1 serves as an introduction). As we conclude, we consider all the events together, in chronological order. Table 9.1 features 18 events from the 1980s and 1990s. These are foundational events: no one event constitutes a transformation on its own, but all were pivotal. Some were planned and others unplanned. Most were at the plant or divisional level, although some—particularly the 1982 Mutual Growth Program and the 1996–1999 Continuous Improvement and FPS rollout—do represent key pivotal events at the enterprise or system level. It is in retrospect that we see the importance of each of these events; at the time, it was not always clear if the potential would be realized.

Two-thirds of the pivotal events in this book were in the 2000s and 2010s. These are presented in table 9.2 in chronological order.

Reviewing the list reveals the broad scale and scope of the transformation—even if this list is incomplete in at least two ways. First, because of the focus on both the UAW and Ford,

Table 9.1

Pivotal Events in the 1980s and 1990s

1. Monroe Stamping Plant, 1981
2. Green Island Plant, 1981
3. Employee Involvement and Mutual Growth, 1979–1982
4. Total Productive Maintenance Roots, 1982
5. Mazda Flat Rock, 1987
6. Romeo Engine Plant, 1988
7. Q1, 1980s, 1998, and 2002
8. Vehicle Operations Modern Operating Agreements, 1990–1995
9. Ford 2000, 1993–1995
10. Plastic and Trim Products Cross-Functional Alignment, 1995
11. Selection of First Female Plant Manager, 1996
12. Continuous Improvement and FPS Rollout, 1996–1999
13. Cleveland Engine Plant I, 1996–2002
14. The Rouge Explosion, 1999
15. Chicago Sexual Harassment Lawsuits, 1999
16. Pivot on Affinity Groups, 1999
17. Team Start and Stop Designations, 1999
18. Policy Deployment—SQDCME, 1999–2002

other complementary developments in the extended enterprise—such as changes in new product development systems, dealer relations, supplier relations, international operations, and government relations—are only partly represented in the events highlighted in this book. Evidence of the transformation into knowledge-driven operating systems with embedded assumptions and which involve the distributed workforce can also be found in these additional settings—each with additional pivotal events that could add up to as many as we have included here. Our primary focus, though, is on transformation at the intersection of the Ford-UAW relationship. Second, the list is incomplete because the story is far from complete. Both Ford and the UAW face ongoing challenges, with more pivotal events to come. Still, the story is sufficiently advanced at this stage to sum up the lessons from these pivotal events and identify the prospects looking ahead.

Of the 56 pivotal events, 34 were planned at the system or enterprise level and another 8 were planned at the division or plant level. This suggests, at least in the case of the UAW and Ford, that the transformation of two organizations and their relationship can be planned approximately three-quarters of the time. In other words, without many system-level planned enterprise change initiatives, a transformation will not take place. However, these data also suggest that relying on planning alone will be incomplete. Indeed, it was in the unplanned events—at the plant/division and system/enterprise levels—where we most often observed courageous leadership that proved to be pivotal. Approximately a quarter of the time, the parties faced pivotal events that were unplanned.

In their book *The Transformation of American Industrial Relations*,[1] Tom Kochan, Harry Katz, and Bob McKersie indicate that a full transformation of labor-management relations requires

Table 9.2

Pivotal Events in the 2000s and 2010s

19. Same Sex-Partner Benefits, 2000
20. UAW-Ford United in Diversity (now Equality and Diversity) Program, 2000
21. Automotive Components Holding (ACH), 2000–2013
22. Fresh Eyes Auditors and QOS Coordinators, 2000–2004
23. 9/11 Zero Tolerance Response, 2001
24. Rouge Revitalization, 2001
25. Atlanta Assembly Plant, FTPM Chartering, 2001
26. UAW FPS Total Cost Stand Down, 2001–2002
27. Dearborn Assembly Plant Chartering, 2001–2003
28. Lean Manufacturing Managers and the Lean Implementation Network, 2001–2003
29. Time and Data Management, 2001–2003
30. Atlanta Zero Tolerance Intervention, 2002
31. UAW Glass Plants, 2002
32. Quality Leadership Initiative, 2002
33. Quality Chartering, 2003
34. Quality Operating System, 2003
35. National Negotiation—Quality, 2003
36. Targeted Training, 2003–2007
37. Hourly Six Sigma Black Belts, 2003–2007
38. Action America, 2005
39. BPR and SAR Processes, 2006
40. Quality Operating Committee, 2006
41. Bargaining Over How to Bargain, 2006
42. UAW-Ford National Joint Program Conference, 2006
43. Voluntary Separation Packages, 2006–2007
44. Competitive Operating Agreements, 2006–2007
45. Ford Puts All Cards on the Table with the UAW, 2007
46. National Negotiations—VEBA, Entry Wage, 2007
47. One Ford, 2007
48. Powertrain Operations Plant of the Future, 2007–2008
49. Safety Chartering, 2008
50. Safety Operating System, 2008
51. National Negotiations—Pattern for crisis negotiations, 2009
52. UAW-HR Change Agents and HR OD Institute, 2009–2010
53. National Negotiations—Health Care, Profit Sharing, 2011
54. Team-Based Agreements, 2011
55. Entry-Wage Team Leaders at Chicago Assembly, 2012–2013
56. Frontline Leadership, 2013

an alignment of changes at the workplace level, collective bargaining level, and strategic level. While we are describing more than just a transformation in labor-management relations—we are also describing a transformation within Ford and within the UAW—the labor-management transformation is an essential part of our focus—transforming work and relationships to deliver results.

Among the pivotal events documented in this book, the collective bargaining events are the most visible. These are some of the most important pivotal events in the Ford-UAW transformation, including the 1979 agreement on Employee Involvement, the 1982 Mutual Growth Agreement, the 2003 negotiation on quality, the 2007 negotiation that produced the VEBA and entry wage, the 2009 negotiation that set the pattern for the industry, and the 2011 negotiation that codified the team-based system and restructured the profit-sharing formula.

What are less visible, but no less important in the transformation, are the pivotal events at the strategic level. These includes Ford putting all the cards on the table, the UAW and Ford launching the Action America forum, the way both parties handled the ACH/Visteon strategic challenge, and the joint commitment to an integrated set of operating systems for the enterprise. It is important to note that these pivotal events are linked and aligned with the pivotal events at the collective bargaining level. For example, Action America set the stage for collective bargaining through information sharing and relationship building. At the same time, collective bargaining has produced agreements that were foundational in advancing the operating systems, such as formalizing the roles of Quality Operating System Coordinators (QOSCs) and team leaders.

Advances at both the collective bargaining and strategic levels align with pivotal events at the frontline workplace level. The personal transformations of individuals such as Armentha Young and Rusty Woolum at the workplace level were enabled by the changes at the other two levels and are instrumental in advancing these collective bargaining and strategic objectives. Unplanned workplace level events such as the Rouge explosion became drivers for collective bargaining and strategic-level initiatives on workplace safety.

It is the combination of these events across the three levels that add up to a transformation—or, more accurately, a *set* of transformations. The story is far from complete, but the message is clear: a transformation does not happen all at once and the many pivotal events in the process represent a complex, interwoven tapestry. Further, the strategic level of the transformation model is limited here to strategy for Ford and the UAW at the level of the enterprise. Additional transformation at the societal level is ultimately needed to sustain transformation, as we will see in the next discussion of the underlying nature of institutions and what we are terming "True North."

Creating Value and Mitigating Harm

When pivotal events—planned and unplanned—combine over time, a transformation is possible. While the UAW-Ford transformation is not complete, it is sufficiently progressed to represent a fundamental change that has been central to the survival and success of both organizations. But the transformation is distinct in the case of each organization.

It is an old adage that a union is a political organization with hidden hierarchy, while a corporation is a hierarchical organization with hidden politics. Historically, the hierarchy in the UAW has not always been so hidden—it is one of the most centralized unions operating in the United States. Nor, historically, have the politics in Ford always been so hidden—the company was riddled with fiefdoms and silos in the 1980s and 1990s. In part, the transformation of the Ford-UAW relationship has required a transformation in the internal operations of each organization.

Given the contrasting structure and mission of a multinational corporation and an international union, what are the overall dimensions on which to measure success? Both have in common the embodiment of institutional arrangements—these are the core institutional characteristics of a corporation and a union. As well, there are the institutional arrangements shared between the two in the form of labor-management relations. One view of the primary functions of any institution is that institutional arrangements must *create value* and *mitigate harm*. In the case of the UAW and Ford, both apply as ultimate standards to measure success, but in different ways.

There are thousands of ways that the Ford Motor Company is legally and morally responsible to mitigate harm—through environmental protection, vehicle safety, employment relations, and other matters. Among the pivotal events documented in this book, the voluntary separation packages covering approximately 50,000 people during the economic collapse in the auto industry is a compelling instance of mitigating harm. If other companies had done likewise, the impact of the recession on the nation would not have been nearly as severe. Similarly, the dedicated focus on workplace health and safety following the explosion in the Rouge complex and the dedicated focus on diversity following the sexual harassment lawsuits in Chicago are also instances of mitigating harm—each with unplanned, harmful precipitating events that led to comprehensive planned change initiatives. The decision not to take the government bailout money represents a proactive decision that mitigated harm (in the form of risk) for the U.S. taxpayer—not taking bankruptcy protection and tax dollars unless it is really needed. The launch of the most environmentally friendly auto assembly plant in the world (now producing high-aluminum-content F150 trucks with greater fuel efficiency) is an example of mitigating harm in the environment.

While mitigating harm is essential, Ford's success as a corporation depends on its ability to create value. The pivotal events centered on quality and successful new product launches are key parts of the value proposition with customers. The pivotal events centered on business success are key parts of the value proposition for investors and the workforce (particularly around profit sharing). Taken together, the transformation documented in this book involves both an increased ability to create value and ways of mitigating harm for Ford that go well beyond what most corporations do.

There are many ways that that the UAW helps create value—through joint programs, for instance, and other means. The union is a full partner driving the value created through continuous improvement in quality, the successful launches of new products, and the many forms of joint community outreach. Indeed, the efforts of the thousands of frontline teams driving continuous improvement in *S, Q, C, D, M, P*, and *E* (Safety, Quality, Cost, Delivery, Maintenance, People, and Environment) have been essential to the value proposition for the business to succeed. Further, the investments in training and development for the workforce (central parts of the *P* in the balanced scorecard) represent value creation for the workforce enabled by the UAW leadership.

Still, the UAW's success as a union and its legal responsibility depend on its ability to mitigate harm. This is evident in the pivotal events around workplace health and safety and diversity in the workplace. It is evident in protecting the wages and benefits of the workforce so that the minimum necessary concessions were made during the recession, as well as in the VEBA that protected retiree benefits (which added value for investors at the same time). It is also evident in the record of continuous improvement by the frontline teams that are driving performance on *S* (Safety). While there is more limited focus by the teams on *E* (Environment), that will be of increasing importance in the years to come. Taken together, the transformation documented in this book involves an increased ability by the UAW to mitigate harm as well as to establish ways of creating value that go well beyond what most unions do.

It is not contradictory that the long-term success of Ford depends more on creating value (though mitigating harm is essential), while the long-term success of the UAW depends more on mitigating harm (though creating value is essential). Indeed, each organization appreciates the distinct role and priority of the other. Leaders in Ford acknowledge that the UAW plays a "checks-and-balance" role in mitigating harm that is in the long-term interest of the company. Leaders in the UAW acknowledge that Ford has to deliver value to its customers, investors, dealers, and suppliers if it is going to deliver value to its workforce.

It is an appreciation of these different yet complementary commitments by each organization that contributes to an institutional transformation—one in which they are truly advancing what in the United States is called the "American Dream." It is a transformation that combines good jobs with high performance. Organizations—unions or employers—that focus only on one of these twin outcomes are at risk of underperforming and imposing extra costs on others in society. Organizations that embrace both are not only creating value and mitigating harm for themselves, but are also doing so in ways that serve society.

While all the other chapters have featured pivotal events, this concluding chapter features key leadership perspectives, as well as our own perspective looking to the future, around what we are calling True North—good jobs and high performance. In this chapter we sum up the legacy of the transformations—enabling continued progress in the future.

True North

The combination of good jobs and high performance, which is sometimes termed the "high-road" strategy or model, is exemplified by the 30 years after World War II in the United States, during which productivity grew at a steady 3 percent each year and wages grew at a similar pace. The result was a period of sustained economic performance by the nation and the development of a strong middle class. The specific employment aspects of this model are sometimes called the "New Deal" model after the key supporting legislation passed in the 1930s as part of President Franklin D. Roosevelt's New Deal.

The subsequent 30 years have seen the collapse of many elements of the New Deal model, but we have also seen the emergence of some new elements on the employment front—such as team-based work systems and continuous improvement tools and methods. The pressures of globalization have, meanwhile, spurred a "race to the bottom" in which some employers try to compete with each other for profits by paying their workforce ever-lower wages and offering fewer benefits.

In this book, we have documented the complex dynamics by which the UAW and Ford have worked together to revitalize a high-road strategy that has indeed combined good jobs with high performance. It has not been easy, and it has not happened all at once. As we conclude, it will be important to identify some of the moral and civil authority that underlies key themes in this transformation story, which begins with dignity and respect, and includes business fundamentals and mutual gains.

A longstanding source of moral authority for these issues dates back to 1891, when Pope Leo XIII issued an encyclical on "rights and duties of capital and labor" to which he gave the Latin title *Rerum Novarum* (revolutionary change). This was the Catholic Church's effort to address a relentless assault against working people in the initial years of the Industrial Revolution. It defends capitalism, but not unrestrained capitalism, argues against radical socialist alternatives, and—in essence—exhorts bosses to respect their workers.

We offer extensive quotes from the document here, with commentary, because it addresses directly several themes that have emerged in this book. Indeed, key elements of the encyclical's message—issues that were a concern in the emergence of the Industrial Revolution—are still a concern in a postindustrial, global economy more than 120 years later.

The encyclical initially states the motivation for addressing these issues as well as the difficulty and importance of doing so:

The elements of the conflict now raging are unmistakable, in the vast expansion of industrial pursuits and the marvelous discoveries of science; in the changed relations between masters and workmen; in the enormous fortunes of some few individuals, and the utter poverty of the masses; the increased self reliance and closer mutual combination of the working classes; as also, finally, in the prevailing moral degeneracy. The momentous gravity of the state of things now obtaining fills every mind with painful apprehension; wise men are discussing it; practical men are proposing schemes; popular meetings, legislatures, and rulers of nations are all busied with it—actually there is no question which has taken deeper hold on the public mind.

... It is no easy matter to define the relative rights and mutual duties of the rich and of the poor, of capital and of labor....

... Some opportune remedy must be found quickly for the misery and wretchedness pressing so unjustly on the majority of the working class: for the ancient workingmen's guilds were abolished in the last century, and no other protective organization took their place. Public institutions and the laws set aside the ancient religion. Hence, by degrees it has come to pass that working men have been surrendered, isolated and helpless, to the hardheartedness of employers and the greed of unchecked competition,... so that a small number of very rich men have been able to lay upon the teeming masses of the laboring poor a yoke little better than that of slavery itself. [2]

Note that the encyclical points to great inequality in society as a motivating concern—an issue still of concern today. The articulation of "mutual gains" in the Ford-UAW case stands in contrast. The encyclical explores the justification for private property and the need for private charity or public aid to the most disadvantaged, and then argues that class conflict is not inevitable:

The great mistake made in regard to the matter now under consideration is to take up with the notion that class is naturally hostile to class, and that the wealthy and the working men are intended by nature to live in mutual conflict....Each needs the other: capital cannot do without labor, nor labor without capital. Mutual agreement results in the beauty of good order, while perpetual conflict necessarily produces confusion and savage barbarity.

The dependence of labor and management on one another is a continued theme in the Ford-UAW case, but there are many other instances in contemporary society of increased polarization between labor and management. The dignity of work is then praised in the encyclical and the role of the state in establishing supportive institutions is identified:

The following duties bind the wealthy owner and the employer: not to look upon their work people as their bondsmen, but to respect in every man his dignity as a person ennobled by Christian character. They are reminded that, according to natural reason and Christian philosophy, working for gain is creditable, not shameful, to a man, since it enables him to earn an honorable livelihood; but to misuse men as though they were things in the pursuit of gain, or to value them solely for their physical powers—that is truly shameful and inhuman....The rich must religiously refrain from cutting down the workmen's earnings, whether by force, by fraud, or by usurious dealing...

...The foremost duty, therefore, of the rulers of the State should be to make sure that the laws and institutions, the general character and administration of the commonwealth, shall be such as of themselves to realize public well-being and private prosperity....It is the province of the commonwealth to serve the common good. And the more that is done for the benefit of the working classes by the general laws of the country, the less need will there be to seek for special means to relieve them....

...The labor of the working class—the exercise of their skill, and the employment of their strength, in the cultivation of the land, and in the workshops of trade—is especially responsible and quite indispensable. Indeed, their co-operation is in this respect so important that it may be truly said that it is only by the labor of working men that States grow rich ... It follows that whatever shall appear to prove conducive to the well-being of those who work should obtain favorable consideration.

For many decades there has been gridlock with respect to the labor and employment laws in the United States such that innovation is only possible at the facility or enterprise level, such as is documented in this book. The encyclical is calling for a more proactive alignment of the institutions at the societal level in order to generate mutually beneficial outcomes. In this context the encyclical offers particular support for the role that unions play in society:

The most important of all are workingmen's unions, for these virtually include all the rest. History attests what excellent results were brought about by the artificers' guilds of olden times. They were the means of affording not only many advantages to the workmen, but in no small degree of promoting the advancement of art, as numerous monuments remain to bear witness. Such unions should be suited to the requirements of this our age—an age of wider education, of different habits, and of far more numerous requirements in daily life. It is gratifying to know that there are actually in existence not a few associations of this nature, consisting either of workmen alone, or of workmen and employers together, but it were greatly to be desired that they should become more numerous and more efficient....

...In order that an association may be carried on with unity of purpose and harmony of action, its administration and government should be firm and wise. All such societies, being free to exist, have the further right to adopt such rules and organization as may best conduce to the attainment of their respective objects.

As we document in this book, it is certainly possible for a union to serve in such a constructive and proactive role in today's economy, though it takes a transformation in a number of key operating assumptions within labor and management. More than a century after being issued, the encyclical provides continuing moral authority for a True North involving courageous leadership, the dignity of work, the value of collective action, and the importance of fair treatment. It has parallels in the civil domain.

Over six decades ago, on December 10, 1948, the United Nations issued General Assembly Resolution 217A (III)—the Universal Declaration of Human Rights. It affirms the dignity of the person, freedom of expression, freedom from slavery, freedom of assembly, and what are seen as other basic human rights, including Article 23, which states:

(1) Everyone has the right to work, to free choice of employment, to just and favourable conditions of work and to protection against unemployment.

(2) Everyone, without any discrimination, has the right to equal pay for equal work.

(3) Everyone who works has the right to just and favourable remuneration ensuring for himself and his family an existence worthy of human dignity, and supplemented, if necessary, by other means of social protection.

(4) Everyone has the right to form and to join trade unions for the protection of his interests.[3]

As we indicate in chapter 2, such dignity and respect is foundational in the Ford-UAW transformation story. Important as these principles are, there are many workplaces in the United States and other parts of the world where such rights are not fully supported. Building on the transformational experience with the UAW and other unions, Ford is a leader in signaling the importance of reinforcing these fundamental rights on a global basis.

In 2012 Ford Motor Company became the first major U.S. corporation to sign a global framework agreement affirming this UN declaration and other key principles. The agreement states, in part:

The achievement of business competitiveness, employee involvement, and employee security are positively influenced by good relations and mutual trust between employees and management within the Company. This requires the on-going cooperation of management, unions, works councils, employee representatives, and employees, ensuring that social dialogue at Ford be characterized by mutual respect and understanding. Procedures for information and consultation provide the opportunity for issues to be raised by either management or employee representatives to ensure that the views of both parties are fully understood.

Ford recognizes and respects its employees' rights to associate freely, form and joint a union, and bargain collectively with applicable law. The Company will work constructively with employee representatives to promote the interests of our employees in the workplace. In locations where employees are not represented by a body of employee representation/unions, the Company will provide opportunities for employees concerns to be heard. The Company fully respects and supports workers democratic right to form a union and will not allow any member of management or agent of the Company to undermine this right or pressure any employee from exercising this right.

Cooperation with employees, employees' representatives and trade unions will be constructive. The aim of such cooperation will be to seek a fair balance between the commercial interests of the Company and the interests of the employees. Even where there is disagreement, the aim will always be to work out a solution that permits constructive cooperation in the long term.[4]

The full text of this framework agreement is presented as Supporting Materials 9.1 and is a testament to Ford's leadership, working with unions and other forms of worker representation around the world. The framework agreement also identifies commitments with respect to wages and hours of work, child labor, workplace health and safety, training and development, supplier relations, and environmental sustainability.

✳✳✳

To conclude the book, we approached a number of the most senior leaders from both Ford and the UAW and asked them to comment on some of the accomplishments to date and the challenges ahead. In some cases, quotes from these interviews have been used earlier and are brought back here to summarize key points. While we feature the remarks of only eight senior leaders here, their comments connect with those of others we interviewed—and, we are sure, would be echoed by the many people we did not interview but who contributed to the many pivotal events featured in this book. We begin with two senior management leaders, followed by three senior union leaders, a former U.S. congressional representative with close ties to labor and a member of Ford's board of directors, and then two more senior management leaders. In each case, key background information is provided to set the stage for the comments.

Mark Fields

Ford's track record since 2008 in job and product creation is exceptional. A projected 18,000 new jobs will have been created in six-year period between 2008 and 2014—an accomplishment that eclipses nearly all other U.S. employers. Some of this is a product of the economic recovery as jobs lost in the recession are replaced—a slow process not yet complete at Ford or in other U.S. workplaces. Other jobs have been created by bringing work back to the United States that had been in Mexico or other countries, or with new jobs in parts sorting centers and other work—some of which has been enabled by the new entry wage and the reduced long-term retiree costs.

In terms of new products, Ford was an early leader in introducing hybrid engines for small SUVs and has continued to pioneer in the use of superchargers and other innovations, such as in the Ford EcoBoost engines, that are also increasing fuel efficiency. The new F150 pickup, with a body that is more than 75 percent aluminum, is a major leap forward in fuel efficiency for trucks—one with a substantial impact across the U.S economy, since this is one of the best-selling vehicles in North America.

Mark Fields was the executive vice president and then the president of the Americas for Ford from 2005 to 2012. In December 2012, he became Ford's chief operating officer, and in June 2014 was elevated to the position of chief executive officer. He has been responsible for, and at the center of, both the job creation and the new products. He leads the weekly Business Plan Review (BPR) and Special Attention Review (SAR) sessions introduced by Alan Mulally. He began his career at Ford in 1989 and previously was president and CEO of the Mazda Motor Company, as well as executive vice president, Ford of Europe and Premier Automotive Group. Fields is a "car guy"—he can be passionate about the latest car and truck designs.

When we asked him to reflect on the important gains since 2008 in job creation and new products, he focused on Ford's unique relationship with the UAW.

"I remember my first day at Ford," he said. "I was told that we had the brand of having the best relationship with the UAW. From the first day that people come into the company, we are bathed in the fact that this is a relationship and you need to work the relationship."

Fields then connected that UAW-Ford relationship with the family ownership of the company, and added, "We are all part of the Ford family. Like any family, there are occasional dysfunctions. You will always have issues, but you are always family."

Finally, he linked both factors to business success. "There is a level of trust between the UAW and Ford. That doesn't mean shying away from the issues. But having the relationships and investing in the relationships is a competitive advantage. Action America amped-up the relationship."

Mark Fields concluded by linking the union and the company even more. "We all have Ford Motor Company on our paychecks," he said. "There is a reason we haven't had a strike or work stoppage since 1976. Our relationship with the union has helped to drive the success of the business. Every year when we can issue the profit sharing checks, it is reinforced. But what is most important is that people are being treated and rewarded on a fair and consistent basis. That is how you should treat people who are family."

Joe Hinrichs

From the early 2000s to 2010, Ford went from near last in global quality to best in class. There are ongoing challenges in maintaining quality leadership—particularly as quality performance depends increasingly on the quality of software, not just manufacturing quality. Still, the transformation in quality has been dramatic; just in the two years prior to 2010, Ford saved over $1.2 billion in warranty costs as a result of quality improvements. In terms of profit and loss, Ford had lost $12 billion in 2006 but, by 2010, Ford's North America

Automotive profits were $5.4 billion. Even during the worst of the recent recession, Ford achieved year-over-year gains in quality and not a single unit was lost during these years.

We spoke to Joe Hinrichs about how he brought the voice of manufacturing to the relationship with the UAW. He was the group vice president of Global Manufacturing and Labor Affairs during some of the most challenging years of the past decade. During these years, he also served as CEO of Ford of Canada, group vice president and president of Asia Pacific and Africa, and chairman and CEO of Ford China. Since December 2012, he has been Ford's executive vice president and president of the Americas.

Hinrichs began working in the automotive industry at General Motors as an entry-level engineer, and joined Ford in December 2000 as plant manager of the Van Dyke Transmission Plant in Sterling Heights, Michigan. Later, he was promoted to serve as a director of manufacturing (DOM). In many ways, Hinrichs is still the engineer who likes to define a problem systematically, collect data, test options, implement solutions, and check to be sure the solutions are working. At the same time, he has expanded his horizons to encompass strategic problems on the scale of the full, extended global enterprise. In our interview, he reflected on being a director of manufacturing facing the economic crisis.

I believe in partnership and working together. It was clear to me early on that we could not do what we needed to do as a business without the UAW as a strong partner. Everything we needed to accomplish with quality, safety, plant closings, and other matters depended on multiple partnerships. That included how the DOMs worked together and then how we partnered with everyone else. This was a true concerted effort to save the company. I have always believed that intelligent people with the same set of facts will come to the same solutions.

Hinrichs initiates Ford's 2009 strategic move to take the lead from GM and Chrysler in negotiating with the UAW—a unique process. "It was a peak moment when Marty and I met with Ron Gettelfinger and Bob King and we agreed that we could do this together in 2009—without relying on government money," he recalled. "We did an agreement in a week with seven people sitting around the table in my office in World Headquarters…based on relationships we had established."

While the 2009 negotiation was certainly a pivotal moment, Hinrichs pointed to the 2006–2007 negotiations as most central to the survival of Ford Motor Company and the UAW.

What we did in 2009 helped to save the company, but perhaps what was equally important was what happened in 2006-2007. It is most impressive that 50,000 hourly people left with voluntary packages—about 40 percent of the workforce—and no unit of production was lost and quality and safety got better. It was because we did this together. All planning was joint in every location. It was an unbelievable feat—accomplished with the same objective in mind—helping people to leave in the best way we could and keeping the customer in mind.

Hinrichs elaborated on the voluntary separation packages.

We offered a number of different packages—more than our competitors. This included educational programs. There was a lot of interest in finding solutions that would be the best—so we could do what we could to help people transition to a different life. We all wanted to help people to be successful in the transition.

Because of how it was done collectively and collaboratively we were able to achieve the needed cost reductions to save the company. We ended up having many more people take the packages than we expected and then we all came together to protect the customer at the same time—amazing!

Delivering on quality and productivity depends on effective communications, Hinrichs notes.

We were investing all of our time in communicating with each other. My role was to communicate directly with the work force. I tried to explain things in a way that was meaningful to the employee and their family. I was careful to not place blame.

In making the case for change, you can't over-communicate—especially when people are worried about their livelihoods. You have to rally the troops and realize that everyone is part of the solution—everyone has a role to play. People will not change just because someone they don't know says they need to change. The foundation of change is trust and you can't start by saying, "Trust me." You have to first invest in a relationship—so you have to invest time and energy in that relationship to understand the issue and concerns. You have to invest in the relationship—so that the relationship works for both parties.

Joe Hinrichs spoke of a continued commitment to being competitive and delivering on the mutual gains promise. He also noted the future will hold challenges.

"Looking ahead," he said, "the key challenge is in how to walk the line and balance being competitive and sharing the benefits. There are still issues to work through together. We have the interests of the entry-wage workers and the traditional work force to take into account. It is back to investing in relationships, trust, and listening. Several of our key assembly plants have a high percentage of entry-wage workers—this is a new world for Ford and the UAW. There's always a solution if we work together to find it."

Jimmy Settles

Valuing work is about much more than economic performance. It transcends issues of cost, quality, schedule, and productivity. Equally important is the quality of working life and the broader impact work has on families and communities. These are all key ingredients in what in the United States is called the "American Dream."

Advancing that American Dream has been a consistent aim for Jimmy Settles, who began has career at Ford in 1968 at the Dearborn Iron Foundry and Michigan Casting Center. Then, African American workers were concentrated in foundry and casting work—some of the toughest jobs in the industry. As he rose in leadership roles in UAW Local 600, Region 1A, and eventually the International vice president, Settles always maintained his focus on the whole person, including family and community. His first inclination was always to do good work quietly, but over time he came to recognize that his leadership role requires him to speak out on behalf of others who may not have the same opportunity for their voices to be heard.

When we spoke with him, he was the UAW vice president responsible for relations with Ford. We asked him the meaning of the American Dream, from his personal perspective.

I can remember back when I was a kid, people who worked at Ford had a badge that they would wear on their suit going to church on Sunday. The kids would shine it up—it was a point of pride. If you went in a store, people saw you with the badge and treated you differently.

Ford paid black workers the same as white workers. There were only limited occupations possible in GM—foundry was immigrants as well as 40 percent African Americans. I worked in a foundry. You had chances to get into plants in Ford, which was not the case at GM. They would not even allow blacks to buy new Cadillacs—had to buy used. At Ford, everyone was paid the same and the chance for advancement was greater—especially for skilled trades. Ultimately, you want every generation to do better than the generation before.

It is not enough for people to have job opportunities. They also have to know what to do to keep a job. They have to understand the idea of getting to work every day.

Once people have a job and then they open up a checking account and pay bills themselves—that is real pride and dignity... . You know what it is to be working and providing for your family.

When someone needs a haircut or a pair of shoes, you do this for your kids before you do it for yourself. Your kids see this. The kids learn that people take their obligations seriously.

I was blessed—my dad worked and had a good job, but where I am now is because of the community. There were lots of activities all the time—opportunities to play sports and positive role models who instilled discipline. This is missing today from many communities. There are video games and music, but kids are not getting the full benefits of the village—what happens when you always have people to help you.

Focusing on the larger context, Settles spoke of his personal sense of responsibility and commitment to giving back. "For most of the workers we hire," he said, "it will be their first experience as employees. Most kids are great kids—you might have 5 percent who are difficult."

He added, "This is our reason for going into the community. We criticize kids, but what are we doing to help them? We all can do something and the position I am in allows me to do more—to give back to the community."

Focusing on the workplace, Settles takes into account production issues like cost and performance as well as caring for the workers who fuel the enterprise. For instance, he spoke of the enhanced health care program.

If we don't change behaviors [health care costs] will just continue to expand. [The agreement we reached is] one of the most important long-term things we have done in negotiations. It is not that it hasn't been done in other companies. Boeing had done something like this, but it is still important that we do all we can. . . .

Some illnesses can be reversed with these coaches—it involves ensuring the right medications, checking for negative effects between medications. People really appreciate this—not just the medical part, but the fact that someone really cares about you. . . . It is the right thing to do and it can be preventative as well.

Settles summed up his views with a comment about what the union does for workers. "Through collective bargaining," he explained, "we are making a difference in people's lives—inside and outside of the workplace. Collective bargaining is about being in the middle class, and it can be more than that. What we have been able to do—the UAW and Ford—is an example for others."

Bob King

Historically, unions derived power by withholding labor (or by threatening to do so). That model, though, may not be the best for the new knowledge economy. The dynamics of a knowledge economy requires that unions learn to derive power by enabling work.[5] This shifts the focus to leadership based on influence and collaboration rather than leadership based on confrontation and power—a particularly complicated shift in a democratic organization such as a union. An elected leader always risks accusations of not being strong or aggressive enough in advancing the interests of the rank and file.

In the UAW, the internal tension between these opposing approaches to delivering the best results for members has always been accompanied by a third consideration: the degree to which the union's focus should be on its current members and its relationship with their employers or on its broader commitment to social and economic justice in society. Some union leaders, including King, believe that these two objectives are inseparable.

Before he became UAW president in June 2010, Bob King served as UAW vice president responsible for the relationship with Ford during some of the most challenging times the union has ever faced. The pressures to navigate among these complex and often competing strategic directions for the union have marked King's time in the union leadership.

Bob King is an inspirational and sometime controversial leader. He is a religious man driven by principles of social justice. His views have been both embraced and challenged for being too progressive or too idealistic. At the same time, he has made tough business decisions that were central to the success of Ford and other automakers.

With respect to Ford, King spoke of positive relationships as the initial point of departure—a view he shares with senior Ford leaders.

A basic principle is to always listen to everyone and treat every person with respect. This has been what has characterized our relations with Ford. We have always had good personal relations with the leadership at Ford and believe strongly that these relationships help us achieve the best results for our members.

We work at maintaining the relationship. It is just like a marriage—you constantly work on it. I refer to the UAW-Ford relationship as creative problem solving.... We both need to focus on how to address the other party's issues—not limited by what the contract does or does not say. Ideally mutually advantageous solutions can be found. Or at least we can find solutions that are not disadvantaging one side.

When I first became the UAW-Ford vice president, there was a history of broken commitments. We have made great progress. The way we handled Visteon is an example of problem solving. The same was true when we were first looking at what we thought would be a [job] reduction [for] 30,000 of our members. Together we created many different and innovative incentives so that all of what turned out to be 50,000 reductions were voluntary—an amazing accomplishment. We then joined with management to put together a team to focus solely on maintaining quality while the reductions were taking place. There had to be discipline in the process. It really was amazing. We had joint strategy sessions and intense discussions—our goal was to not have quality slip and it actually improved.

Beyond the UAW-Ford relationship, however, King told us of the considerable challenges he sees in society.

The challenge looking ahead is the demise of democracy and a strong middle class in the United States. The shrinking of the middle class and the lack of affordable education and "a going backwards" in so many areas of social and economic fairness—all are connected to attacks on workers collective bargaining rights and attacks on workers right to organize. There are some very wealthy individuals and corporations who do not value collaboration with workers or their unions—all are connected to a tendency of management to be shortsighted. This is in contrast, for example, to the German model, which is more focused on collaboration, joint commitment, and joint decision making at all levels, and ensuring high skills in the workforce.

I sit on the Opel supervisory board and get to experience the German collaborative, co-determination approach first hand. The union representatives really know the business—these guys are really smart. We can learn from this model. Steve Girsky [GM's head of European operations] would say, "Labor was more honest open, and correct in their analysis than my management."

There is a realization that there has to be a new system. We have brought what will likely be 18,000 jobs in here at Ford. Initially, Ford had promised 12,000 and then 15,000. We could not have achieved this and exceeded the goals if we had kept wages at traditional rates. The challenge is how to figure out a system with a clear path to top wages for the entry-level workers and still maintain different rates of pay to remain competitive on all the work we have insourced, and to allow us to insource more work creating more jobs and more job security for current members.

King concluded our interview by highlighting the particular challenge within labor—"everyone learning how to build cultures of strong collaboration."

A major challenge from both labor and management involves everyone learning how to build cultures of strong collaboration. This includes operating in an environment of transparency—full information sharing. It also includes openness from both sides to look at each other's ideas.

There is an ongoing challenge, which is building this approach into the structure of the union. Some want to slip back into the more positional stance. Together with management we have to create a problem-solving culture, so that it is engrained at every level. We have to spread the culture to suppliers and other industries and relationships.

Ron Gettelfinger

The Louisville Assembly Plant (LAP) was among many UAW-Ford locations more fully valuing the knowledge of production, material handling, and the maintenance department at the launch of a new product. The launch of the Ranger pickup truck at LAP in the 1980s was but one example. Ford management displayed prototype sections in the body, paint, trim, and chassis departments. Employees in each department could examine the product, physically touch it, compare production requirements, and make suggestions for improvements. Workers turned in more than a thousand suggestions for improvements, many of which were adopted.

In the 1980s, when Ford was exploring innovative approaches to maintenance involving input from the workers, Ron Gettelfinger was the local union leader at the Louisville Assembly Plant (see chapter 5). He was mentioned as someone who would give the idea appropriate, thoughtful consideration. And, indeed, maintenance workers then at LAP made important progress.

Gettelfinger left LAP to join the staff of the international union in December 1987 and was elected Region 3 director in 1992, responsible for Indiana and Kentucky. In 1998, he was elected UAW vice president with responsibility for the Ford, Aerospace, and Chaplaincy departments. In that role, he joined with Ford executive chairman Bill Ford, Local 600 president Jerry Sullivan (who represented the Rouge Complex), and other local union and company leaders to launch a system-wide joint safety initiative. The catalysts for this action was the Rouge power plant explosion on February 1, 1999, which claimed six lives, and it was further driven by fatalities at Sterling Axle and Nashville Glass.

Between 2002 and 2009, Gettelfinger served two terms as president of the UAW. He appointed individuals to leadership roles who were instrumental in transforming work to enable continuous improvement and employee involvement. During this time, he also represented the UAW when the nation's spotlight was on the auto industry, demonstrating the courage to make the necessary concessions required to save the industry. As a result, with the recovery, auto workers are better off than they would have been had the initial government plan been imposed.

Gettelfinger's approach to leadership comes down to one word: "integrity." His reputation is for never tolerating misrepresentation and always insisting people do what is right. On behalf of the UAW, he initiated monthly Action America meetings with Ford's high-level leadership that kept the top leadership of the UAW abreast of what was going on throughout Ford's operations. In addition, regular meetings with Bill Ford were instrumental in keeping a strong relationship with the company. Gettelfinger also held top leadership meetings with GM and Chrysler, but not as frequently as at Ford. While he found all three companies respectful, he reports a different feel at Ford—where the relationship continued to strengthen over time.

Gettelfinger's deep personal sense of integrity was most evident (as we saw in chapter 8) in his October 25, 2000, address in Romulus, Michigan, to a joint Health and Safety meeting involving plant managers, human resources managers, local union presidents, and plant chairpersons from all locations. Gettelfinger stated at the time that he "accepted the responsibility for safety" and added: "If we do not fix safety, the delegates to the next UAW

Convention are obligated to vote against me." Following this meeting, on November 2, 2000, every U.S. Ford location held a "safety stand-down" that began with meetings of the Ford management plant operating committees and all elected and appointed UAW representatives, with UAW appointed staff and their Ford counterparts in attendance. It was made clear that if an employee was caught working in an unsafe manner he or she would be penalized and their immediate supervisor would be penalized equally.

Summing up his priorities as a leader, Ron Gettelfinger worked with management to have 4 x 8–foot banners in the plants with the UAW and Ford logos stating:

Safety—it's about our lives and our families
Quality—it's about our job security and our future
Diversity—it's about our dignity and our respect for each other

The survival of the auto industry during the 2008 and 2009 national recession, Gettelfinger has often said, would not have been possible without the sacrifices of active and retired members in all three companies. He has stated publicly that these were the people who were the real heroes. He also challenged those in the media who blamed the UAW for the bankruptcy of Chrysler and GM, pointing out that Chrysler, Ford, and GM had the same contract and the same union. Ford avoided bankruptcy.

Ron Gettelfinger reminds us that the UAW membership has been recognized by Detroit's Channel 7 and by Crain's Automotive News as "Newsmaker of the Year" and by *The Detroit News* as one of the "Michiganders of the Year."

The theme of this chapter is "True North: combining good jobs and high performance." Gettelfinger has never wavered from his commitment to this goal.

Dick Gephardt

Richard "Dick" Gephardt represented Missouri 3rd District in the U.S. House of Representatives from January 3, 1977, until January 3, 2005. A Democrat, he was majority leader from 1989 to 1995 and as minority leader from 1995 to 2003. When he retired from the House, he accepted a position on the Board of Directors of the Ford Motor Company—at the behest of both Ford and the UAW. He was in this role during the economic collapse and was a key sounding board for Ford and UAW leaders as they navigated Washington's intervention into the auto industry.

We asked him to reflect back on that pivotal moment from his unique perspective as a former congressman then serving on the board of an auto company. "There was a sense of disbelief," he recalled. "No one could bring themselves to think that GM in particular could go bankrupt. Some of us had seen what happened with Chrysler in the 1980s. But not all had seen that and that sense of disbelief made it hard for people to see what needed to be done."

The Chrysler bailout, Gephardt noted, "was highly controversial in the 1980s. On the right, people said government should not intervene, and on the other side there were people, myself included, that said we can't give up these good jobs and let the Japanese take over our market—especially when they wouldn't let us in their market and were playing with the currency."

Gephardt was critical of the initial response from Washington in 2009, as we note in chapter 1. "Once people went past the state of disbelief, which went on too long, then there was blame," he recalled. "There was blame for the business people and blame for the unions. When enough people confronted the fact that it is really going to happen if you don't do something—that jobs will be lost, the supply chain will go down—then we started to see action. You can blame later, but deal with the issues."

As Gephardt saw it, the history of the UAW and Ford was "a big factor" in Ford not taking the bailout money. He observed:

Ford had the benefit of this for decades, [it was] a huge benefit for the workers to be with you. It doesn't mean that they don't fight—that happens in any family. [But] right after Alan [Mulally] arrived, Ford made what was called the biggest home improvement loan in history. That was pivotal. Ford had cash, which was vital in getting through the bad times. They also had the backing of the Ford family—that is very important in the whole equation. Alan could cut the dividend and invest in the company. Again, the good relationship with the union was also vital.

More broadly, said Gephardt, "The CEO and business school culture in most companies puts a premium on finance and does not give enough attention to how we lead people. The board backed management because of the way they were leading. You can't do something like this without the board being with you." But, as he noted, the UAW's role should not be discounted.

I am still in awe of what Gettelfinger and the union did. If they had not made the hugely painful concessions, all three companies would have gone down.

Policy makers in Congress have no clue of what unions are doing on a day-to-day basis to make companies more successful and to work with leaders of companies in a different and better way. There is huge role for unions in the modern world. In this highly competitive world workers can't figure all this out individually. Unions need to better communicate to policy makers and to the public the importance of their role.

Gephardt summed up his reflections.

We pay a lot of attention to the bad things. We don't study sufficiently what happens when things work pretty well. Nothing is perfect in life and none of it is easy. But getting the Ford-UAW story across to people is really important to do.

This can help a lot of other companies and unions and other workforces in the country and the world. Labor relations—how we treat people at work—is the issue of the time and will be forever. In order to hold your standard of living and enhance it you have to have highly productive workplaces—that is how we achieve shared growth for all.

Alan Mulally

Alan Mulally is appropriately celebrated for his service as one of the most successful CEOs in the United States today. The Business Plan Review (BPR) and Special Attention Review (SAR) processes he brought to Ford not only introduced much-needed structure and discipline to the company's operations, but signaled a culture change centered on open problem solving and a shared commitment to "One Ford."

Discussing the lessons of these changes with Mulally was an extraordinary experience. He began with a handshake, a touch on the shoulder, and then came a constant flow of observations and questions. Some were prepared; some were spontaneous. He would be sitting and then suddenly jump up to point to a picture or artifact. All he said was delivered with a combination of joy in the moment and unrestrained intensity.

Mulally highlighted four key elements of success. The first is a *compelling vision.*

All stakeholders need to know why they are coming together. This is the compelling vision. The vision sets you free. It is all stakeholders—customers, the company, its workers, the unions, the suppliers, the dealers, and all others. Seventy percent of the dollar value of a car comes from our suppliers. It has to be everyone who shares in the compelling vision.

The second, a *comprehensive strategy*, builds on the compelling vision.

We have the core strategy on a wallet card. Everyone knows the plan. The strategy centers on success as measured by our customers, our employees, our suppliers, our dealers, our unions, our investors. It is a strategy of profitable growth for all. At 87 percent, we have some of the highest employee satisfactory scores of any major corporation. Working with the union we have been able to create a projected 18,000 new jobs. Our investors have realized massive gain in the value of our stock. Our dealers and suppliers are doing well. Our success in all markets has been to work together. We have to deliver value through our strategy on a consistent basis—year after year.

The comprehensive strategy, though, is nothing without *relentless implementation.*

To realize the strategy, we have had to aggressively restructure the company. That included selling nearly all of the brands we had acquired. We learned that you have to pay people appropriately to leave on a voluntary basis. That was needed, along with massive borrowing, in order to have the cash to invest in new products. BPR provided the road map, premised on continuous improvement in the plan.

The fourth and final element integrates the other three—*working together.*

It is all about people working together. It is about committing to the behaviors. It is about technical excellence. It is about shared responsibility for the results. It is about working together to find a way to make the bar on a graph go up. This is what has made possible transformational agreements between the UAW and Ford. This is what makes it possible for us to build world-class vehicles. This only happens with profitable growth for all—PGA—that is the only way that everyone can benefit.

Mulally was delighted to share with us a 1925 Ford advertisement from the *Saturday Evening Post* (figure 9.1). The text of the ad celebrates the mission of the Ford Motor Company, which was to provide the mobility to open new horizons for the public. That broader conception of a societal purpose—one that echoes Henry Ford's $5 day and the notion that people should be able to buy the product they build—has been the driver for Mulally.

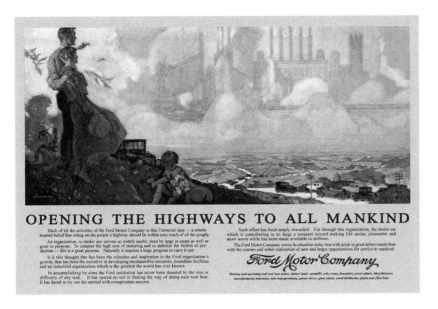

Figure 9.1
1925 Advertisement on "Opening the Highways to All Mankind." *Source:* Ford Motor Company.

Bill Ford

Over the years, many members of the Ford family have worked for and helped lead the company that bears their name. Indeed, tracing the intertwined genealogy of the family and company is quite a complex undertaking.

Edsel Ford, the son of Henry Ford, was the first to carry forth his father's legacy. He had a passion for car design and was instrumental in purchasing and building the Lincoln brand. During his tenure as company president, he spent many years working to overcome his father's objections to building anything other than the Model T, and he ultimately succeeded with the Model A.

Henry Ford had grandchildren—Henry Ford II, Benson Ford Sr., Josephine Clay Ford, and William Clay Ford Sr. At various times prior to his death in 1987, Henry Ford II—known as "HF2" and "the deuce"—was president, CEO, and chairman of the board, and was responsible for the Ford Motor Company becoming a publically traded company. Benson Ford headed up the Lincoln-Mercury Division and chaired the Dealer Policy Board. William Clay Ford Sr. served as chair of Ford's Design Committee for 32 years and chaired the board's Finance Committee.

Today, other members of the family have key roles in the company. William Clay Ford Jr.—or Bill Ford, as he prefers to be called—has served as CEO and is currently executive chairman of the board. Edsel Bryant Ford II, a great-grandson of Henry Ford (and the son of

Henry Ford II), is a member of Ford's board of directors. Elena Ford, vice president of the Global Dealer and Consumer Experience for the company, is the first member of the family's fifth generation (i.e., beginning with Henry Ford) to hold an executive position with the company and the first women from the Ford family in management. Others from the fifth generation include Henry Ford III, who contributed to the 2007 negotiation (in chapter 6).

Our focus here is Bill Ford. As a student at Princeton, he wrote his senior thesis on the history of the UAW. When he first went to work for the company, he did so under the name William Clay to avoid drawing attention to himself. One of his first experiences as a Ford employee was to serve on one of the subcommittees supporting the 1982 negotiation that generated the Mutual Growth framework. Over time, he rose in the company to become CEO and board chair. In these roles, he emphasized environmental issues—both in the products produced and in the factory operations—in the late 1990s and early 2000s when it was seen as outside the mainstream of the business. In retrospect, his focus was prescient.

In a rare move for a leader of his stature and authority, Bill Ford voluntarily gave up the CEO role to bring in Alan Mulally. Although he offered Mulally the board chair role as well, Mulally made an equally rare move by insisting that Bill stay in the role of the executive chairman. Together, they were at the helm during a period in which the very survival of the enterprise was at stake.

Reflecting on these challenges, Bill Ford focused first on the people in the company. "I have always realized that this company is not about what we make," he said. "It is about who does it. I don't think about the launch of a given product. What is most important is people. If we ever lose sight of that—and we have at times—it hurts the company."

Ford then highlighted the crisis years. "Back in 2006 and 2007," he recalled, "I received letters from people who were laid off that were thanking me. I would have understood anger. There are many letters instead saying that this is a great company. I have to say that those were awful years. It was the worst time ever. I spent night after night lying in bed thinking it can't end this way. We did want to make sure we treated people right in the crisis. Once we got the plan together, the only issue was do we have enough time."

Bill Ford had specific praise for the relationship with the UAW in meeting the challenge during the crisis period.

What was most important was the recognition that we were fighting for something that was worth saving. If you believe, then you will do the right thing.

[UAW president] Ron Gettelfinger doesn't get near the credit he deserves for his pivotal role in saving the industry. When the 2006 crisis hit, we already had many years of building the relationship—Marty and others and maybe me, too. That went a long way to enabling him to act decisively. He knew we were telling the truth. At the same time, it is important that Ron was as strong as he was. The decision on the VEBA and the entry wage were critical. The decisions to close facilities were painful....

Ron could have laid in the tracks and it would have been a different outcome. He didn't roll over. Anyone who knows Ron knows that he is principled and tough. But he cared about the future for his members and the future of Ford. His leadership was pivotal.

In union-management relations it is essential to have a level of trust and honest dialogue. We realize that negotiations start the day the contract is signed. It can get heated, but it doesn't get overblown. If Jimmy Settles or Bob King is having a bad day, we have to be careful to not overreact. It begins with really getting to know someone. I really appreciate how Jimmy is interested in the city of Detroit and bringing the city up. Some of his counterparts at the other auto companies are dealing with people who haven't taken the time to get to know them. As a result, when issues come up, they are more volatile.

Ford emphasized just how fragile continued business success can be. "For quality and safety," he noted, "it takes years to get it right and you can lose it quickly. We have had huge change in moving to global platforms. In addition, we have been working with nontraditional suppliers like Microsoft, Google, and others. There are great reasons to do so, but we do have quality challenges that come from these new technologies. This is after we had made great progress in figuring out quality. The lesson is that you have to be vigilant every day. You are never done. The same is true with safety."

Having seen the strategic importance of an environmental orientation long before other leaders in the auto industry, Ford spoke of an additional focus now on how technology is a strategic challenge for the industry as it looks ahead. "The opportunity and challenge looking ahead is that changes are coming like we have never seen," he pointed out. "Self-driving vehicles are coming. Vehicles will be connected to the cloud. We will be transitioning into being a technology company as a result."

Technology can be cold. If we don't do it correctly, we can end up severing people's emotional connection to the car itself. [We can't] all retreat to our laptops and iPads and forget to treat the human element....

I was just at a conference in Silicon Valley. People were there with all their technology, but the quality of interaction was terrible....

Relationships take time and need full attention, which is in short supply now. People are interactive with the technology, but it lacks humanity....

I believe that people still want to have positive human relationships—even if it is redefined today with technology. Any company should exist to make people's lives better. We have done that and with all the new technology we still need to be doing that.

We asked Ford about the role of a family-owned firm in society. He began his answer by focusing on how family ownership is connected to the relationship with the UAW.

I care about the relationship with the UAW—it is all part of being in an extended family. There is good will. I am not sure about the broader impact in society of our being a family-owned firm, but I can say that it humanizes us. It is also reassuring to the stockholders that we are not going to take a golden parachute and run. Families can also turn negative, so maintaining the good will is key.

In the next generation it is not just about who has the skill set, but also the right empathy and people skills and attitude.

Henry Ford III (great-great grandson of his namesake and son of Edsel Ford II), part of the next generation from the Ford family after Bill Ford, came to appreciate the connection between family ownership and family in general after coming to work for Ford in 2006.

"Employees at all levels feel the connection to Ford Motor Company," he noted. "The dedication, loyalty and passion for the company was often the legacy of their families. I can't say how many people I met whose mother or father had worked for Ford. Family is such a universal concept—it connects and binds us. It is a real asset for Ford and the UAW that I didn't appreciate until I began to work for Ford. It keeps our focus on long-term success."

Bill Ford concluded our interview by highlighting the challenge to maintain the family culture with each new generation in the workforce.

It is true that most other firms don't work at it like we do—they don't come at it like we do. We believe that we are a large family company, but we don't just define it as my family, it is the Ford family.

I speak to the new employees often, both in large and small groups. I have challenged the top management to make our culture relevant to the people coming in....Cultures are not static, but truths continue. These truths have to be re-expressed for the next generation. We have to keep it relevant.

Weaving a Tapestry of Pivotal Events

Returning to the full list of pivotal events, examining the way they interweave provides important insights into the integrated nature of the transformation. In chapter 1, we provided three examples that illustrate how the pivotal events in early chapters built a foundation for pivotal events in later chapters. We offer here a closer analysis of the third example, figure 9.2 (which is a reprint of figure 1.4) to show how this works.

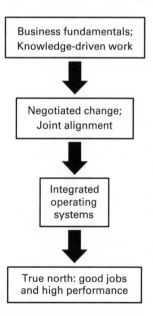

Figure 9.2
Connecting Chapter Themes (beginning with Business Fundamentals and Knowledge-Driven Work).

This chart illustrates one set of pathways to True North—combining good jobs with high performance. The two boxes on the left of the chart group the four themes (i.e., the titles) of chapters 4 and 5 and chapters 6 and 7, respectively; the third box contains the theme of chapter 8. The actual interweaving of these grouped themes, however, takes place at the level of the pivotal events in their respective chapters. Consider the first box on the left in figure 9.2, which combines "business fundamentals" with "knowledge-driven work" (chapters 4 and 5). If we unpack the pivotal events in these two chapters it becomes clear that many of the pivotal events placed in one chapter overlap to a considerable degree with the theme of the other chapter.

Figure 9.3 presents all the pivotal events in chapters 4 and 5, with the pivotal events that are more distinct in either the left or the right column and those that overlap in the middle column. For example, the SQDCME policy deployment is a pivotal event we classified as "business fundamentals," but it is also the framework guiding continuous improvement efforts in the work system. Similarly, the FPS roll out was classified as part of "knowledge-driven work," but it is a core building block for delivering business results.

This presentation has two important implications. First, the Ford-UAW transformation rests on a foundation in which business fundamentals interweave with a distributed, knowledge-driven form of work organization. In the process, the way the business is conducted changes (with a focus on mutual gains) and the way work is oriented changes (with a focus on continuous improvement in operations). Second, at a deeper level, domains that might be separated in a traditional business become interconnected in new ways as part of the transformation in the nature of the work itself.

The same story can be told at the level of the pivotal events in other parts of figure 9.2. For example, figure 9.4 shows the interweaving of "negotiated change" and "joint alignment," the themes of chapters 6 and 7.

While the initial negotiated-change events involve management-led restructuring that was distinct from the joint alignment efforts, the negotiated change events from 2003 onward feature an interweaving of attention to joint alignment as part of the bargaining process—both during negotiations and in anticipation of implementation after negotiations. While most of the pivotal events we highlighted as part of joint alignment are separate from formal negotiations, the quality chartering clearly built on the 2003 quality negotiations. The 2006 UAW-Ford National Joint Program Conference would normally be formally separate from the 2007 collective bargaining negotiations, but in this case the interweaving of business fundamentals ended up setting the stage for the Competitive Operating Agreements (COAs; presented in chapter 2 as part of the case for change), which then led into the 2007 negotiations.

The interweaving in figure 9.3 points to two fundamental changes in the labor-management relationship. First, collective bargaining is no longer a periodic adversarial contest, separate from the ongoing alignment between labor and management. Second, joint alignment comes about though a cyclical "cause and effect" process; it is enabled by agreements reached in collective bargaining and serves as well an input into future bargaining

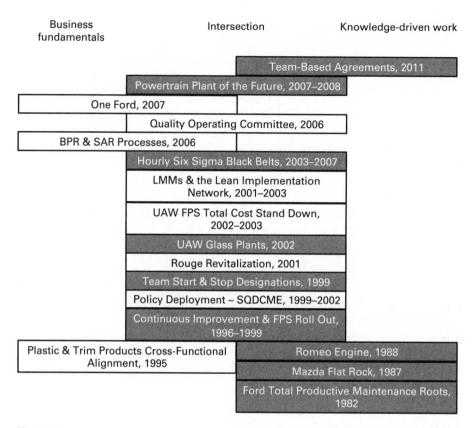

Figure 9.3

Pivotal Events from chapters 4 and 5: Interweaving of Business Fundamentals and Knowledge-Driven Work.

Legend: *white boxes*: "Business Fundamentals" pivotal events (chapter 4); *shaded boxes*: "Knowledge-Driven Work" pivotal events (chapter 5); *left column*: pivotal events that are primarily about the business; *right column*: pivotal events primarily about the work system; *middle column*: pivotal events in which business fundamentals interweave with the work organization and job design.

processes as new opportunities for joint alignment are identified. Ultimately, the interweaving of these two themes represents a transformation in relationships that increases the capacity of both parties to advance their separate and shared interests.

An interweaving of the pivotal events in other combinations of chapters could also be developed. As figure 9.2 suggests, it is the sum of these transformations that has made possible the emergence of "operating systems" (see chapter 8), which in turn sets the stage for the True North vision of good jobs and high performance. We conclude the book with that vision and the way it relates to the guiding principles in each chapter.

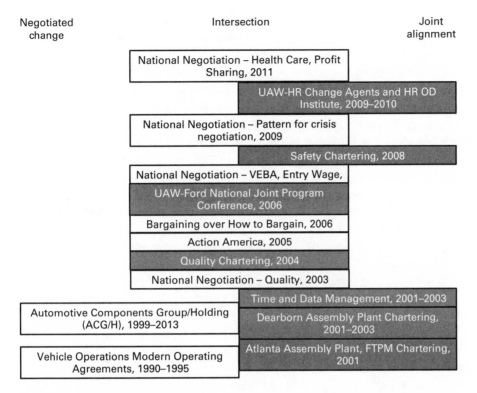

Figure 9.4
Pivotal Events from Chapters 6 and 7: Interweaving of Negotiated Change and Joint Alignment.
Legend: *white boxes*: "Negotiated Change" pivotal events (chapter 6); *shaded boxes*: "Joint Alignment" pivotal events (chapter 7); *left column*: pivotal events that are primarily about the negotiated change, including collective bargaining; *right column*: pivotal events primarily about joint alignment, including chartering; *middle column*: pivotal events in which negotiated change interweaves with joint alignment.

Vision for Good Jobs and High Performance

"True North" for Ford and the UAW combines good jobs and high performance. As the pivotal events in this book indicate, these twin objectives can complement and reinforce one another. The knowledge-driven aspects of good jobs are both responsive to deep human needs and central to continuous improvement in the organization. The integrated operating systems that deliver high-performance results depend on widely distributed engagement of the entire workforce. Some of what makes a job good is integral to high performance, and high performance makes it possible to avoid a race to the bottom in pay and benefits.

In the United States, the combination of good jobs and high performance fuels what is referred to as the American Dream, in which each generation has the potential to do better than the next—by virtue of education and hard work. Versions of this dream have taken hold around the world to a remarkable degree, even as the dream is at risk in the United States. How can the dream be revitalized in the United States and sustained around the world?

The Ford-UAW pivotal events help point the way forward, while also providing evidence that the path is neither easy nor quick. The way forward is not simply a list of good things to do or a single reengineering initiative, but involves rethinking deeply embedded assumptions about work and relationships while simultaneously ensuring the infrastructure to support new ways of working. If W. Edwards Deming's injunction is correct—that transformation is everyone's business—then we must operate from the assumption that everyone (or at least the vast majority of people) want to contribute to the transformation and that they are capable of doing so. While working in a high-performance work system can be intense, it can also be highly engaging and rewarding. In contrast, as Lee Sanborn observed in the Romeo Engine Plant pivotal event (chapter 4), "Bad systems will beat good people every time."

Thus, integrated operating systems become key. If we assume people want to be part of the transformation, then the way we deliver results on safety, quality, cost, delivery, maintenance, environment, and other factors depends on how we deliver results for the "people" side of the enterprise—the P in Ford's SQDCMPE. In each case, processes of alignment and stabilization are needed as the foundation to enable the integration and innovation—hence our guiding principle in chapter 8 of "align and stabilize, then integrate."

In turn, to align key stakeholders—whether it is union and management, various functions within management, original equipment manufacturers and suppliers, or other combinations—the principle in chapter 7 of "disciplined standardized processes" is essential. This includes the chartered forums that bring the stakeholders together, the time-and-data management to support the SQDCMPE balanced scorecard in the chartered forums, and the targeted training to ensure that the right people with the right knowledge and skills are in the right place at the right time.

In the process, there are collective interests best addressed through negotiation, but it can't be traditional adversarial collective bargaining. As Bill Dirksen observed in discussing the 2007 negotiation (chapter 6), the definition of "insanity" is doing the same thing over and over but hoping for a different result. Bargaining over how to bargain leads to the use of tools and methods from interest-based bargaining—and they extend beyond formal negotiation to inform the principle in chapter 6 of "interest-based relationships." In the process, collective bargaining becomes a platform for innovation—codifying past innovations and providing a framework for future innovations. Thus, collective bargaining served to codify innovations such as the roles of quality operating system coordinators (in 2003) and team leaders (in 2011), as well as setting the stage for future innovations advancing mutual growth (in 1982), increasing operational flexibility (in 2006–2007 COAs), and ensuring retiree health care coverage (in 2007).

The innovations enabled by collective bargaining require the distributed knowledge of the entire workforce—that is, knowledge-driven work systems. These systems involve workplace teams, continuous improvement suggestion systems, and the many lean and Six Sigma tools and methods. The key point is that the principle in chapter 5 of "continuous improvement" depends on the lean and Six Sigma tools and methods being driven on a widely distributed basis, rather than with a more narrow, expert-driven approach. That is the way to engage *everyone* involved in the generation of products or services—and not just the small set of so-called knowledge workers. The global knowledge economy has the potential to encompass all workers and managers.

The business fundamentals do matter—getting functions aligned to deliver value to customers requires the unified focus enabled by Ford's Business Plan Reviews and Special Attention Reviews. Moreover, the BPR and SAR help to build a culture of responsibility and action by managers at all levels, an aspirational goal for many corporations. Attending to business fundamentals also requires an underlying assumption of and commitment to the principle in chapter 4 of "mutual growth." Aspects of the business, such as the Quality Operating Committee for the corporation and the use of charters in the various operating systems, benefit by the engagement of the union, which sees the delivery of business objectives as in the interests of the workforce.

At an even deeper level, there is an essential underlying assumption around the dignity of work—guided by the principle in chapter 3 of "dignity and respect" in the workplace. Transformations in the workplace ultimately involve our very identity as human beings. That is why we have, at various points in the book, reached beyond the scholarly literature to include relevant language from the traditions of human rights, social justice, and even religion.

The foundations of "mutual growth" and "dignity and respect" mean that change should not be imposed. The "case for change" needs to be made to engender voluntary engagement and, ultimately, commitment. This rests on the principle in chapter 2 of "courageous leadership"—where the courage is to operate on the basis of transformational principles that value work and relationships in new ways.

When Ford didn't take the government bailout money, it was a pivotal event that was enabled by many dozens of preceding pivotal events—some planned and some unplanned. Viewing transformation through the lens of pivotal events helps reveal the underlying guiding principles and essential dynamics of change. Today, Ford, the UAW, and the Ford-UAW relationship have changed in fundamental ways—though the transformation is not and cannot ever be complete. Indeed, it is always at risk of pivots that move away from True North—the combination of good jobs and high performance—just as it always has the potential for future pivots that more fully deliver on the promise.

Transforming work and relationships can indeed deliver results for all. In documenting this particular journey, we sincerely hope we have honored Bill Ford's call to "re-express" the truths experienced by one generation in ways that keep it current for the next.

SUPPORTING MATERIALS

9.1 International Framework Agreement

International Framework Agreement
Ford Motor Company
and
Global IMF / Ford Global Information Sharing Network
Agreed upon Social Rights and Social Responsibility Principles

Preamble

The diverse group of men and women who work for Ford is our most important resource. In recognition of their contributions, policies and programs have been developed to ensure that our employees enjoy the protection afforded by principles agreed upon in this document (the "Principles"). While these principles are not new to Ford, they are vitally important to what we stand for as a company.

The Principles are based on a thorough review of labor standards espoused by various groups and institutions worldwide, including those outlined by the International Labour Organization and stand as a general endorsement of the following human rights frameworks and charters:

- The UN Universal Declaration of Human Rights
- The ILO Tripartite Declaration of Principles concerning Multinational Enterprises and Social Policy
- OECD Guidelines for Multinational Enterprises
- The Global Sullivan Principles of Social Responsibility

These Principles are, however, intended to represent a statement of Ford's own high standards.

The universe in which Ford operates requires that these Principles be general in nature. In certain situations national law, local legal requirements, collective bargaining agreements and agreements freely entered into by employees may be different than portions of these agreed upon Principles. If these principles set higher standards, the Company will honor these Principles to the extent which does not place them in violation of domestic law. Nevertheless, we believe these Principles affirm important, universal values that serve as the cornerstone of the relationship between employees and management for us.

Ford and the signatories to this document confirm their support for these Principles and for the Company's Code of Basic Working Conditions, Business Principles, and Corporate Citizenship strategy.

Freedom of Association and Collective Bargaining

The achievement of business competitiveness, employee involvement and employment security are positively influenced by good relations and mutual trust between employees and management within the Company. This requires the on-going cooperation of management, unions, works councils, employee representatives and employees, ensuring that social dialogue at Ford be characterized by mutual respect and understanding. Procedures for information and consultation provide the opportunity for issues to be raised by either the management or employee representatives to ensure that the views of both parties are fully understood.

Ford recognizes and respects its employees' right to associate freely, form and join a union, and bargain collectively in accordance with applicable law. The Company will work constructively with employee representatives to promote the interests of our employees in the workplace. In locations where employees are not represented by a body of employee representation/ unions, the Company will provide opportunities for employee concerns to be heard. The Company fully respects and supports workers democratic right to form a union and will not allow any member of management or agent of the Company to undermine this right or pressure any employee from exercising this right.

Cooperation with employees, employees' representatives and trade unions will be constructive. The aim of such cooperation will be to seek a fair balance between the commercial interests of the Company and the interests of the employees. Even where there is disagreement, the aim will always be to work out a solution that permits constructive cooperation in the long term.

Timely information and consultation is a prerequisite for successful communication between management and employee representatives. Information will be provided in good time to enable representatives to appropriately prepare for consultation.

Collective bargaining on conditions of work is the expression in practice of freedom of association within the workplace, a responsibility to bargain in good faith in order to build trust and productive workplace relations. Even when disagreement occurs, all parties will be bound by group collective and legislative requirements and the aim will be to reach adequate solutions.

The signatories respect the employees' democratic rights to determine representation and will not use tactics of harassment or discrimination to influence employees' exercise of these rights.

Harassment and Unfair Discrimination

The signatories will not tolerate harassment or unfair discrimination on the basis of race, religion, color, age, sex, sexual orientation, union activity, national origin, or against any employee with disabilities.

Ford acknowledges the rights of its employees to raise concerns. From this it follows that any worker who, acting individually or jointly with other workers, considers that he has grounds for a concern should have the right to raise such concern without suffering any prejudice whatsoever as a result, and to have such concern examined pursuant to an appropriate procedure.

Forced or Compulsory Labor

Ford will not use forced or compulsory labor regardless of its form.

Child Labor

Ford opposes the use of child labor. In no event will the Company employ any person below the age of 15, unless this is part of a government-authorized job training or apprenticeship program that would be clearly beneficial to the person participating.

Wages and Conditions

Ford will promote its employees' material well being by providing compensation and benefits that are competitive and comply with applicable law, and acknowledges the principle of "equal pay for work of equal value" in that the Parties affirm their commitment not to discriminate because of race, religion, color, age, sex, sexual orientation, union activity, national origin, or against any employee with disabilities.

Hours of Work and Vacation

Ford will comply with applicable law regulating hours of work and vacation periods.

Occupational Safety and Health Protection

Ford will strive to promote the safety and health of those who make, distribute or use its products.

The Company will provide and maintain for all employees a safe and healthy working environment that meets or exceeds applicable standards for occupational safety and health. Management and employee representatives work jointly regarding considerations and measures in the field of occupational safety and health protection to eliminate workplace accidents, injuries and fatalities as detailed in Ford Motor Company's Safety Operating System.

Education, Training and Development

Ford promotes and supports appropriate education, training and development for its employees, and will continue to establish beneficial ties with institutions with expertise in this area, such as universities, research and training facilities.

Continued dialogue in this area between employee representatives and management assists the early identification of employee adaption needs, ensuring appropriate skills upgrading and improved employability, to meet long-term business requirements.

Suppliers and Business Partners

Ford will encourage business partners to adopt and enforce similar policies to those contained in these Principles, as the basis for establishing mutual and durable business relationships. The Company will seek to identify and utilize business partners who aspire in the conduct of their business to standards that are consistent with this document and will provide the network an opportunity to raise issues for discussion and resolution.

The Company conducts assessments of selected existing and prospective Tier 1 suppliers in multiple countries. The assessments provide feedback to Ford and suppliers about how well they are meeting legal requirements and Ford's expectations. They also provide insight into the effectiveness of our training programs. Assessments consist of a detailed questionnaire, a document review, factory visits, and management and employee interviews, and are conducted with the assistance of external auditors. Ford will review such assessments with the Network, as requested, in connection with its regular meetings and will respond to issues raised.

Sustainability and Protection of the Environment

Ford will respect the natural environment and help preserve it for future generations by working to provide effective and practicable environmental solutions and avoiding waste. The Company will work to continuously reduce the environmental impacts of our business in line with our commitment to contribute to sustainable development. The Company will measure, understand and responsibly manage its resource use, especially the use of materials of concern, and the use of non-renewable resources.

Ford seeks to ensure coherence between social, economic and environmental objectives.

Integrity

Ford will be honest, open and transparent and model the highest standards of corporate integrity. The Company will compete ethically and avoid conflicts of interest and have zero tolerance for the offer, payment, solicitation or acceptance of bribes.

Accountability

The signatories to this agreement commit themselves to these principles on a global, national, and local level.
The ongoing compliance of these Principles can be raised and discussed between the Company and Union in the Regions or at the Ford Global Information Sharing Forum. When issues are identified, the Parties will work together to find mutual solutions. In addition a more detailed monitoring process will be discussed by the parties at the next Global Information Sharing Forum meeting.

General

Ongoing compliance with these Principles will be reviewed at the annual meeting with management.

April 25   , 2012

Source: Ford Motor Company

Postscript: How We Wrote the Book

The impetus to write this book began with the view that there were important past pivotal events that needed to be understood if the recent success of Ford and the UAW were to be fully appreciated. Thus, from the beginning, we organized the preparations for the book around pivotal events.

We followed a systematic process in selecting the pivotal events, conducting the interviews, and writing the text. Our initial outline for the book featured approximately twenty-five pivotal events, all points in the history at which one or more of us had direct personal experience. We focused on pivotal events that were building blocks in what we had come to see as three transformations—that of Ford, that of the UAW, and that of the Ford-UAW relationship. These were all pivots that involved what Douglas McGregor called the human side of enterprise.[1] Additional developments in automotive design, globalization of markets, and new technology do enter the story in various ways, but are not the primary focus.

We then identified individuals at all levels of the enterprise with direct personal involvement in one or more of the pivotal events. Overall, we sought a balance of union and management perspectives. While eight enterprise leaders are featured by name in sections of chapter 9 (Ron Gettelfinger, Bob King, and Jimmy Settles for the UAW; Mark Fields, Bill Ford, Joe Hinrichs, and Alan Mulally for Ford; and Dick Gephardt for both Ford and the UAW), many more individuals from all levels of both organizations are featured. Still, these perspectives are not exhaustive; there are many more such individuals throughout the enterprise who could also comment on these pivotal events—distributed knowledge is a key point of the book. If only time and space permitted, we would welcome the chance to include these additional comments—it seems that every conversation about a given pivotal event reveals a new dimension of what was at stake and why things happened as they did.

Some pivotal events, such as the Rouge explosion or the 2007 negotiations, were cited by many of the people we interviewed. In some cases, we interviewed an individual with a focus on one pivotal event and that person would suggest other events—sometimes confirming our own selections or compelling us to add something to the book. For example, we interviewed Jim Quinlan because we know he had played a central role in a pivot around the way the corporation was addressing the emergence of what are known as affinity groups (presented in chapter 3). During the interview, Jim asked if we also wanted to know about the meeting when the first female plant manager was selected, which provided insight into a pivotal event that was not initially on our list but that represents an important addition to the book. Some pivotal events were identified as we went through our files. By the time we were done, the number of what we saw as essential pivotal events had more than doubled.

Not all pivotal events identified are included in the book. For example, we initially identified the first job-share promotion as pivotal—two individuals sharing a job for work-life balance who performed so well that they were able to apply for and receive promotions. While it is interesting from a work-life perspective, it is not clear what previous pivots led to this or what subsequent pivots built on it. Future developments around the importance of work-life balance with the next generation workforce may reveal this to be an important part of ongoing transformation, but at this stage we decided it is not sufficiently central to the story. A focus on "frontline stability" involving the roles of team leaders, supervisors, and other aspects of frontline leadership could have been included, but was not distinct enough to stand as a separate pivotal event. These issues show up in many other pivots, of course. Much earlier events could have been separate pivots, but instead we integrated them with parts of the book: for example, the pay equity policy for black workers and the five-dollar day are integrated into the introduction to chapter 3, the "treaty of Detroit" is integrated into the introduction to chapter 4, and the "battle of the overpass" is integrated with the presentation of the Rouge revitalization in chapter 4. There are historical events that could have been presented separately since they are certainly foundational pivots, but we have focused primarily on the past 30 years.

The pivotal events are organized in chronological order within each chapter. In many cases, we reference events across chapters or people in their quotes will reference events covered in other chapters. As a result, the reader may find that some events presented early in the book are clarified by pivotal events presented in other parts of the book. Indeed, in writing the book we saw connections among events that we didn't fully appreciate at the time.

The pivotal events have been written to be relatively self-contained, engaging stories—each of which could be interpreted in multiple ways. We sought to provide "thick" descriptions grounded in the industry and organizational contexts.[2] While we do draw lessons and principles from the events, we have attempted to present the material in a not-too-heavy-handed way, allowing for dialogue and the identification of additional lessons and implications.

Some interviews were conducted in person, but most were by phone. Each was approximately an hour long and was highly open-ended. At least two of the co-authors conducted each interview. At the outset, we explained the aim of the book and indicated one or more pivotal events on which we would like to focus. After that, each individual would tell us his or her story, with only occasional prompts by one of us. While the interviews were not recorded, one of the co-authors regularly serves as a process facilitator capturing brainstorming dialogue in real time, so we had notes nearly at transcript quality. The write-ups of the pivotal events were shared with the individuals interviewed to check on the accuracy of quotes and the sequencing of the story.

Generally, pivotal events at the system or enterprise level feature multiple perspectives, whereas those at the plant level are mostly told from one person's point of view. Since we were familiar with nearly all of these pivotal events, our narrative provides additional perspective and a form of triangulation on the pivots. In a number of places, we quote ourselves—in those places where one of us has a unique role or perspective in the story and where a quote from one of us helps to bring that perspective out. In some places where we initially quoted ourselves, we converted the material to narrative to minimize the number of self-quotes. Also, places where interviewees praised specific accomplishments by Marty or Dan were edited out—neither felt comfortable keeping those quotes in.

Serving as co-authors when we were all contributors in the transformation poses special challenges. Joel Cutcher-Gershenfeld deliberately kept his consultant role with the UAW and Ford separate from his scholarly role for nearly two decades. It was only with the 2007 negotiations experience that he concluded that key information would not see the light of day if it were not written up.[3] The same "separate hat" principle came into play with this book, though the process in both cases has shifted him into a role that involves the many challenges and dilemmas associated with action research[4]—particularly being mindful of bias associated with his consulting role. For Dan Brooks and Marty Mulloy the writing did not begin in earnest until both were retired. Still, Dan approached the writing mindful of his brothers and sisters in the UAW (as well as the many folks who consider themselves his colleagues at Ford) and Marty approached the writing mindful of his colleagues at Ford (as well as the many folks who consider themselves his brothers and sisters in the UAW). While this does represent a positive bias, both were also determined to present the materials—including pivots that fell short of their potential—so that lessons could be learned by future generations. As well, there was triangulation among the three of us—each with our own perspectives—all of which does serve to neutralize some of the positive bias. There were certainly many times in which one of us pushed back on a given interpretation or way of telling the story in order to get beyond the superficial. Any remaining bias that does come with our insider experiences can be balanced against the unique insights, in the tradition of action research, that come from having been directly involved in leading or facilitating change within the system.

Here is a tally of the pivotal events, classified by the type of event and the level at which it occurred:

	Plant/Division Level	Enterprise/System Level
Planned Pivotal Events	8	34
Unplanned Pivotal Events	9	5

As the table indicates, most of the pivotal events documented in this book were planned at a system/enterprise level, as would be expected. A transformation of the scale and scope experienced by the UAW and Ford requires many instances of planned change at that level. On their own, events at the plant/division level would not add up to a transformation without changes at the system/enterprise level. The events at the plant/division level were all selected as harbingers of larger system-level changes, many of which were codified through collective bargaining or other institutional and policy decisions.

Note that this classification is necessarily imprecise: as we indicated in chapter 1, the same pivotal event will be experienced by some as planned and by others as unplanned. We have classified them here based on the perspective from which we have presented the story. Thus, the Cleveland Engine Plant 1 story is classified as a plant/division level, unplanned pivotal event since we have presented the story from the perspective of those in the plant. Of course, at a higher corporate level there was advance planning, though this too had an unplanned aspect in that it was driven by a market downturn.

The classification was completed individually by each co-author and then reviewed jointly. There was very high inter-rater reliability initially with the separate classifications and complete agreement through the joint classification. The process helped clarify how we were operationalizing the concept of a pivotal event and highlighted the ways a pivotal event can be experienced as planned by some and unplanned by others.

While most of the pivotal events were associated with consequential change, our definition of a pivotal event as "a time-bound situation with highly consequential potential" makes clear that pivotal events do not always result in change. That most events were highly consequential is not a surprise—this is, after all, a successful transformation story. Still, at least a half dozen of the pivotal events presented fell well short of their potential. In some cases, such as the Plastic and Trim Products offsite meeting (chapter 4) and early FTPM initiative (chapter 5), ideas that would later prove essential were not able to overcome cultural and organizational barriers at the time. In other cases, such as Ford 2000 (chapter 2) and QLI (chapter 8), the more top-down reengineering approach to change was incomplete as a change strategy—it was missing the distributed engagement of the workforce and a full partnership with the union. We have included these pivotal events to provide as complete a picture as we can. Indeed, they help make clear that the transformation process is not deterministic and could have been derailed at these or other junctures.

The organization of the pivotal events at the conclusion of chapter 9 reveals how the themes of the chapters interweave. It also shows that many of the pivotal events could have been presented in more than one chapter. Of course, all the pivotal events in chapter 2 on the case for change also involve substantive changes that relate to the themes of various other chapters. More important, many of the pivotal events on "knowledge-driven work" in chapter 5 could be in chapter 4 on "business fundamentals," many of the pivotal events on "negotiated change" could have been in the chapter on "joint alignment," and the same could be said for the intersection of many of the chapters. This is a key implication of the book—that is, transformation is evident as the component parts (pivotal events and underlying assumptions) interconnect in new ways.

Tracing transformations in work and relationships through the lens of pivotal events has helped highlight the ways in which transformation is long-term, multidimensional, and interconnected. The methods in preparing the story have involved new thinking on how best to organize and present the material. We sincerely hope readers have found our approach engaging and informative. Indeed, for the next generation of scholars and practitioners we hope we have provided insight and inspiration that is sufficient foundation to navigate the pivotal events ahead.

List of Pivotal Events and Supporting Materials by Chapter

Chapter 1: Pivotal Events: Introduction and Industry Context

Pivotal Events

- Monroe Stamping Plant, 1981
- Green Island Plant, 1981
- Employee Involvement and Mutual Growth, 1973–1982

Supporting Materials
1.1 Green Island Archive

Chapter 2: The Case for Change

Guiding Principle
- Courageous leadership

Pivotal Events
- Ford 2000, 1993–1995
- Cleveland Engine Plant I, 1996–2002
- The Rouge Explosion, 1999
- Competitive Operating Agreements, 2006–2007
- Ford Puts All Cards on the Table with the UAW, 2007
- Frontline Leadership, 2013

Supporting Materials
2.1 Ford Executive Education Transition Curve
2.2 U.S. Assembly Plants 2002 vs. 2009/2010 Comparison

Chapter 3: Dignity of Work

Guiding Principle
• Dignity and respect

Pivotal Events
• Selection of First Female Plant Manager, 1996
• Chicago Sexual Harassment Lawsuits, 1999
• Pivot on Affinity Groups, 1999
• Same-Sex Partner Benefits, 2000
• UAW-Ford United in Diversity (now Equality and Diversity) Program, 2000
• 9/11 Zero Tolerance Response, 2001
• Atlanta Zero Tolerance Intervention, 2002
• Voluntary Separation Packages, 2006–2007

Supporting Materials
3.1 Sample United in Diversity Materials

Chapter 4: Business Fundamentals

Guiding Principle
• Mutual growth

Pivotal Events
• Plastic and Trim Products Cross-Functional Alignment, 1995
• Policy Deployment—SQDCME, 1999–2002
• Rouge Revitalization, 2001
• UAW FPS Total Cost Stand Down, 2001–2002
• Lean Manufacturing Managers and the Lean Implementation Network, 2001–2003
• BPR and SAR Processes, 2006
• Quality Operating Committee, 2006
• One Ford, 2007

Supporting Materials
4.1 Support Function Alignment
4.2 Sample Business Fundamentals Briefing Materials

Chapter 5: Knowledge-Driven Work

Guiding Principle
• Continuous improvement

Pivotal Events
- Total Productive Maintenance Roots, 1982
- Mazda Flat Rock, 1987
- Romeo Engine Plant, 1988
- Continuous Improvement and FPS Rollout, 1996–1999
- Team Start and Stop Designations, 1999
- UAW Glass Plants, 2002
- Hourly Six Sigma Black Belts, 2003–2007
- Powertrain Operations Plant of the Future, 2007–2008
- Team-Based Agreements, 2011

Supporting Materials
5.1 Sample Romeo Engine Plant Root Cause Analysis Charts
5.2 Week in the Life for a Team/Work Group Leader

Chapter 6: Negotiated Change

Guiding Principle
- Interest-based relationships

Pivotal Events
- Vehicle Operations Modern Operating Agreements, 1990–1995
- Automotive Components Holdings (ACH), 2000–2013
- National Negotiation—Quality, 2003
- Action America, 2005
- Bargaining Over How to Bargain, 2006
- National Negotiations—VEBA, Entry Wage, 2007
- National Negotiations—Pattern for Crisis Negotiations, 2009
- National Negotiations—Health Care, Profit Sharing, 2011
- Entry-Wage Team Leaders at Chicago Assembly, 2012–2013

Supporting Materials
6.1 Appendix "S" Collective Bargaining Language, 2003
6.2 Letter on "Best Options for the Auto Industry Crisis"
6.3 Briefing Slide on Working Together

Chapter 7: Joint Alignment

Guiding Principle
- Disciplined, standardized processes

Pivotal Events
- Atlanta Assembly Plant, FTPM Chartering, 2001
- Dearborn Assembly Plant Chartering, 2001–2003
- Time and Data Management, 2001–2003
- Quality Chartering, 2003
- UAW-Ford National Joint Program Conference, 2006
- Safety Chartering, 2008
- UAW-HR Change Agents and HR OD Institute, 2009–2010

Supporting Materials
7.1 Mutual Growth Forums, Five Ws & How, 2005
7.2 Joint Alignment and Implementation "Engine"
7.3 Joint Safety Simulation Exercise, "Role Conflict"

Chapter 8: Integrated Operating Systems

Guiding Principle
- Align and stabilize, then integrate

Pivotal Events
- Q1, 1980s, 1998, and 2002
- Quality Leadership Initiative, 2002
- Fresh Eyes Auditors and QOS Coordinators, 2000–2004
- Quality Operating System, 2003
- Targeted Training, 2003–2007
- Safety Operating System, 2008

Supporting Materials
8.1 Operator Instruction Sheet (OIS)
8.2 Quality Hot Line
8.3 Error Proofing Single Point Lesson—Basic
8.4 Error Proofing Instructor's Guide—Basic
sessment—Basic
ar Miss Report

th: Good Jobs and High Performance

nitigate harm

Concluding Comments
- On "True North"
- On "Creating Value and Mitigating Harm"
- Mark Fields
- Joe Hinrichs
- Jimmy Settles
- Bob King
- Ron Gettelfinger
- Dick Gephardt
- Alan Mulally
- Bill Ford
- On "Vision for Good Jobs and High Performance"

Supporting Materials
9.1 International Framework Agreement

Abbreviations, Acronyms, and Terminology

ACH	Automotive Components Holdings, LLC, a Ford-managed temporary business entity comprising former Visteon Corp. plants and facilities in the United States and Mexico*
AIF	Annual Improvement Factor, an annual wage increase of 3 percent to match the 3 percent rate of productivity growth (initially instituted in the 1950s)
APA	Asia Pacific and Africa, a Ford region*
BPR	Business Plan Review meetings, one of Ford's key management processes*
CAFÉ	Corporate Average Fuel Economy, a U.S. regulation requiring auto companies to meet certain sales-weighted average fuel economy levels for passenger cars and light trucks and report these numbers annually*
CAW	Canadian Autoworkers Union, which was formed in a split from the UAW in 1982
CBA	Collective Bargaining Agreement
CIWG	Continuous improvement work group, the model for a team-based work system adopted under the Ford Production System
CPU	Cost Per Unit, a measure of productivity
DAP	Dearborn Assembly Plant
DART	Days Away, Restricted, and Transferred (a health and safety measure)
DCP	Dimensional Control Plan, defining key dimensional specifications for component parts
DfE	Design for Environment, a tool for bridging the gap between product development and environmental management*
DfS	Design for Sustainability, a tool similar to DfE but broader in scope*
DMAIC	Define, Measure, Analyze, Improve, Control—Six Sigma model for process improvement
DTP	Dearborn Truck Plant
EDTP	UAW-Ford Employee Development and Training Program
EI	Employee Involvement

EOS	Ford's Environmental Operating System, which is integrated with ISO 14001 and used for driving environmental compliance*
ERC	Employee Resource Coordinator
ERGs	Ford's Employee Resource Groups, affinity networks at the company that help to foster diversity and inclusion*
FCSD	Ford Customer Service Division
Flexible manufacturing	The use of common platforms and shared manufacturing technologies that allow a single plant to make multiple models and switch relatively rapidly between them, allowing faster response to changing customer demand*
FPDS	Ford Product Development System, an integrated approach to new product development*
FPS	Ford Production System, a continuously improving, lean, flexible, and disciplined common global production system*
GQRS	Ford's Global Quality Review Survey
HIC	High-Impact Characteristic, an aspect of a component part that would have a high impact on product quality
IMT	Integrated Manufacturing Team, utilizing skilled trades integrated with production operations
ISO 9001	The leading global quality standard, developed by the International Organization for Standardization
ISO 14001	The leading global environmental management system standard, developed by the International Organization for Standardization*
JAI	Joint Alignment and Implementation model
LAP	Louisville Assembly Plant
LTCR	Lost Time Case Rate (a health and safety performance measure)
MAP	Michigan Assembly Plant, a Ford facility that is being transformed from a large SUV factory into a modern, flexible, small-car plant*
NFD	UAW National Ford Department, the staff within the UAW, led by a vice president, responsible for the union's relationship with Ford
NJCHS	UAW-Ford Joint Committee on Health and Safety
NJEDC	UAW-Ford National Joint Equality and Diversity Committee
NPC	UAW-Ford National Program Center
NQC	UAW-Ford National Quality Committee
OCM	Operating committee meeting, which could be a plant, divisional, or corporate levels
OEE	Overall Equipment Effectiveness, a key measure of machine reliability that takes into account "uptime" and "downtime" that is planned and unplanned

OEM	Original Equipment Manufacturer*
OHS policy	Ford's Occupational Health and Safety policy
OIS	Operator Instruction Sheet, providing standardized guidance to an operator on the proper performance of a given job
ONE Ford	Ford's accelerated restructuring plan; One Team unified in pursing One Plan to deliver One Goal: An exciting, viable Ford*
OPEB	Other Post-Employment Benefits (beyond pensions, such as retiree health care)
PDCA	Plan, do, check, adjust (continuous improvement process pioneered by W. Edwards Deming—sometimes "act" is used instead of "adjust")
PTO	Powertrain Operations, a division of the Ford Motor Company
Pulse survey	Ford's annual, voluntary survey of salaried-employee satisfaction*
Q1	Ford's "Best-in-Class" quality certification initiative
QLI	Quality Leadership Initiative
QOS	Ford's global Quality Operating System, used in our manufacturing to develop, measure and continuously improve robust processes*
QOSC	Quality Operating Systems Coordinator
QR	Quick Response Code, notifying suppliers of time-sensitive quality concerns
SAAR	Seasonally adjusted annual rate, for North American car sales
SHARP	Ford's Safety and Health Assessment Review Process*
SMF	Synchronous Material Flow
SOS	Safety Operating Systems
SQDCPME	A scorecard that helps Ford keep focused on the vital components of a sustainable business: Safety, Quality, Delivery, Cost, People, Maintenance and Environment*
SRP	Sheldon Road Plant, a Ford components manufacturing facility
Stakeholder	Anyone who is impacted or believes they are impacted by the operations or practices of the Company, including customers, employees, business partners, shareholders, governments, communities and nongovernmental organizations. Some also consider the environment a stakeholder.*
Stamping	A division of the Ford Motor Company
Sustainability	A business model that creates value consistent with the long-term preservation and enhancement of environmental, social, and financial capital (also, meeting the needs of the present without compromising the future).*
TGW	"Things Gone Wrong," a metric measured by the GQRS*
Tier 1 Suppliers	Suppliers sourcing directly to an OEM*

Tier 2 Suppliers	Suppliers not sourcing directly to an OEM*
UAW	The International Union, United Automobile, Aerospace and Agricultural Implement Workers of America*
VEBA	Voluntary Employee Benefit Association trust, an independent trust designed to ensure health care coverage for current and future Ford employees*
VO	Vehicle Operations, a division of the Ford Motor Company
VRT	Vehicle reduction teams, operating within a production facility to implement the Quality Operating System

*Entries for these terms are part of Ford Motor Company's official list of acronyms, retrieved from http://corporate.ford.com/microsites/sustainability-report-2011-12/glossary. Additional entries without the asterisk cover other terms or acronyms used in the book.

Notes

Chapter 1

1. Wall Street Journal Staff, "Congress Members Criticize Auto Executives' Corporate Jet Travel," *Wall Street Journal*, November 19, 2008, blogs.wsj.com/autoshow/2008/11/19/congress-members-criticize-auto-executives-corporate-jet-travel.

2. See, for example, Elaine Romanelli and Michael L. Tushman, "Organizational Transformation as Punctuated Equilibrium: An Empirical Test," *Academy of Management Journal* 37, no. 5 (1994): 1141–1166. Based on their research in the computer industry, Romanelli and Tushman introduced the concept of "punctuated equilibrium," summarizing their findings as follows: "Supportive results showed that (1) a large majority of organizational transformations were accomplished via rapid and discontinuous change over most or all domains of organizational activity, (2) small changes in strategies, structures, and power distributions did not accumulate to produce fundamental transformations, and (3) major environmental changes and chief executive officer succession influenced transformations."

3. Michael Hammer and James Champy, *Reengineering the Corporation: A Manifesto for Business Revolution* (New York: HarperCollins, 2001).

4. Joel Cutcher-Gershenfeld, "Xerox and the ACTWU: Tracing a Transformation in Industrial Relations," in *Human Resource Management: Text and Cases*, 2nd ed. (New York: Prentice-Hall, 1987), 348–373.

5. Thomas A. Kochan, Adrienne E. Eaton, Robert B. McKersie, and Paul S. Adler, *Healing Together: The Labour—Management Partnership at Kaiser Permanente* (Ithaca, NY: Cornell University Press, 2009).

6. Fred Stahl, *Worker Leadership: America's Secret Weapon in the Battle for Industrial Competitiveness* (Cambridge, MA: The MIT Press, 2013).

7. Eric Reis, *How Today's Entrepreneurs use Continuous Innovation to Create Successful Businesses* (New York: Crown Business, 2009); Steve Blank and Bob Dorf, *The Startup Owner's Manual: The Step-by-Step Guide for Building a Great Company* (Pescadero, CA: K&S Ranch, 2012).

8. Rosabeth Moss Kanter, *When Giants Learn to Dance* (New York: Simon and Schuster, 1989). Kanter signaled the challenge. Kanter identifies synergies, alliances, and partnerships as enabling large corporations to succeed in an increasingly interconnected and complex global economy. These forms of "lateral

alignment" among stakeholders are indeed essential if organizations are to be agile in the context of accelerating change. We add that each engagement along these lines will involve one or more pivotal events. Kanter concludes that the new corporate context is not conducive either to what she terms "cowboys" or "corpocrats." We concur; what we identify as "courageous leadership" in chapter 2 requires individuals to step beyond either "shooting from the hip" or reifying bureaucracy.

9. Charles L. Van Doren, *A History of Knowledge—The Pivotal Events, People, and Achievements of World History* (New York: Ballantine, 1991); Nick Yapp, *100 Days in Photographs: Pivotal Events That Changed the World* (Washington, DC: National Geographic, 2007).

10. B. Peter Riesch, J. P. Assal, and G. Reiber, "Pivotal events: A neglected field of factors leading to major diabetic foot complications," *Diabetologia*, vol. 39 (August 1996).

11. Pamela Sloan and David Oliver, "Building Trust in Multi-Stakeholder Partnerships: Critical Emotional Incidents and Practices of Engagement," *Organization Studies* 34, no. 12 (2013): 1835–1868.

12. Thomas A. Kochan, Harry Katz, and Robert B. McKersie, *The Transformation of American Industrial Relations* (New York: Basic Books, 1986).

13. William K. Roche and Paul Teague, "Do Recessions Transform Work and Employment? Evidence from Ireland," *British Journal of Industrial Relations* 52, no. 2 (2012): 261–285.

14. Douglas McGregor, *The Human Side of Enterprise*, annotated edition, ed. J. Cutcher-Gershenfeld (New York: McGraw-Hill, 2006.).

15. Ed Schein, *Organizational Culture and Leadership* (New York: John Wiley & Sons, 1985).

16. Wanda J. Orlikowski, "Improvising Organizational Transformation Over Time: A Situated Change Perspective," *Information Systems Research* 7, no. 1 (1996): 63–92; Samuel B. Bacharach, Peter Bamberger, and William J. Sonnenstuhl, "The Organizational Transformation Process: The Micropolitics of Dissonance Reduction and the Alignment of Logics of Action," *Administrative Science Quarterly* 41, no. 3 (1996): 477–506.

17. Robert J. Thomas, *Crucibles of Leadership: How to Learn from Experience to Become a Great Leader* (Cambridge, MA: Harvard Business Review Press, 2008).

18. For more information on individual agency within institutional arrangements, see: P. H. Thornton, W. Ocasio, M. Lounsbury, *The Institutional Logics Perspective: A New Approach to Culture, Structure, and Process.* (Oxford: Oxford University Press, 2012); Steven R. Barley and Pam S. Tolbert, "Institutionalization and structuration: Studying the links between action and institution." *Organization Studies* 18, no. 1 (1997): 93–117.

19. Peter Drucker, *Concept of the Corporation* (New York: John Day, 1946).

20. Sanford M. Jacoby, *Employing Bureaucracy: Managers, Unions and the Transformation of Work in the 20th Century*, 2 ed. (Mahwah, NJ: Lawrence-Erlbaum Associates, 2004). Jacoby counts General Motors and the Goodyear Tire and Rubber companies among the handful of bellwether firms of mid-twentieth century organizational form.

21. Estimates from the Auto Alliance industry trade organization, www.autoalliance.org/auto-jobs-and-economics.

22. Cited in Gary B. Hansen, "Ford and the UAW have a better idea: A joint labor-management approach to plant closings and worker retraining," *Annals of the American Academy of Political and Social Science* 475, no. 1 (1984): 158–174.

23. Arlena Sawyers, "1979 Oil Shock Meant Recession for U.S., Depression for Autos," *Automotive News,* October 13, 2013.

24. Ernest J. Savoie, "The New UAW Agreement: Its Work Life Aspects," *Work Life Review* 1, no. 1 (July 1982): 1–10.

Chapter 2

1. For more on letting go before embracing what is new, see William Bridges, *Managing Transitions: Making the Most of Change* (Cambridge, MA: Da Capo Press, 2009).

2. This internal negotiation is the focus of Erica Ariel Fox, *Winning from Within: A Breakthrough Method for Leading, Living, and Lasting Change* (New York: HarperBusiness, 2013).

3. Michael Hammer and James Champy, *Reengineering the Corporation: A Manifesto for Business Revolution* (New York: HarperCollins, 2001).

4. James L. Nevins, Robert I. Winner, and Danny L. Reed, "Ford Motor Company's Investment Efficiency Initiative: A Case Study," Institute for Defense Analysis IDA Paper P-3311 rev. (1999).

5. CNN, "At least one dead, dozens injured in Ford plant explosion" February 1, 1999, edition.cnn.com/US/9902/01/ford.explosion.02.

6. CNN, "Ford identifies victim in plant explosion as longtime employee," February 2, 1999, edition.cnn.com/US/9902/02/ford.explosion.03.

7. The write-up of this pivotal event draws on Joel Cutcher-Gershenfeld, "Bargaining When the Future of an Industry is at Stake: Lessons from UAW-Ford Collective Bargaining Negotiations," *Negotiation Journal* 27, no. 2 (2011): 115–145.

8. This quote and many others draw on 2008 and 2009 panel presentations cited in the 2011 *Negotiation Journal* article (ibid).

9. Warren G. Bennis and Robert J. Thomas, "Crucibles of Leadership," *Harvard Business Review* 80, no. 9 (2002): 39–45.

Chapter 3

1. Max Weber, *The Protestant Ethic and the Spirit of Capitalism: Translated from the German by Talcott Parsons* (London: Allen & Unwin, 1930), translation of *Die protestantische Ethik und der Geist des Kapitalismus* (1904–1905), workethic.coe.uga.edu/history.htm.

2. Henry Ford, *My Life and Work: In Collaboration with Samuel Crowther* (Garden City, NY: Doubleday, 1922).

3. United Automobile, Aerospace, and Agricultural Implement Workers of America, "Constitution of the International Union," Amended June 2010, uaw.org/page/uaw-constitution.

4. Christopher L. Foote, Warren C. Whatley, and Gavin Wright, "Arbitraging a Discriminatory Labor Market: Black Workers at the Ford Motor Company, 1918–1947," *Journal of Labor Economics* 21, no. 3 (2003): 493–532.

5. Forrest Briscoe and Sean Safford, "Employee Affinity Groups: Their Evolution from Social Movement Vehicles to Employer Strategies," *Perspectives on Work* 14, no. 1 (2010): 42–45; Michael Piore and Sean Safford, "Changing Regimes of Workplace Governance, Shifting Axes of Social Mobilization, and the Challenge to Industrial Relations Theory," *Industrial Relations: A Journal of Economy and Society* 45, no. 3 (2006): 299–325.

6. "Employee Resource Groups," corporate.ford.com/dynamic/metatags/article-detail/ergs-442p.

7. Alex Taylor III, "My Life as a Gay Executive," *Fortune* 136, no. 5 (September 8, 1997): 106–109.

8. Briscoe and Safford, *Employee Affinity Groups*.

9. UAW-Ford National Diversity Committee (developer) and Tim Kelly (producer), *Introduction to the United in Diversity Training*, Video (UAW-Ford National Joint Programs, 2002).

10. Ibid.

Chapter 4

1. John Barnard, *Walter Reuther and the Rise of the Auto Workers*. (New York: Little, Brown and Company, 1983).

2. We have not included health care and pensions for the UAW-Ford assembly worker in figure 4.1 since there are aspects that do not lend themselves to being calculated in ways equivalent to the U.S. totals. Including health care and pensions would shift this line up further as an even greater year-to-year rate of change.

3. 1999 UAW-Ford National Agreement, Letter of Agreement on Mutual Growth.

4. For additional background on the balanced scorecard, see Robert Kaplan and David Norton, *Alignment: Using the Balanced Scorecard to Create Corporate Synergies* (Cambridge, MA: Harvard Business Press, 2006).

5. UAW-Ford 2003 National Collective Bargaining Agreement, Letter of Agreement on VO Cost Objective Efforts.

6. This incident is documented in greater detail in Bryce G. Hoffman, *American Icon: Alan Mulally and the Fight to Save Ford Motor Company* (New York: CrownBusiness, 2012).

7. We would like to thank Rob Scott and Will Kimball of EPI and Kristin Dziczek of CARS for assistance in this analysis. We would also like to thank Carola Frydman, Northwestern University, and Taekjin Shin, University of Illinois, Urbana-Champaign, for parallel data and analysis on executive compensation that is mentioned in the text, but not included in the chart.

Chapter 5

1. Joel Cutcher-Gershenfeld, Michio Nitta, Betty J. Barrett, et al., *Knowledge-Driven Work: Unexpected Lessons from Japanese and United States Work Practices* (Oxford, UK: Oxford University Press, 1998).

2. James P. Womack, Daniel T. Jones, and Daniel Roos, *The Machine That Changed the World* (New York: Macmillan, 1990).

3. Seiichi Nakajima, *Introduction to TPM: Total Productive Maintenance* (New York: Productivity Press, 1989).

4. Edward Hartmann, *Successfully Installing TPM in a Non-Japanese Plant: Total Productive Maintenance* (Allison Park, PA: TPM Press, 1992).

5. Janet Braunstein, "Ford to Close Romeo, Mich., Tractor Plant by 1989," *AP News Archive* Nov. 11, 1986, www.apnewsarchive.com/1986/Ford-to-Close-Romeo-Mich-Tractor-Plant-by-1989/id-0907c79b79 f3aa0f6ff25e8b2dd5e61e.

6. For more information on alternative models for team-based work systems, see: Joel Cutcher-Gershenfeld, Michio Nitta, Betty Barrett, et al., "Japanese Team-Based Work Systems in the United States: Explaining the Diversity," *California Management Review* 37 (1994): 42–64.

7. Gerald D. Bantom, November 24, 2002, quoted on Zoom.Info, www.zoominfo.com/p/Gerald-Bantom/3453389.

8. UAW-Ford 2003 Letter of Agreement, Book IV, p. 50.

9. John P. Kotter, *Leading Change* (Cambridge, MA: Harvard Business Press, 1996).

10. Cutcher-Gershenfeld et al., *Knowledge-Driven Work*.

11. UAW-Ford National Collective Bargaining Agreement (2011).

Chapter 6

1. Mary Parker Follett, "Lectures Inaugurating the Study of Management at the London School of Economics" (1933), cited in *Mary Parker Follett: Prophet of Management*, ed. P. Graham (Cambridge, MA: Harvard Business School Press, 1995).

2. Richard Walton and Robert McKersie, *A Behavioral Theory of Labor Negotiations: An Analysis of a Social Interaction System* (New York: McGraw-Hill, 1965).

3. Roger Fisher and William L. Ury, *Getting to YES: Negotiating Agreement Without Giving In* (New York: Penguin, 1981).

4. UAW-Ford National Agreement, Book IV (2003).

5. Joel Cutcher-Gershenfeld, "Bargaining Over How to Bargain in Labor-Management Negotiations," *Negotiations Journal* 10, no. 4 (1994): 323–335.

6. This quote, other quotes in this section, and major portions of the text are taken from Cutcher-Gershenfeld, "Bargaining Over How to Bargain," ibid. The quotes are either from the "bargaining over how to bargain" session notes or from two presentations made on the 2007 negotiations in 2008 and 2009.

7. This quote, other quotes in this section, and major portions of the text are taken from Cutcher-Gershenfeld, "Bargaining Over How to Bargain," ibid. The quotes are either from the "bargaining over how to bargain" session notes or from two presentations made on the 2007 negotiations in 2008 and 2009.

8. Walton and McKersie, *A Behavioral Theory of Labor Relations*; Richard E. Walton, Joel Cutcher-Gershenfeld, and Robert B. McKersie, *Strategic Negotiations: A Theory of Change in Labor-Management Relations* (Cambridge, MA: Harvard Business Review Press, 2004).

9. Walton, Cutcher-Gershenfeld, and McKersie, ibid.

10. Ibid.

11. Because confidentiality was promised when conducting these focus group sessions, no names are included with the quotes.

Chapter 7

1. Milton Derber, *The American Idea of Industrial Democracy, 1865–1965* (Urbana-Champaign: University of Illinois Press, 1970).

2. Robert Michels, *Political Parties: A Sociological Study of the Oligarchical Tendencies of Modern Democracy*, trans. Eden Paul (Whitefish, MT: Kessinger Publishing, 2010). Originally published as *Zur Soziologie des Parteiwesens in der modernen Demokratie: Untersuchungen über die oligarchischen Tendenzen des Gruppenlebens* (1911), and then in an Italian translation by Dr. Alfredo Polledro as *Sociologia del partito politico nella democrazia moderna: studi sulle tendenze oligarchiche degli aggregate politici* (1912), from which the English version—first published in 1915—is translated.

3. Peter Drucker, *Concept of the Corporation* (New York: John Day, 1946).

4. John Kay, "Salutary lessons from the downfall of a carmaker," *Financial Times,* June 2, 2009, www.ft.com/cms/s/0/b66cd19a-4fb4-11de-a692-00144feabdc0.html#axzz35yr1tzc2.

5. Frederick E. Emery and Eric L. Trist, *Toward a Social Ecology: Contextual Appreciation of the Future in the Present* (New York: Plenum Press, 1973).

6. These quotes from Bob King are from the session notes.

7. Comments by Marty Mulloy, Dan Brooks, and Tom Kochan are from session notes.

8. The original acronym, developed by Walter Shewhart, Deming's mentor at Bell Labs during WWII, was "Plan, Do, Check, Act." In addition to the shift over time from "Act" to "Adjust," Deming did advocate for a shift to "PDSA" for "Plan, Do, Study, Adjust," though the PDCA abbreviation is that has continued in common usage.

9. Stephen Clibborn, "Managing from Afar: International Transfer of Employment Relations Policy and Practices in US Multinational Corporations" (PhD diss., University of Sydney, 2014).

Chapter 8

1. See chapter 4 in Earll Murman, Tom Allen, Kirkor Bozdogan, Joel Cutcher-Gershenfeld, et al., *Lean Enterprise Value: Insights from MIT's Lean Aerospace Initiative* (New York: Palgrave Macmillan, 2002); and Fred Stahl, *Worker Leadership: America's Secret Weapon in the Battle for Industrial Competitiveness* (Cambridge, MA: MIT Press, 2013).

2. Joel Cutcher-Gershenfeld, Michio Nitta, Betty J. Barrett, et al., *Knowledge-Driven Work: Unexpected Lessons from Japanese and United States Work Practices* (Oxford: Oxford University Press, 1998).

3. This is the central thesis in Clayton Christensen, *The Innovator's Dilemma: When New Technologies Cause Great Firms to Fail* (New York: Harper Business, 1997), though the supporting evidence has been challenged in Jill Lepore, "What the Theory of 'Disruptive Innovation' Gets Wrong" (*The New Yorker*, June 23, 2014) and the Ford-UAW case is a counter example.

4. Michael Piore and Charles Sable, *The Second Industrial Divide* (New York: Basic Books, 1984).

5. James P. Womack, Daniel T. Jones, and Daniel Roos, *The Machine That Changed the World* (New York: Macmillan, 1990).

6. Murman et al., *Lean-Enterprise Value*.

7. IBM, "Service Science," researcher.watson.ibm.com/researcher/view_group.php?id=1230.

8. Cutcher-Gershenfeld et al., *Knowledge-Driven Work*.

9. Henry Ford (with Samuel Crowther), *Today and Tomorrow* (New York: Doubleday, Page & Co., 1926).

10. W. Edwards Deming, *The New Economics: For Industry, Government, Education* (Cambridge, MA: MIT Press, 1993).

11. This is aligned with Douglas McGregor's "Theory Y" assumption that people want to do a good job and that the job of management is to provide the needed support (in contrast with the "Theory X" assumption that people need to be monitored and controlled to do a good job).

12. John P. Kotter, *Leading Change* (Cambridge, MA: Harvard Business Press, 1996).

13. As reported by an executive at the Young and Rubicon (Y&R) ad agency at the time. The executive was meeting with Joel Gershenfeld and Susan Cutcher from the Michigan Quality of Work Life Council, providing pro bono support arranged courtesy of Ernie Savoie from the Ford Motor Company and Don Ephlin from the UAW. The Y&R executive also offered praise for whatever copywriter had come up with the idea of "employee involvement" which he said was great for selling cars.

14. There are roots to this standard that go back at least two decades earlier around military quality standards for procurement.

15. When ISO environmental standards (14000 and 14001) are established, they too become entry criteria for Q1.

16. Ford Motor Company, *Q1: Setting the Standard*, 2002, elsmar.com/pdf_files/Q1_2002-Final_Aug.pdf.

17. CEBOS, "The Top Five Automotive Quality Management Failures of All Time," undated, www.cebos.com/the-top-5-automotive-quality-management-failures-of-all-time.

18. Shortly before his death, Deming stated that Stevens had, in fact, been his best student.

19. For more on this topic, see Joel Cutcher-Gershenfeld and Kevin Ford, *Valuable Disconnects in Organizational Learning Systems: Integrating Bold Visions and Harsh Realities* (New York: Oxford University Press, 2005).

20. Dennis O'Connor and Penny Drain, *Targeted Training: A "How To" Guide for Changing Employee Behavior in 30-Minute Intervals* (Xlibris, 2009).

21. "Ford Motor Company Vision for Health and Safety," 2012/2013, http://corporate.ford.com/microsites/sustainability-report-2012-13/people-workplace-health.

22. Ed Schein, *Process Consultation Revisited* (Boston: Addison-Wesley, 1999).

23. "FPS: Global Ford Production System Introduction," September 16, 2013, www.at.ford.com/news/Plants/Pages/Global-Ford-Production-System-Introduction.aspx.

24. Ibid.

25. Chris Shunk, "Ford Global Warranty Costs Slashed by $1.2B Over Last Two Years," *autoblog,* February 3, 2009, http://www.autoblog.com/2009/02/03/ford-global-warranty-costs-slashed-by-1-2b-over-last-two-years.

Chapter 9

1. Thomas A. Kochan, Harry Katz, and Robert B. McKersie, *The Transformation of American Industrial Relations* (New York: Basic Books, 1986).

2. *Rerum Novarum,* 1891, www.vatican.va/holy_father/leo_xiii/encyclicals/documents/hf_l-xiii_enc_15051891_rerum-novarum_en.html.

3. United Nations, "Universal Declaration of Human Rights," 1948, www.un.org/en/documents/udhr.

4. "International Framework Agreement: Ford Motor Company and Global IMF/Ford Global Information Sharing Network," 2012, www.google.com.au/url?sa=t&rct=j&q=&esrc=s&source=web&cd=2&ved=0CC4QFjAB&url=http%3A%2F%2Fwww.global-unions.org%2Fspip.php%3Faction%3Dacceder_document%26arg%3D454%26cle%3D1fabbd3c625d984e7f26e3b42c99f3bc65f657c7%26file%3Dpdf%252Fifa_ford.pdf&ei=doKKU-bfG8HsoASn54HACQ&usg=AFQjCNHruHj3Z6l3PssEAFm3sY35y7mg0A&sig2=ZwoW94iwPetoMkohrf6jfg&bvm=bv.68191837,d.cGU.

5. Joel Cutcher-Gershenfeld, Michio Nitta, Betty J. Barrett, et al., *Knowledge-Driven Work: Unexpected Lessons from Japanese and United States Work Practices* (Oxford: Oxford University Press, 1998).

Postscript

1. Douglas McGregor, *The Human Side of Enterprise*, annotated edition, ed. J. Cutcher-Gershenfeld (New York: McGraw-Hill, 2006.)

2. Clifford Geertz, *The Interpretation of Cultures: Selected Essays* (New York: Basic Books, 1973); Barney G. Glaser and Anselm L. Strauss, *The Discovery of Grounded Theory: Strategies for Qualitative Research* (Chicago: Aldine, 1967).

3. Joel Cutcher-Gershenfeld, "Bargaining When the Future of an Industry is at Stake: Lessons from UAW-Ford Collective Bargaining Negotiations," *Negotiation Journal* 27, no. 2 (2011): 115–145.

4. For more on action research see: Chris Argyris, R. Putnam, and D. Smith, *Action Science: Concepts, Methods and Skills for Research and Intervention* (San Francisco: Jossey-Bass, 1985); and Ed Schein, *Process Consultation Revisited* (Boston: Addison-Wesley, 1999).

Index